GOVERNING THE MODERN CORPORATION

GOVERNING THE MODERN CORPORATION
Capital Markets, Corporate Control, and Economic Performance

Roy C. Smith and Ingo Walter

OXFORD
UNIVERSITY PRESS
2006

OXFORD
UNIVERSITY PRESS

Oxford University Press, Inc., publishes works that further
Oxford University's objective of excellence
in research, scholarship, and education.

Oxford   New York
Auckland   Cape Town   Dar es Salaam   Hong Kong   Karachi
Kuala Lumpur   Madrid   Melbourne   Mexico City   Nairobi
New Delhi   Shanghai   Taipei   Toronto

With offices in
Argentina   Austria   Brazil   Chile   Czech Republic   France   Greece
Guatemala   Hungary   Italy   Japan   Poland   Portugal   Singapore
South Korea   Switzerland   Thailand   Turkey   Ukraine   Vietnam

Published by Oxford University Press, Inc.
198 Madison Avenue, New York, New York 10016

www.oup.com

Oxford is a registered trademark of Oxford University Press

Library of Congress Cataloging-in-Publication Data
Smith, Roy C.
Governing the modern corporation : capital markets, corporate control
and economic performance / Roy C. Smith and Ingo Walter.
    p. cm.
Includes bibliographical references and index.
ISBN-13 978-0-19-517167-9
ISBN 0-19-517167-5
1. Corporate governance. 2. Capital market. 3. Corporate
governance—United States. 4. Capital market—United States.
I. Walter, Ingo. II. Title.
HD2741.S635 2005
338.6—dc22   2004028386

9 8 7 6 5 4 3 2

Printed in the United States of America
on acid-free paper

Preface

The corporate and financial scandals of the late 1990s and early 2000s in the United States have elicited a broad range of reactions. "A few bad apples," said some, "that have distorted the picture of the world's best performing economic and financial system." "An unfortunate legacy of the greatest financial bubble in history," said others. Still others suggested that the conduct of major American corporations revealed fundamental weaknesses at the heart of the free market system—flaws that have always lurked just below the surface of the country's overly triumphal, self-absorbed capitalist approach to economic organization.

The truth surely contains elements of each. What is certain is that the faith most people had in the integrity and discipline of market-based finance and capital deployment was severely shaken. The magnitude of the losses and the extent to which these losses reached ordinary citizens, along with the cynical disregard by senior business and financial leaders of legal or ethical constraints pressed home a need for reform. A sense of public outrage developed that motivated government officials and regulators to move quickly to "restore confidence" in the markets and prosecute some of the most visible offenders.

Before the 1930s, neither government regulators nor the courts had much of a role in enforcing checks and balances in the U.S. economic and financial system. Boards of directors were appointed by knowledgeable investors and constrained by fiduciary duties. The boards would select people to manage their firms and achieve the objectives the board had established. If they failed, they could expect to be replaced. Such enlightened self-interest might not be a sufficient restraint on management under some circumstances, so both companies and investors could be expected to exercise discipline upon each other. Powerful figures in business and finance sought the support of banks, insurance companies and other investors, who in general would avoid or liquidate positions in companies run by those whom they did not trust. Key investors would also monitor corporate executives to be sure they were performing up to expectations. The executives had to negotiate loans, stock issues, and credit facilities. Financial intermediaries sought to provide these facilities, and to be appointed to manage investments for large public institutions such as municipalities, universities, and charitable endowments. Senior representatives of many of the intermediaries involved at the time—bankers, brokers, insurers—were appointed to boards of directors or were otherwise sufficiently well plugged into the system to be able to use their vantage point to look after their own interests, which focused on steady and predicable results.

The system essentially consisted of a self-regulating cohort of knowledgeable insiders that was based on the old doctrine of *caveat emptor*. The government's role was largely one of establishing fiduciary and property laws. What derailed the system in the 1920s turned out to be a fantastic stock market bubble, in the course of which rising share prices drew thousands of unsophisticated investors into the market, where, in search of quick and sure profits, they could be relied upon to make unwise and ill-informed investment decisions. Under such circumstances, there were plenty of opportunities for them to suffer serious losses, often promoted by people and firms who were well entrenched in the inner circle of the time.

The "modern" corporation was defined during this era by Adolph Berle and Gardiner Means in their classic 1932 study of the business organization model of the large publicly owned company that was managed by professional executives who owned very little of its stock but had great incentives to maximize its profits. Such corporations, they reported, dominated the economic landscape of the time, and their governance represented a potential problem for society that only the federal government was powerful enough to address.

After the market crash in 1929 and the Great Depression that followed, the federal government, acting in the public interest, became heavily involved in regulation of both corporations and markets. The government imposed a variety of laws on corporations affecting market shares and competitive structures, labor relations, workplace safety, and periodically even prices and output. The government's regulatory powers peaked during World War II, after which they were gradually (sometimes very gradually) withdrawn. The heavy regulatory role on the part of the government had two immediate effects. It bureaucratized broad reaches of the national economy, suppressing growth and initiative, and it shifted attitudes away from self-regulating checks and balances to widespread mistrust of corporate management who, it was thought, needed to be watched carefully to be sure they did not abuse the public trust.

Financial market regulation at the time was based on a simple concept of accountability for full disclosure of material information, together with "fair" trading practices, with the intent of protecting unsophisticated investors who were inadequately prepared to look after themselves. However, from the very beginnings of key legislation, notably the Securities Act of 1933 and the Securities Exchange Act of 1934, there were exemptions from the disclosure laws for sophisticated investors who were thought not to need them. Government securities (including municipal bonds) were exempt from Securities and Exchange Commission (SEC) registration; so were securities of government agencies and certain bank stocks. Corporate securities had to be registered only if they were to be offered through public distributions. If not, they could be sold to sophisticated investors as "private placements" without complying with the disclosure rules. Mutual funds sold to public investors had to be registered, but private investment funds investing in venture capital, leveraged buyouts, real estate, or other "private equity" investments did not. *Caveat emptor* still applied for sophisticated, wealthy investors able to look after themselves, but *full disclosure* had become the necessity for all stocks initially sold or resold in the public markets.

The SEC believed that transparency would be the best approach to fair and efficient markets, and by insisting on full, accurate, and timely disclosure of large quantities of corporate information, the market players could check and balance themselves. The large institutional purchasers of publicly traded stocks would keep their eyes on aggressive corporate executives to be sure they were credible and honest enough to merit their trust. In response, a "golden era" developed in the stock market in the 1960s that greatly encouraged the development of mutual funds and pensions, and greatly increased the importance of institutional investors in the stock markets, making the checks and balances seem even more secure.

The 1970s, however, were the most difficult years in the stock market since the 1930s. Many things went wrong then, discouraging investors. Corporate scandals were plentiful, some of them tied in with senior government officials, some involving bribing foreign governments, and some involving juicy cases of fraud and misconduct. New laws were passed, adding to the layers of regulation that corporations had to comply with, and enforcement was tightened. The economy was caught in a low-growth inflationary spasm that pushed interest rates to 20 percent and threw almost the entire corporate community on to the defensive. Corporate expansion and development was no longer the objective. Survival was.

The government's grip began to relax at the end of the 1970s decade of abysmal economic performance, and government regulation was increasingly portrayed as clumsy and an impediment to growth. Antitrust rules were relaxed in the 1980s and regulations were withdrawn in transportation, broadcasting, telecommunications, and other key sectors. Resistance to hostile takeovers and leveraged corporate reorganizations (very unpopular at the time) was suppressed, and such transactions were permitted to flourish, offering renewal to much of the corporate landscape that had been devastated in the 1970s. The federal government—under great pressure from record fiscal deficits—neglected regulation in general, especially in the banking sector, which helped create a wave of banking and savings-and-loan failures that devastated those industries and resulted, after massive taxpayer losses, in much more intensive regulation. The banks recovered in the 1990s, and used their experience as evidence of the need for extensive deregulation and consolidation in financial services, a view that was ultimately ratified by congressional action in 1999.

Indeed, in the 1990s, during an eight-year Democratic presidency, transportation, energy, telecommunications, and health care, as well as all forms of banking and financial services, were fundamentally deregulated in order to attract the stimulating—if disorderly—effects of increased competition. The deregulation was not accompanied by sufficiently alert market and institutional oversight, perhaps contributing both to the stock market bubble of the late 1990s and to the bust of the early 2000s.

By the 1990s, world financial markets had been revolutionized by a heady mix of technology advances, globalization, and a decade of significant growth in household wealth. The market value of financial assets and real estate, minus mortgage, credit card, and other household debt, grew from $8.2 trillion in 1980 to $37 trillion in 1999 in the United States alone. Financial markets expanded at an exceptional rate, about twice the rate of nominal economic growth. Not only did they grow rapidly but they also had become "democratized" by extensive participation on the part of ordinary people, not just skilled financial practitioners. By 2000, half of all American households owned stocks in one form or another, and the same households participated fully in the market crash of 2000–2002. While deregulation was in vogue, millions of new investors were pouring into the markets with little idea of what to do. Most purchased mutual funds, which had become more numerous than the number of stocks available in the market. Some tried their luck as on-line day-traders—largely without much investment knowledge at all—at deeply discounted commission rates. As in the 1920s, many of these individuals fell victim to the half-baked or fraudulent investment schemes that usually surface in the excitement of an ever-rising market.

The corporate and financial scandals that emerged in the bubble and were subsequently revealed unleashed a public uproar that called for action, immediate action to address the outbreak of "corporate greed" that had created such havoc across the American financial landscape. With this came an urgency for corporate governance reform unseen in the United States since the 1930s. A variety of actions were taken, first and most important by market investors, who corrected prices of all financial assets quickly and stubbornly kept them in the grip of a bear-market decline for three years, forcing everyone to share in the pain. Despite a decade of diminishing regulatory activity on the part of Congress and the Securities Exchange Commission (SEC), the system responded with a vengeance to punish those who had allegedly transgressed, and to warn off those who might be tempted in the future, by requiring complex procedural reforms in the way corporations, financial institutions, and markets are governed.

The effort was understandably politicized, uncoordinated, and rushed, driven by breathless media reports. So it was no surprise that the collective efforts contained many flaws. The 2002 Sarbanes-Oxley Act led to a wave of rule-tightening and enforcement actions that placed all of America's public corporations on the defensive, with a heavy burden to adapt to new and costly compliance standards and to review their own internal corporate governance practices. Nor did it stop there. Legal actions were taken by prosecutors and regulators in an effort to punish a variety of financial intermediaries, advisers, and investment managers. Some of these actions contained provisions designed to bring about reforms, but how effective many of them might be remained in doubt. The pendulum had swung, but the law of unintended consequences hovered in the background.

By 2004, the stock market had recovered much of its loss of the previous three years and returned to more or less normal operations. But there was a lingering suspicion that not enough had been done to identify the causes for the avalanche of corporate and financial misconduct that occurred in the late 1990s and early 2000s, or to prevent them from reoccurring down the road. Standing back a bit from the drama of rapidly unfolding events following the Enron collapse, almost anyone could recognize that things had been allowed to run amok for a few years, and that those who allowed them to do so included the market's key "gatekeepers"—its experts, advisers, intermediaries, and regulators—who seemed to disappear entirely during much of the period, along with sound judgment among supposedly savvy, well-informed institutional investors. What could they have been thinking? What happened to the checks and balances? What happened to market discipline?

In this book, we examine the central dimensions of effective governance, monitoring, and control of corporations and financial markets, both with an eye on the lessons of history and a firm focus on the future. We argue that the effective functioning of the market-driven financial system basically rests on a number of assumptions.

First, the market-driven system assumes that managers consistently strive to maximize risk-adjusted total returns to shareholders, and that they do so within an accepted set of legal, regulatory, and ethical constraints. It also assumes that boards of directors, as elected representatives of the shareholders, supervise management effectively, see to it that they are compensated appropriately, and assure that a company's accounts fairly reflect the financial reality of the business as a going concern. The critical managerial issues are shareholder value and discipline in resource allocation, incentive-compatibility of management contracts, and organizational and financial transparency.

Second, external to the firm, the market-driven system assumes that effective monitoring by auditors, investors, analysts, bankers, and others takes place, and that material developments are communicated to the market in an accurate and timely way, so that they can be reflected in the "correct" price of the firm's securities held by investors.

Third, the market-driven system assumes that both business firms and their financiers, advisers, and monitors are in compliance with laws and regulations, and are subject to private legal redress to assure appropriate business conduct—and that these constraints are fair and reasonable, set in the realm of politics and anchored in the overall social context. The rules of the marketplace should center on safety, soundness and fairness of the financial and business system, balanced against its ability to deliver economic efficiency, and therefore regulatory constraints should evolve in a deliberate way to help concentrate the power of the marketplace in achieving the greatest good for the greatest number. This, after all, is an essential requirement for maintaining a market-based economic system within a popular democracy— it is what is meant by "democratic" free market capitalism, which its advocates are fond of recommending to virtually all societies in order to foster sustainable economic development.

Some of those who had long placed their bets on the superiority of the market-driven system against competing models—as well as those who had been more skeptical of the proposition—were taken aback by the size and frequency of the revelations of corporate wrongdoing that surfaced beginning in 2001, following the most dramatic stock market bubble of all time. Suddenly all of the assumptions of how things are supposed to function were called into question. The market seemed less an institution than a game, one that was neither fair nor efficient. Management seemed shocked by the growing public revulsion toward business practices that were widely known and accepted yet were now seen as treacherous and untenable. A maelstrom had developed that would die out in time, as maelstroms invariably do. But its ferocity and political resonance invited a serious review of the operation of the public corporation in the modern free-market economy.

The objective of this book is to provide a useful framework for thinking about these issues after the dust has settled. We focus in particular on the role of financial markets and their respective institutions (asset managers, banks, securities firms, advisers, lawyers, auditors, and others)—the key intermediaries in capital allocation, generating and distributing information, and setting securities prices—and the fault-lines in the system that have come to light.

All financial intermediaries have somewhere in their statements of business principles or mission statements words to the effect that "Our reputation is our most important asset." Yet many ended up in trouble with the regulators, their clients, and their own shareholders—and in some cases were accused of aiding and abetting serious corporate misadventures. How could this happen to supposedly independent, sophisticated, reputation-sensitive institutions?

A number of regulatory or legal solutions to such problems have already been put in place, and these need to be examined as well in order to determine how effective they are likely to be and what effect they may have on the free-market system. We shall explore just how robust the new regulatory initiatives are likely to be in the thick of the hypercompetitive financial markets that are sure to dominate going forward.

We have written on these subjects before. Virtually all of the problems enveloping financial firms today were discussed in our 1997 book *Street Smarts: Linking Professional Responsibility and Shareholder Value in the Securities Industry.* That book was written to lay out many of the performance-tensions that confront management of financial intermediaries and to suggest the key managerial and leadership requirements for creating valuable and durable business franchises in tough and volatile financial markets. This book is intended to focus on how corrections in the market and regulatory environment and within the sphere of corporate governance can restore the healthy balance needed between firms pursuing their own objectives and the overriding interests of the public.

We are grateful to William Allen, Paul Brown, Charles Ellis, Sy Jones, George Smith, Richard Sylla, and Lawrence White for helpful comments and suggestions on various chapters during the course of writing this book, as well as to Gayle DeLong, Vivek Pradhan, and Neela Saldanha for help with data, analysis, fact-checking, background research, and preparing the index. Research support from the R&D Committee at INSEAD in Fontainebleau, France, is gratefully acknowledged. The authors alone are responsible for any remaining shortcomings.

Contents

Part I

Corporation, Governance, and Capital Markets in Perspective

In 1932 Adolph Berle and Gardiner Means described the "modern" corporation as one owned by public shareholders but controlled by an elite group of managers empowered to run the corporation largely at their own discretion. Much of the American economy at the time was made up of such corporations, which Berle and Means believed needed to be restrained by regulation and enforcement, not necessarily by relying on internal practices that have come to be known as "appropriate corporate governance." The abuses of power they feared were broadly economic, not financial: monopolies, restraint of trade, price-rigging, and union-busting.

In the 1930s, many abuses of the previous decade were revealed and hotly debated. But these were largely financial, not economic, issues. And they were blamed mainly on financial market intermediaries—much more than on corporate executives. So in due course, the financial market was subjected to an entirely new, tight-fitting regulatory regime that was naturally resisted in some quarters. But in time it was accepted, and for 50 years the financial market regulation set in place during 1933–1940 seemed to work effectively in providing a safe, transparent environment for financial transactions of all kinds, including many new financial instruments that came along. Large corporations continued to dominate American business. Occasionally they would tap the financial markets by issuing stocks or bonds, but the daily lives of senior managers were not especially affected—certainly not mesmerized—by capital market activity. Executives were seen as respected professional managers, wielding great responsibility generally in a responsible way. Most were not entrepreneurs or (with a few exceptions) business tycoons, and most owned very little stock in the companies that employed them.

All of this changed in the early 1980s, when a 20-year era of financial prosperity that fundamentally changed how American corporations conducted themselves got underway. More wealth was created in this time than during any other period in history, and most of it was driven by the stock market, which for nearly two decades grew at twice the rate of gross domestic product (GDP). Many factors contributed to this unique dynamic, as a result of which the capital markets exploded in power and importance—and enormously impacted the opportunities and strategies of business executives, who remained fully empowered to run things more or less as they liked. The executives, of course, responded to the changed environment and the signals it was sending. Their conduct changed in many ways, and so did the managerial qualities needed to get to the top and stay there.

Then came the "bubble"—like a hurricane rising up from a vast and turbulent ocean. There have been plenty of other financial bubbles. But the impact of this one, because of the enormous capital market energy from which it developed, was by far the most powerful. The collateral damage eventually extended to the reputations of all the principal players of the time—corporations, auditors, bankers, and investors—forcing the public to seek changes in the rules of the game and assurances about the future.

Part I of this book consists of two chapters. The first considers the nature, effects, and consequences of the bubble of 1995–2000. The second chapter assesses the more fundamental effects related to the evolving dominance of capital markets, which has changed the way corporate executives perceive their role and the expectations they are required to meet.

1

Irrational Exuberance

The buzz from Silicon Valley was that Netscape was the newest thing—a real "killer application." It would popularize and democratize the Internet, allowing anyone to have instant access to websites that would connect to all the world's information sources. True, the Internet had already existed for a while, but it was mainly confined to universities and the military. Now, by making this new form of communication available to anyone with a personal computer, it could change the way business was done—all business: wholesale, retail, services—because everything depended on information, and now information would be delivered differently, in an architecture available to everyone. Netscape offered a free "browser" to "surf" the Internet over telephone lines, and was building a network that would attract millions of users, and businesses would pay to access it.

Netscape was offering shares of stock to the market in an "initial public offering" (IPO) to be priced in August 1995. All of the proceeds would be new money to be invested in the business. No shares were being offered by existing investors—who included Jim Clark, a founder of Silicon Graphics, a previous Valley money-maker, and backed by the famed venture capitalists Kleiner Perkins Caufield & Byers. So all the right people were involved. And the deal was to be underwritten by one of the country's most prestigious investment banks, Morgan Stanley, whose technology team was headed by Frank Quattrone.

Morgan Stanley was really taking a chance with this issue. Netscape was less than two years old. It had no profits and no immediate expectation of profits. Its most recent 12-month revenues were less than $25 million. It was run by an unknown, 24-year-old Illinois computer science graduate, Marc Andriessen. But Quattrone believed the deal would jumpstart the market for technology stocks, which had been listless for a year or so. Total U.S. IPOs had amounted to only $46

3

billion in 1994, down from $64 billion in 1993, and technology deals had hit a three-year low of $8.5 billion—only 18 percent of all 1994 IPOs. Morgan Stanley had a new technology stock analyst, Mary Meeker, who was enthusiastic about Netscape but admitted that valuing such companies was very difficult. It was really a "concept stock." Morgan Stanley said it expected to offer stock at about $12 per share, which would make the Netscape offering the third largest IPO in the history of the National Association of Securities Dealers Automatic Quotation system (NASDAQ.)

A BUBBLE FORMS

Netscape aroused a broad range of interested investors, notably the most aggressive, performance-driven mutual and hedge funds and the technology-investing world as a whole. Some would plan to acquire shares from the underwriters and sell them later the same day if the stock spiked, although such immediate IPO gains as a whole had averaged only about 15 percent in recent years. Others, like Microsoft, watched carefully as a new player ventured into its PC software domain. The buzz fed on itself, and indications of orders flowed into Morgan Stanley. Afraid the deal would be greatly oversubscribed and that they might not be allocated many shares, investors tried to exert pressure on Morgan Stanley by reminding the firm of what good brokerage clients they were. Netscape and its advisers saw what was happening as well, and pressed for an increase in the offering price. Morgan Stanley, recognizing the building market for the new company, agreed to increase the price to $28, based on the unusually strong order book. But the firm knew that it had endorsed an almost indefensible price for the stock, based on classic valuation approaches. It also knew that a great deal of Netscape stock would be dumped by the lucky IPO investors as soon as a significant price premium was reached, and Morgan Stanley would essentially have to sell the offering all over again to keep it from collapsing entirely under the selling pressure.

Morgan Stanley's worries proved unfounded. The stock opened at $58 and rose from there. At the close of trading on the first day, the tiny, profitless company was valued by the market at $2 billion, and its young CEO was worth more than $80 million. Those who were allocated shares by Morgan Stanley had made a profit of more than $30 per share on a one-day investment that had required putting up no money of their own, since both their purchases and sales would close on the same day. Suddenly, the whole financial community— investment bankers, analysts, brokers, mutual and hedge funds, and venture capitalists—began a rush to find other Internet companies. If it could work for Netscape, it could work for others. Perhaps another hundred companies could similarly capture the imagination of investors. The Internet was perceived as being able to change the world, like the automobile, or electric power, or television had done. Besides software suppliers, it would turbocharge demand for various types of computer and telecommunications equipment, including digital high-speed networks—"broadband" that could carry all of tomorrow's information over cable and wireless communications systems. A "new" economy was seen as being fashioned by fusing these technologies with the media and entertainment, advertising, and retail sales industries, and it was not long before the market had other Internet stocks to consider. Search engine companies came next—Lycos, Excite, and Yahoo in 1996, followed by a seemingly endless series of dot-com "B to B" or "B to C" companies. Virtually all had hot, wildly oversubscribed IPOs.

About the same time as the Netscape IPO, another new "concept company" was making a move. Long-Distance Discount Services (LDDS) was formed in the early 1980s to take advantage of the newly deregulated long-distance telephone market, following the breakup of AT&T, by offering steep discounts in phone rates. LDDS acquired several similarly entrepreneurial telephone service companies and, as a result of one of these acquisitions, had become publicly traded in 1989. Four years and several additional acquisitions later, LDDS operated the fourth largest long-distance network in the country. In 1995, after further acquisitions of network companies and fill-ins, it acquired the voice and data transmissions company Williams Telecommunications for $2.5 billion in cash. Later than year, LDDS, based in Jackson, Mississippi and run since 1985 by Bernie Ebbers—a former high-school basketball coach who had owned a string of local motels before joining the company—changed its name to WorldCom, Inc.

Within the next three years, WorldCom would make several more large acquisitions of local access facilities, fiber-optic cable networks, and Internet access providers for businesses, culminating in a $40 billion acquisition of MCI Communications, Inc. in 1998. The acquisitions were made possible by a rising stock price—from $8 in early 1995 to $50 after the MCI deal—and access to substantial credit facilities from banks.

Ebbers was assisted in developing and executing his strategy by an enthusiastic PaineWebber Group, Inc. telecommunications analyst, Jack Grubman, a former AT&T employee who understood the basic model of challenging the behemoth and enthusiastically recommended first LDDS shares, and later WorldCom shares, to investors. In 1994, Grubman left PaineWebber, a retail brokerage, to join Salomon Brothers, Inc., a major investment bank. He was soon encouraged both to do stock analysis work, as he had before, and to assist Salomon's investment bankers with their mergers and corporate finance activities. Soon thereafter, Salomon Brothers became the principal investment bank to WorldCom, advising on various mergers and arranging the financing for them while continuing to recommend the stock to investors.

In 1997, Salomon Brothers was acquired by Travelers Group, Inc., and was merged with Smith Barney & Co., a large stock brokerage business. Travelers was controlled by Sandy Weill, a former Wall Street star, who the following year engineered the merger of Travelers and Citicorp Inc., the country's most successful commercial bank. A major objective of the merged businesses—now called Citigroup Inc.—was to cross-sell products and services across the two units. Citigroup soon formed a corporate banking division that combined the lending capacity of its banking unit, Citibank, with the investment banking and brokerage ability of the combined Salomon Smith Barney. It was a merger made in heaven for Jack Grubman, who now had enormous financial resources to offer an insatiable client, Ebbers, and to his other telecom industry favorites, including Global Crossing Ltd. and Qwest Communications International Inc.

BUBBLES, PAST AND PRESENT

The market capitalization of all publicly traded common stocks in the United States on December 31, 1999, was $16.7 trillion, up from $1.3 trillion, its 20-year low point, in 1981.[1] The gain over the period—$15.4 trillion—reflected an 18-year compound annual increase in the value of stocks of 15 percent. This was over twice the 7 percent nominal rate of U.S. GDP growth, indicating the extent to which this nearly fourteenfold increase in stock market capitalization had created wealth in excess of underlying economic activity.[2] As one observer of the 1990s put it, it was the "greatest flood of liquidity since Noah,"[3] and people all over the world plunged into the action in search of investments in the new economy—what was also being called the next industrial revolution.[4] The technology component of the boom was dominant. A nearly seventeenfold increase in market capitalization of technology-laden NASDAQ stocks occurred from 1991 through 1999, changing what was a mere bull market (as represented by the fourfold increase in the market capitalization of all NYSE listed companies) into a "bubble," a runaway euphoria about the future of the stock market driving speculation to extraordinary levels.

The NASDAQ index was a little over 900 in August 1995, and it would close the decade, the century, and the millennium on December 31, 1999, at 4,069, on its way to an all-time high of 5,048 in March 2000. Much of this rise in the index occurred in 1999, when it jumped 85 percent, contributing to a compound growth rate during this four-and-a-half-year period of nearly 50 percent. In 1999, the S&P 500 index, much less concentrated in technology stocks, rose 19.5 percent.

During the twentieth century there were four exceptional stock market booms in the United States that in retrospect have been called "bubbles." Economist Richard Sylla describes these periods (1905, 1928,

1958, 1998) as times when the 10-year moving averages of real rates of return on stocks reached peaks from which they rapidly descended (or "crashed") a year to two later.[5] The crashes, of course, involved large losses and other forms of collateral damage, although the losses were calculated using inflated market values registered at the market's peak. Of these four bubbles, the ones that peaked in 1928 and 1998, leading to crashes in 1929 and 2000, respectively, were the ones of greatest significance.

The 2000 crash involved more financial wreckage—however it is calculated—than earlier crashes, even the crash of 1929, given the extraordinary levels stock prices had reached. Although the Dow Jones Index fell about 90 percent from its peak in 1929 to its low in 1933, the total amount of market capitalization lost was about $70 billion, or about 59 percent of 1929 GDP. By contrast, the loss of market capitalization in 1987, following the celebrated 22.6 percent Dow Jones one-day crash on October 19 of it year, was about $585 billion, only 12.4 percent of 1987 GDP, and most of that was restored by a swift market recovery in the following months. However, even though the S&P 500 index plunged by 48.9 percent from its high in September 2000 to its low in October 2002 (the Dow Jones, now a less used index, dropped by 29.4 percent), the estimated loss in total U.S. market capitalization was over $8 trillion, or 80 percent of GDP in 2000. These figures represent only the loss in equity values during a period when bond markets also shed about $100 billion in value and bank loan losses were estimated at more than $50 billion.

The difference in loss experience between 1929 and subsequent crashes largely reflects the growth of securities markets as repositories for savings and investments of American financial institutions and individuals. In 1929, institutional investors were just developing and had not become powerful, important players in financial markets. Individuals, for the most part, kept their savings in banks. During the 1930s, $1.3 billion of deposits were wiped out as a result of some 9,000 bank failures (40 percent of all banks). Such an enormous financial collapse was a major cause of the Great Depression and the high levels of unemployment that followed for nearly a decade.

Another indicator of the magnitude of the effect of bubbles bursting is the amount of public attention and regulatory and legislative response that was generated. Lost market values, bankruptcies, and scandals lead to cries for punishment of the "guilty" and improved regulation to prevent future recurrences. The 1929 crash was a watershed event because it was seen at the time as the cause of the ruinous economy that followed a decade of prosperity. It led to the election in 1932 of Franklin Roosevelt, who promised extensive reforms. The Roosevelt administration pushed through Congress (among many other measures to reform the American economic system) the Banking Act of 1933 and the Securities Act of 1933 and the Securities Exchange Act of 1934, which instituted a totally new regulatory and enforcement regime, one that fundamentally changed the way American capital markets would operate in the future. The emphasis of reformers in the 1930s was to prevent a recurrence of the situation rather than to seek retribution and punishment for those held to be responsible.

In the 1960s, there was no government response to that decade's bubble, other than the passage of the Williams Act to slow down the pace of hostile takeovers (discussed in chapter 3).

In the 1987 crash, the federal government only formed a commission to look into the causes of the large one-day price collapse on October 19, and some technical reforms were later adopted by the New York Stock Exchange and by the stock futures markets.

In 2000, however, the market crash and the scandals that soon followed were front-page stories for months. Public interest in the market collapse and its causes and consequences was intense—public ownership of stocks had reached an all-time high in 1998, when the Federal Reserve announced that 48 percent of all American households owned stocks, either directly or through mutual funds and pension funds. Congress hurriedly passed the Sarbanes-Oxley Act in the summer of 2002 to substantially reregulate corporate activities and securities markets; the Justice Department appointed a high-profile corporate fraud task force; the attorney general of the state of New York organized an omnibus $1.4 billion settlement of charges to be brought by various regulatory bodies against the leading Wall Street investment banks; and the Securities and Exchange Commission (SEC) and its designated self-regulatory cohorts, the New York Stock Exchange (NYSE) and the National Association of Securities Dealers (NASD), began to introduce a number of new regulations to be followed by all 15,000 publically traded corporations in the United States and by the financial services community. The principal stated objective of these efforts was to restore investor confidence in the financial system, which many observers believed required the apprehension and punishment of those responsible and some far-reaching changes in how the system functions.

ANALYSIS OF A MARKET COLLAPSE

The 2000–2002 crash had several causes. There was growing recognition that the high-growth economy of the 1990s was slowing, that stocks—particularly technology and new economy companies—were overvalued, perhaps by a great deal. But there was also considerable public anxiety reflected in the markets after the attack of September 11, 2001, about international terrorism, global instability, and the apparent rapid unraveling of relatively benign conditions in longtime trouble spots. Further, there were charges of fraud and serious abuses of corporate governance practices at many large and respected companies that made many investors very skeptical of all investment information and advice they received.

Overvaluation or a Change in Risk Premium?

Peter Lynch, the famous manager of the Magellan Fund at Fidelity from 1978 to 1990, frequently reminded viewers of television ads for the mutual funds group during the late 1990s that "earnings drive the stock market." They do, but not entirely. Corporate earnings (measured by analysts' forward-looking estimates) in fact increased only about threefold between 1981 and 1999. Interest rate changes are also important. The future earnings of companies are capitalized by the stock market at discount rates that are determined in part by government interest rates—the lower the rates the better the stock prices. Interest rate changes indeed played a very important role in the 1990s because of their significant decline beginning in December 1981, when two-year government bonds traded at a yield to maturity of 14.5 percent. On December 31, 1998, two-year Treasuries traded at a yield to maturity of 5.1 percent. (A year later, interest rates rose, and the two-year Treasuries traded at 6.3 percent.) The overall decline in rates was almost two-thirds by the end of 1998 and almost 60 percent by the end of 1999.

The increased earnings, together with the lower interest rates, should explain all, or almost all, of the large increase in stock market values during the 18-year period ending in 1999. But they don't quite. According to one study, these two variables only explained 70 to 80 percent of the growth in the S&P 500 index between 1981 and 1998. The 20 to 30 percent of market value increase that was unexplained was attributed to "overvaluation."[6] However, by this the author meant to include all the many other things that might affect the market but had not been directly measured in the study. Such things as (1) the dramatic decline in inflation, (2) improvements in productivity and generally strong and continuing growth across all sectors in the economy, (3) a very positive outlook for increased business in the newly deregulated, privatized, and integrated global economy, (4) structural imbalances in the supply and demand for equities that can affect pricing, and (5) changing attitudes about risk on the part of investors. According to some observers—one of whom predicted a Dow Jones level of 36,000— the so-called overvaluation might simply be explained by a reduction in the amount of risk that equity market investors perceived themselves to be taking when they bought stocks, possibly because of the considerably lowered difference in the volatility of stock prices as compared to the volatility of debt prices, which were presumed to be less risky. Investors in stocks during the 1990s seemed to treat the market as if it were less risky than in earlier periods, and therefore they were willing to pay higher prices for stocks and bought more of them. This change in attitude toward risk (called a "risk premium") might be enough, some said, to explain all the supposed overvaluation.

However, some other more traditional market observers noted that as much as 60 percent of the stock market's gains were the result of one-time events (tax cuts, the end of the Soviet Union, corporate mergers and restructuring, low inflation, etc.) that probably would not be repeated in the future. Many investors, despite the euphoria, became convinced that the market had leapt into unreality and that a strong correction was due. Indeed, a sharp correction in stock prices did occur in the summer and fall of 1998. The market shuddered with concerns about future corporate earnings, debt default in Russia, and worrying economic conditions in Japan and Brazil. Stock market indices dropped almost 20 percent as a result, but recovered by year-end to midyear levels, where the S&P 500 was presumably overvalued again, but somewhat less so, because, in the meantime, more earnings had been realized and interest rates had dropped a bit more. But after the short, sharp drop and a rapid recovery, many of the more experienced investors wondered whether indeed a new set of forces now set market levels.

Even if stocks were still overvalued at the end of 1998, and due for a further correction, they experienced just the opposite in 1999, a year in which the technology-laden NASDAQ composite nearly doubled, while the yields on two-year Treasuries actually increased. In the first quarter of 2000, some correcting took place, but it was still overwhelmingly clear that an extraordinary amount of personal wealth had been created by rising stock prices during the previous two decades. This wealth was the reward for individuals willing to take greater risks (by staying invested even when "experts" were sounding dire alarms) and for institutional investors who felt they too had to stay invested because their competitors were and they could not afford to look bad relative to them for fear of risking major fund withdrawals.

Excitement of New Technologies

With the rising market came many stories of the period about the new alchemists of the times—the entrepreneurs of the new economy who had created dynamic new companies, such as Microsoft, Cisco, Dell, and now Netscape, Amazon, and a variety of other "dot coms." The Internet had only become available for public use in 1995, and the extraordinary usage that developed exceeded the velocity of all previous technological introductions. The economic potential of the Internet seemed unlimited, and although it was well understood that many of the early companies would fail in the bloody competition among them that was to come, a few would survive to become the Microsofts of tomorrow. To find those companies now, one had to invest in a variety of possibilities and to expect some casualties and do so in a market of constantly rising prices. However, the investment returns enjoyed by the early investors were staggeringly good, and these attracted other investors to try their luck as well.

There were at least five different types of new economy stocks in the late 1990s. First, there were the "backbone" stocks, that is, the companies that had a strong manufacturing base to supply the hardware needs of those utilizing the Internet. These companies did not have to be located after long searches; they were obvious, existing high-tech manufacturers (Cisco, IBM, Intel, Hewlett Packard, Lucent, Motorola, etc.) who were going to benefit from the Internet revolution no matter which companies led it. Second and third, there were the Internet marketing companies—those that set up special websites to sell directly to the growing number of web users. The companies were the "B to B" (business-to-business) and "B to C" (business-to-consumer) companies that made up the bulk of the new Internet startup companies with revolutionary new ideas, such as web-based supply chain management, online retailing, and a variety of free information and services. Fourth, there were the "old economy" businesses that found ways to transform themselves into the stars of the new economy. Such companies would include not only old-economy adapters such as Ford, General Electric, and WalMart but also former public utilities such as Enron, WorldCom, and Qwest. The telecom industry suddenly entered the technology field because it had to adapt existing systems to enable and utilize Internet capability for others, and to compete on the basis of faster, cheaper communications for their customers. But this industry, and subsequently the power industry also, had only recently been turned loose from nearly a century's rule by public (i.e., government) commissions, to compete with one and all in the free market. Finally, there were companies proposing to use the Internet to do things that had not been done before—such as using auction sites to allow customers to bid for unsold hotel rooms and airline seats and to buy or sell miscellaneous items all over the country.

One result of this investor excitement was the availability to many new economy companies of capital at a very low cost. If a company could raise substantial amounts of equity at generous prices in the stock market, despite its lack of earnings, then the cost of that equity capital (and of any debt capital the equity might enable) was very low. The lower the cost of capital, the less the return on the investment would have to be for new projects demanding investment. And these companies had plenty of projects.

Computer companies were investing heavily to bulk up for the Internet and to address the special problems of adapting old software to accommodate the new 2000 dates of the millennium ("Y2K"). Equally, the telecom companies went on a building spree of historic proportions. By the time the Internet bubble burst, there were 40 million miles of fiber-optic cable installed in the United States alone—enough to make 80 round trips to the moon.[7]

Most of the "new" technology companies (i.e., not the reworked old-economy companies) became available to the public only after initial public offerings of stock. Before that they were expensively funded by venture capitalists who helped season and develop the companies before bringing them to the market, a process that a decade before took about seven to ten years and required a history of at least a year or two of profits to accomplish. However, the investor demand for IPOs by the mid-1990s was off the charts. Not only was the underlying investment potential thought to be great (because of the potential of the Internet) so too was the potential gain from buying an issue and reselling it almost immediately at a much higher price to investors unable to accumulate any shares in the initial offering. Realizing the premium available to investors favored by generous IPO allocations became a way to lock-in solid investment profits, and as a result, most large institutional investors began to demand IPO allocations from the investment bankers handling the sales. The value of technology IPOs offered in 1994 was $8.5 billion. In 1996, it was $25 billion and represented about a third of all IPOs; another third was from health care, and the last represented all other sectors. In 1999, tech IPOs were valued at $40 billion, and in 2000 at $55.6 billion, before falling off sharply in 2001.

As demand for IPOs surged during the 1990s, the underwriting standards declined for companies going public. By 1999, they no longer needed to demonstrate earnings at all—or even revenues. With such low standards, almost any company with a connection to the Internet could be taken public, and as a result, investment bankers looked everywhere for companies they could feed into the virtually mindless demand for IPOs that developed at the market's peak (see table 1.1).

In the 1990s, much of the "mindless" demand for securities related to the Internet and the new economy came from sophisticated financial institutions. To get into the better opportunities, they often had to rely on the IPOs underwritten by particular investment banks. Most of the companies launching IPOs were young and had not developed a stable, profitable business, but because the excitement about the technology sector was so great, investors were willing to buy these companies even well before they had matured. Many of these companies were still in venture capital stages, but the Internet itself was doubling every year, and investors did not want to wait. To satisfy the large demand for technology IPOs, the investment banks had to develop capability within new industries that no one really knew very well, and to locate companies that otherwise were invisible to the market because they were not public.

As the IPOs that were brought to market in the late 1990s were in great demand, and almost all went to a large premium in the aftermarket, as noted in table 1.2.

To gain mandates for IPOs, the banks had to promise the new companies that they would wholeheartedly sponsor the IPO, by making

Table 1.1. IPOs in the 1990s

Date	Total IPOs (number)	Value (US$ millions)	Tech IPOs (number)	Value (US$ millions)	Tech IPOs Percent of total number	Percent of total value
1991	457	26,872	167	5,857	36.5	21.8
1992	742	45,652	240	10,487	32.3	23.0
1993	945	64,370	236	8,945	25.0	13.9
1994	855	46,302	238	8,518	27.8	18.4
1995	656	33,711	308	11,858	47.0	35.2
1996	1028	55,146	469	24,809	45.6	45.0
1997	785	46,557	326	14,107	41.5	30.3
1998	609	58,412	231	16,843	37.9	28.8
1999	707	68,248	487	40,361	68.9	59.1
2000	764	72,228	631	55,581	82.6	77.0

Source: Thomson Datastream

an extra effort to distribute the shares to investors all over the world, by following the company in research after the issue, and by making a secondary market (for block trades) in the stock for institutional investors. Often mandates for IPOs were only awarded after extensive "beauty contests" among investment banks, in which these and possibly other promises were extracted. Without question, the high level of competition for IPOs resulted in unusual advantages for companies seeking to go public, including many that would not under normal practices have been deemed to be ready for public ownership, and that later proved not to be.

Table 1.2. Average First Day Return on IPOs

Year of filing	First day return (%)
1991	16.4
1992	12.3
1993	13.9
1994	18.9
1995	26.0
1996	18.1
1997	21.1
1998	53.3
1999	99.5
2000	47.0

Source: Thomson Datastream

Supply and Demand for Shares

With such powerful market conditions—falling interest rates and rising stock prices and trading volumes—corporations raised an abundance of capital in the 1990s: nearly $17 trillion, more than during any other decade by far. Of this amount, the bulk was in the form of *debt* securities, but $1.2 trillion was from the sale of common stock, of which somewhat more than one-third ($470 billion) represented the volume of initial public offerings during the decade. Although only a modest portion of all capital raised, this was by far the largest volume of IPOs ever handled in a 10-year period. During the 1990s, however, corporations were also very active in repurchasing their own shares in the market (despite rising prices), usually to acquire shares to be reissued under employee stock option plans without increasing the total number of shares outstanding. As a result, the *net* new issues of common stock during the 1990s was nil—new issues had been completely offset by repurchases.

In addition, approximately $5.2 trillion of U.S. mergers and acquisitions were completed in the 1990s. The peak year for mergers was 2000, when $1.8 trillion of transactions were completed, more than five times the volume of the peak year of the merger boom of the 1980s. In the 1990s, very large mergers took place in transactions involving exchanges of shares. Approximately 65 percent of the larger deals done in the 1995–2000 period involved the issuance of new shares, and the rest were for cash.

Thus, at a time when new money was flowing into stock market investment pools such as mutual funds, the actual supply of shares available to purchase in the market was diminishing from cash mergers and corporate repurchases, and these retirements significantly, on balance, reduced the supply of shares, just when the demand for them was soaring. As suggested in table 1.3, this dynamic had an effect on stock prices, further forcing prices upward.

Table 1.3. Supply and Demand for Equities, 1997–2000 ($ Billions)

	1997	1998	1999	2000
Gross New Issues	161	207	284	351
Corporate Demand for Shares (Stock Repurchases, Cash Acquisitions)	−247	−432	−395	−470
Net Change in Supply of Shares	−86	−225	−112	−118
Net Acquisition of Equity Securities by Institutional Investors	213	169	292	453

Source: Federal Reserve Board, Flow of Funds Accounts

Media Attention and Public Relations

The stock market was rising fast enough in the mid-1990s to begin to attract considerable attention in the media—which had expanded to include extensive broadcast and cable television reporting. But also there had been a great expansion of the print media covering mutual funds and other investment topics since the 1980s. All of this coverage intensified with the commercialization of the Internet and the many changes in the telecommunications sector. Biotechnology, medical devices, and wider healthcare service businesses also excited public attention. The appetite was satisfied by interviews with CEOs and market analysts and by talk shows with portfolio managers and market watchers. During the late 1990s, it was possible to fill one's day with live market information and commentary put on by 24-hour televised coverage, or by information posted on the Internet or published in newspapers or magazines. The media would bring the "experts" to the attention of the public, and the public would join in the excitement of investing in a rising market by purchasing mutual funds, or individual common stocks they had heard about, or by undertaking a program of day-trading using their desktop computers, the Internet, and the services of discount brokers. Most individual investors relied on others to suggest stocks or funds to buy—usually their brokers or friends with good access to advice. Most did not bother to read the lengthy legal-offering documents provided to them. They were relying on others to manage their investments and trusted these others to do as well for them as they did for themselves. People believed they had little choice if they wanted to invest in the stock market but to do so through the advice or agency of others. Some of these advisers were well known to the investors as longtime investment counselors, or brokers, but others were people they had just met or seen on television. Many individual investors in the 1990s were simply free-riders who did little to protect themselves through independent research or inquiry.

Analysts, Brokers, and Underwriters

In the late 1990s, the securities industry was nearing the end of a 25-year period of deregulation, consolidation, growth, and competition that changed the industry beyond all recognition. Chapter 8 discusses these changes and the subsequent creation of a globalized capital market of enormous size, scope, and capacity to provide low-cost capital financing for many thousands of corporations.

In general, by the end of the twentieth century these markets were dominated by highly sophisticated financial institutions—both investors and service providers (who were often investors themselves)—that were largely regarded by regulators as being able to look after themselves. Institutional investors (principally pension and mutual funds, insurance companies, banks, and investment advisers, both do-

mestic and foreign) were the decision-makers in the markets—the largest players that tended to set prices for trades. These institutions understood the power of competition (they themselves were under
considerable competitive pressure for accumulation of assets to manage) and played financial service providers off against each other whenever possible.

To earn a portion of an institution's commission business, a broker-
dealer would have to struggle to make a short-list of preferred vendors—instead of what had once been a lengthy list to provide access
to all sorts of ideas. Most investment institutions had culled these lists
to concentrate on the most important brokers who could, and would,
be motivated to help them the most. To earn a disproportionate share
of the institutions' business, the broker-dealer had to be willing to do
three things: (1) provide analytical research on hundreds of companies
whose stock the institutions owned (to spare the institutions the effort
of doing this work for themselves and by economizing on the broker's
ability to offer the research to hundreds of different investors); (2) trade
large blocks of stock at competitive prices; and (3) offer its best investment ideas—either for new stocks to buy or sell, or advantageous
trades to make—to the institution before offering these ideas to the rest
of the market, which would spoil the opportunity. Institutions referred
to this as providing the "first call" to them. The broker-dealers did their
best to satisfy these demands, and in doing so substantially increased
the level of competition in the market for stocks and other securities.

Broker-dealers were thus required to maintain large investment research organizations at their own expense, to use a portion of the firm's
capital to underwrite block trades, and to be sure that their sales representatives were in instant contact with institutions as soon as any
new development or idea occurred. The requirement to supply so much
research (the major firms by 2000 had research department budgets
nearing $1 billion per year, covering hundreds of individual companies,
along with fixed income, commodity, and foreign exchange markets
around the world) to some extent imposed an economic hardship on
the brokers. This was because the direct return on their investment in
high-caliber personnel and support systems paid in commissions on
trades in the stocks they covered was often meager at best. Indeed, it
was usually less after applying the net gains or losses on facilitating
block trades for the institutions, which were often losses. But these
institutions did trade in large volume, and they traded often, so the
brokers could make money from institutions if they secured a large
enough piece of their business. However, most firms realized that research analysts were useful in their investment banking business as
well—in advising on the future prospects of a potential client, and in
providing research coverage for important companies that needed such
coverage for their shares to be traded at their full potential. Analysts

were also helpful to investment banks that were advising on mergers and acquisitions and in identifying potential IPO candidates. Most firms believed that assisting investment banking was an appropriate part of the job of the analyst and that individual analysts should be compensated for their investment banking contribution. The average analyst might expect 10 to 30 percent of his or her compensation to come from assistance to investment banking efforts, but the analysts whose sectors were hot and involved in numerous, large investment banking transactions (such as Internet and telecom) could expect a much greater compensation from their investment banking contribution. In a small number of cases (a handful, perhaps, out of thousands of analysts), the individual analyst was so well known and regarded by clients as to become more important than the firm's own investment banking team.

The requirement of analysts to notify clients first became more important to institutions, as many found themselves increasingly following a "market momentum" investment strategy. In a market environment such as that of the late 1990s, when average stock prices might rise by 25 percent and favored technology stocks by 75 percent, few mutual fund managers felt they could afford to ignore the technology stocks, because only through them could their funds deliver the high returns that investors expected. To protect themselves against withdrawals from their funds ("redemptions"), they stayed invested in the most volatile parts of the market—knowing that the slightest disappointment in quarterly earnings could cast a company off the high-valued favorites list and plunge its stock into a one-day free fall of 20 to 30 percent. Investment managers had a difficult task: to stay invested, but not too long, and to be prepared to get out of certain stocks at the first sign of trouble. Thus the importance of the "first call" requirement was greatly increased. An analyst covering a technology sector would closely watch for trouble signs and be prepared to call up his or her best clients as soon as anything was known. Such analysts, however, to get the jump on other analysts and on the company's own announcements, had to be plugged in to the company's chief executive officer (CEO) and chief financial officer (CFO) closely so as to receive information that not everyone was getting. Many CEOs believed that such close information sharing with star analysts would be to their advantage. On the other hand, sharing price-sensitive inside information with a favored few could be against the law—the insider trading rules expressly forbid such conduct on the part of both executives and analysts. The "first call" requirement also imposed conflicts of interest on the broker-dealer. Who actually should get the first call? Was speed more important than the validity of the idea communicated? Was the trade to be made to be satisfied from the firm's own inventory? Could the firm trade first on the information, before the client could act on it? The SEC detected the practice of offering first calls to preferred clients and in October 2000 imposed "Regulation FD" (for fair disclosure), which required companies to release no investment information without simultaneously posting it to a company website that would make it available to all investors at the same time.

ASSESSING THE DAMAGES

Beginning in mid-2001, for about a year, public attention was drawn to series of corporate disasters that are probably best evoked by the bankruptcies of Enron and WorldCom[8] and the liquidation of Arthur Andersen, one of America's five largest and most distinguished accounting firms, following criminal conviction for obstructing justice by destroying documents.[9] Enron and WorldCom, however, were only two of many large corporate bankruptcies that occurred in 2001 and 2002. Others included Global Crossing, Kmart Corporation, UAL Corporation, Adelphia Communications Corp., The Finova Group, Inc., Reliance Insurance Company, and Consolidated Freightways Corp. Some of America's most highly paid executives were among the leaders of the bankrupt companies.[10] Further, executives of several of these and other high-profile companies were arrested and faced criminal charges. Other companies that have avoided bankruptcy also underwent criminal investigations—AOL–Time Warner, Computer Associates, HealthSouth, Imclone Systems, Rite-Aid, Tyco International, Qwest, and Xerox among them, followed later by AIG, Marsh & McLennan, and others.

Bankruptcies, Accounting Failure, and Litigation

The problems of failed or wounded corporations extended much further than these high-profile cases. In 2001, there were 171 large corporate bankruptcies involving liabilities of $230 billion, more than twice the level of bankruptcy liabilities in 2000, the previous record year for bankruptcies. During 2002, 122 bankruptcies involving liabilities of $338 billion occurred, thus establishing a three-year series in which American bankruptcies—the ultimate form of corporate failure—broke all previous records.[11]

In addition, instances of accounting failures (in the form of "restatements" of prior audited financial results due to accounting errors) nearly quadrupled in the four-year period 1998–2001 to 616 cases.[12] Restatements continued to occur at a record level during 2002, when 330 cases were reported, 22 percent more than in 2001). As a consequence of these failures, federal securities-fraud class-action lawsuits seeking damages from officers, directors, and advisers of the companies exploded. In 2001, 493 such suits were filed (of which 312 were related to initial public offerings), and in 2002, 270 more, as compared to an average of 194 filings per year during the three years prior to passage of the Private Litigation Reform Act of 1995, a bill that was designed to substantially limit the number of such class-action lawsuits.[13] Many of these lawsuits were the consequence of stock prices that fell rapidly, causing losses (damages) to investors, when such stock price declines followed sudden news of changed financial information.

Market Losses

Although the number of corporations associated with investigations, restatements, and litigation was comparatively small as a percentage of all 15,000 publicly traded corporations (the number reflected a much higher percentage of those companies included among the S&P 500), the losses they caused were disproportionately large. Bank loan write-offs for 2001–2002 were in the tens of billions of dollars. Publicly traded noninvestment grade bond defaults for 2002 were (at par value) $96.9 billion—the highest level of such defaults then recorded—representing 12.8 percent of all such outstanding issues. In 2001 the default rate of these bonds was 9.8 percent, the highest since 1999. On the assumption that the bond defaults would result in recoveries (through bankruptcy or other work-out arrangements) equal to the 10-year historical average of about 30 percent, then the expected losses from loan loss write-offs and from bond defaults for the two-year period would be about $100 billion.

Equity market losses in 2001–2002 attributable to fears of corporate failures were even greater: the S&P 500 index peaked at 1527 in March 2000 and then fell steadily to 966 in September 2001, but it recovered by year-end 2001 to nearly 1200. But, even after clear signs of recovery in the economy and in corporate earnings were evident early in 2002, the influences of the Enron bankruptcy in December 2001 and other corporate surprises affected the market, and the S&P 500 index reversed direction and fell further. Unlike the periods following recovery from previous recessions, the stock market continued to sag, with the S&P 500 index reaching a five-year low of 798 on July 23, 2002, down 33 percent for the year (reflecting a loss of $4 to $5 trillion of market capitalization) and down more than 47 percent from its all-time high two and a half years earlier. For many industries suspected of account-ing or governance shortcomings (e.g., telecom, health care, energy serv-ices, and technology), share price declines were greater. By the end of July 2002, the NASDAQ index had declined more than 75 percent from its peak, and the Chicago Board of Options Exchange's stock market volatility index (VIX) reached a 14-year high. The storm continued to blow through the rest of the year. By the end of 2002, the stock market had experienced three consecutive years of negative returns for only the second time since the 1930s. These losses, of course, were mainly absorbed by sophisticated, well-informed institutional investors, but of course they were ultimately passed on to the nearly half of American households that owned stocks in 2001–2002.

Regulatory Failure

In addition to corporate failures during this time, there were associated failures in the accounting profession (see chapter 7) and failures on the part of the SEC, the regulatory agency empowered by Congress to monitor and enforce fair market conditions. The SEC has the power to decide what adequate auditor independence is, and to refuse to accept financial statements certified by firms deemed to be inadequate. It also has the power to set accounting principles and standards, which it had delegated to the Financial Accounting Standards Board (FASB) but could take back if it found the FASB to be too slow, too vague, or too influenced by others. The SEC has similar powers to refuse to allow mutual funds that are inappropriately controlled by their management companies to be sold to the public. Its powers are potentially vast, and perhaps for this reason they are rarely fully employed—the Commission and its chair are appointed by the president and are not beyond the reach of political considerations. Arthur Levitt, SEC chairman during the latter 1990s, claims that the SEC's failures to catch all that was going on was because of insufficient budgets, inadequate staff, and a lack of will to battle severe political pressure from members of Congress influenced by vigorous lobbying efforts by corporations and accounting firms. Altogether, the events of the late 1990s and early 2000s, according to Levitt, caused "an emerging . . . crisis of confidence in our [financial] market [system]. What has failed is nothing less than the system for overseeing our capital markets."[14]

Further, a decade of deregulation in financial services had increased competition to levels that were beginning to both outgrow and to strain the existing regulatory system. Many of the abuses alleged in the 1990s were related to conduct that was not clearly covered by existing regulations and regulatory precedent.

For example, banks and investment banks were no longer separated, and many had merged together to form large lending and underwriting institutions with a great appetite to use their balance sheets to increase the volume of transactions they managed even though, at the time, such "tied" lending by banks was to some extent prohibited. The banks found ways to get around the existing rules.

Accountants were now engaged in a broader range of financial services businesses, but conflicts between these businesses and the firms' essential independence from auditing clients were left to a vigilant market to detect and correct, which it did not do.

Unregulated derivative financial instruments had developed to allow trading in a variety of totally new investment vehicles involving contracts in electric energy, oil and gas, telecom bandwidth, and credit risk. But regulatory and accounting measures lagged well behind these powerful innovations.

There was a confluence, therefore, in the late 1990s of opportunistic

corporate actions that were rewarded by rising stock prices, of deregulation that had introduced new competitors and ways of transacting
business with the corporations, and of a laxity by regulators due to
underfunding, political interference, and possibly insufficient understanding of all that was going on. This confluence ended in a "perfect
storm" that did great damage, for a time, to the American corporate
and financial market system.

Effects on the Market System

The numerous business and accounting failures of the 1990s, when
they became known, were subjected to severe price changes—as
market-based systems are supposed to produce when they need correction. Market failures occur from time to time in the United States,
where robust economic activity sometimes results in excessive levels
of speculation, careless investing, or misconduct, even by sophisticated
investors. Such ebullient periods preceded the corrective market activity of the 1930s and the 1970s and the stock market crash of 1987.
Despite the damages and scandals in such periods—including the recent one—that embarrassed (if not surprised) American capitalism's
many supporters, the essential principles of free-market activity and of
rewarding managers for delivering shareholder value have been successful in creating the growth and prosperity in the modern American
economy that exceeds that of all other countries. Indeed, Federal Reserve chairman Alan Greenspan delivered an address at New York
University in the spring of 2002 on the subject of corporate governance,
a topic he normally did not discuss. Because some excesses had occurred that affected the quality of financial markets, he said, he felt he
needed to speak out. Despite many imperfections that need to be addressed, he said, the American system of market capitalism still clearly
worked better for the economy and society than any other. And American financial markets, characterized by openness, fairness, active competition and the efficient distribution of information, have for many
years set the standard for the world. But they can go awry and, when
they do, cause a lot of damage.

Ultimately, the burden of restraining corporate actions falls upon
investors themselves—those who buy and sell corporate securities.
They, after all, are the ones who gain or lose directly from the market's
actions, and they must look after themselves. Credit markets in America are almost entirely made up of banks and sophisticated bond market
investors. Approximately 80 percent of stock market trading is performed by equally knowledgeable institutional investors. These investors not only have access to information and analysis sufficient to warn
them of deteriorating investment conditions in many companies in
which they were invested in the 1990s but also, collectively, they pos-
sess massive amounts of share voting power with which to express
their wishes for correct corporate governance actions and procedures.

It is clear now that these banks and institutional investors, sometimes conflicted by relationships with corporations in which they invest, did little to protect themselves or their clients and shareholders during this chapter in financial history.[15] The responsibility for the failures is not, therefore, that of errant corporations alone.

It is also clear that the bubble of 1995–2000 distorted much of the clarity of vision and efficiency of markets that people have come to depend on to preserve fairness and integrity in their financial system. Bubbles are fundamentally psychological events that turn skeptical individuals into crowds of true believers. Apparently we are not immune, even today with our vast marketplace dominated by professional investors, from the effects of bubbles. But bubbles can perhaps be prevented from forming by sensible and well-enforced regulation, and by ensuring that the markets we rely upon to defend us from irrational exuberance are themselves cleansed of the harmful viruses of conflicts of interest and self-dealing.

Not least is the recognition that capital markets have achieved a power and importance in economic life that is vastly greater than at any time in history. Twenty years ago, depository institutions claimed this distinction, but now as a result of many factors, the dominant financial resource for large corporations has moved to capital markets. Huge amounts of money move daily into and out of securities traded actively in at least a dozen major locations around the world. Corporations seek access to this stream of investment demand, and hope to capture a share of it to boost share prices and to empower corporations, and their managers, to expand their strategies and dreams for enrichment well beyond anything that was available to them before financial markets became so large and powerful. The bubble of 1995–2000 was the first to occur in such a vast and global marketplace, and although it contributed its own distortions, the marketplace itself demonstrated that it could host, or tolerate, elements of market failure under severe stress. This enormous, ebullient, ever-shifting marketplace needs to be better understood if we are going to rely upon it as our first line of defense against fraudsters, manipulators, and spin doctors.

2

The New Financial Markets

During the last two decades of the twentieth century, financial market activity expanded at a pace nearly twice that of nominal economic growth in the United States—nearly 15 percent per year. This expansion was reflected in stock market prices both in the United States and Europe, in stock trading volumes and the volume of mergers and acquisitions, corporate restructurings, and related transactions. Sustained rapid growth in financial markets was in part an accident of the times that developed into a speculative frenzy before the bubble it formed burst in 2000.

But the times were not simply a bubble, to be dismissed not long afterward. These were the times when the forces of economics and history combined in an unprecedented period of disintermediation, deregulation, globalization, innovation, and confidence in market-oriented economic policies. They were also times when financial markets, not banks or insurance companies, came to be relied upon to supply the bulk of the world's finance.

By the end of the twentieth century, the proportion of all financial assets held by banks had declined to approximately 30 percent from 45 percent in 1980, and the difference had shifted into global financial markets that had developed to an extraordinary, completely unprecedented size—with market capitalization of stocks and bonds exceeding $72 trillion in 2000.[1] These markets contained powerful forces that could quickly move funds in large quantities around the world to jump into (or out of) a suddenly discovered investment opportunity. These forces were energized by enormous turnover volumes—the value of consolidated world stock trading in 2000 was more than $47 trillion, one and a half times its market capitalization. About half of this trading occurred outside the United States, in stock markets in Europe, Asia, and Latin America.

Table 2.1. Global Market Capitalization, 2000 (US$ Billions)

	Bonds				Total Market Cap
	Domestic	International	Total	Equities	
USA	14,500	1,845	16,345	16,635	32,980
Europe	7,174	2,765	9,939	8,408	18,347
Japan	6,014	105	6,119	4,547	10,666
Rest of the World	2,471	1,651	4,122	6,441	10,563
Total	30,159	6,366	36,525	36,031	72,556

Source: BIS, IFC

In 2000, more than $4.4 trillion of new corporate debt and equity securities were issued, including some $2.3 trillion of investment grade debt securities, $460 billion of asset-backed securities, $800 billion of medium-term notes, and $100 billion of high-yield debt securities, as compared to $1.9 trillion of new syndicated bank loans and note issuance facilities. In 2000 as well, gross purchases and sales of U.S. securities (stocks, bonds and government securities) by foreigners totaled $7 trillion, and gross purchases and sales of foreign securities by U.S. investors exceeded $3.6 trillion. Foreign investors, in the aggregate, owned about 10 percent of all U.S. stocks in 2000, the third highest ownership after mutual and pension funds. Markets were well connected internationally and were linked by arbitrage opportunities and financial derivative instruments, such as interest rate and currency swaps, of which $66 trillion in notional amounts were outstanding in December 2000, and by a daily turnover in foreign exchange markets of more than $1.5 trillion, over 80 percent of which was attributed to financial transactions, as opposed to trade.

The growth of the financial markets, as well as the scale they achieved, was well beyond anything imaginable a generation earlier. In most of them, the volume attributed to transactions completed outside the United States was 30 to 50 percent of the world total, indicating that the rest of the world was quickly catching up with American financial market capacity. Overseas markets today provide virtually unregulated, fully competitive "alternative marketplaces" that can be easily used by U.S. corporations. The existence of such large, global financial markets, their trading power, and their changeable demands and whims make them a challenge for all corporations seeking to utilize their sources of low-cost capital, and to banks and others seeking to provide access to them.

US has 50% to 80% of financial transactions

Table 2.2 Nongovernment Capital Market Activity—1993–2004 ($ billions)

	2004	2003	2002	2001	2000	1999	1998	1997	1996	1995	1994	1993
U.S. Domestic New Issues												
US MTNs	57.6	370.6	357.0	429.2	372.8	397.9	308.6	284.7	255.3	404.9	282.8	260.3
Investment Grade Debt	2,086.8	2,323.6	1944.1	1,851.5	1,579.6	1,195.8	504.2	726.1	518.9	417.3	342.5	389.2
Collateralized Securities	1,394.8	1,359.1	1154.2	841.1	479.0	559.0	560.9	378.0	252.3	154.1	252.5	478.9
High Yield Debt	141.0	147.5	77.1	109.0	70.3	108.7	149.9	125.3	121.4	30.2	36.4	69.5
Municipal Debt	264.4	331.5	346.1	320.8	204.0	219.3	279.7	214.8	181.7	154.9	161.3	287.8
Total Debt	**3,944.6**	**4,532.3**	**3,878.5**	**3,551.6**	**2,705.7**	**2,480.7**	**1,803.3**	**1,728.9**	**1,329.6**	**1,161.4**	**1,075.5**	**1,485.7**
Preferred Stock & Convertibles	52.1	93.1	66.5	137.9	87.6	68.3	74.5	91.3	45.6	16.3	15.5	22.4
Common Stock	170.1	121.1	117.8	128.6	206.9	171.9	114.8	120.1	115.4	81.7	61.6	101.7
Total Equity	**222.2**	**214.2**	**184.3**	**266.5**	**294.5**	**240.2**	**189.3**	**211.4**	**161.0**	**98.0**	**77.1**	**124.1**
Total U.S. Domestic	**4,166.8**	**4,746.5**	**4,062.8**	**3,818.1**	**3,000.2**	**2,720.9**	**1,992.6**	**1,940.3**	**1,490.6**	**1,259.4**	**1,152.5**	**1,609.8**
International Issues												
Euro MTNs	609.9	514.2	390.9	484.0	440.2	607.8	598.0	420.0	392.6	251.6	257.2	149.8
Euro Investment Grade Debt	1,979.2	1,641.6	1,044.5	910.3	779.8	815.5	553.4	573.4	563.3	398.2	385.9	421.4
Euro Collateralized Securities	341.6	243.7	146.8	130.8	78.9	103.4	60.6	65.6	31.5	8.4	21.3	8.3
Euro High Yield Debt	102.6	66.4	32.6	34.0	50.6	46.1	41.0	40.7	27.0	17.6	6.9	6.3
International Equity	151.9	59.4	53.7	82.8	98.9	181.0	74.1	75.0	51.0	32.1	32.4	27.7
Total International	**3,185.2**	**2,525.3**	**1,668.5**	**1,641.9**	**1,448.4**	**1,753.8**	**1,327.1**	**1,174.7**	**1,065.4**	**707.9**	**703.7**	**613.5**
World-Wide Total	**7,352.0**	**7,271.8**	**5,731.3**	**5,460.0**	**4,448.6**	**4,474.7**	**3,319.7**	**3,115.0**	**2,556.0**	**1,967.3**	**1,856.2**	**2,223.3**
Global Syndicated Bank Loans & NIFs	3,076.0	2,166.3	1,860.2	2,359.0	1,789.2	1,750.0	1,223.0	1,265.8	1,400.0	1,098.0	785.6	555.4

Source: Thomson Financial Securities Data, Investment Dealer's Digest

Table 2.3. Financial Derivative Instruments Outstanding

	Notional Principal Amount (US$ billions)			
	1998	1999	2000	2001
Exchange Traded Instruments	13,932.4	13,521.7	14,303.2	23,717.3
Interest Rate Futures	8,020.0	7,913.9	7,891.9	9,234
Interest Rate Options	4,624.0	3,755.5	4,734.2	12,492.6
Currency Futures	31.7	36.7	74.4	65.6
Currency Options	49.2	22.4	21.4	27.4
Stock Index Futures	290.7	334.3	393.2	334
Stock Index Options	916.8	1,458.9	1,187.1	1,563.7
Over the Counter Instruments	38,515.0	46,380.0	51,962.0	62,839.0
Interest Rate Swaps	36,262.0	43,936.0	48,768.0	58,897.0
Currency Swaps	2,253.0	2,444.0	3,194.0	3,942.0

Source: BIS

AN EXTRAORDINARY TIME

Events came together in the 1980s and 1990s in ways that provided an unusually fertile environment for the global financial marketplace to develop.[2] These consecutive decades were the only time in the twentieth century in which the United States was not at war, or in economic crisis, or just recovering from one or the other. And some special conditions did materialize during these two decades that significantly accelerated financial market developments: (1) changes in economic policy initiated by governments; (2) the release of market forces resulting from these changes; and (3) technology developments that not only occurred simultaneously and greatly extended the effects of the other two developments but also created myriad institutional changes.

New Economic Policies

A new set of economic policies emerged in the United States during the 1980s and 1990s, the essence of which was that the government's intervention in the economy would be less than before. The private sector was recognized as the principal source of job and wealth creation, and the free market was acknowledged as the best of alternative mechanisms for allocating economic resources. These policies were accepted by both of America's major political parties, mainly because people believed they worked. Unless some large problems requiring government intervention arose (and they do), the consensus appeared to be that arm's-length government involvement in economic affairs works well, so the market should mainly be left to its own devices.

But it was not always so. The role of the federal government in the prosperous Kennedy-Johnson years loomed large in American economic life, and was very hands-on. The government's role, it was thought, was to promote balance and fairness in the economy by interventions that would assist and encourage some sectors (e.g., labor, the poor), while restraining or constraining others (business, finance). This was to make society more democratic, but not necessarily more efficient. Such policies resulted in large government budgets that were extremely difficult to manage. Accordingly, economic policy initiatives were almost impossible to fine-tune. Toward the end of the 1960s, the government had simultaneously become committed to a war in Vietnam and to a wide range of expensive new social policies. It was struggling hard to control inflation and defend the value of the dollar, ultimately without success. The stock market, which enjoyed strong performance during the first half of the decade of the 1960s, was much less confident during the second half. Despite outstanding performance in some sectors of the economy, the Dow Jones Industrial Average did not quite double during an 11-year period, encompassing a low of 536 in June 1962, and a high of 1,053 in January 1973. During this time, the index flirted with 1,000 on several occasions, only to fall off again. Things were much worse in the 1970s, a period of economic difficulty not experienced in the United States since the Great Depression. Inflation, seemingly out of control, rose into double digits for the first time in anyone's memory. After the decade's effects of inflation averaging about 8 percent, an investment made in the stock market in 1970 had lost more than 40 percent of its economic value by 1981.

Ronald Reagan ran for the presidency in 1980 at a time when the country had lost confidence in the government's ability to manage the economy and to maintain its position in the world. He was elected because of the appeal of his basic values and a well-communicated, popular platform of economic renewal, a reduced government role in the personal and corporate lives of Americans, and a robust and confident stance against the Soviet Union. Reagan's skillfully conducted campaign offered images of a new "morning in America," and it was successful. In 1984, he was elected again. Reagan's simple economic ideas appealed strongly to those faithful to the conservative school of the Nobel laureate economist Milton Friedman, the reigning prince of monetarism and laissez-faire. His supporters believed that governments were incapable of managing the economy to maximize growth and prosperity, because the political arena required too many compromises and economically wrongheaded detours. The country should leave growth and prosperity to the private sector, a natural marketplace, and everyone would be better off—including the poor, who would benefit from more jobs and other opportunities that would "trickle" down to them.

Reagan came into office with a landslide victory and a powerful mandate for economic change. Much of his work, however, had already been done for him by Paul Volcker and the Federal Reserve Board, which had turned inflation around by an extraordinary, Friedman-like tightening of the money supply in 1979. But the country was still in recession in 1981, so the first action of the new Reagan economic team was to offer an economic stimulus program that included a major tax cut—not unlike the Democratic Kennedy-Johnson plan that had worked so well 20 years before.

The tax cut was a large one, and it was accompanied by an increase in defense spending, and no appreciable reduction in the rest of the budget, so a large deficit was unavoidable. However, the first effect of the 27 percent personal income tax cut enacted in 1982 was the encouragement of a sudden burst of consumption, which, combined with a steady lowering of interest rates, enabled the economy to grow at real rates above 4 percent for four years. The early Reagan years were heady ones, and created conditions that pushed stocks and other financial markets into sudden recoveries. The economic success would last for several years, until the stimulus wore off and the heavy burden of the deficits started to take hold, by which time Reagan's time in office was about to end, and George H. W. Bush's presidency was about to begin.

The economy briefly fell back into recession as Bush, Sr., was running for reelection in 1992. Conservatives Reagan and Bush were criticized for having wrecked the country's financial position by overborrowing, and putting the burden for repaying the national debt on their children and grandchildren. A lack of confidence in Bush's ability to regain control of the economy surfaced, and he was beaten by Bill Clinton, who, predictably, promised—as John Kennedy had done in 1960—to "get the economy moving again" and to undertake significant spending programs that were popular with the voters. Clinton was easily able to ride out the recession, which ended before he was inaugurated. But he had no convincing mandate and soon found his legislative ideas blocked by Congress. He nevertheless made a significant contribution to the economy by focusing on interest rates, not the budget.

All Bill Clinton had to do was stay away from all the temptations that had beset Democrats from the days of Franklin Roosevelt. With reducing the deficit being seen as the necessary and patriotic thing to do, there was no room for new social programs or reforms, even if the Republican Congress would have allowed them. Clinton did narrowly pass a tax increase for further deficit reduction, and reappointed conservative Republican Alan Greenspan as chairman of the Federal Reserve, on whom he relied to keep interest rates down. But mainly he just waited for the deficit to reduce itself, as economic growth, responding to the check on the money supply, began to resume. Economic value popped back into the system and helped to fuel a continuous period of growth in the economy that was even longer than the 106 consecutive months of the golden years of the 1960s. But unlike the earlier growth period, the Reagan-Clinton expansion was not accompanied by a prolonged war or ambitious spending programs that would reignite inflation. The Clinton stock market (1993–2000), in which the Dow Jones tripled, was able to do so well because no such big spending programs loomed ahead and, in any case, any major Clinton spending programs would be blocked by a Republican-dominated Congress. To many, Clinton's economics seemed to be about what one would expect from a steady, mainstream Republican. The stock market felt it had nothing to fear from Clinton's administration, and it continued to expand until his last days in office.

The 1980s and 1990s were also important years in Europe, and in many other parts of the world, for the amount of radical changes that occurred in political-economic systems. As unpleasant as the 1970s were in America, they were perhaps worse in Europe—trade union disputes became increasingly common, productivity declined, inflation and unemployment rose, and in many countries, concern about the increasing influence of the "Euro-communists" was expressed. The "mixed-economy" plan of the early postwar years had been very disappointing, and finally provoked a response from the Right, as Margaret Thatcher was chosen to lead the Conservative Party in Britain and soon afterward, in 1979, became prime minister—a position she held powerfully and influentially for 10 years. Thatcher was an admirer of Milton Friedman and Ronald Reagan and wasted no time implementing plans both would approve. She abolished Britain's foreign exchange controls, which had been in place since 1914—an astonishing 85 years—and lowered taxes. She immediately challenged the principal trade unions and successfully endured their strikes. She initiated actions that completely reformed the ancient ways of the City of London's financial district, and paved the way for a decade of privatizations—the sale of government-owned shares in industrial corporations that were being denationalized and returned to the private sector. Before long, Britain's economy began to respond, and its economic indicators began to rise, and with it the stock market.

On the European continent during this time, many were watching Britain in quiet disbelief. By the mid-1980s, enough of Thatcher's magic had worked to cause the other countries of the European Union (EU) to take a fresh look at the 1958 Treaty of Rome, which had fallen well short of its goals of creating the unified and transparent market for goods and services that had once been envisioned. A study was commissioned, supported by many important business and academic leaders, that recommended that the EU remove the national restrictions on the free flow of goods and services that were impeding European growth and dissipating the principal advantages of membership in the EU. They resolved to create a unified market, which would establish, in a Europe of 325 million people and combined GDP equal to that of the United States, an "area without internal frontiers in which the free movement of goods, services, persons and capital is ensured." The "Single Market Act" was approved by European heads of state in 1985 and by national legislatures in 1986, and went into effect in 1992.

But before it did, many other reforms were gathering steam. Following Britain's lead, privatization programs were undertaken by virtually all European countries, and a great many outside Europe as well. Privatizations became the rule in many countries in the 1980s and 1990s; they raised funds for governments in developed and developing countries, enabled improvements in the operating results of the former state-owned enterprises that were being privatized (thus becoming part of the taxpaying economy), and spread ownership of the shares widely among the investing public, thereby helping to build up national capital markets.

There were other reforms, too. In 1986, the central bankers of 12 leading financial powers agreed on a system for assuring a risk-adjusted minimum level of capital for banks that went into effect in 1992. Stock exchanges in Europe, Japan, and other countries entered into major technical reforms to be able to keep up with the advances in London, since its dramatic financial overhaul in 1986 ("Big Bang"), which had uniformly lowered commission rates and improved trading and settlement arrangements.

In 1989 and subsequently, the Soviet Union and its eastern European satellites disintegrated, creating an end-of-the-Cold-War optimism in Europe that had not been seen for decades. The regime had imploded bloodlessly as a result of the failure of its economic system, and the new governments rising up afterward chose to rely on a free-market capitalist system to replace it. Watching closely, the governments of China, India, and many Latin American countries decided to adopt their own forms of market capitalism as well. By the mid-1990s, it could be argued that nearly half the world's population had experienced a nonviolent, voluntary conversion of their underlying economic systems from a socialist to a free-market orientation. Nothing like this had ever happened before. Next came the Economic and Monetary Union within the EU, in which initially 11 (and later 12) of the 15 member countries elected to exchange their currencies for the euro; the launch took place at the start of 1999.

Releasing Market Forces

Beyond the budget, a fundamental belief of "Reaganomics" was that the government should get out of businesses and functions it had no good reason to be involved with. The idea, originally called "deregulation," actually began during the Carter administration, when airline rates and routes and a number of other industrial sectors subject to direct government regulation were set free. Reagan's policies went further, and were more vocal. America would participate in "privatization" efforts, just as Margaret Thatcher was beginning to do in Britain. Unlike Europe, however, the United States owned relatively few commercial businesses that could be privatized—Conrail was one, and it was privatized in 1988. Americans instead settled for deregulating a number of industries in the transportation, telecommunications, and defense sectors, in which a great deal of merger and acquisition activity subsequently took place. But foremost among the affected sectors was financial services.

The Reagan administration also extended its deregulatory reforms to accommodate a significant relaxation in antitrust enforcement actions by the federal government. Since the 1950s, even during robust Republican years, the government's view of antitrust violations was much more restrictive than it has since become. Bigness was bad in itself, because it *might* restrict competition. This forced companies that wanted to grow by acquisition to become conglomerates instead— mostly inefficient ones—by buying a large variety of smaller, nondominant companies in vastly different businesses. In the early Reagan years, however, the government reset its antitrust positions, and substantially reduced its objections to business combinations on the grounds of market dominance. When it did intervene, it allowed companies to negotiate a solution based on selling off businesses in overlapping sectors. This policy was eroded a bit during the Bush and Clinton administrations but not substantially. Huge transactions involving direct competitors with large market shares (Exxon and Mobil, for example) were allowed to go ahead all through the 1990s, although the government did try (unsuccessfully) to break up Microsoft. Nevertheless, the lessening of antitrust policy restrictions on corporate combinations created many restructuring opportunities for larger companies in the 1980s and 1990s, undoubtedly to a far greater extent than might have been imagined at the beginning of the period.

In 1980, a great many American companies were in need of serious restructuring. They had lived through the 1970s, when it was difficult to make any money—let alone grow their businesses—and the markets had been especially cruel to their shareholders. Domestic economic conditions worsened, and they lost ground, encountering tough competition at home and abroad from Japanese and other foreign rivals. They did what they could in the context of the prevailing management model they were used to—in bad times, reduce debt, hunker down, and avoid big risks or major changes in the business unless absolutely necessary. By 1980, corporate debt, as a percent of total capitalization, had dropped to its lowest level since the Eisenhower years. At many companies, executive stock options had not been worth much for years, and the CEOs—who owned little stock anyway—were not thinking like aggressive institutional investors looking for high returns on investment. The managers were trying to *protect* the great American companies and the environment they knew (including their own jobs and perks) from external dangers, such as "unfair" foreign competitors and corporate raiders seeking to rip apart and destroy them. Many such companies were thought to be cheap in 1980—the price—earnings ratio of the S&P 500 composite of publicly traded companies at the time ranged between a high of 9.5 and a low of 6.6. (In 1970, the S&P 500 p/e ratio ranged between 18.2 and 13.5. By 1990, it would return to and exceed these levels.)

But a company could be considered cheap only if an investor knew how it might be returned to fair value. A takeover could be an opportunity only if there was a plan for changing things so significantly that the company could come to trade at a maximum valuation—a level reflecting what it would be worth if the best reorganization plan imaginable was adopted, and implemented effectively and completely. The trouble was, existing management groups were not about to undertake such drastic reorganizations without being absolutely sure that the best plan had been identified and that it could be implemented without damaging the company or its managers. Such plans were subjects of endless meetings and debates that often were left unresolved or ended in debilitating compromises. Indeed, little might have happened to change things if the corporate raiders had not appeared.

The raiders were a group of opportunistic capitalists—bright, insolent, confident individuals responsible only to their financial backers—who didn't much care if corporate America liked them or not. They bought stock in companies they thought could be improved, issued press releases criticizing management, made threats and trouble at annual meetings, and sometimes launched tender offers to achieve control. The idea was that the targeted companies had been badly managed in the past and, if new management was brought in, could be completely restructured in the interest of increasing shareholder value. "Restructuring" meant selling off divisions and other assets that no longer fit into a highly focused, "back-to-basics" strategy. The raiders also wanted to increase leverage, run companies for cash (not just accounting profits), milk all possible tax benefits, and provide substantial incentives to management to work hard to make all this happen. And they insisted on layoffs of unnecessary personnel, a process later called "downsizing."

At first, the business establishment reacted negatively to these ideas, suggesting instead that stockholders accept that management knew best and criticizing the motives, reputations, and integrity of the raiders. But stockholders were often bought out for cash, at a substantial premium over the market value of the company before the offer. Institutions saw the value in these deals right away, but it took longer to convince the general public. But ultimately people began to see the raiders as actually doing some good, in their much-publicized quest to uphold shareholders' rights. Before long, a consensus was formed that all companies needed to examine shareholder value issues and either initiate self-restructuring measures themselves or otherwise expect a hostile group, with shareholder support, to come after them.

MERGERS AND RESTRUCTURING

From 1982 through 1988, more than 10,000 mergers took place in the United States, valued at over $1 trillion, including the largest ever completed, the acquisition of RJR Nabisco by KKR for $30 billion in 1988. About a quarter of the merger transactions during this period were initiated by a hostile bid, and one in six was in the form of a leveraged buyout. The vast majority of transactions were neither hostile nor leveraged. But all the corporate combat going on around them made managers and boards of directors distinctly nervous. This led to an increase in self-initiated actions to cure the problems that made companies attractive to others. Some observers believed that more overdue corporate restructuring took place during this time as a result of management's own efforts than in response to takeover attempts.[3]

Arguably, the strong stock market performance during the 1990s was a result of the large-scale corporate restructuring (and accompanying increases in productivity) that began during the 1980s. Improved corporate profits had certainly been helped along by the takeover struggles and threats of the 1980s. By the 1990s, it was well understood that companies were required to produce returns on investment that would be acceptable to investors, or face the consequences. The stock market, in fixing new price levels, was in fact capitalizing expected future earnings improvements, which for many companies were now a permanent, systematic recurring event. In 1980, the return on equity of the S&P 500 index of companies was only 11 percent; by 1998, it had increased to 18 percent.

During the first years of the 1990s, the pace of merger-and-acquisition activities fell off sharply. The junk bond market collapsed in 1989, and banks became much more cautious about making highly leveraged loans, so financing for deals became scarce, and the "financial entrepreneurs" who were acquiring companies quit the scene. In light of the rising stock market values, there were no longer many low-priced, easy restructuring deals to be found. By 1994, however, the merger market was back in business, at an even faster pace than before. This time financial entrepreneurs played only a small role. The big deals were being done by companies seeking strategic partners, or repositioning themselves for the future in their changing industries. In the five-year period from 1996 through 2000, $3.1 trillion of U.S. domestic and cross-border merger-and-acquisition deals involving more than 10,000 companies took place, making this the most merger-intensive period of all times—in terms of five-year combined merger volume as a percent of GDP. The activity in the 1996–2000 period eclipsed the much acclaimed merger intensity of the 1898–1902 period, which had never been equaled even during the heyday of the 1980s.[4] The merger boom reached its peak in 2000, when nearly a trillion dollars of domestic transactions were completed in the United States, the record year by far. It fell precipitously thereafter.

Outside the United States, market forces were also mounting. In Japan, the 1980s was a boom decade, in which money poured into financial markets from the country's enormous depository institutions and from pension funds beginning to set aside the assets needed to care for the aging population. Many of these assets were directed into Japanese stocks and real estate, creating a bubble that burst in late 1989, followed by economic flame-out and a decade of efforts to restart the economy that did not begin to bear fruit until the early 2000s. In the 1980s, Japanese overseas investments had been highly visible, but by the 1990s they largely dried up. The stress on the underlying system bankrupted many companies and financial institutions and forced Japan to adjust, restructure, and redeploy assets.

Meanwhile, in Europe, the need to adapt to the new economic

Table 2.4. Completed M&A Transactions 1985–2004 (US$ Billion)

		US Domestic		Non-US Transactions		
		%LBOs	%Hostile	Value Completed	%LBOs(a)	%Hostile
1985	192.3	13.4	22.3	24.8	8.7	13.1
1986	200.9	16.5	17.7	54.6	3.8	8.0
1987	203.9	19.7	25.0	96.2	9.9	8.5
1988	293.2	31.1	19.8	140.3	12.1	10.6
1989	250.1	11.2	20.9	227.8	14.5	10.1
1990	124.9	6.6	24.0	236.2	11.1	8.4
1991	108.5	4.6	19.3	202.4	8.5	6.5
1992	119.3	6.6	14.1	163.8	15.0	7.0
1993	101.1	5.4	12.4	125.8	7.9	10.1
1994	199.8	3	14.4	148.7	10.0	10.1
1995	218.5	1.4	14.2	227.8	7.2	7.4
1996	330.7	0.3	15.1	298.6	5.8	8.6
1997	488.3	1.3	7.2	388.3	14.6	6.3
1998	801.8	0.4	6.1	505.6	8.1	7.0
1999	588.7	1.3	4.2	797.5	15.2	11.3
2000	930.9	2.6	3.5	1,143.90	7.5	15.9
2001	379.0	1.9	2.5	713.0	13.6	7.8
2002	220.9	4.8	3.2	546.6	13.2	13.3
2003	264.1	5.0	3.3	564.0	8.8	4.1
2004	474.5	8.2	2.5	719.1	8.9	4.6

(a) based on European sellers

Source: Thompson Financial Securities Data

realities of the single market of 1992 required that companies restructure as well, and Europe's first merger boom began in about 1985. Within the next 15 years, during which mergers valued at $9.9 trillion were completed globally, Europe became as active a venue for mergers as the United States, with almost half of the deal volume. In 1985, only $25 billion in mergers occurred outside the United States, about half of that in Europe. In 2000 alone, $1.1 trillion in mergers were completed outside the United States, of which about two-thirds involved intra-European transactions. This greatly expanded level of activity accompanied growth in European stock, bond and bank financing markets enabling them to grow in capacity and in capability and sophistication.

NEW TECHNOLOGIES

The bull market of the 1990s occurred during times of major change in technology, which greatly improved productivity in large sectors of the economy and also created entirely new industries and applications. Three new industry groupings, in particular, emerged as a result—electronics and related fields (hardware, software and applications); the telecommunications field (embracing cellular systems, cable, and the Internet); and the reconfigured healthcare industry (drugs, biotechnology, and healthcare delivery systems). Together, these industries made up about a quarter of the stock market capitalization of all of American industry at the end of 1998.

The computer industry was especially expansive, particularly in terms of new companies, products, and services being introduced to the market. A Goldman Sachs study of the industry in June 1998 suggested that 56 companies in this industry group accounted for almost $1 trillion of market capitalization.[5] Of this, less than 22 percent was made up by the eight companies that had been market leaders in the industry in 1981 and were still independent. The rest of the group's market capitalization was attributable to new companies like Cisco Systems, Compaq Computer, Dell, Microsoft, Oracle, and Sun Microsystems. Of the 30 largest computer/communications companies by market capitalization in June 1998, only 5 were listed on the *Fortune 500* list in 1981. IBM was the leading computer-technology company in 1981, and its market capitalization at the end of 1998 was $170 billion. Microsoft's was $343 billion. Dell Computer's was $93 billion. The bubble saw technology valuations soar even further—Microsoft was valued at $550 billion and Dell at $141 billion, on December 31, 1999, after the NASDAQ index had risen by more than 80 percent in that year.

Similarly, in the high-tech sectors of the telecommunications industry (leaving aside the traditional telephone businesses), 31 companies contributed $340 billion of market capitalization in 1989. This did not include another $133 billion of market capitalization of MCI WorldCom, which came together that year in an exchange of shares. Of the 31 companies, more than three-quarters of the market capitalization was contributed by companies that were either nonexistent or insignificant in 1981, such as AOL, Comcast, Netscape, and Yahoo!

Similar high-tech communications companies were sold in an effort to pass their market capitalization on to larger, long-established companies. Examples included the purchase of McCaw Cellular Communications by AT&T in 1993 for $12.6 billion; Time-Warner's acquisition of Turner Broadcasting for $6.7 billion in 1995; and U.S. West's acquisition of Continental Cablevision for $5.3 billion in 1996. In 1999, Bell Atlantic merged with GTE in an $89 billion transaction, and Airtouch Communications, the West Coast cellular phone company, was merged into the British communications company, Vodafone, in an exchange of shares valued at $58 billion. Olivetti, an Italian manufacturer that had converted itself into a telecommunications company, acquired control of the much larger Telecom Italia for $60 billion. Later in the year, Vodafone-Airtouch made a surprise hostile takeover attempt to acquire Mannesmann, a German cellular company, which finally agreed to a friendly merger for a price of $180 billion, the world's largest deal up to that time. In January 2000, AOL organized a friendly merger with Time Warner in a transaction valued at $165 billion. AOL, one of the country's first Internet portal companies, had already acquired Netscape and Compuserve, two star performers of the Internet era.

All of these mergers, of course, were affected at high valuations, reflecting very high price-earnings ratios by ordinary standards. Accordingly, they created and released a great wealth to founders, key employees, and initial investors of the companies involved. They also provoked a substantial amount of postmerger restructuring, management changes, and asset sales. The merger wave of technology deals continued unabated into 2000, with dozens of deals completed.

The healthcare industry was another to explode in the 1990s. At the end of 1997, this industry, which was loosely defined as consisting of pharmaceutical companies and healthcare service providers, represented more than $900 billion of market value. The 11 pharmaceutical companies among the *Fortune* 500 contributed most of this value, but in 1997 there were also 13 health-care service companies, such as hospital management companies and HMOs, among the *Fortune* 500, worth more than $60 billion in market capitalization. None of these companies were among the 500 largest American companies in 1981. In 1999 and 2000, massive mergers occurred between the leading pharmaceutical companies, such as the $93 billion combination of Pfizer and Warner-Lambert, and the $75 billion merger of Smith Kline-Beecham and Glaxo-Wellcome in January 2000.

TRANSFORMATION OF THE FINANCIAL SERVICES SECTOR

In the mid-1960s, the U.S. financial services industry consisted of three solid and separate parts—insurance, banking, and securities. Insurance was divided between property and casualty and life insurance, although some companies offered both. Banking consisted of deposit-taking and commercial lending, and included savings institutions as well as commercial banks. The securities business was focused on brokerage, underwriting, and advice. All three managed pension and non-pension assets, as did independent fund-management firms. These industry segments were all highly regulated, usually by both state regulations and federal statutes enacted in the early part of the Roosevelt administration. They were generally thought of as low-growth, conservative businesses.

All of this changed as the separate segments began to experience both growth and convergence, and a firestorm of competitive dislocations took hold that entirely transformed the old regime. Among the reconfigured firms that emerged were some that not only originated and distributed loans, securities, derivatives, and a variety of other financial products and services but also traded in them on behalf of clients and for their own account and managed large pools of assets for others. These "integrated" financial firms acted as both agents and as principals as they performed the functions of the modern "lender-broker-dealer-adviser." The single-function ("monoline") firms of the past—which acted uncomplicatedly as bankers, or brokers or underwriters—were no longer considered by some to be viable in the fluid and highly competitive financial markets that developed in the 1980s.

By the end of the 1990s, fewer than a dozen integrated firms dominated the industry, accounting between them for market shares of well over 80 percent in capital raising, wholesale lending, and merger advice, expanding their activities to a very large range of securities, commodities, and derivatives and operating all over the world (see table 2.5). Firms that were not so integrated acted mainly as "niche players," offering a specialized set of products and services. But they too had to compete in the broader market with the integrated firms.

By the end of the 1990s, financial services had evolved into two large and distinct markets—retail (consumers and local or regional businesses) and wholesale (corporations, banks, and governments with access to capital markets). Some firms endeavored to address both markets. Others preferred specialization in one market or the other. The major developments that have transformed the wholesale financial services industry, and thus the financial marketplace, consist primarily of institutionalization, deregulation, and consolidation over a period of three decades.

Table 2.5 Global Wholesale Banking Origination Rankings, 2004

Firm Rank 2004	Syndicated Bank Loans	Global Debt U/W & Private Placements	Global Equity U/W & Private Placements	M & A Advisory Completed	MTNs Arranged	Total	Market Share
JP Morgan	543,021.0	341,091.6	31,890.1	594,936.0	1,000.0	1,511,938.7	13.25%
Citigroup	376,028.0	461,421.3	50,565.9	525,611.1		1,413,626.3	12.39%
Goldman Sachs & Co	34,395.9	207,530.4	48,588.2	688,087.4		978,601.9	8.58%
Morgan Stanley	16,473.1	305,881.0	52,657.5	495,562.4		870,574.0	7.63%
Merrill Lynch & Co Inc	29,826.6	269,804.7	56,222.9	404,864.2	17,410.0	778,128.4	6.82%
Deutsche Bank AG	122,304.3	298,896.8	25,087.5	259,108.5		705,397.1	6.18%
Lehman Brothers	30,377.6	300,945.9	29,750.8	320,268.1	6,000.0	687,342.4	6.02%
Banc of America Securities LLC	319,643.3	222,419.9	11,532.9	73,749.1		627,345.2	5.50%
Crédit Suisse First Boston	63,644.4	306,437.1	32,119.4	208,086.3		610,287.2	5.35%
UBS	24,520.8	244,668.2	33,314.7	233,464.0		535,967.7	4.70%
ABN AMRO	70,425.7	111,162.6	7,800.0	166,133.1	11,380.0	366,901.4	3.22%
Barclays Capital	139,249.3	189,190.1	575.3		2,497.5	331,512.2	2.91%
Bear Stearns & Co Inc		192,587.2	6,194.7	102,830.5		301,612.4	2.64%
BNP Paribas SA	100,261.5	89,957.8	5,950.6	96,864.2		293,034.1	2.57%
Royal Bank of Scotland Group	80,877.6	186,640.9				267,518.5	2.34%
Rothschild				242,236.4		242,236.4	2.12%
Lazard			940.7	240,699.9		241,640.6	2.12%
HSBC Holdings PLC	61,531.1	123,286.8	3,008.5	45,949.9		233,776.3	2.05%
Wachovia Corp	85,112.6	66,448.7	3,290.9	39,549.7	200.0	194,601.9	1.71%
Societe Générale	50,529.0	77,534.3	7,158.8			135,222.1	1.19%

Note: Full credit to bookrunners only, and named advisors to merging companies. Completed deals only.

Data: Thomson Financial Securities Data.

INSTITUTIONALIZATION

This transformation had its origin in the rise of the importance of institutional investors in the stock market during the 1960s. These institutions—banks, insurance companies, foundations and endowments, pension funds and investment managers—were large enough to employ professional investment managers using modern portfolio concepts that had become the foundation of their profession. The central idea was to find the optimum balance between risk diversification and return on investment, or perhaps, put another way, how to invest aggressively but safely. A Ford Foundation study of university endowments in the 1960s concluded that too few of them invested their endowment funds aggressively enough, and the Foundation threatened to cut off future funding until they did. Corporate pension funds also became interested, knowing that the better the investment returns, the less the parent companies would have to contribute to their pension plans in the future.

Once some of the institutions became known for investment performance, it was not long before all of the rest had to emulate them. Many in-house managers decided to hire professional firms specializing in equities to take over for them. Trustees and directors of all sorts of fiduciary institutions began to look for investment performance that could balance risks with rewards. These trustees and directors, in turn, began shopping around for better investment managers. In 1959 three recent Harvard Business School graduates founded the firm of Donaldson, Lufkin & Jenrette & Co. to provide institutional managers with the detailed, analytical company research reports that they would use to make investment decisions. Soon similar research efforts were undertaken by other securities firms that were pursuing the institutional business.

In 1974 Congress passed the Employees Retirement Income Security Act (ERISA), which compelled corporations that had fallen behind in making contributions to their pension funds to bring them up to date and to reduce the share of assets in the pension funds that were represented by their own company stock. This increased the flow of funds going into managed pension plans. Congress also allowed a variety of tax-deferred individual retirement accounts, which added to this flow. By 1989, institutional holdings of equities accounted for 49 percent of all American equities, and half of these were owned by private and public pension funds. In 2001, combined institutional holdings exceeded 61 percent of all equities, although pension funds only accounted for about a third of these holdings.

Institutional holdings of equities were further boosted by the rapid expansion of mutual funds in the 1980s and 1990s. Although mutual funds had existed since the 1920s, they only became popular in the late 1960s when individuals became aware of skilled money managers whose talents they could purchase for the price of a management fee through a mutual fund. Still, mutual funds did not amount to more than 5 percent of household liquid assets until 1986, after which they began to rise in popularity, reaching a peak of 49.9 percent of household liquid assets in 1999.

This extraordinary acceleration in the role of mutual funds was partly caused by the shift by many corporations to defined contribution plans—including 401k programs that allowed pension plan participants to select mutual funds for investment—which grew to 55 percent of all private pension assets in 2000. Mutual fund growth was also assisted by an exceptional effort to distribute and market such funds, which were being offered in the mid-1990s not only by the original mutual fund management companies but also by banks, Wall Street broker-dealers, independent financial advisers, and market-index fund managers. By 2000, mutual funds owned 18.4 percent of all equities outstanding in the United States; private pension funds 12.5 percent, public (i.e., state and municipal) pension funds 7.6 percent, life insurance companies 5.4 percent, and bank trust companies 1.6 percent. The institutions were often not buy-and-hold investors. They were active traders, frequently buying and selling stocks, as new funds had to be invested and new opportunities pursued. As a result, institutional investors dominated the trading markets in stocks, and were most influential in establishing the prices at which stocks traded.

DEREGULATION

Until the mid-1970s, block trades generated exceptionally large commissions for the brokers handling them under the NYSE rules that prohibited discounting of commissions, regardless of the size of the trade. Some institutions objected and sued the NYSE to abandon practices that restrained trade, and the Justice Department joined the suit, ultimately ensuring its success. Fixed stock-brokerage commissions were ended on May 1, 1975—remembered as "Mayday," a maritime distress call—and dropped sharply as they were quickly cut by competitive firms eager to gain institutional business. They hoped to make up the lost revenues from greater trading volume, and many did. Not all firms could manage this well, and many failed as price competition intensified. The result was a number of mergers and takeovers in the securities business to create larger firms capable of integrated operations in which one firm's brokerage, research, trading, back-office, and underwriting and corporate finance businesses could be managed effectively under one roof.

The brokerage business, however, had become commoditized, and for a broker to succeed, it was necessary to come up with new ideas, new insights, or new forms of access to information about companies they were recommending. What the institutions valued most was a leg up in the ongoing battle for performance so one firm could distinguish its investment management process from that of its many competitors. For some brokerage firms, being first to call with new information or some other service or benefit could determine whether an institutional investor traded with the firm or not.

Securities researchers became increasingly important to institutional investors. In the late 1970s, *Institutional Investor* magazine devised the first effort to rank research analysts according to their popularity with institutions in an "All-American" poll. Once the list was created, every analyst aspired to be on it. Emphasis was also placed on building up distribution power with retail customers (for whom higher commissions could be maintained), especially as these customers began to become acclimated to investing in mutual funds, whose business could not survive without distribution, no matter how good or bad their investment management skills.

In the search to replace income lost to lower commissions, many Wall Street brokers also became dealers—that is, both market-makers and proprietary traders. With the savings-and-loan crisis of the 1980s, soaring fiscal deficits and the developing merger boom provided a large field of opportunity for traders. Some simply accommodated clients in providing liquidity. Others devised techniques for taking advantage of market anomalies with arbitrage trades for their own account. Trading activities substantially increased the capital requirements of broker-dealers and also increased the risks that the firms had to learn to manage.

In 1982, two other changes occurred to increase competition in the integrated securities business. After 1979, exchange controls affecting cross-border capital flows were removed in most of the European Union countries, and markets became globally integrated again for the first time since before World War I. By 1982, a rising dollar and falling interest rates attracted European investors to Eurodollar bonds offered through subsidiaries of well-known U.S. and foreign corporations and public-sector entities. Indeed, because Swiss investors, for example, saw an advantage in the rising dollar, they and other Europeans bid up the prices of Eurodollar bonds, encouraging United States-based issuers to float new issues in the Eurobond market instead of the U.S. domestic bond market. Issuers could access the unregulated market instantly, unlike issuers in the United States, who had to wait for the SEC to process a registration statement, requiring about three weeks. Instant access meant that issuers in a seller's market could auction off their securities to the highest bidders, and a truly competitive offshore market developed. In the United States at the time, companies selected their bankers before the securities were registered, severely limiting their ability to generate any sort of competition for the bonds when they were issued. Eurobond interest rates, therefore, fell well below corporate bond rates in New York, companies flocked to the unregulated London market, and regulators at the SEC wondered what had happened. Now that markets had become global, investment bankers had to be competent in the Eurobond market or they could not offer a full set of services to their clients. They had to be prepared to bid for their clients' business in an open market or lose it to someone who was.

The SEC intervened, with what was possibly an unintended deregulation, by introducing its Rule 415, permitting registration in advance ("shelf registration") so companies could access markets without a registration delay, and could auction their issues to the highest bidder if they wanted to. Many did, and the U.S. bond market was transformed quickly into one resembling (and keeping up with) the Eurobond market. This change (and a vigorous merger-and-acquisition market, discussed earlier) brought about the end of the practice of appointing one or two investment banks to be a company's "exclusive" bankers, and brought a premium to the bond business for those firms that were capable of moving quickly and had good knowledge of foreign markets and the latest innovations. No longer could broker-dealers rely on traditional relationships or provide indifferent client coverage, or fail to be on top of all markets anywhere in the world where it might matter. To be fully competitive was much more costly than before, and the profits earned on individual deals were much lower. The underwriting business had to rely on lower rates and better service to clients, which often meant absorbing more of the clients' risk. The best way to make money involved innovative ideas, and often these were the result of introducing a new accounting or tax feature that had not been tried before. The clients expected such service, and extracted it from those with whom they did businesses. Underwriters, like the brokers, became accustomed to giving their clients what they wanted, and what they wanted was lower costs of capital, less risk in raising it, and new ways to use it.

CONSOLIDATION

After being prohibited for more than 70 years, interstate banking was again allowed by repeal of the McFadden Act, and after 60 years, the Glass-Steagall Act was repealed by Congress in 1999. There was a period of about five years during which the Federal Reserve Board allowed banks seeking to engage in businesses otherwise prohibited by the Glass-Steagall law to carve out a permitted amount of such activities that they could engage in. The repeal of these two laws enabled healthy banks to grow into much bigger, more diversified businesses by entering new markets in different areas of the country and by capturing cost savings through mergers with other large banks in their principal markets. Some entered previously prohibited businesses, exemplified by the landmark 1998 combination of Citibank,

Created Mergers as companies tried to become one-stop-shops

Salomon Smith Barney, and Travelers Insurance into a massive financial conglomerate, Citigroup.

As a result of finally being permitted to do just about anything, and because of serious competitive threats in their industry that many felt required banks to be bigger and more streamlined, the banking sector began to consolidate in the early 1990s. Indeed, the banking industry was one of the most active of all U.S. industries in mergers and acquisitions activity and general corporate restructuring since then. As a result, the banking industry was able to offer one of the highest returns to investors during the 1990s. Citicorp stock, which traded at $8.25 per share in December 1991, was valued at $168 when its $74 billion merger with Travelers Group was announced. Chase Manhattan, which was a veteran of several large mergers since the 1980s, and traded at a low of $9.63 per share in 1991, reached a high of $149.50 in 1998. Although many banks that have had aspirations to secure a major share of the securities business have failed to do so, a few, like Citigroup and JP Morgan Chase, have succeeded, and others, like Bank of America and Wachovia, have aspirations.

The repeal of Glass Steagall has certainly added further to the intensity of competition in investment banking. This was one of the reasons justifying repeal preached by its supporters for many years, and it has come to pass. However, in the process, investment banks have been forced to rely on different activities to rebuild the profits lost to the competitive pressure—for commissions, for underwritings, and for challenges from new entrants into the business—by increasing their trading risk exposures, and being more innovative in developing new products, such as derivatives (which brought Bankers Trust to its knees in 1995) and "structured" products.

Deregulation did not make these things happen by itself. But it did remove barriers that had stultified the banking industry for many years before the bad loans and poor management caught up to it in the 1980s. Altogether, $558 billion in banking industry mergers took place in the United States from 1985 through 1999. There was a further $187 billion of mergers in the insurance industry, and $57 billion of mergers in the (global) investment management industry. Altogether, the 1980s and 1990s saw more than $800 billion of mergers in the U.S. financial services industry. As a result, the firms that survived were bigger and stronger and are now competing intensively to offer lowest prices and newest ideas to customers and to find ways to accommodate new customers that might have been excluded before.

The massive shift of wholesale banking to the capital markets is one example of this. Another is the increase in consumer credit facilities being extended by banks and other providers. The result is that access to capital has expanded enormously, and financing costs to end-users has declined significantly. Needless to say, a large, low-cost, flexible capital market is indispensable to changing the performance of an entire economy and fueling future growth. As interest rates declined and stock prices rose during the 1980s and 1990s, the corporate cost of capital dropped to historically low levels. But this did come with some baggage. Competitive conditions became tight enough to encourage firms to take more risk—both with regard to the positions they put on their books and with the schemes they devised for giving their clients what they wanted and for making what was left on the table into as profitable a business as possible for themselves. In both areas, corners were cut, and some standards were lowered.

SYSTEMIC CHANGE

By the end of the 1990s, financial markets were vast, innovative, aggressive, and highly competitive. Pension and mutual fund managers had melded into giant investment management companies that competed fiercely for assets to manage. They devised new funds aimed at exploiting the trends of the times, and paid handsomely to have them distributed by broker-dealers searching for more volume to turn over to their highly "incentivized" sales forces. Hedge funds had developed for wealthy individual investors to back bold investment managers who might try just about anything.

All of these players depended upon short-term results to continue to attract the assets from which they could draw fees. Investment results were published by numerous periodicals and by professional consulting companies with access to information about all competitors' performance. Performance was the key—and to gain the necessary performance, increasingly aggressive fund managers were appointed, and these managers looked increasingly for special "edges" that research analysts and underwriters with technology IPOs could provide. Indeed, the market became obsessed with quarterly performance to such an extent that any company (including *Fortune* 100 companies) "missing" targets—that is, failing to post the quarterly earnings result expected by the Street—might see its stock tumble instantly by as much as 25 percent or more.

For CEOs of companies benefiting from market attention, the 1990s were a perilous paradise. Market valuations and low interest rates combined to produce extremely low costs of capital for companies with access to the markets, and many individual CEOs were privately worth many hundreds of millions of dollars as a result of compensation arrangements tied to stock price performance that their boards had offered them. It was also perilous because the market might be disappointed and the stock might drop into free fall, possibly resulting in the dismissal of the CEO. No matter how philosophical and long-range the thinking of individual CEOs, the market environment in which he or she worked was what it was. Great incentives were in place to motivate all CEOs to maximize their stock prices by pleasing market analysts, reporters, and an increasing number of financial broadcasters that the 1990s had produced, and to make sure that these relationships did not turn sour.

Operating within the capital markets of the 1990s were scores of vendors and service providers seeking to please their clients. Any corporation or investment manager could turn to a different vendor if the service wasn't up to par, and the way to gain more of a client's business was to be creative, responsive, optimistic, and willing to take risk and to offer packages of some important services bundled together that tied the client to the vendor. The vendors included banks, broker-dealers, and underwriters of course. But they also included accounting firms, law firms, consultants, lawyers, and various other professional service providers. These professional service providers were captivated by a system in which consistent double-digit growth was expected from the best companies, the rewards of which to investors and the managers could be enormous. But the ability to sustain double-digit growth was well beyond the essential economics of most companies; only those with better ideas, more aggressive acquisitions, and special rapport with investors could be expected to survive this difficult challenge.

Part II

Corporations and Their Governance

The invention of the corporate form of business organization was a development of singular importance. Corporations could raise permanent capital by selling shares to the general public. These investors could sell to others in a market for shares if they wanted to exit the business, something that partnerships or proprietorships could not do. And investors' liabilities are limited to the investment itself—the corporation might fail, but creditors could not pursue individual investors for the repayment of debts beyond their stake in the company. Corporations became the principal vehicle through which the vast American railway industry was financed, and around the turn of the twentieth century had become a common form of organization in most other capital-intensive industries. Because of the corporation, American "big business" was born.

By the early 1930s, public corporations, as the dominant players in American industry, had concentrated great economic power into the hands of a few professional managers who themselves were not significant owners of the companies they led. They served as "agents" for the public shareholders who owned the company but did not manage it. A growing segment of American economic life, and the risks associated with it, had become subject to "agency conflicts"—potential conflicts of interest between corporate managers and their owners.

The corporate form of organization, however, anticipated such conflicts. Corporations were authorized when a business entity applied to a state government for a license. Under that license, the corporate entity would agree to abide by and "incorporate" the state's business laws into its charter. All U.S. corporations today are incorporated under state laws—there are (with a very few exceptions) no federally incorporated corporations. The state laws all require that a corporation's shareholders elect a board of directors that is required to bear fiduciary duties of care and loyalty to the shareholders whom they represent. The board of directors then appoints a chief executive, to whom it delegates a great deal of the corporation's powers to set and execute policy and strategy.

Corporations and their officers and boards are subject to many additional laws and regulations, both federal and state. These laws were enacted over the years to limit corporate freedom of activity in areas where it might come into conflict with the public interest. Corporations and their officers and boards are also subject to civil litigation that may be brought by private parties with complaints against a corporation. And they are subject to pressure from the news media and "public opinion," which can affect their business franchise. As was not the case in the days prior to the 1930s, American corporations are now required to satisfy a broad constituency of so-called stakeholders, and they are regulated and scrutinized more intensely than ever before.

This being so, how could the events of the 1990s that spawned a host of corporate scandals have occurred? Many corporate failures can be attributed to suddenly changed economic conditions, which can drive even well-run businesses into bankruptcy, honestly if not honorably. But we have also seen an uncomfortable array of corporate failures that resulted from fraud, malfeasance, or obfuscation, caused by management, that was approved, tolerated, or undiscovered by boards of directors.

The vital role of governance of modern corporations in the avoidance of agency problems can be examined both internally and externally to the firm. Part II of this book consists of three chapters that explore the internal governance function of corporations. First, we trace the development of the "modern corporation"—as the dominant institution for raising capital and conducting business—and the parallel development of ideas about how that structure should be governed. Next, we examine the two key agents of corporate governance, the board of directors and the chief executive. What are the duties and responsibilities of directors with respect to the corporate owners and to other stakeholders in the firm, and where have the principal failures occurred? And, how do modern CEOs define their role in corporate governance and their relationships to boards of directors, and how is this reflected in their power and their compensation?

3

Legacies of the Corporation

Corporations have a long history in the English-speaking world. They were originally conceived in medieval times as a means by which a group of private citizens could combine their interests under a royal charter to differentiate (and protect) themselves from the changeable interests of the government. The formation of municipalities and other public-interest entities was often accomplished through corporations.

Early in the seventeenth century, the concept was broadened to permit individuals to combine resources into a single entity to exploit opportunities made available to them by a government concession or license, thereby creating "corporate charters." Early examples of chartered corporations include the East India Company, formed in 1600 to hold a monopoly on trade with India, and the Virginia Company, formed in 1606 to develop the land and trade opportunities in North America. Valuable monopoly provisions were included in a charter granted to the original founders of the Bank of England in 1694, which was quickly capitalized by public subscription of shares in the London market. The overriding idea was to let private money fund investments necessary to develop economic and financial activity while retaining a royalty interest for the Crown. The investors were well-known, influential figures who could be relied upon to "get things done," a phrase associated with corporations ever since.

The incorporated form of business organization was soon copied in various other trading cities in Europe. For example, the Bank of Amsterdam was founded in 1609 to help finance corporate trade with the East Indies.

By the late seventeenth century, a variety of commercial corporations were being formed and successfully capitalized in financial markets to pursue all sorts of ventures beyond those with state-granted monopoly rights. English trade, merchanting, and finance began to outdistance much of the rest of Europe and other economies around the world, partly because of the use of corporations to organize and capitalize new ventures. These ventures included water companies, toll roads, treasure-ship recovery projects, and light manufacturing companies (metal works, glass, linen) and some that were more far-fetched and speculative.

In 1711, the South Sea Trading Company was formed to exploit such opportunities as might be found in South America. This company was all illusion but nevertheless generated an overwhelming response from investors—the euphoria became known as the great "South Sea Bubble" after it collapsed in 1720. There were many other failures of companies traded on stock exchanges at the time, and much anger and recrimination developed in their aftermath over the role of the public corporation as a form of business organization. As a consequence, the corporation—as a legal form under which to do business and subscribe funds was suppressed and did not resurface in England for the next hundred years.

Indeed, Adam Smith was highly critical of the East India Company and other incorporated monopolies in *The Wealth of Nations*, published in 1776. He saw the corporation then as a creature of privilege that was able to ignore the laws of market economics and to depend on taxpayer bailouts when it faced financial failure. In fact, a large bailout of the East India Company was undertaken in 1773, after which the government intervened more extensively in its management. The East India Company was dissolved in 1858 after the Indian Mutinies, which led the British government to step in and assume direct governance of the colony.

The corporate form of organization was revived in Britain later in the nineteenth century, during the Industrial Revolution, in order to raise the large amounts of capital that industrialization required. Without corporations to attract that capital, organize management, and finance the opportunities envisioned, it is doubtful that the process of industrialization in Britain or the United States during the nineteenth century would have been much of a revolution at all.

AMERICAN CORPORATE CAPITALISM

Colonial charters (and land grants) were abolished after the American Revolution. Although few colonial corporations existed at that time, they were subsequently encouraged, especially by Alexander Hamilton, as a way to establish and finance the private sector of the American economy. Initially, corporations were local, intrastate enterprises, and were not thought to be important enough to rise to the level of federal attention and supervision. So they were left by the Constitution to the individual states to authorize and control. Corporate forms of business organization—chartered by the states—were utilized in America by banks, insurance companies, transportation companies, and public utilities before 1800, by which time there were about 300 in total.

The New York Stock Exchange was founded by merchants in 1792 to trade corporate securities. Industrialization came almost immediately afterward—the textile industry was formed in New England in the 1790s, the steam engine was produced commercially in the United States in 1805 and the steamboat in 1807, the Erie Canal was opened in 1825, and the first (of a great many) railroads appeared in 1830. Gold was discovered in California in 1849 and attracted a vast migration of prospectors and settlers, who opened a new market in the West that was connected to the east by a pioneering transcontinental railroad 20 years later. Oil was found in Titusville, Pennsylvania, in 1859, and kerosene was produced as a cheap illuminant, replacing whale oil. The Rockefeller-controlled Standard Oil Company was set up not long afterward. Private businesses flourished throughout the country. In Pennsylvania, for example, more than 2,000 business corporations were chartered from 1790 to 1860, of which 65 percent were in transportation, 11 percent in insurance, 7 percent each in general manufacturing and banking, and 3 percent each in water, gas and other utilities.[1] Much of the new investment in transportation involved railways or steamships, each requiring large quantities of coal, iron, and steel, and the corporate form of organization dominated.

After the Civil War, American industries sought to become national by combining with other businesses. But state corporate law at the time did not permit interstate holding companies, so acquisitions for stock were difficult to execute. John D. Rockefeller invented the "trust" as a workable interstate alternative to the federally chartered corporation. He formed the Standard Oil Trust in 1882, and issued trust certificates to acquire other oil companies around the country. Rockefeller's move was copied in several other industries and by 1889, when the last of the trusts was formed, there were 350 of them, including several other large, consolidated national commodity trusts in sugar, beef, tobacco, and so on. Trust certificates soon became the most actively traded securities on the New York Stock Exchange. In this way, the trusts gained an "acquisition currency" with sufficient liquidity to appeal to shareholders of companies they were seeking to buy out (or squeeze out) as part of their aggressive consolidation strategy. As their market power increased, so did their opportunities to capture economies of scale, bulk purchases of raw materials, discounts on rail shipping rates, and the ability to influence prices. Sometimes this meant selling below cost to force a competitor out of business, or into selling out to the trust.

During the 1880s, public opinion in America turned sharply against trusts, although the offenses they allegedly committed were against other businesses (albeit smaller ones) rather than against the public itself. The public in fact benefited by investments made by the trusts, by the economies of scale they achieved, and by their price wars. But to a great many, the trusts seemed unfair and un-American. They smelled of great and dark powers being preserved for the privileged and the rich at the expense of everyone else—complaints that were amplified by journalists and politicians who spoke out against them as evil monopolies. Fearful of such large concentrations of power and wishing to constrain or reverse them, Congress for the first time intervened directly in business activity by passing the popular Sherman Anti-Trust Act in 1890.

The Sherman Act outlawed "restraint of trade" and the attempt to form monopolies, but it took a while to work its way through Congress. In anticipation, New Jersey in 1889 passed a new, flexible corporation law permitting interstate holding companies. To avoid the Sherman Act, most of the trusts in the 1890s transformed themselves into New Jersey corporations by exchanging their trust certificates for shares of stock.[2] Nevertheless, it is customary in American economic history to refer to these New Jersey companies also as "trusts," and for trusts in general to mean a very large consolidation of many companies in the same industry into a centrally managed enterprise with considerable market share and market power. In 1910, Woodrow Wilson became governor of New Jersey and began a series of legal reforms that made many companies that had recently incorporated in the state nervous. Soon many of them had reincorporated across the river, in Delaware, where the original New Jersey holding company law had been adopted but where there was little pressure to change the rules of the game. Delaware has remained the preferred state for incorporation of large businesses ever since. reason — To promote competition and benefit society through surplus

The "Premodern" Corporation

By the end of the nineteenth century, a few hundred large corporations ruled the economic landscape in the United States, and had amassed powers that were unimaginable just 25 years before. In 1877, Cornelius Vanderbilt, the founder and principal owner of the New York Central railroad, died and left a fortune of $100 million to his son William, making him the richest man in America. But beyond the railroads, corporations were at that time much less developed. "Before 1880, the largest manufacturing companies were capitalized at less than one million dollars, yet within a single generation all of this had changed," noted business historian Thomas McCraw. The American Tobacco Company completed a series of mergers in 1904 that took it to a capitalization of $500 million (up from $25 million in 1890), more than three times the size of Standard Oil.[3] In 1901, J. P. Morgan organized a merger of Carnegie Steel into a group of other steel companies to form U.S. Steel, with a value at the time of $1.4 billion, making the deal (in terms of current dollars) the largest merger ever done in the United States until the $30 billion RJR Nabisco leveraged buyout that was completed in 1986.

Corporations were understood to be vital to American economic development, in part because they provided entrepreneurs with a means to secure needed financing but also because they offered choices to investors and thus a value-based system for allocating private capital. Investors outside the control group, of course, had no influence on corporate policies or conduct. They were only interested in securing profitable returns by backing new industries early, or by free-riding on the coattails of the great industrialists. In the nineteenth century, the investors were largely wealthy individuals (some of them industrialists in their own right) looking to risk their savings in dynamic new ventures. Large numbers of these investors were European, as were many of the engineers, managers, and other professionals and the thousands of low-cost laborers who migrated to America during this period. The business environment at the time was totally opportunistic and laissez-faire—the rough rules of the unregulated marketplace prevailed, and these included bribing corrupt state and local officials to assure a benign regulatory climate. The federal government at the time was thought to be constitutionally above most business and commercial issues.

By the end of the nineteenth century, a great deal of credit for economic development but also blame for economic brutality were attributed to corporations. They engaged in epic battles with other businesses to assemble the parts of their large, dominating national enterprises. They also battled with their employees over worker's rights and wages, and there were many reports of price gouging, misrepresentation, and abuses of consumer health and safety by the some of the large firms.

It became clear that if there were objections to the exercise of the power of corporate entities, these would have to be met by the power of the federal government to legislate and enforce new sets of laws to regulate private-sector economic activity. There were no other powers—in the market itself or at the state level—that could do this. So the issue fell to the federal government by default. Of course, not everyone agreed that federal intervention was called for. Corporate activity was left to the states by the Constitution, but the country and its economy were nothing like what they had been when the Constitution was ratified. There were also many who wondered how the government—however well-intentioned—could accurately assess what was wrong with the system and how to fix it without seriously harming the extraordinary economic engine that had accomplished so much for American society as a whole.

The Beginnings of Regulation

The great corporations at the time were controlled by hard-driving, self-made tycoons with reputations for ruthlessness who became the world's richest men. The last quarter of the nineteenth century was an unprecedented time of growth and prosperity, but it was also a time referred to by Mark Twain in *The Gilded Age* as a period of exceptional glitz, greed, and immorality. Monopolies with the power to squeeze both consumers and competitors were widely thought to exist everywhere. The singularly bare-knuckled capitalism of the era was dominated by a handful of men like Rockefeller, Carnegie, and Morgan, whom Matthew Josephson, writing during the Great Depression, called "robber barons." But it was also the period of rugged individualists described by Horatio Alger, the bestselling author in the 1890s whose rags-to-riches stories offered a new notion of what it was like to be American—to pursue self-advancement and individual economic opportunity with perseverance and determination in a land of liberty. If entrepreneurs like Rockefeller, Carnegie, and the others who started with little could do so well, why not everyone? Such opportunities were uniquely American, a key reason why so many had migrated to America from Europe, where such opportunities were scarce and the mentality far different.

As the contrast between Twain and Alger suggests, the public had mixed feelings about corporations at the turn of the century, but the accumulation of so much power in a few hands and the forceful, and sometimes irresponsible, application of that power increasingly drew unsympathetic public attention. Labor disputes involving strikes, repression, and violence had already broken out in the 1880s. The deadly workers' uprising against Carnegie Steel's Homestead Mill occurred in 1892, and against the Pullman Company in 1894.

Morgan's U.S. Steel deal outraged many—here was yet another trust being formed, a much larger and more dangerous one (as some said at the time) arrogantly engineered by Wall Street's most powerful banker, who didn't seem to realize that the public strongly opposed such enterprises and that the government (in the Sherman Act) had attempted to constrain them. Newspaper criticism of the steel merger was extensive, even in London. The president of Yale University said that unless the abusive power of large corporations was soon restrained, there "would be an emperor in Washington within 25 years," suggesting that the American democracy itself would be overthrown by revolt.[4]

These views encouraged investigative journalists to publish exposés of the business practices of some of the country's largest corporations in popular newspapers and magazines with large audiences. Early in the1900s, articles on the beef trust, Amalgamated Copper, Standard Oil, and the life insurance industry did much to create public demand for regulation of these and other great business combines. In 1906,

Theodore Roosevelt labeled the journalists "muckrakers," saying he agreed with many of the charges but thought some of their reporting was sensational and irresponsible.

In 1900, the railroad industry had been the most important sector in the economy for 50 years—many of the larger railroads employed over 100,000 workers[5]—and, as such, it attracted not only determined entrepreneurs and financiers but also an endless supply of market speculators and corrupt and disreputable characters. By the 1880s, the industry's economics had become very uncertain, buffeted by over-investment, duplicate facilities, cutthroat pricing, and predatory (frequently dishonest) activities. By then, railroads were typically operating across state lines, confusing whatever regulatory controls states may have been able to apply. In 1886, a seminal Supreme Court ruling (*Wabash, St. Louis and Pacific Railroad Co. v. Illinois*) held that commerce originating and terminating outside a state's borders could not be regulated by the state, even though the federal government had no capability at the time to regulate such commerce. Largely as a result of this ruling, the Interstate Commerce Commission (ICC) was created in 1887 (to require "just and reasonable" rate-making by the railroads) and served as a prototype for other forms of government regulation by commission that would follow. The ICC got off to a slow start, as subsequent court rulings reduced its powers to little more than those of a recordkeeper. When the national economy sank into depression in 1893–1897, the ICC had done little to improve the industry, and 169 railroad corporations—nearly 25 percent of the industry—were forced into bankruptcy.

After the railroads were reorganized, Congress attempted to inject new life into the ICC, passing five laws from 1905 to 1935 to increase its powers and the scope of the firms it regulated to include, in addition to the railroads, roadways and waterways. Never an effective body, the ICC was torn by its political mandates to attempt to be fair (i.e., "just and reasonable," as the statute required) even at the cost of impeding efficiency. In effect, however, the government, through the ICC, was setting prices for transportation in the United States, which in turn affected the allocation of transportation between the different modes, without a good economic understanding of what it was doing. But the popular idea had arisen that railroads were abusive and unstable, and had to be controlled. This control was achieved by setting freight rates, which in turn affected other competitive industries, so these industries and their pricing were thrown into the expanding regulatory pool as well.[6]

Antitrust Actions

Meanwhile, the Sherman Anti-Trust Act got off to a very slow start. The Act did not create an enforcement agency. Instead, it relied on the Justice Department to bring suits against offending parties. There was no clear idea of how to define some of the illegal monopolization activities, or to measure trade restraint, so the attorneys general of the 1890s did not prosecute aggressively. When they did, they picked cases they thought they could easily win—mostly against weaker, peripheral companies, not those at the center of the industries that were thought to be monopolized. In that sense, some economists suggested that the government was suing the victims of monopoly rather than the perpetrators. Then, in 1893–1897, a severe economic depression occurred, which the public to a large extent was encouraged to blame on the trusts. Although enforcement was initially ineffective—between 1890 and 1904, only 22 Sherman Act cases were brought by the Justice Department—the issue did not die away, and the trust question dominated public debate until the beginning of World War I.[7]

Theodore Roosevelt helped to energize an era of proactive federal intervention in the affairs of business. President from 1901 to1909, he encouraged the formation of the U.S. Bureau of Corporations to gather information and to conduct industry studies to identify cases of systematic restraint of trade. As a result, 130 Sherman Act cases were brought between 1905 and 1914. Roosevelt also urged Congress to authorize the ICC to regulate rates charged by railroads and to pass the Pure Food and Drug Act in 1906. The Supreme Court had begun to hear Sherman Act cases and by 1903 forced the dissolution of the Northern Securities Company (a railroad holding company). Perhaps most important, after many years of litigation, it forced the dissolution of the Standard Oil Company and the American Tobacco Company in 1911. The ruling was considered a great victory for the government. Standard Oil was required to distribute shares in 33 large subsidiary oil companies directly to its shareholders, an event that in the end only made them richer.[8] In 1914 the Federal Trade Commission was established to consolidate antitrust activities.

The "New Economy" of the Early Twentieth Century

While these efforts to harness the power of large, consolidated corporations were underway, some of the greatest technological developments of all time were beginning to affect American business, and new corporations were being created that would change permanently the character of the American economy. Electric light and power had become an industry in 1890. Spindletop, the greatest of Texas oil wells, began to gain traction in 1901. The Wright brothers took off in 1903, and in the same year the first motion picture telling a complete story, *The Great Train Robbery*, was produced. Life insurance was a big business by 1905. Transatlantic radio communications were launched in 1905. The first hotel with private bathrooms was built in 1907, and the Model T Ford was introduced in 1908. These and many other developments, such as the growing use of telephones and business machines, would change the pace and the character of private business in ways that could hardly have been imagined before. The catastrophic war of 1914–1918 in Europe enabled America to emerge as the world's leading economy, and its financial markets proved to be robust and deep enough to finance government requirements from all over the world, including those of the Allied powers in the war.

By 1920, it was generally thought that the sort of abuses attributed to corporations in the last quarter of the previous century had been successfully curtailed by government intervention in the public interest, so it seemed that the new century was off to a good start. The U.S. market-based system had been strengthened by the curtailment of corporate monopoly power and through the regulation of interstate commerce. The rapid growth of important new industries was further diluting the economic power of the old trusts. But powerful new monopolies, under regulatory control, were already starting to emerge.

 In 1892, Thomas Edison merged his Edison General Electric Company (a manufacturer of turbines and electric transmission equipment formed in 1889) into the Thomson-Houston Company to form the General Electric Company. Three years later, Edison's protégé, the English immigrant Samuel Insull, resigned from the new company to become president of Chicago Edison Company, one of a hundred power stations franchised by Edison all over the country to promote the sale of electricity. This new industry, Insull knew, was too capital-intensive to avoid consolidation. But consolidation would subject the major companies almost immediately to the Sherman Act, or might result in the government's nationalizing the industry to protect the public's interest in the availability of low-cost power. Insull successfully promoted the idea of consolidation being permitted under the aegis of a state or local public utility commission that would allow but control local or regional power monopolies. Insull's company, renamed Commonwealth Edison in 1907 after several mergers, became the largest regulated public utility monopoly in the Chicago region. In 1912, he formed Middle West Utilities, which owned or controlled several regulated utility companies all over the country. From then on, through the bull markets of the 1920s, Insull acquired more companies, often doing so by issuing bonds or preferred stock against expected cash flow. During the 1920s, the utility holding company became the norm, accounting for approximately 80 percent of the national electric power industry. Insull was the industry's most important and admired figure, and Middle West Utilities one of the bluest of the blue chips. However, the increasing use of leverage to affect these mergers turned the largest of such companies into financial "pyramids" that sank in the aftermath of the stock market crash of 1929.

The Great Crash

The market collapse that started in October 1929 closed a decade of financial activity in the United States that had never been experienced before. During this period financial markets boiled with activity—with new issues stocks, bonds, and emerging market securities, a "new economy" mentality as new technologies were absorbed, consumer products supplied in abundance, and individual investors flocking in to buy "investment trusts." These were closed-end investment companies (mutual funds) that were first launched in substantial quantity in 1927. Many of these investment trusts were leveraged several times and invested in holding companies that were themselves highly leveraged. These were times of "exuberant expectations" and "infectious greed." Financiers and speculators did what they could to pool resources and manipulate markets through bull or bear strategies. Throughout it all, the Dow Jones Industrial Average rose 15 to 20 percent per year from its low point in 1921 to mid-1928, after which the index doubled by August 1929 to reach a high of 381. Three years later, it would stand at 41. Investors in leveraged investment trusts, of course, did much worse. One popular fund, the Blue Ridge Trust, which invested in pyramided utility holding companies, plunged from a price of $24 in September 1929 to about $3 on October 29, before sagging to a price of $0.63 in July 1932.[9]

The stock market crash was held at the time to be responsible for the Great Depression that followed during the 1930s, although many subsequent studies have by and large concluded that structural imbalances in the economy and missteps by the Federal Reserve and the White House were as much to blame for the general economic collapse that followed the crash as was the sudden loss of confidence in the market and the capitalist system it represented.

This was not the first market crash in American history, or the first one that was followed by a depression, but it was the first time that millions of ordinary citizens, enticed into the markets by the attraction of investment trusts in a time of bull market speculation, lost substantial amounts of their assets—compounded by losses in their (uninsured) deposits during the widespread bank failures that followed in the early 1930s. These events, added together, amounted to an economic and political disaster for the United States, one that assured a change of political leadership and a long train of new laws and regulations to prevent a recurrence of the events that had been so destructive. Many of the principal figures of the euphoric 1920s lost their wealth and their reputations, and some took their own lives. But few were convicted of criminal activity.

Samuel Insull, as chairman of the failed Middle West Utilities a highly visible public villain, was charged with securities fraud three times but acquitted in all three cases. The heads of New York's two most powerful banks, Albert Wiggin of Chase National Bank and Charles Mitchell of National City Bank (a predecessor of Citigroup), were found to be engaged in speculation in concealed investment pools (including one that shorted the stocks of their own banks) and beneficiaries of large undisclosed compensation arrangements. Wiggin was urged to step down from his position in 1933 at the age of 65 and granted a salary for life of $100,000 per year, although under pressure he later renounced it. Mitchell, a much more flamboyant, publicly visible, and notorious character, was even more deeply involved in the shady, complex deals of the times. He was arrested in 1933 by assistant U.S. district attorney Thomas Dewey (later governor of New York and opponent of Harry Truman for the presidency in 1948) on charges of tax evasion. He was subsequently acquitted on all counts. Richard Whitney, once president of the New York Stock Exchange, went to jail in 1938 for embezzling funds (not for fraud or market manipulation) but the rest of the corporate and financial crowd of the times could not be charged with activities that were legal at the time.

EARLY NOTIONS OF CORPORATE GOVERNANCE

Before 1900, there was no sense that corporations served any purpose other than to make money. Before the creation of the trusts, corporate directors were frequently seen as swashbuckling financiers, jumping into and out of deals and schemes with great ease and dexterity, but risking only their own fortunes and prospects. The trusts were more orderly, professional, and systematic. They organized their businesses to maximize their market power, and attempted to use that power effectively—and legally—to make money. Still, industry in the nineteenth century was very unevenly developed, and major business cycles periodically resulted in crashes and recessions that dried up business for everyone. Most businesses were more concerned with survival than with growth, and competition was plentiful in most sectors (despite the ideas of monopolies dominating in particular industries), sometimes triggering price wars and discounting that caused losses for producers but benefited consumers. The unstable, boom-bust character of business was broadly discouraging to investors, creditors, employees, suppliers, and customers.

Surveying the wreckage of the railroad industry during the late 1890s, J. P. Morgan must have thought that there had to be a better way for business to function. As Morgan (then in his sixties) immersed himself in the restructuring of the railroads his clients had invested in, he attempted to undo some of the excessive overlaps in rail lines and to leave the industry in a more orderly state from which to work itself into recovery. The restructuring was regarded as a great success, and made Morgan's name. Years later, when he considered the fragmented, underperforming steel industry, Morgan believed that the sad condition of the industry was the result of the same sort of excess competition and profiteering that had earlier affected the railroads, and that the appropriate remedy for this was for the financial community to rescue the industry from itself by forcing consolidations and sensible industry discipline. He must have thought that he would be doing the nation a favor by rationalizing this important industry so that it could operate safely and at its full potential.

Morgan's offer to buy out Andrew Carnegie (on behalf of a large syndicate of banks that would finance the transaction) and merge the company with a dozen or so lesser steel companies to form a dominant player, U.S. Steel, was no more than another effort to reorganize an industry in the public interest. Morgan thought the consolidation of the steel industry would preserve it from the fate of the railroads. He backed the $1.4 billion deal with his own money, and his fee, paid in the stock of U.S. Steel, was $12 million. Morgan was well aware of— but rather contemptuously dismissed—public criticism of the deal.

Equity ownership of early American corporations was relatively concentrated in the hands of founders and early-stage entrepreneurs. Carnegie, for example, owned 59 percent of his company at the time of its sale to Morgan. But as the companies grew and needed more capital, or merged into larger units, the shareholdings of the original capitalist entrepreneurs declined, and board seats were filled with a more diverse set of investors and advisers. Indeed, for railroads and other capital-intensive industries, seats on boards of directors were often occupied by representatives of past and future *bondholders*. J. P. Morgan and his partners, for example, sat on the boards of many of the railroads that went bust in the 1890s. Morgan and his partners developed such a reputation on behalf of bondholders that they had the power to deny access to the bond markets to companies they disliked, and as such were very influential. One academic study showed that the market value of companies on whose board a Morgan partner sat significantly outperformed comparable companies.[10]

Legally, corporations are created with an infinite life and limited liability for their shareholders. The corporation exists as long as the shares are outstanding, and these shares may be sold or exchanged, so shareholders come and go over time, but the corporation itself persists. Corporations may raise new money by selling shares to the public. Shareholders are only liable for their own investment, however, unlike a partner in a partnership whose liabilities are unlimited. Founders and major investors in corporations may sell their shares to public investors when they want to cash in or retire, and over time their share of the corporation is reduced. New managers of the corporation eventually are appointed who become successors to their founder's powers—that is, the exclusive right to control the company—while at the same time having limited ownership of shares themselves. Professional managers operate as *agents* for the shareholders as a whole.

This creates an asymmetry between the power of controlling shareholders (and/or their management agents) and all the rest of the shareholders.

Economists call conflicts between owners and their agents (managers) "agency conflicts." Controlling agents may not themselves own more than a modest percentage of the stock, but by controlling the board (and denying control to others), such individuals can appoint and remove directors, management, and advisers and can allocate corporate resources. Those in control are inclined to favor their own interests, policies, or points of view in all things that touch the corporation. They may believe that the actions they take on behalf of the company are in the company's best interest and that as a result minority shareholders without board representation should have no complaint. The interests of minority shareholders may therefore be ignored by the majority. After all, they might say, minority shareholders can always sell the stock if they don't like the way the controlling parties manage things.

Some managers, however, make major strategic errors or allocate company funds inappropriately—actions that the minority shareholders are powerless to prevent. However, in a landmark 1919 case, the Dodge brothers in the auto industry sued their business partner, Henry Ford, the principal founder and then chief executive of the Ford Motor Company, to force payment of dividends from a great cash horde that Ford had accumulated. The brothers believed that the dividends where the natural entitlement of investors, but Ford wanted to save the cash to reinvest in the company. The Michigan Supreme Court upheld the Dodges on the grounds that the primary duty of the corporation was to its investors, and neither principal stockholders nor management could unreasonably divert funds for any other purpose.[11] This was the first important ruling that constrained powers of management in public corporations.

The "Modern" Corporation

In 1932, Adolph Berle and Gardiner Means first called attention to the concentration of American industrial power that had come to be controlled by large publicly owned corporations. They undertook extensive statistical work to ascertain that in 1930 the top 200 publicly owned industrial companies controlled about 50 percent of all corporate wealth, representing 38 percent of business assets in the country; that these 200 companies were vastly larger than all the rest of America's corporations combined; and that they were generally controlled by groups or individuals owning only a small minority of shares. The Rockefellers, they noted, in 1930 owned only 14 percent of Standard Oil (and a much smaller share of almost all the other publicly traded oil companies created when the Standard Oil Company was broken up) but fully controlled the corporation and its subsidiaries. The management group at AT&T owned only a small percentage of the stock, yet governed a company with more than 400,000 employees.

Berle and Means termed such large, publicly owned enterprises with widely dispersed shareholder influence "the modern corporation." The potential for conflict between the owners of these modern corporations and their agents was considerable. Giant public companies not only were already dominant, but as a group they were also growing faster than the rest of the economy.[12] The new controlling groups of managers, Berle and Means argued, were not like the capitalists of earlier times, whose personal interests and corporate wealth were one and the same and whose business appetites were held in check by both competition and the fear of losing money, friends, and reputation. The modern corporations, lacking these inhibitions, Berle and Means feared, would be interested only in business efficiency and making profits, and thus (because of the concentration of national economic power in their hands) they represented a new, potentially very powerful force in American society.

> There may be said to have evolved, a "corporate system"—as there once was a feudal system—which has attracted to itself a combination of attributes and powers, and has attained a degree of prominence entitling it to be dealt within as a major social institution. . . . We are examining this institution probably before it has attained its zenith. Spectacular as its rise has been, every indication seems to be that the system will move forward to proportions which would stagger imaginations today. . . . For that reason, if for no other, it is desirable to examine this system, bearing in mind that its impact on the life of the country and of every individual is certain to be great; it may even determine a large part of the behavior of most men living under it.[13]

They further pointed out that the purpose of the corporation is such as to cause it to resist regulation that might interfere with its economic objectives, but equally, the duty of the state was to put in place regulations that would protect society from corporate excesses. Berle and Means thus looked forward to the development of a robust corporate law, one that could be as important to the country as constitutional law. They recognized that no law could prevent every possible abuse, but as long as investors had the good sense to be alert and keep themselves well informed, they could avoid abuses by selling their shares in a liquid public market. The governing law they envisioned for the modern corporation was one that would also assure effective, accessible, honest financial markets into which dissenters would always have the option to sell their stakes. No such federal law existed then, and state laws that governed securities markets were limited, ineffective, and seldom enforced.

Berle and Means's view was that the emerging system of public corporations, as good as it was as an engine of economic growth, would have to be restrained for its own good and for the good of society. They saw the issue much as Morgan did, but did not believe an elite of wealthy insiders would invariably act neutrally for the benefit of society, so that the government had to step in. However, they also held that shareholders of public corporations did not have the same (more protective) legal rights as did the beneficiaries of a trust—and indeed, by knowingly and voluntarily forgoing managerial power by investing in a public corporation for the investment benefits alone, the shareholder was acting as a free-rider—and therefore had only a diminished claim to insist on profit-making as the only justifiable activity of the corporation.

Berle and Means thus saw the modern corporation as an entity solely devoted to maximizing its own power and profits, regardless of the public interest, and as an entity that had to be restrained by powers of equal magnitude, powers that only government could exercise. There was no suggestion that the directors of the corporation should change roles and begin to restrain themselves in the public interest. By being solely devoted to maximizing market power and profits, the corporate officers and directors were only doing their jobs. Berle and Means called instead for the federal government to use its powers to check the forces of capitalism, which, by evolving into an economy of large, interstate public corporations, had escaped the bounds that more than a century of local governance had placed upon them. They were well aware that the power of the federal government was subject directly to the vicissitudes of American politics, and that neither appropriate legislation nor its accompanying enforcement powers could be guaranteed. But in the end, they were connecting the restraint of corporate power to American democracy itself, as inefficient, uneven, and unpredictable as it was. Berle and Means believed that in the long run, if corporate power was thought, rightly or not, to be abusive to society as a whole, then the people, exercising their political rights, would take that power away from the corporations.

In 1932, Austrian-born Joseph Schumpeter joined the economics department at Harvard University, bringing with him a rich academic resume along with the experience of having served as finance minister of Austria and president of an investment bank. Schumpeter was a powerful teacher, with two Nobel Prize–winners among his students, and a dominant figure at Harvard during the depression years. In 1942, he published *Capitalism, Socialism and Democracy*, in which (surprisingly, for a champion of capitalism) he noted that "the capitalist order tends to destroy itself and centralist socialism is a likely heir apparent."

Schumpeter did not believe, as some of his colleagues did, that capitalism would wear itself out according to a theory of "vanishing investment opportunity," as returns on investment were worn away by competition. He believed instead that there would always be a supply of new opportunities and entrepreneurial energies to challenge the established players, and create a beneficial condition of "creative destruction." However, he did believe that the structure and pace of corporate capitalism was its own enemy. There were three phases to its development: (1) the entrepreneurial phase in which values and new opportunities are created, and then (2) the bureaucratic phase that succeeds the first as the successful companies become large and institutionalized. In this phase, the corporation absorbs and threatens its competitors and their infrastructure—small businessmen and proprietors who were historically the source of entrepreneurial energy—as it evolves the kind of modern corporation with diffused ownership that Berle and Means observed. As all this happens, Schumpeter suggested, the corporation destroys too much of the social and political support for capitalism in society, and little by little, (3) "an institutional pattern in which control over means of production and over production itself is vested in a single authority" emerges in the third phase. Socialism, in other words, was not an ideology but a form of institutionalization of a controlling role of government in the economic affairs of the private sector.

Schumpeter died in 1950, having observed 20 years of economic life in America that he believed justified his views. Not only were corporations hamstrung by antitrust enforcement from the early part of the century but also, during the depression, the war, and the postwar recovery, the government's role in economic life became swollen beyond the recognition of someone who had operated a business before 1930.

That this development might actually be a good thing was suggested in 1952 by Schumpeter's younger Harvard colleague, John Kenneth Galbraith. In his book, *American Capitalism,* Galbraith described how as a result of their wartime experience, American corporations had become successful because they had consolidated into powerful oligopolies that represented a formula for growth because the large corporations had the resources necessary to enable technical innovation. Galbraith insisted that this power had to be balanced by a "countervailing power" against potential abuse, in the form of labor unions, consumer groups, and the government; he repeated some of these themes—and suggested that the countervailing force was not up to the job—in his book, *The New Industrial State,* published in 1967.

Perhaps the countervailing force was falling behind Galbraith's expectations, but certainly by the end of the 1960s and the long period of economic growth enjoyed during that decade, the essential ideas of Berle and Means, Schumpeter, and Galbraith had become a large part of the public understanding of how corporations did and should operate in America. They should operate in a free market for goods and services, although they did have to be large, powerful, and professionally managed to be able to be effective in contributing to national economic growth. But by being restrained through countervailing forces that transferred authority away from corporate managers, they were compelled to behave in a way that would be acceptable to democratic society, even if that meant a sacrifice of some portion of the potential contribution to growth. This uneasy equilibrium seems to have emerged today in the United States as a system of "democratic, free-market capitalism," one that is paralleled in various ways in most successful economies around the world.

The Rise of Government Power over Corporations

Berle and Means seem to have correctly predicted the future intervention by government in corporate matters in the 70 years that followed their seminal book. Following the market crash and the numerous bank failures in the early 1930s, the Roosevelt administration pushed through Congress an entirely new legal and regulatory regime to control corporations. The emphasis was placed on creating a federal system for protecting ordinary citizens from abuses or misconduct of powerful business and financial interests. The Banking Act of 1933 instituted deposit insurance, strengthened the regulatory powers of the Federal Reserve System, and, in its "Glass-Steagall" provisions, separated investment and commercial banking to prevent abuses of corporate lending being tied to mandates to issue new securities (they were reconnected by the "Gramm-Leach-Bliley" Act in 1999). The Securities Act of 1933 and the Securities Exchange Act of 1934 required truthful, complete disclosure of corporate information and audited financial statements for new securities issues, a level playing field in secondary financial markets, and created and empowered the Securities and Exchange Commission to regulate the system and enforce the rules. The National Labor Relations Act, which affirmed the rights workers to organize in unions, was passed in 1935. The Public Utility Holding Company Act of 1935 redressed many of the problems of the pyramided utility holding companies, and the Investment Company Act of 1940 attempted to apply the same principles to the investment management business. To this body of law was added the 2002 Sarbanes-Oxley Act, the most extensive piece of federal securities legislation since the 1934 Act. This newest of comprehensive federal laws was presumed to assure good corporate governance by the specificity and clarity of its dozen or so implementing regulations requiring actions of corporations and their boards and by insistent pressure for greater transparency.

All of these laws and regulations, however, aggravate an old and serious dilemma—the dual system of federal and state laws affecting corporations. The duties of corporations and their directors are established by the law of the state in which the corporation is incorporated. Yet all the new laws intended to restrain corporations were federal. The federal corporate laws—centered on antitrust, labor relations, banking and securities—were justified as being within the scope of constitutional powers provided to the federal government to regulate interstate commercial and financial activity. As such, these laws and powers gradually crowded the states out of the corporate governance picture. Notwithstanding this crowding-out, the federal laws were not underpinned by the basic statutory fiduciary duties of corporate officers and directors to their investors, a key link needed to enforce laws related to corporate conduct at the level of the individual director.

The economic malaise of the 1930s provided few opportunities to test the new federal regulations that had been imposed. Corporate opportunities revived with the coming of the world war in Europe in 1939 and U.S. entry in 1941. The 1940s and 1950s were times of war and emergency that increased and centered economic power in Washington as never before. Defense mobilization and production, rationing and price controls, and massive, sudden shifts in the labor market were necessitated by the war effort. After the war, Americans expected their larger, much more powerful federal government to return the economy to peacetime conditions, arrange employment for returning veterans, and encourage global economic recovery and reconstruction in the war-devastated areas. This challenge was compounded by another war in Korea in 1950–1953, to be followed by nearly 40 years of national security concerns related to the Cold War struggle with the Soviet Union—which by then had emerged as a rival power to the United States—and yet another war, in Vietnam.

The Cold War conflict was partly ideological, pitting the merits of free-market capitalism and centrally planned socialism against each other. By the 1950s, the two systems—often described as being the fruits of the philosophic labors of Adam Smith and Karl Marx, respectively—were already very far from their founders' ideals. Capitalism had been very substantially curtailed by government regulations put in place by democratically elected representatives who interfered with the natural forces of the free market and its invisible hand in the public interest. And the crude and cumbersome economy of the unelected Bolsheviks behind the Iron Curtain appeared to have all the disadvantages of socialism with few of the advantages, but was nevertheless capable of developing and supporting formidable military power to be reckoned with.

In 1959, the Harvard University historian Alfred Chandler published a seminal article, "The Beginnings of Big Business in American Industry," emphasizing the unheralded importance of the development of business organization systems and a managerial class to American economic growth.[14] To Adolph Berle, also writing in 1959, the modern corporation he had described in 1932 had evolved into a tamer, less rapacious, "institutionalized" version. "Slowly," he said, "or perhaps not so slowly, industrialized United States is moving toward a form of an economic republic, without historical precedent. The system [is] in effect new, leaving [both] nineteenth century capitalism and European socialism behind."[15] Schumpeter might have added, however, that the system may actually have left capitalism behind—with its vibrant entrepreneurialism acting as the true source of economic growth—as it descended further into de facto socialism.

But there was no doubt in Berle's mind as to which system—capitalist or communist—would ultimately prevail. The American system of market capitalism had matured and evolved to accept a natural tension—a sort of benign, permanent conflict—between competitive corporations looking out for their own economic interests and a powerful government seeking to advance a balanced social and economic agenda, partly at corporate expense. Berle's 1959 essay was one of several included in an influential book edited by the Harvard professor Edward Mason, *The Corporation in Modern Society,* in which most of the writers took a similar view. Mason himself observed that it had become *de rigueur* for managers "to deny . . . exclusive preoccupation with profits and to assert that [they] are really concerned with the equitable sharing of corporate gains." Corporate power was potentially vast, but the institutionalization of "big business" that these essayists observed made it socially acceptable and beneficial. Such policies might smooth the hardest edges of pure laissez-faire economics, but would they unacceptably interfere with optimal allocation of economic resources within the society to maximize growth and "opulence" (Adam Smith's term for national wealth)? This was a question that would be put back on the table in the 1970s and 1980s.

The 30 years from 1930 to 1960 were economically abnormal in almost all respects, and corporate power relative to the power of government shrank to a mere shadow of what it had been in the 1920s. That power was a long time recovering. The government had become accustomed to directing a planned wartime economy, and vestiges of that central planning persisted throughout the 1950s. Government retained the earlier tradition of reliance on enforcement of tough antitrust policies (Alcoa's control of primary aluminum production was broken up in 1945) and expanded industrial regulation (in the manner of the Interstate Commerce Commission; such regulation was extended to railroads, public utilities, banking and finance, shipping, airlines, oil and gas, broadcasting, and food and drugs). Labor relations also were delicate during this period, when union power was at its peak (the manufacturing sector employed about 40 percent of American workers in 1940).

Most large corporations responded by participating in the system rather than opposing it. The new institutionalized corporations Berle described were poised to exploit postwar business opportunities at home—there was a vast demand for consumer products, and many new technologies developed during the war, waiting to be commercialized—and abroad, where entire economies had to be rebuilt and serious local competition had yet to mature. There was plenty of good business for everyone, as long as everyone knew how the game was played—avoid being too greedy or too radical or too conspicuous, and things will take care of themselves. And there were still plenty of government contracts in defense, transportation, telecommunications, and other sectors, available through friendly connections, subsidies for favored industries (such as oil and gas), and other forms of trade and regulatory intervention (steel, textiles) that increased competitive barriers and protected the competitive positions of American corporations.

These companies were now run by invisible, grey-flanneled, salaried men, who usually worked their way up in the company over a long bureaucratic career in time to run it as chief executive for five or six years before a dignified and comfortable (if not especially enriched) retirement. Economic growth in the United States was robust in the first Eisenhower term, and sluggish in the second. President Eisenhower warned Americans of the growing threat of the "military-industrial" complex. John F. Kennedy, as a candidate to succeed Eisenhower in 1960, spoke repeatedly of the need to "get the economy moving again."

The Emerging "Postmodern" Economy

In the 1960s, during the Kennedy-Johnson years, which featured two substantial income tax cuts and a recovery of world trade and investment, the U.S. economy experienced another boom, one that some economists at the time called a "golden age." Growth averaged over 5 percent for nearly a decade, and productivity and family incomes grew at rates not since equaled. Unemployment declined to 3.4 percent in late 1968, even after the economy had expanded for a record 106 consecutive months. Confidence emerged in the ability of the government to keep the economy growing and prosperous, with the help of established business management systems and top executives, two of whom were in President Kennedy's cabinet. Government economic planning, regulation, and intervention were still prominent in an era when it was assumed that output could be managed by a combination of enlightened, government-directed fiscal and monetary policies.

A series of "voluntary restraints" on cross-border funds transfers were imposed in the early 1960s to protect the balance of payments. Large corporations were expected to defer to government requirements in the national interest, and if they were unwilling to do so, they were subject to public shaming by officials and the press. Roger Blough, then chairman of U.S. Steel, received a severe public dressing-down from President Kennedy for introducing a price increase at a time when the government was trying to reduce inflation. President Johnson repeatedly intervened in labor disputes by inviting the parties to the White House where he could lock them in a room until they settled things in a way acceptable to him.

Meanwhile, the stock market discovered young nonlegacy corporations with new technologies (Polaroid in photography, Xerox in copiers, as well as a variety of players in semiconductors and pharmaceuticals) and growth strategies (Litton Industries, ITT, Textron) that were exciting to investors. Wall Street enjoyed its first bubble market since the 1920s—the 1960s were dubbed the "Go-Go Years," for their youthful, uninhibited style. However, antitrust enforcement remained intense. It seemed to have a nonpolitical momentum of its own, flourishing in the 1950s and 1960s regardless of which political party controlled the White House or the Congress, and probably fathered the decade's newest technique for creating wealth through mergers and acquisitions of unrelated businesses—the "conglomerates"—as one of the only ways for large corporations to be able to grow faster than the economy as a whole. The pace of mergers and acquisitions accelerated, fueled by conglomerates run by sophisticated financiers who were much admired at the time. Some of them were able to attract funding for aggressive takeover exploits and became known as corporate "raiders," who threatened established public corporations with surprise cash tender offers to purchase control on a first-come, first-served basis. These "hostile" takeover bids were sometimes called "Saturday Night Specials," and in time they attracted a mild form of federal regulation (the Williams Act of 1968, the first new federal securities law since the 1934 Act) that was designed to slow hostile bids down so their defenders could act before it was too late.

Also during the 1960s, the stock market was fueled by increased funding for corporate and state pension funds, and by the rapid growth of mutual funds. Together these "institutional investors" were managed by younger, bolder, smarter, and more demanding people than their predecessors, who still had vivid memories of the 1930s and 1940s. They were active, dynamic traders who bought and sold shares in large blocks (10,000 shares or more) and soon became the dominant figures in the investment world. In 1965, institutions owned 16 percent of all outstanding stocks, and block trades comprised a negligible portion of total NYSE volume. By 1975, when the same institutions pressured the New York Stock Exchange to discontinue fixed (minimum) commission rates, they controlled 41 percent of outstanding shares, and block trading had grown to 25 percent of total NYSE trading. The fund management institutions recruited even younger, more aggressive portfolio managers to compete with each other in order to attract still more funds to manage. It was not long before these new portfolio managers, called "gunslingers" by some (they shot first, asked questions later), attracted the attention of senior corporate executives whose stocks they were buying and often pushing to premium prices. Suddenly corporations discovered that they had a new set of constituents to please, ones whose importance was tied to their abilities to affect stock prices.

The market, however, reversed direction in 1969, and the next de-

cade began with a stock market slump, followed by a brief recovery,
and then a fall into a deep malaise caused by the wars in Vietnam and
the Middle East, the Nixon political crisis and resignation, a sudden
quadrupling of oil prices, and a withdrawal by the United States from
the gold standard to allow for a freely floating exchange rate system
in which the dollar depreciated against the currencies of major trading
partners. These were times of low economic growth in the midst of
high inflation (called "stagflation"), low productivity growth, penetration of imported products such as automobiles from Japan, and a general sense of economic discouragement. The Republican Nixon administration responded with wage and price controls that made matters
worse. Not surprisingly, one of the worst bear markets since the 1930s
developed, severely reducing confidence in the government's ability to
manage the economy.

Corporations suffered economic and competitive pressures that
forced many of them to lay off employees, shut factories, curtail social
programs, and reduce pension and healthcare benefits. The institutionalized corporations of Adolph Berle's new economic era became conservative, stagnant, and apparently more concerned (as their predecessors had been in the 1890s and 1930s) with mere survival than in
increasing growth. Some large corporations, including several well-
known companies, turned to illegal political contributions (at home)
and bribery (abroad) to obtain business and to acquire favors and
privileges. This period was also the beginning of the environmental
movement, in which protesters publicly objected to various "irresponsible" forms of corporate activity, especially those related to natural
resources (logging, mining, oil and gas) and called for companies to be
more socially responsible.

Milton Friedman was one of several famous economists (others included Kenneth Arrow and Friedrich Hayek) who jumped in to oppose
this line of argument. In a short 1970 essay, "The Social Responsibility
of Business Is to Increase Profits," Friedman maintained that, although
corporations must follow the law and "ethical custom" in the management of their businesses, the essential argument of Berle that a corporation has inherent social obligations is false, and he asserted that if it
did, it was not at all clear who should decide what and how extensive
these obligations were. He added that the cost of meeting social obligations would necessarily come out of the pockets of owners or customers or employees, and would thereby reduce the corporation's ability to perform its free-market economic functions. Friedman did not
explain what he meant by "following ethical custom," or whether that
involved some degree of permissible board-determined social responsibility. Notwithstanding Friedman and the other economists, however,
the idea of social obligations of public corporations by this time had
developed in the public mind and in the law, although it was still
ambiguous, and outcomes in contested cases seemed to be based more

on any particular circumstances than on the application of particular social or legal doctrine.

Jimmy Carter, a Democrat, served as president during the last four years of the 1970s. The economy continued in its doldrums, and Carter was unable to do much about it. He did, however, appoint Paul Volcker as chairman of the Federal Reserve Board. A few months after taking office in 1979, Volcker reversed monetary policy and doubled interest rates over just a few months, beginning a slow turnaround of the inflationary spiral of the 1970s that had peaked at about 13 percent in the consumer price index. When Ronald Reagan was elected president in November 1980, some of the economic and political effects of the prior decade had reached their worst point. Iran and Iraq were waging an all-out war, with Iran still holding American hostages. The Soviet Union had invaded Afghanistan, and gold reached an all-time high of $850 per ounce in January 1981. The prime interest rate quoted by banks rose to 21 percent after Reagan's election, and the price of oil exceeded $40 per barrel. But the economic turnaround began to be reflected in stock prices by mid-1982. The market also admired Reagan's intent to continue Carter's policies of reducing government regulation of industries (begun with the passage of the Airline Deregulation Act in 1978, the first ever deregulation law) and to be more tolerant in antitrust enforcement. So stock prices reversed direction and began a 20-year rise that would lift the Dow Jones index from 821 to a high of 11,723 in January 2000. The dismal 1970s were over, and brighter, more optimistic times—inspired by a major tax cut in October 1981— lay ahead.

The Dominant Influence of Financial Markets

In the two decades after Ronald Reagan took office, American capital markets surged as never before. The market capitalization of all outstanding corporate stocks and bonds in 1981 was just under $2 trillion, and the total value of all U.S. government securities outstanding was $1.4 trillion. In 2001, corporate securities outstanding were valued at about $21 trillion, and government securities stood at $8.3 trillion. In 1999, the high point, stocks alone were worth nearly $20 trillion, and the value of all outstanding corporate securities was $24 trillion. From 1981 to 1999, stock prices rose at a rate exceeding 14 percent per year, more than twice the nominal growth rate of the GDP. Thousands of new millionaires were created during this period, a great many of them corporate executives benefiting from mergers and compensation programs that were generously laced (as should be expected in a bull market) with stock grants and options. The boom became the speculative bubble discussed in the last chapter, and stock prices rose to unsupportable levels—from which they sharply fell away in 2000, when the market began its downward adjustment of about 30 percent. Some of the more overheated sectors—Internet technology and telecommunications companies in particular—plunged by much more, and many firms slid into bankruptcy.

This was the most extraordinary period of capital market expansion in American history. It was driven by several factors unrelated to the bubble itself. There was the continuing rise in ownership of stocks by financial institutions, which exceeded 60 percent of all equities in 2001. There was the growing ability of the capital markets to offer lower cost financing than traditional bank or insurance company lenders, thus leading to disintermediation of funds from traditional savings institutions to financial market instruments. There was the development of all kinds of financial derivatives allowing investors and corporations to better manage risks related to interest rates, stock prices, and exchange rates. There were technology advances that allowed trading volumes to reach record levels (well over a billion shares traded every day just on the NYSE). And there was globalization and deregulation abroad that created instantaneous linkage of major foreign investors to markets in the United States through a foreign exchange market of almost $2 trillion per day, with about 90 percent of its volume identified with cross-currency investment transactions.

Financial markets today play the vital roles of reflecting—instantly and globally—values of companies and their securities and in determining the success or failure of management teams and corporate policies. No public company can operate successfully without taking financial market pricing information into account. So the corporation has to be attentive to all of the market's requirements and to satisfy them, whether they seem foolish or not. These requirements differ over time, and always reflect fashionable notions and trends, which is what markets do. But they always involve, at minimum, an evaluation of corporate performance over a measurable time period against investor expectations.

Consequently, corporations at the start of the new millennium had become very different from what they were at the beginning or the middle of the twentieth century. They now had a new constituency to satisfy—the fluid and demanding financial market—and this new constituent had shown itself to be unavoidable, exceptionally demanding, mercurial, and quick-acting. More than anything else (except perhaps a criminal indictment) the markets determined a CEO's success or failure, and there have been many who have been turned out of their jobs because of it. Satisfying the market is difficult to do, and sometimes had to be accomplished by suppressing long-term corporate plans and objectives to favor more immediate results. Sometimes it required appearing to "go with the flow" and to comply with a latest trend, and by continually and professionally promoting the company to investors. In extreme cases, the perceived need to satisfy the market even affected the truthfulness of financial reports or resulted in deliberate actions of fraud to cover up earnings shortfalls of balance sheet problems.

When Berle and Means described the "modern" corporation in 1932, they meant the large, publicly held corporation managed by professional managers who were subject to agency conflicts but whose purpose nevertheless was to run the company to maximize its profits and not necessarily its share price. They did not expect the corporation as they conceived it to restrain itself through corporate governance efforts to conform to unwanted noneconomic pressures. But they did expect (and predicted) that the federal government would step in to regulate corporations so that corporate operations would be consistent with the wider public interest. After 25 years of regulations aimed at controlling corporations, and a much larger economic presence of the federal government, Berle concluded that corporations had become "institutionalized." They had become good citizens and cooperated with government in their own interest. This, he felt, was likely to be the way the story would end—in an unprecedented new arrangement with a strong government and benign corporations working together to bring prosperity and stability to the country in the next century (then still 40 years away).

Today it is clear that the "postmodern" corporation must face two different and powerful constituents at the same time, the government and the market. Their interests may frequently collide and conflict with one another. Both can affect the corporation in truly meaningful ways—and both are subject to their own inefficiencies, distortions, and corruptions. Both have multiple elements. The government constituent operates at both state and federal levels, and includes not only regulators and administrators but also law enforcement agencies that use the courts, civil or criminal, to bring actions against corporations. The government constituent is subject to political influence and the confusion and unpredictability of competing ambitions, as well as the lobbying power of corporations themselves. The market constituent is made up of national and international credit and equity markets, which in turn consist of institutional and individual—short- and long-term— investors. These investors can be acutely sensitive to trends and fashions, and can sometimes set unreasonable expectations. They can also be volatile, and both overreward companies and overpunish them, causing stock prices to jump or fall by 30 percent or more on the basis of a quarterly earnings report. The dilemma of the postmodern corporation is learning to manage these difficult and conflicting constituents—the regulators and the investors—without giving up the essential energy and purpose of a corporate organization to maximize long-term, risk-adjusted returns for shareholders.

4

The Role and Duties
of Corporate Directors

A corporation is formed to allow a number of investors to do business together with their individual risk-of-loss limited to the amount of their investment. The corporation raises capital by selling shares of stock to other investors, who may resell them to yet others. The interests of the corporation are entrusted to a board of directors, who are the elected representatives of stockholders (the members of the corporation), who in turn appoint senior management who direct the business of the firm. Generally, stockholders owe each other few legal duties, unless they assume a controlling position in the firm. There is no U.S. federal corporation law applicable to private-sector corporations, although there are a small number of special-purpose federally chartered corporations. The federal government does, however, seek to regulate and protect "interstate" commerce in a variety of ways—particularly through extensive regulation of the capital markets—and these affect state-created corporations significantly.

STATE AND FEDERAL CORPORATION LAWS

Generally, state corporation laws were never intended as regulations. Instead, they provided a legal framework within which business people may structure semipermanent private enterprises. The idea of corporate directors having a *fiduciary* duty to stockholders developed, but this meant little more than a director's being obligated to be careful in discharging the duties of the office, and in not putting his or her own interests ahead of other shareholders. A substantial body of state case law has developed to clarify directors' *duties of care* and of *loyalty*. These have their origins in English common law and in the notion of the *prudent man* rule, that is, that the standard of conduct used to judge negligence or disloyalty should be the same as a wise and experienced person would employ in managing his or her own affairs.

Many years ago, the Delaware Chancery Court adopted the idea of the *business judgment rule,* which held that in cases where a board had acted carefully and in good faith, the court would not second-guess the board's judgment on business matters. Thus the burden of proof rested on plaintiffs to demonstrate negligence, bad faith, or unreasonableness in the process of decision-making by a board of directors. In most instances of conflict, this was difficult to prove.

Directors' Liabilities

Prior to the late 1920s, when investment trusts began to be sold to individuals, stockholders were understood to be sophisticated, wealthy people who knew those they were dealing with and had accordingly chosen to invest voluntarily, despite a lack of full information about the companies involved. However, as the market evolved and expanded, it became possible to sell securities of an increasingly diverse set of companies to a broader range of investors. The "modern" corporation described by Berle and Means in 1932 came into being, and as the extent of public ownership increased, the position of the minority stockholder in general became so diluted as to have little influence on the managers who controlled the corporations. Moreover, the power of corporations—lacking any serious restraining influence from major investors—grew to the extent that abuses of minority shareholder interests occurred. The only legal remedy available to them was to sue for restitution of losses caused by the breach of fiduciary duties of the board, based on a demonstrable violation of the business judgment rule. But only very large shareholders could justify the expense and time for such litigation, and as a result very few suits were brought by individual investors.

Things changed after 1966, when change in federal rules allowed a new device for obtaining relief for general shareholders to develop—the shareholders' "class action" that permitted the aggregation of hundreds or thousands of claims into a single, large, and powerful plaintiff that could motivate, finance, and manage a highly professional lawsuit. These suits were organized by law firms prepared to finance the litigation themselves in exchange for a contingency fee, an agreed percentage of the judgment or settlement received. The law firms would have to identify the claim (from some perceived misconduct by officers or directors), organize the class (often in competition with other law firms doing the same thing), and manage the litigation (and the public relations) until the case was tried or settled. The plaintiffs would have their eyes focused on the amount of insurance carried by the corporation against litigation and settlement expenses, and on the depth of the pockets of other parties involved in the disputed transaction, such as bankers and accountants. The process might take a year or two to complete, but could be very lucrative for the law firms that bore the full expense and risk of the litigation from the beginning.

Unlike the lawyers' fees, the settlements received by individual shareholders in class actions are usually modest relative to the amounts lost. Plaintiffs' attorneys, however, are not regulators and have no obligations to anyone other those who sign up for their suit, and other shareholders are not obliged to participate in the suit at all. The plaintiffs' lawyers benefit only when they have organized a substantial class and can settle or prove misconduct in court, so law firms are always on the lookout for such misconduct, and many corporations understand that they should avoid conduct that might provoke such lawsuits.

In the period after 1980, shareholder class-action suits flourished. There were many suits alleging losses caused by the failure of management, and the volume of settlements achieved increased considerably. The business community in general thought many of these suits were frivolous and unfair and significantly raised the cost of doing business in America. The law firms involved in bringing (and in defending) the suits and many influential academics and politicians held that securities class actions helped to police the marketplace. Frivolous and unfair suits would most likely be unable to meet the standards required to secure a successful judgment, so the law firms would be unlikely to risk their own capital in bringing them. Still, the volume of these suits and the settlements or judgments they produce have become so large as to be a significant force of their own in constraining the actions of corporations, their boards, and their management.

Corporate directors are the individuals responsible under the law for corporate conduct. Suits therefore typically name individual officers and directors in their complaints. The directors, of course, are not eager to personally bear the burden of any judgments or settlements, or legal expenses incurred in the course of carrying out their duties to the corporation.

Director Indemnification

Anyone becoming an officer or director knows that he or she may be sued for a variety of alleged offenses. In America, such suits are an ordinary part of business, although occasionally they can become major, expensive issues for corporations and the individuals named in the suits. Neither officers nor directors can be expected to be willing to meet these frequent challenges—some of which are spurious or minor, but some are not—at their own expense. Such a burden would include payment of judgments, settlements, and legal expenses incurred by them in the course of carrying out their duties to the corporation. They are entitled to expect the corporation to indemnify (or shelter) them for any and all such costs, except in the case of negligence on the part of individual directors.

For directors, the indemnification (and insurance to back it up) has thus provided a necessary safety net that limits personal damages any individual director might incur to those that could be attributed to his or her negligence. Further, directors have succeeded in persuading their corporations to set the level of negligence at "gross negligence," which is defined in such a way as to mean a very high degree of personal negligence, not merely negligence resulting from unintended carelessness or neglect.

The Federal Role in Corporate Securities Law

The crash of 1929 changed the state and federal roles in securities law profoundly. Great financial losses resulted from the crash, mostly experienced by sophisticated individuals of sufficient wealth as to be able to absorb them. Other investors, however, generally a rash of speculators trying to participate in the rising market as best they could, lost more than they could afford. There were many stories of suicides and families thrown into distress by the crash, some of which suggested that the responsibility for these tragic events lay with the ways in which securities were created and distributed by Wall Street brokers and dealers. Such stories often made the case for greater government involvement in the securities markets to protect the public from dishonest corporations and brokers, as noted in chapter 3. But the association of the crash with the general economic depression that followed generated a fundamental shift in political-economic thinking from one that was essentially laissez-faire to one that accepted that the federal government was the only power capable of repairing the economic damage done by the crash, and preventing its recurrence in the future. The Roosevelt administration that took office in 1933 entered the fray by recruiting some of the best legal talent in the country to draft the new securities laws.

The regulatory philosophy behind the Securities Act of 1933 and the Securities Exchange Act of 1934 was brilliantly conceived and anticipated future developments by many years. This philosophy held that the federal government cannot (under the Constitution), nor does it want to, regulate everything that companies do. If it tried, it would probably make the cost of regulation prohibitive, and business activity (the source of almost all the country's growth and prosperity) would certainly suffer. However, if it regulated only very selectively, too many things would get by. So government decided to use its powers to regulate one thing, but to regulate it thoroughly. It would ensure a fair and honest market in which investors could buy and sell securities. To do so, it would force companies to disclose, at least annually, all information that a reasonable investor would need to make a well-informed investment decision. As markets grew and there were more and more transactions, the ability of the market to absorb material information—and to assess the correctness of this in-

"freedom of exit"

formation—would be central to assuring fair and honest prices for traded securities.

To assure this fairness and honesty in the financial markets, the securities laws were constructed in two parts. The 1933 Act focused on "truth in new issues," requiring prospectuses to be distributed containing all material information about the company issuing securities, and making underwriters and accountants share the liability for the accuracy of prospectus information with the company, in order to increase the scrutiny they would give their clients. The 1934 Act required fair and honest secondary market conduct that would prevent market rigging and manipulation, and created and empowered the SEC to enforce both the 1933 and 1934 Acts. Officers and directors are required to direct their companies to comply with these laws, but otherwise they were not required by the Acts to be good directors or to discharge their fiduciary duties responsibly.

Over the 70 years since the passage of these federal securities laws, the SEC has continually interpreted the 1933 and 1934 Acts, tried thousands of cases to enforce them, and issued hundreds of rules establishing correct procedures and practices for companies to follow in complying with them. Congress has also, on the whole, supplied the SEC with a sufficiency of funds to provide for a comparatively thorough enforcement capability, something state securities regimes and many foreign countries acutely lack.

The body of laws, procedures, and practices is broad, and also covers accounting matters that affect audited financial statements required by the Securities Acts to be published annually. The SEC may refuse to accept audits prepared by particular firms that it does not believe practice high standards, and will publish what auditing and accounting standards it regards as acceptable.

Over the years, the SEC has adapted to financial innovations and market changes in a variety of ways. It has issued rules to increase the volume of corporate information and the speed at which it reaches the market in takeover cases. It has defined and proscribed insider trading. It has forced more extensive disclosure of complex securities. It has allowed preregistration of securities, so companies can bring issues to market whenever it is opportune, and has allowed exemption from registration for certain private placements. The SEC's powers have also enabled it to prevent new issues from coming to market, stop transactions in process, and bring civil (not criminal) cases for infraction of its rules in federal courts or negotiate settlements with those involved.

The SEC also certifies stock exchanges, credit rating agencies, and "self-regulatory organizations" (SROs), to which it delegates some of its powers. In the 1930s, certain regulatory powers and functions were delegated to the New York Stock Exchange and the National Association of Securities Dealers. While federal law is supreme in areas where it overlaps with state laws, such as laws defining corporate organization, the SEC must respect the state laws, and in practice it does not bring suits in state courts, or attempt to enforce or modify state corporation or securities laws.

The Concept of "Due Diligence"

In 1968, an important legal case was decided in a federal court in New York state that affected the duties of directors of public corporations (*Escott v. BarChris Construction Corp.*).[1] The case involved fraud and false accounting in a company selling securities to the public, and the court found against the company's independent directors, accountants, and investment bankers. Under the Securities Act of 1933, underwriters share liability with the company and its advisers for the accuracy of all offering documents. The defendants claimed they had been lied to by management and therefore did not know, and could not have known, of any fraud. The 1933 Act does prompt underwriters to perform independent investigations responsibly but does not establish how directors of issuers subject to the law are to do so. The court held, however, that the defendants had failed to demonstrate that they had made a significant effort to discover the facts for themselves. Therefore, they had not been "duly diligent" in making all appropriate efforts to inform themselves of the true facts in the case, thereby breaching their duties of care under the 1933 Act.

This case, very importantly, put the burden of proof as to satisfactory due diligence on the defendants. *BarChris* changed the securities underwriting business fundamentally and lastingly by putting directors and advisers directly on the line. The ruling made them fiduciaries with a federally imposed duty to investors for the first time. In the future, they would have to be able to demonstrate a due diligence defense if a prospectus should turn out to be defective. This was a worrisome thing to many professionals. What exactly was satisfactory due diligence? How often did it have to be conducted? To ease the difficulty, board members and underwriters began to insist on indemnification by the company for any costs or damages borne by a director while fulfilling his or her duties (except in the case of gross negligence). To ensure that this protection was available even if the company was unable to satisfy its indemnification obligations, companies began to acquire liability insurance for directors and officers ("D&O insurance"). Although the due diligence standard remained, the availability of indemnification and insurance actually meant that, to protect themselves, officers and directors only had to meet the gross negligence test, a comparatively easy one to satisfy.

As a result, very few corporate officers or directors have personally suffered any kind of financial damage as a result of class-action litigation in the last 40 or 50 years. Some in the corporate governance community have suggested that directors should forego or be pre-

vented from receiving such extensive indemnification from the corporations they serve, as an incentive to keep them alert and concerned.
Such an incentive might be welcome, the corporate community has
observed, but it would no doubt come at the cost of removing the most
competent and experienced corporate directors from those willing to
serve.

EVOLVING STANDARDS OF DIRECTOR CONDUCT

Neither state nor federal law has much to say about corporate governance. The presumption has always been that the two sets of laws are
there to be complied with, and if there is compliance, then the governance of corporations will be satisfactory. Ethical issues have always
confronted corporations, and have changed and developed along with
American culture, social values, and principles. Failure to meet contemporary ethical standards might result in some degree of customer or
investor rejection, or, if the situation were serious enough to receive
high levels of media attention, it could attract litigation or adverse
legislation. But corporate and securities laws do not impose requirements to comply with ethical standards of any sort—whether a company does or does not do so is the company's own business, for which
it may be rewarded or punished by the markets it serves.

On occasion, however, Congress has become convinced that existing
rules and regulations do not provide the level of protection needed to
assure that the public is not exploited by out-of-control market practices
that may be legal but do not seem to be ethical. The spate of new laws
following the crash of 1929 and the ensuing depression is an example
of government intervention to fix a problem that was not understood
to exist before. In 1968, Congress passed the Williams Act to affect the
pace and processes of unsolicited (i.e., unwanted, or "hostile") tender
offers, the first federal law affecting securities markets in 34 years.

Thirty-five years after the Williams Act, Congress passed the
Sarbanes-Oxley Act of 2002 to address a public perception of serious
corporate governance failure after a series of scandalous cases of corporate bankruptcies, investor losses, and executive self-enrichment.
This intervention was driven as much by media attention and politics
as it was by conclusions drawn from careful economic and financial
analysis. Still, the effort was to protect the "level playing field" that
Congress wants public securities markets to be. But new regulations
always have economic costs, and sometimes these added costs can
exceed the benefits that are realized.

Corporate Performance, Takeovers, and Entrenchment

"Corporate governance" became a term in general public use (perhaps
for the first time) in the 1980s, when the evolution of capital markets
and institutional investors described in part I of this book permitted

the appearance of so-called corporate raiders (for the third time in the twentieth century). These raiders sought to acquire companies that were underperforming, and therefore undervalued. There were many of these around at the time—business conditions had been very difficult in the preceding decade, and many large public corporations had become more survival oriented than growth oriented. Boards of directors rallied behind their CEOs in loyal opposition to virtually all such efforts. But many raiders—persistently calling for new management and increased "shareholder value"—succeeded nonetheless, through unsolicited cash tender offers made directly to investors (at a price reflecting a premium over the prevailing market) sufficient to purchase a majority of the stock and vote in a new board. The Williams Act did not prevent any of these offers, but it did require bidders to adopt procedures other than sudden, first-come, first-served tenders.

The 1980s represented an era of colorful tactical maneuver—but it was an era in which shareholders began to see more clearly that a challenge to management (however prestigious and well accepted) might be in their own interest. A bidder could be expected to offer a premium over the existing market price, or a change in management might result in increased earnings that would be reflected in the value of their shares. Interest rates were declining during much of the decade, stock prices were rising, new financial instruments were being created (notably junk bonds), and even unknown operators seemed to be able to secure financing for takeover bids. Many tactical and strategic innovations were devised to help win battles for corporate control—and there were many in the 1980s, one of the largest merger booms in American history.

At the beginning of this period, the attacker would select a company with a comparatively low stock price that was thought to be performing poorly and decide what could be done to improve both its competitive performance and the company's stock market value in the future. The attacker would quietly buy stock up to 5 percent of the shares outstanding (at which point such holdings must be made public) and arrange financing based on plans to acquire and restructure the company. A maximum offering price, reflecting a significant premium over the present market price, would be agreed, and a bid would be made for something less than this price. The announcement of the bid would be accompanied by a press release that criticized the company's performance, its management, and its board, and insisted on shareholders' having the right to a choice. If management attempted to block this choice, then management was obviously entrenching itself to protect its privileges, but was doing so at the expense of the interests of its own shareholders.

The classic defense against hostile bids was for management to do whatever it could to slow the process down to provide time for a well-considered defense to be communicated to investors. The 1968 Williams

Act provided more time (all offers must remain open for a minimum of 20 days) but not always enough. To gain the time needed, defenders would counterattack with a battery of lawsuits, often on antitrust grounds, sometimes on the basis of alleged violations of securities law. The defender would then try to persuade its investors that the price offered and the bidder's true motivations were exploitative and socially unacceptable. Efforts were made to scandalize bidders, and to inflame employees, customers, suppliers, politicians, and others among the company's constituents to protest what was characterized as a reprehensible, greed-driven attack on "one of America's great corporations."

Very often the defense failed, and the defender was either forced to accept a somewhat higher final price or to sell out to another company (called a "white knight") instead. By the end of the 1980s, hostile bids no longer had the fiercely pejorative tint to them that they did when the Williams Act was approved. These battles simply became "contested bids" in which one side would make an offer, the other would try to block it, usually by producing a shareholders' rights plan, or "poison pill," that would prevent an offer being accepted by shareholders without first obtaining the consent of the board.[2] Thus deadlocked, the two parties would sue each other, usually in the state court in which the company was incorporated. As a result, a decade of intense litigation ensued, which helped to create guidelines for the takeover activity that would assure a level playing field for the market for corporate control.

Delaware Makes the Rules

As many important public companies were incorporated in Delaware, that state's Chancery Court heard and decided a large number of these cases. The Delaware court soon developed the ability to receive complaints, conduct a trial, hear from all sides, and then produce a ruling (often with a completed appeal) all in the course of a month or two. These rulings frequently focused on the powers of boards acting on behalf of shareholders to obstruct offers to acquire control of their companies. During the 1980s, hundreds of such cases were heard and resolved, and a pattern of case law establishing the rules for takeovers (limiting the powers of boards to obstruct them) was developed.

The Delaware Chancery Court applied state laws regarding directors' fiduciary duties, along with their standards of care and loyalty, to these cases and relied upon the business judgment rule in formulating its opinions. But these issues proved to be much more complex, and contradictory, than anyone had expected at the beginning of the period, and the cases came fast and furiously as the takeover boom reached full stride in the mid-1980s. In the end, the court had occasion to revisit and refine all of the basic concepts of fiduciary duties of corporate directors. The rulings it produced were often based on previous rulings, so that the system of board governance that emerged a decade later was both progressive and cumulative.

In 1984, the business judgment rule was put to a test, in a case (*Moran v. Household Finance*) in which a poison pill issued by Household Finance Corporation (HFC) was contested for the first time. A poison pill was created by the HFC board (without a shareholder vote) when it decided to issue shareholder rights to all stockholders to buy additional HFC shares at a large discount from the market price, but only if activated by the accumulation of a threshold level of ownership (e.g., 30 percent) by another party without the consent of the HFC board. The rights, however, would not be made available to the threshold-crosser, whose ownership position would be so diluted by the newly issued shares as to prevent indefinitely acquisition of a control position. The idea was that the raider would have to negotiate with the board to get it to lift the pill, and therefore would be blocked from approaching shareholders directly—presumably with an inadequately priced offer.

At first, the poison pill was seen by other companies as a kind of last-ditch, scorched-earth effort to entrench management. But soon they began to see it as a workable device to protect a company from opportunistic takeover efforts. Institutional investors were not especially opposed. They saw it as a way to gain higher prices (through a subsequent negotiation process, the defending company could force the buyer to pay more) when a takeover bid was contemplated, not necessarily as a method to entrench management or an impediment to a free market for corporate control.

There was only one problem—the pill severely discriminated against the threshold-crosser, denying it the principle of one-share, one-vote that the New York Stock Exchange and the SEC (enforcing federal securities laws) had endorsed for years. So, when the issue reached the Delaware Chancery Court, the question was whether the business judgment rule would be applied even if the judgment in question was unfair to a single shareholder and contrary to the public interest. The court decided that it did indeed apply—under Delaware law, the board had acted in good faith and without self-interest, which was all that had to be demonstrated to allow its judgment to go unchallenged. HFC had won.

The ruling resulted in a cascade of poison pill adoptions, and it became much more widely employed as a takeover defense. By 1992, over a thousand publicly traded companies had adopted poison pills in one form or another. Respectability had been gained by popularity, even though it was understood that a company could sit behind its poison pill and "just say no," which became the colloquialism to describe a no-negotiation defense that could logically be considered management and board entrenchment.

Next, the issue turned to determining the conditions under which the Delaware Chancery Court would *not* allow the poison pill to remain in place. The court did not have long to wait. In 1985, Mesa Petroleum launched an aggressive, two-tiered, front-end-loaded offer for Unocal Corporation, in which cash was offered for a controlling position that, when achieved, would be followed by a forced issue of junk bonds for the remainder of the shares. Unocal's defense was to offer to buy back its own shares at a higher price in cash, except that Mesa's shares would not be accepted. Mesa sued (*Unocal Corp. v. Mesa Petroleum*), asserting that the action unfairly discriminated against it, and denied Unocal shareholders any choice in the matter. The SEC, reflecting the federal point of view, objected to the defense at the time, and would subsequently disallow selective self-tenders.

Despite the SEC's position, the Delaware court upheld Unocal, arguing that the business judgment rule applied, but adding that it must be applied differently depending upon whether the contested matter was an *enterprise* issue or an *ownership* issue. If it was deemed to be an ownership issue, then a higher standard—an *enhanced business judgment rule*—would have to be applied. The higher standard involved a difficult determination of balance and proportion. Henceforth, the court decided, in a contested ownership situation, the takeover defenses employed by the target company's board must be "reasonable in relation to the threat to shareholder interests posed by the challenge," which in the Unocal case the court found to be the case.

This ruling changed everything. Before, the plaintiff had to prove that the defendant failed to meet the prerequisites for the business judgment rule to get anywhere, even if the business judgment taken by the board might be demonstrably unreasonable. After the ruling, the burden of proof fell upon the defender. The target corporation would have to demonstrate (and quantify) the threat, and convince the court that its actions were not disproportionate in the light of that threat. For example, if a defender had good reason to believe its stock was worth $60 a share, but a bidder had offered only $40, then vigorous no-holds-barred defenses could be justified. However, if the offer were at $56 a share, the defenses had to be more moderate. If the enhanced business judgment rule was not to apply—because the company could not satisfy these rather obscure proportionality tests—then the court would be required to determine for itself whether the actions taken by the board to defend the company in fact reflected good business judgments, based on whatever standards it wanted to adopt.

The consequences of the imposition of the enhanced business judgment rule were several. First, it resulted in almost automatic litigation in all takeover cases in which a poison pill and certain other defenses existed. The defender has 10 days in which to respond to the bid, and it must do so in the presence of legal and financial advice from outside the company (which diminishes the board's own role in deciding the company's destiny).

Second, in defining the threat posed by the bid, the company must rely on the adequacy of the bid price relative to the long-term potential value of the stock if the company were left alone. Investment bankers had to be recruited to give "fairness opinions" as to the future value of the stock, and these bankers could be deposed and cross-examined in court.

Third, once the theoretical difference between the future value and the bid price was established, the company had to decide what magnitude of defense was proportionate to the differential. Clearly, this was a very convoluted task, but most executives believed that the ruling limited the flexibility and ferocity that they could employ in defending their companies. The court, in the end, would judge for itself whether or not a defending company complied with its requirements. Because they were so abstract, this meant that the court could decide any way that the judges chose, based on whatever factors impressed them the most. If they did not, then the court could go into—and perhaps repudiate—bona fide business judgments made in good faith by a properly constituted board. The enhanced business judgment rule effectively nullified the traditional business judgment rule whenever a takeover of a company incorporated in Delaware occurred.[3]

The next case to come along clearly demonstrated that the powers of directors to decide a company's future had been curtailed by the Delaware court. Ronald Perelman was a successful but dreaded corporate takeover specialist, and when he announced a bid in 1985 for Revlon, the cosmetics giant, its board invited a leveraged buyout (LBO) firm to organize a management-led buyout of the company. The board committed itself to dealing with the LBO firm exclusively, and to sell to it certain key assets of the company if Perelman acquired as much as 40 percent of Revlon. As the transaction progressed, Perelman's bid price was always somewhat higher than the LBO price. Perelman claimed (*Revlon v. McAndrews & Forbes*) that the Revlon board inappropriately showed favoritism to its own LBO, even though it was priced lower than Perelman's offer. He also claimed that the various side deals that locked Revlon into the LBO were illegal under the enhanced business judgment rule. The court agreed with Perelman (and the Delaware Supreme Court upheld the decision on appeal), disallowed Revlon's defenses, and threw the victory to Perelman. The court noted that once Revlon "put a 'For Sale' sign on the firm" by deciding to take the company private through an LBO, then the role of the directors changed from defenders to that of auctioneers, in which the duty of loyalty to shareholders required that the main goal be to secure the highest price for its shareholders, not to favor a deal in which management had an interest.[4]

Another case in the same year reexamined directors' duties of care in takeover situations. In a landmark (and highly controversial) case, the board of Trans Union Corporation was sued by a shareholder plaintiff group (*Smith v. Van Gorkom,* 1985) for having agreed too readily to a merger proposal that was presented suddenly and would expire within a few days.[5] The board reasoned it could always accept a higher bid if one came along, and if none did, it could claim to have got the best possible price at the time. The Delaware Supreme Court, however, held that the board had failed to perform its duties of care by failing to conduct a thorough analysis of the "low-ball" takeover proposal with the assistance of professional advisers and experts. How could they know what the company was worth without undertaking such an analysis? If they did not know what it was worth, how could they accept an offer for the company? Indeed, the court went further, holding that the board had so neglected its duties as directors that it voided Trans Union's officer and directors' indemnification and D&O insurance policies. In the end, the buyer paid the individual judgments against the board members, so none of them suffered personally. Still, for all future takeover cases, the board of a target company would have to be able to demonstrate that it had performed its duties carefully by seeking expert advice and conducting a thorough analysis of the proposal. The new rules had to be followed, whether boards agreed with the ruling or not. It also guaranteed that every merger proposal from then on would be carefully studied by boards and their advisers—and that all companies would have to engage such advisers.

Three years later, a 1988 case of a contested takeover similar to the Revlon case occurred in which the defender—the publishing house Macmillan—attempted to escape the clutches of a distinctly unwanted and unsavory suitor by organizing an LBO. In this case, Macmillan was being pursued by the notorious British rogue entrepreneur Robert Maxwell. An intense battle ensued, in which the board of Macmillan backed a management-led LBO and a bidding war followed, with Maxwell's price always a bit higher. In the process, Macmillan engaged in a number of actions that Maxwell claimed were unfair and corrupted the auction process, such as spying on Maxwell and leaking mischievous information. The Chancery Court did disallow Macmillan's poison pill but left a one-sided asset-sale defense intact. This defense would probably have been enough on its own to block the Maxwell deal from proceeding. However, the Delaware Supreme Court was so offended by the conduct of the Macmillan board that it threw out the other defense, too, leaving the victory to Maxwell. In its decision, the Delaware Supreme Court said: "There must be the most scrupulous adherence to ordinary principles of fairness in the conduct of an auction" for the auction to be legal in Delaware.

For the first time, the court was requiring that standards of "fairness" also be applied in determining the legality of a takeover—in the past, it was understood that vigorous, hard-knuckle tactics were part of the free-market system and should not be interfered with in contests between professionals. The court in the future would look not just to proportionality in defense but also to *fairness*, another abstract concept that added to the discretion of the courts at the expense of that of the boards.

Within just a few years, the Delaware Courts had cut deeply into the freedom of boards of directors to utilize their powers as they saw fit. Their rulings affected not only the thousands of companies incorporated in Delaware but also companies incorporated elsewhere. Many states adopted Delaware law in corporate matters, but the high level of publicity the court's rulings were getting was entering the minds and expectations of institutional investors around the country. The Delaware decisions were having a major affect on corporations all across the country by limiting the freedom and independence of boards to govern themselves as they wished and by introducing abstractions to the process of determining a fair response to unwanted takeover efforts. Corporate sentiment began to build against Delaware as the preferred state of incorporation. If corporations abandoned Delaware (has they had New Jersey earlier in the century), the move would have a devastating impact on the state's economy.

But the court managed to offer corporations a break in 1989, just before the overheated market exhausted itself and brought the merger boom of the 1980s to an end. At the time, there was still a great deal of concern about excesses in the financial markets, which crashed in October 1987 and later recovered. Treasury secretary Nicholas Brady was worried about America's loss of international competitiveness if the country's great corporations were going to be destroyed as a result of the excessively "short-term profit motivations" of the merger craze.

An announced plan to merge Time Incorporated and Warner Communications on a friendly basis was challenged by a competing offer from Paramount Communications. A protracted struggle followed, and the Delaware Chancery Court, in a decision noted for its puzzling inconsistency with the prior pattern of its decisions, decided in favor of Time-Warner, disallowing a higher valued offer from Paramount. Time, the Court held, had not put up a "For Sale" sign. Instead, it was carrying out a long-term business strategy to merge with a company like Warner Communications. In such cases—when the ownership issue was unexpectedly raised as a challenge to a bona fide, long-term strategic move—the board was authorized by the court to set aside the (short-term) ownership issue in favor of the boards' long-term plans to develop the company's future vitality and shareholder value by prudent strategic development. Normally the court ruled in favor of private property rights, wrote William Allen, former chief judge of the Delaware Chancery Court. But occasionally, as in the Time-Warner case, it decided in favor of the merger, construing the corporation as an entity with many interests, not just property interests. In this case, the "long-term" interests of Time and its shareholders justified a decision by the board that might not have been superior to its "short-term interests."[6]

Many institutional investors objected to the Time-Warner decision, which deprived them of an opportunity to tender their shares at a higher stock price than they had ever seen for the company. But boardrooms welcomed the idea that they might rely on long-term strategic plans to avoid unwelcome takeover efforts. However, it was still up to the court to decide what a defensible long-term strategy was and how it was to be weighed against all other factors. And the court had become very hard to read.

The Changed Scene for Class-action Litigation

During the 1990s, when technology stock prices were soaring, many executives chose the opportunity to cash-in stock options to extract some of their wealth from the company they had helped build. They did this by converting options into shares, selling the shares and retaining for themselves the often substantial difference between the exercise price of the option and the market price. Virtually all companies did this, and it was thought to be normal. However, many of the companies involved were both speculative and fragile, and the stock prices were subject to huge swings, especially if disappointing news was released. Sometimes, just at the moment when an executive would be selling his or her own shares, an adverse event or disclosure would occur that caused the stock price to drop suddenly.

Specialist law firms began to pursue such cases by filing lawsuits against the company and its executives in federal court for securities fraud, or in a state court for breach of fiduciary duties. The charge would be that the executives or directors knew or should have known of the coming adverse events and discontinued trading in their own stock, or otherwise acted to prevent the adverse event from occurring. These cases would be handled with as much publicity as possible so as to keep the burden of proof on the defendant, and usually the case would be settled, both to dispose of it and to avoid an uncertain jury trial. The law firm bringing the action and organizing the plaintiff class would then attempt to convince the judge to approve an appropriate legal fee, usually between 10 and 20 percent of the amount collected, but sometimes more.

Reported settlement amounts in such cases may seem large to the public, but they represent only a token recovery for individual shareholders, often less than a dollar a share. From 1991 through 1995, an average of approximately 180 federal securities class-action suits were brought each year (representing about 2 percent of all publicly listed companies, but a very much higher percentage of high-tech companies). The smaller, entrepreneurial technology companies complained to their political representatives (to whom they also made campaign contributions) that their industry, vital as it was for America's future, had enough troubles competing successfully without being ravaged by plaintiff lawyers.

The result was the passage in 1995 by Congress of the Private Securities Litigation Reform Act, which was designed to make it much more difficult for trial lawyers to bring such suits against corporate officers and directors. The law was reinforced in 1998, by another law that required that all securities-fraud class-action suits be brought in federal court (not state courts), which effectively eliminated the ability to charge breach of fiduciary duties to shareholders. The two laws were thought to have done their jobs of discouraging such suits, until 2001 and 2002 and the overlapping cases of alleged corporate fraud and misconduct in the accounting and investment banking industries, which included cases charging misallocation of IPOs.

In the period after the Litigation Reform Act in 1995, the average annual number of class-actions suits actually increased only modestly (if one adjusts for an extraordinary 312 filings in 2001 related to allegations of abuses by underwriters in the initial public offerings of high-tech companies in the late 1990s). As of March 2, 2005, according to a report prepared by Cornerstone Research, 620 cases had been settled since the 1995 Reform Act, with settlements totaling $5.5 billion in 2004, $2.1 billion on 2003, and $4.5 billion in 2000, the previous record-setting year. These settlements include a number of very large cases involving high-visibility defendants, such as WorldCom and Enron, more than 65% of all settlements in 2004 were for less than $10 million and 80% were for less than $30 million.[7]

These settlements motivated law firms to be more aggressive in bringing suits, and in pursuing deep-pocketed parties connected to fraudulent transactions (such as banks and accountants) through agency or principal relationships. Several such banks were required to reserve funds for possible litigation settlements from these suits. They also experienced substantially increased costs (and tightened the terms) for D&O insurance, and have made corporations operate their business with an even keener eye to the details of compliance with both the spirit and the letter of regulations.

State Antitakeover Statutes

In 1989, Armstrong World Industries, a Pennsylvania corporation founded in 1860, was a leading manufacturer of flooring materials and one of Pennsylvania's most important companies. When it was suddenly subjected to a raid by the Belzberg Brothers of Canada, the company chose to call in its local political chips and lobbied for a state law that would block any takeover effort of a Pennsylvania corporation that did not have the support of its board. Such a bill (which nevertheless allowed Pennsylvania corporations to opt out of its provisions) passed in the legislature and became law in April of 1990. Soon after-ward, many other states followed suit, and by 1990, 42 states (including Delaware) had enacted similar laws, effectively incorporating the poison pill into the charters of corporations under their jurisdiction. These laws immediately became controversial. Businessmen, institutional investors, and academics argued that by taking the company out of the free market for corporate control, or the market to acquire companies, the firm would depress its own share price, unless it chose to opt out of the law.

A number of academic studies demonstrated this point, but no state has attempted to remove the law from its books. State officials are determined to protect the large employers that are chartered in their states (and contribute to election campaigns) and are less interested in share prices. Like the poison pill, these statutes are effective in deterring takeovers. But they also interfere with the free-market process, and by the end of the 1990s, such interference was seen to justify a lower share price. Since then, many companies have opted out of state antitakeover laws, guided by their boards or by pressure from institutional investors, to return their shares to normal trading.

Independence of Directors and Other Reforms

During the last two decades of the twentieth century, some institutional investors and corporate governance experts have tried to restrict excessive concentration of powers in management by increasing the powers of nonexecutive directors. They attempted to do this by insisting that a majority of the members of boards be independent directors, by tightening the duties and standards of the audit and compensation committees, and by increasing disclosures concerning management conflicts of interest, compensation, and benefits. After the cataclysmic events of the failures of Enron and WorldCom, some of these ideas were incorporated in provisions of the Sarbanes-Oxley Act and in new standards for director independence and conduct promulgated by the New York Stock Exchange and the National Association of Securities Dealers.

Although efforts to increase director independence have been under way for many years, a 2002 study by the Investor Responsibility Research Center indicated that two-thirds of all New York Stock Exchange companies (about 4,000 companies) would have to make changes to their boards to meet the new standards, which require a majority of all directors and all members of audit, compensation, and nominating committees to meet elevated standards for director independence.[8]

A variety of other governance proposals have also surfaced over the years to augment these provisions (although few have been adopted), including the separation of the jobs of chair and chief executive, designation of a "lead" outside director, performance reviews and term limits for outside directors, and solicitation of feedback and suggestions from institutional investors. The heart of the effort is to minimize agency conflicts by having all important corporate activities be monitored and supervised by disinterested and competent directors who are truly independent of management. If this single requirement for true independence could be assured, many governance experts have insisted, the balance of power necessary for good corporate governance would be achieved, and the rest of the reforms would be comparatively unimportant.

In the "premodern" corporation discussed in chapter 3, directors were rarely independent. They all had stakes or otherwise vested interests in the companies they directed. By the time Berle and Means published their classic work in 1932, some independent directors had appeared—as an effort to obtain adjunct talents and resources that the company would need. Bankers, lawyers, suppliers, and customers were recruited, as were others with useful connections—all had an interest or stake or some sort in the company. Such nonmanagement directors were well represented on the boards of the larger, "modern," and "institutionalized" corporations by the 1960s. The trend was largely driven by an effort to satisfy institutional investors, the New York Stock Exchange (which had urged more independent directors since the 1960s), and the companies' various public audiences. However, during the 1970s, an outbreak of weak corporate performance and corruption led to demands for greater independence and a reduction in cronyism. Increasing competition in the financial services industry also resulted in a reduction in boards on which bankers were represented. Nevertheless, by the beginning of the 1980s, when the great takeover boom began, most directors were thought to be part of the system of entrenchment. Takeovers were a persistent threat to management, which wanted to be able to address the threat, if one arose, with all the resources available to the company.

Indeed, most analyses of director independence fail to recognize the social dynamics of corporate boards, which often serve to persuade their members that the real purpose of outside directors is to support management and the company as good team players. Board members usually have little contact with each other outside the boardroom, but each has a personal and carefully cultivated relationship with the CEO, who usually has recruited some of the board members—often selecting those who have reason to appreciate the appointment. The CEO can usually influence which committees board members are assigned to, and can set the agendas and the style of committee and board meetings. Any board member who may prove to be difficult can be isolated, given less information than others, or not nominated for reelection. Few CEOs would prefer a truly independent but potentially troublesome board over one that was more supportive, compliant, and reliable.

But the effects of Delaware takeover litigation in the 1980s changed all that for many companies. To protect themselves against charges of unreasonable entrenchment and adverse court rulings, boards were required to make major changes in the ways they governed themselves during takeover bids. Independent directors, not CEOs, would make crucial decisions, and to do so they would have to be afforded their own outside counsel and financial advisers. The outside directors probably did not want or ask for this additional power, but found it forced on them by court rulings. The Delaware rulings reduced the agency conflicts by shifting authority from CEOs and management to independent, professionally advised, outside directors.

After the 1980s, a vocal and vigorous corporate governance advocacy developed in the United States to discourage such agency abuses as entrenchment, excesses in compensation, and other problems that might endanger the welfare of the corporation. This community, made up of academics, journalists, and public-interest officials, has long supported the idea that the greater the percentage of independent directors on a board, the better, although there is no factual evidence to support the belief that independence improves either economic performance or ethical conduct, or that any kind of generalized requirement for board composition would be effective for all of the country's several thousand public companies.

Indeed, there may be contrary evidence in the abundant history of successful startup companies and partnerships that have been governed entirely by insiders prior to becoming public companies or maturing into institutional corporations. In theory, independent directors are free of management pressure and powerful enough to remove a CEO, so they can have a controlling influence. In practice, however, many independent directors do not have significant enough investments in the companies on whose boards they serve to really care about performance, and have difficulty following company operational details. Many are not experienced business executives, or if they are, they may be too busy to keep themselves well informed.

CEOs also have a great deal of influence on independent directors, even those who have served a long time, and can influence their loyalty and support. Moreover, it has been widely observed that in a rising market, CEOs have very few critics—even the most vocal of independent directors are silenced by the immediacy of success. And, of course, rational CEOs are inclined to get rid of troublesome, overly critical directors by arranging for them not to be reappointed. So it may be that the theoretical benefits of independence are fully offset by their practical limitations. Such arguments notwithstanding, after the corporate scandals of the late 1990s, the public policy position of the Congress, the SEC, and the New York Stock Exchange was to insist on independent directors as one of the most important steps to prevent future abuses.

Finally, there is an issue of jurisdiction. Does the Congress (in passing the Sarbanes-Oxley Act) or the SEC have the constitutional authority to impose regulations concerning the composition of boards of directors of companies legally incorporated by the states? Is the purpose of federal intervention the improved regulation of interstate commerce, and not to intrude into the very nature of the corporation's organization for the purpose of performing its functions? This is an argument that is yet to be heard in court.

Federal Regulation and Boards of Directors

The SEC must restrict itself to civil lawsuits in federal court to enforce only federal securities laws. In pursuing this mandate, the SEC has brought and won many lawsuits over the years, and been awarded disgorgements of profits (turned over to the U.S. Treasury) and penalties (retained by the SEC).[9]

The SEC's effective (if checkered) record in bringing such actions to court has sometimes produced important rulings, such as *BarChis*, which then create new standards of compliance. On other occasions, the SEC has won its case only to be overturned on appeal. Two significant insider trading cases that were tried and won by the SEC were overturned by the Supreme Court in the 1980s, and in 1990 an important shareholder voting case brought by the Business Roundtable and won by the SEC in federal court was reversed on appeal. These were cases that the SEC thought were important tests of the law, but the reversals (which still helped establish the law, although in a different way) brought criticism of the SEC, either for excessive enforcement zeal or incompetence. During the late 1990s, the SEC preferred to avoid testing its authority in court, and instead pressured corporate defendants into settlements, hoping these would act as deterrents in the future. These cases have not involved individual directors.

In other instances, however, the federal government has pursued corporate directors for failure to perform their duties. In the 1980s, the Federal Deposit Insurance Corporation (FDIC) and the Federal Savings and Loan Insurance Corporation (FSLIC) were required to expend more than $100 billion (a net figure, after substantial recoveries) to fulfill deposit guarantees for a multitude of failed U.S. savings-and-loan associations and banks. A public furore resulted, and Congress in 1989 passed the Financial Institutions Reform, Recovery and Enforcement Act (FIRREA), which tightened regulations, increased deposit insurance premiums, and established new enforcement and financial recovery machinery. Among these was the creation of the Resolution Trust Company (RTC) to recover funds advanced by the FDIC to insure deposits.

Over a six-year period, the RTC liquidated banks, sold assets, and routinely sued officers and directors of the failed savings-and-loans and banks, on the grounds that they had failed in their *fiduciary duties to depositors* and the FDIC. According to L. William Seidman, chairman of RTC during this time, approximately 1,000 such directors of savings-

and-loan corporations were sued, and substantial sums were collected from them, mainly by "outsourcing" the legal work to private-sector law firms.[10] Many of these cases resulted in settlements with directors who feared they would be unable to convince juries that they had been duly diligent in informing themselves about the affairs of the financial institutions on whose boards they served. Some were also charged with putting their own interests ahead of the depositors and shareholders. This is one of the few times when federal law has been successfully applied to fiduciary duties—but banks insured by the FSLIC and FDIC were "special" and in many ways different from nonfinancial corporations.

RETHINKING THE ROLE OF DIRECTOR

Within a period of about six months in 2001 and 2002, the two biggest corporate bankruptcies ever to occur in the United States—Enron and WorldCom—galvanized public opinion into a powerfully negative view of all boards of directors, as well as accounting and banking firms dealing with corporations. The media—particularly the cable television and network shows—broadcast the views of angry critics of American business who were quick to blame the high-visibility bankruptcies, the sudden collapse of the Internet and telecom industries, and the corresponding drop in stock prices on corporate greed, arrogance, and disregard of public investors.

There were about 15,000 publicly traded companies in the United States at the time, about half of which were listed on the NYSE or NASDAQ. Perhaps three dozen of these companies became the subject of criminal fraud investigations—an unprecedented number. Many more companies—a few hundred or so—had been named in class-action suits, most of which had not been resolved by the time the Sarbanes-Oxley Act was signed into law in mid 2002. Some of these cases would be thrown out by unsympathetic judges. Others would advance but have to await resolution until other investigations and charge-making by the SEC or other government bodies were completed.

Nevertheless, it would be very difficult to compile a list of as many as 200 public companies that could be seriously accused of abusing the public trust by their actions (beyond making business mistakes and the practice of overpaying their executives). Perhaps a finer net would pick up as many as 2 to 3 percent of all traded companies for some form of misconduct or other actions for which boards of directors might be held responsible, if not punished. So only a small percentage of public boards could be said to have gone astray during the latter years of the 1990s, one of the most speculative and overheated times in all financial history. This may actually suggest that 20 years of discussion of corporate governance and enlightened regulation has produced an essen-

tially well-behaved and compliant corporate sector, rather than a sav-
age and fundamentally unethical one. Of course, among those
companies that imploded after the bubble were some gigantic failures
that cost investors many billions. Failures of this magnitude could
hardly go unnoticed or, in the bright light of intense public scrutiny,
unpunished.

After Enron

Sarbanes-Oxley was passed at the height of the public corporate governance frenzy and was reinforced by new rules issued by the SEC, the
NASD, and the NYSE (see chapter 9). Among other things, the law
tightened standards for directors' independence, imposed requirements for "financial literacy," and enhanced the duties of members of
audit committees. It was observed, however, that the boards of several
of the companies that had failed, including Enron, would have met
even these higher standards of qualification for board membership.

The climate in the early 2000s also called for regulators and officials
to demonstrate that they had the public interest at heart and would act
accordingly (and some cases dramatically). The Justice Department
created a new task force devoted to prosecuting corporate fraud, and
brought criminal charges against several managers of well-known companies (including WorldCom, Enron, Xerox, Adelphia, HealthSouth,
and Rite Aid, among others). It also moved against Arthur Andersen,
a leading accounting firm that (with other auditors) had a 15-year
history of losing class-action suits for improper accounting (see chapter
7). In a 12-month period, the Justice Department task force announced
that it had obtained more than 250 corporate fraud convictions, including those of 25 former CEOs.[11] Conspicuously absent from such successes, however, for the first two years following its collapse, were the
chairman of Enron (Kenneth Lay) and its CEO (Jeffrey Skilling), neither
of whom by that time had been charged with an offense by the Justice
Department or the SEC, though both were later indicted on criminal
charges. No one who served as an independent director of any of these
companies was charged by the Justice Department.

There was, however, considerable pressure on the SEC, at the time
chaired by a highly experienced corporate lawyer, Harvey Pitt, to bring
civil charges against board members of companies that had collapsed
because of fraud or corporate wrongdoing. The public appeared to be
disappointed when the SEC announced that it would not bring charges
against the Enron board, despite several credible reports (including a
report by the Enron board itself) of only halfhearted efforts by its
members, and members of the company's audit committee, to identify
and correct the accounting practices that were said to have misrepresented Enron's true financial position. But the SEC would have had a
hard time bringing a case against these individuals, because it could
not prove that they had themselves personally committed or condoned

fraud as it was defined in the securities laws. The SEC could not charge the directors for any failure to perform their fiduciary duties in a diligent and prudent manner since this is a matter of state law. Conceivably, the SEC could have invoked *BarChris* to get a broad-minded and sympathetic federal judge to accept a case based on the audit committee members' failure to be duly diligent in assuring that financial information reported by the company to investors (and to the SEC) was accurate and provided a fair picture of the company's situation, as required by federal law. After all, if they are not going to be responsible for the accuracy of financial information they oversee, what were they good for?

The SEC's announcement, however, suggested that Pitt was giving a pass to responsible directors. Overwhelmed by negative press and unable to deal with it skillfully, Pitt resigned in late 2002. To date, the SEC still has brought no charges against any outside board member of companies that it investigated for fraud or other violations of securities laws.

Meanwhile, plaintiff lawyers had to bring class actions on behalf of equity owners in federal court, and to demonstrate a violation of federal law. One such firm brought a suit on behalf of Enron creditors (but not a class action) in state court, where fiduciary charges could be pursued. Often all of the companies' board members would be named in such suits and their indemnification and D&O insurance provisions would kick in. But quite frequently in such cases, the main targets of the litigation were the large banks and accountants and others with deep pockets whom the plaintiffs hoped to make responsible in some way for their damages. Compared to the banks and accounting firms, individual directors were far less lucrative targets for plaintiff's lawyers, especially when the suits had to be brought in federal courts and either fraud or a violation of securities law had to be proved.

In one such case, however, a different result occurred, with significant consequences for all directors in the future. In March 2005, a class-action suit brought by Alan Hevesi, Comptroller of New York State and sole trustee of its pension funds, against the bankers, accountants, and directors of WorldCom was finally settled. The suit was based on violation of federal securities law in connection with underwritings of WorldCom bonds in 2000 and 2001, and Hevesi was able to achieve a settlement of about $6 billion from more than a dozen banks, a record sum for a securities class action. The settlement, however, upon the insistence of the New York Comptroller, included a requirement that individual board members of WorldCom pay a total of $25 million from their own pockets, and that the company's liability insurers pay an additional $35 million. The board members might have refused to settle, but then they would have been forced to go to trial as the only defendants not to have already settled, a proposition they considered too risky. So they agreed to the unprecedented settlement. Indeed, board members have almost never paid money in settlements from their own pockets in the past. They may not have in this instance either (a $25 million contribution in a settlement of $6 billion is insignificant) had not the plaintiff Alan Hevesi (an elected official) insisted on it.

The Future of Corporate Directors

The regulatory changes in the post-Enron era will certainly affect the role and the impact of outside directors in the future, at least for a while. Sarbanes-Oxley, the SEC, the NYSE, and probably the D&O insurance companies are all asking for more independence among directors, and charging them (particularly regarding accounting issues) with enhanced duties and reporting obligations. Sarbanes-Oxley also provides boards with additional resources to accomplish their duties— such as requiring that outside counsel and financial expertise be made available to audit committees. This is similar to the expanded role of outside directors in merger situations that developed for Delaware companies, which enhanced their independence. For most companies, of course, the enhanced powers will be unnecessary, since there are no accounting irregularities to detect and rectify. For those that have them, the enhancement of independence and resources available to audit committees should help in rooting out and correcting problems.

However, none of the new laws and regulations make independent directors any more liable to penalties for misconduct than they were before. The Sarbanes-Oxley Act did not require directors to bring their fiduciary duties into the federal realm. Nor were any new standards applied to the performance of duties by nonmanagement directors. Indeed, directors' liabilities for failure to perform their duties is likely to remain minimal and may be reduced further by extra efforts on the part of management teams to comply with new standards that affect them. Whereas the regulators have called loudly for more independence on boards, they have not required any increased accountability. As this reality sets in, corporate directors will most probably breathe easier and revert to their pre-Enron willingness to serve on boards. A year after the passage of Sarbanes-Oxley, the National Association of Corporate Directors reported a registry of 2,000 potential candidates for board seats, and the Financial Executives Institute had a list of 300 "financially literate" individuals willing to serve on audit committees.[12]

Perhaps an attitude change caused by enhanced financial powers of independent directors will occur and pass over into nonaccounting areas as well, but in general the sociology of boards is not likely to be transformed by the new requirements. Directors continue to have personal, sometimes beholden, relationships with CEOs that put a premium on loyalty to the management team. Many directors have very limited business experience, and all are dependent on management for the information they receive about the company's business. The dynamics of board meetings are more passive than active—directors listen to reports without subjecting them to vigorous challenge, they ratify and endorse resolutions put forward by management, often with little discussion. Directors do not insult management or each other by public challenges. Individually, some directors give advice to the CEO privately, but in general the only time true independence is felt as a restraint on the powers of the CEO is when something has already gone wrong and the board is called upon to do something about it, including possibly the replacement of the CEO. Most individual members have little ability to influence the future actions of the company, if it requires opposing the CEO and other board members publicly. To expect boards to function otherwise would be unrealistic. Board members do the job required of them by their corporate charter simply by showing up and voting on matters that require board approval. The corporate governance community places great weight on the role of boards in assuring effective as well as ethical actions by corporations, but this confidence may be unrealistic—the dynamics of board composition and relationships with CEOs just don't work that way.

Over the years some states, like Delaware, have charged boards with the additional task of "monitoring" the actions of managers, but what this means or how it is to be accomplished has not been made clear. Federal law requires due diligence on the part of directors, but only when issuing securities. If American investors want their independent board members to be responsible for corporate conduct, then they should look to a change in the laws that now tolerate a confusion of state and federal jurisdiction and effectively limit directors' liabilities. Before doing so, however, it would be wise to consider the consequences of such actions—transferring more power to part-time independent board members may also nullify the authority of executives to act quickly and opportunistically in the shareholders' best economic interest. Boards may deny this authority to competent CEOs while they argue over merits of particular actions and consider their personal liabilities. Perhaps more can be achieved by better understanding the CEO, the one individual to whom shareholders entrust all forms of corporate action and conduct.

5

Evolution and Powers of the CEO

U.S. corporations are not required by law to have a chief executive officer. They are required to have a board of directors. How the board arranges things beyond that is up to it. In the "pre-modern" days, most large corporations were dominated by their founders. But these people had a loyal cadre of assistants, associates, and protégés whom they relied upon to manage their businesses. Many became rich and successful in their own right. By the time of the "modern" public corporation described by Berle and Means in 1932, most of the old magnates, entrepreneurs, and promoters who had built successful companies before the 1920s had left the scene and been replaced by hired professional managers.

CEOs

EVOLUTION OF THE MODERN CHIEF EXECUTIVE

Perhaps the best known hired manager before World War II was Alfred P. Sloan, a precocious MIT engineer who in 1916 sold a roller-bearing business he and his father had bought to General Motors. This was not long after GM had been organized, by a dazzling but unreliable and erratic business booster, William Crapo Durant, who persuaded Sloan to join the GM management team as a vice president. Sloan described himself as well-to-do but not rich—but certainly not one of the "Alger boys" (self-made successes glorified in the novels of Horatio Alger). Sloan was dry, controlled, extremely rational, and a workaholic with no outside interests or bad habits. He shunned personal attention and publicity, and in many ways seems the prototype that Berle and Means had warned of in 1932—the faceless professional manager with no interests beyond the company and its profits. Serious reversals occurred at General Motors not long after Sloan joined the company. Durant was thrown out, and Sloan was made president of the company at age 48,

99

serving under nonexecutive chairmen until 1937, when he was designated "chairman and chief executive officer"— one of the first uses of the term, which was adopted to indicate that he was not being "pushed upstairs." He served in that capacity until 1946, and afterward as chairman of the board until 1956.

Throughout most of this time, Sloan was an extremely powerful man in American business, but he was never flamboyant or excessive; he quietly went about his business and kept himself out of the limelight, just as a hired employee should do. His ownership of GM stock enabled him to become very wealthy, and he became extremely active as a philanthropist. With the exception of his contemporary, Herbert Hoover, who chose to purse a career in public service after a career in business, neither Sloan nor any of the other professional managers of the time before World War II were well known to the public. Sloan founded a school of industrial management at MIT in 1952 to help in the development of more professional managers like himself.[1]

The Establishment Corporation

During World War II, businesses learned to work closely with the government under the auspices of the War Production Board, which was established in 1942 by executive order and assumed sweeping powers over economic activity. The board controlled access to raw material and other resources and could prohibit nonessential industrial activity in the interest of maximizing war production. It soon became by far the largest customer of all major industrial companies. War production greatly increased the scale of manufacturing operations and reliance on sophisticated management practices.

After the war, a great reorganization of American industry was required to shift from military production back to consumer products and capital goods, imposing a need for managers to navigate treacherous channels of change in the demand for their products and services. Five years of warfare had also introduced a new style of effective leadership in corporations—the Eisenhower-like "commanding officer" who could strategize, organize, delegate, appoint and remove subordinates from powerful positions. Generals had to be tough and results-oriented. They had to deliver or be replaced.

After the war, a number of former generals—Omar Bradley, Lucius Clay, and James Gavin, among many others—became heads of corporations, or members of their boards of directors. The wartime experience of generals and their civilian counterparts in business had emphasized cooperation and teamwork (and penalties for those who did not go along) and created a "military-industrial complex" of the sort that President Eisenhower had warned Americans about in his 1961 farewell address. Eisenhower was concerned about excessive influence on the part of the defense industry on American foreign policies, but in another context, his warning suggested a business-political "establishment," which developed as large businesses recognized that they had to deal not only with competition to succeed but also with the war-expanded powers of the U.S. government, powers that were not likely to recede very quickly. Members of the establishment, therefore, needed to be patriotic, cooperative, connected and influential both in government and corporate circles, and sensitive to public images. These were new additions to the skill set required of top management.

The large corporations of the late 1950s and early 1960s became the "institutional" corporations that Adolf Berle described at the time. Their existence was not only defined in economic terms—maximizing returns on investment for shareholders or competing successfully to gain market share—but also in terms of preserving their places in the pantheon of great American corporations (such as the *Fortune* 500 list) that signified success, respect, and importance. Often such distinction was associated with government or other establishment support, contracts, subsidies, or legislation that favored and protected the companies. To some, perhaps, this was considered as valuable as high returns, dividends, and growth.

For a generation, business executives followed similar career paths. They would join major corporations as management trainees or as personal assistants to senior executives. Engineers would be sent off to make things, but the rest of the intake pool—liberal arts graduates, lawyers, and a few MBAs—would spend several years rotating through different jobs and gaining exposure to various executives as they did so. Some would be selected for accelerated promotion, but most generally remained through a fairly predictable career that led to a well-pensioned retirement at the age of 65. Those who succeeded and rose in the ranks often became members of the company's board of directors. Businessmen understood that success at higher altitudes involved a lot of committees, reports, planning and staff work, and deftness at operating within the company's political and social environment. Top jobs, including that of CEO, were usually awarded to those from within the company, often as a result of orderly succession planning. The skills required for advancement were largely those of preserving the corporation's place and position, and of sensible, well-planned development of new business and investment opportunities. These skills would be applied across the various constituencies that the company's activities included—to customers and suppliers, labor unions, and community groups in the locations where the company had facilities, and in government and media circles. To assist them in developing the necessary behavior and contacts, many companies encouraged their chief executives to participate in business leadership associations, and to serve on boards of directors of other corporations.

Many institutionalized corporations fostered a practice of upward mobility that produced new leadership at the top every six or seven years or so. It took a long time to get to be named CEO of a large company, but not very long after that, one was required to retire and make way for a successor. The retired individual would remain on the board for a few more years, perhaps serving as chairman. But it was quite unusual for hired managers of institutionalized corporations to rise to the top at a young age and remain there for a long period. Most companies during this time (from the 1950s through the 1970s) recognized the president as the chief executive. Many of them had different individuals serving as chairman of the board, sometimes yet another as chairman of an executive committee (the function of which was not clear but implied great importance), with the two respected individuals serving as a pair of wise uncles who could guide, but also restrain, the CEO's actions. The board would certainly reflect any large family ownership, but otherwise it would comprise a cadre of rising executive vice presidents or other senior executives and a selection of outside directors chosen because of their close association with the company (as bankers, suppliers, or customers) and a few chief executives of other corporations. When new directors were needed, board members would look to their own connections to suggest replacements.

Not all companies in this era were establishment corporations. Many were new enterprises exploiting technologies or business ideas that had not been around long enough to become institutionalized—companies that were focused on internal growth and expansion. Other companies were controlled by their founding families, or by brash financial entrepreneurs and wheeler-dealers. Companies were either in a high internal growth mode, or they were not. Those that were not included many of the older, more established companies that were limited in their opportunities to grow because of continuing tight antitrust policies left over from the 1920s, which precluded most major companies from acquiring others within their own industry. There were very few mergers of any size until the late 1960s. Many companies attempted to grow overseas instead, which turned a number of them into multinational corporations, a term that reflected the projection of corporate power and resources into markets around the world. But wider international activities of corporations also increased their complexity and dispersed their authority in ways that required even more professional management which inevitably increased the corporate bureaucracy. There seemed to be an understanding that large corporate organizations, like the government or the army, could only be managed through well-organized administrative layers.

Whiz Kids and Corporate Raiders

The preferred phrase for management of a business bureaucracy was "business administration," which was thought to be a set of skills performed by educated business managers. The Harvard Business School was founded in 1910 just for this purpose—to train a group of young men to become business administrators who might rise to pro- vide the leadership needed to head large corporations in the future. These managers were trained in top graduate schools of business administration. The model of the successful modern professional manger was Robert McNamara, a 1939 honors graduate of the Harvard Business School who served as an analyst in the army air force during World War II and was subsequently part of a group of "whiz kids" recruited by Ford Motor Company to reorganize its operations after the war. There he rose to the presidency of the corporation in 1960, soon after which he was selected by President-elect John Kennedy (to whom he was not previously known) to become secretary of defense of the United States at the age of 44.

Business conditions changed dramatically in the 1960s. The economy had entered a high-growth phase again, averaging over 5 percent for a decade, with GNP expanding each month for nearly nine years. New business opportunities were emerging, and the Dow Jones Industrial Average reflected them, nearly doubling during the decade. Growth was what investors were looking for, particularly growth in earnings per share. Those companies that could show annual earnings per share growth of 15 percent of so could aspire to see their stocks trade at 15 or 20 times earnings, a significant improvement over price-earnings multiples of the past. Institutional investors for the first time had become a significant factor in setting stock prices, and mutual funds managed by professionals proliferated to an extent not seen since the 1920s. The stock market went into an exuberant period, and soon afterward the long-dormant mergers-and-acquisitions market entered a boom period as well. Mergers, of course, were the way for companies to grow faster than they could from internal growth alone. Large corporations were still restricted by antitrust policy from participating in the merger boom in a significant way, so the real opportunities were left to a new kind of entrepreneur who appeared at the time and started the multibusiness enterprise, or "conglomerate." One of the earliest of these, Litton Industries, was founded by Charles "Tex" Thornton, a contemporary and fellow whiz kid of Robert McNamara.

Thornton's idea was to create a company that could grow annually at 15 percent more or less indefinitely. It would do so through a holding company structure that would acquire a variety of unrelated businesses at a pace sufficient to reach its growth objectives. Once acquired, the companies would be subject to operational discipline and cost-cutting to improve performance and eliminate any activity that would be duplicated by the holding company, which itself would be run in a lean way by a group of highly talented, well-educated, young and energetic business professionals. With appropriate marketing effort, Thornton was able to persuade investors to buy into his idea, and Litton's stock price rose in anticipation of his achievements. With a higher stock price, Thornton could acquire other companies (any kind of company) that traded at lower price-earnings multiples than Litton, and in doing so would enable Litton to consolidate the acquired company's earnings on a basis that increased Litton's earnings per share, and thus justified its stock price. The technique seemed to work. Litton's stock price rose dramatically in response to the strategy, and various other conglomerate companies were formed to do the same thing.

Many of the companies that followed Litton were inclined to make takeover offers whether they were welcome or not. They came to be seen as "corporate raiders" and "asset strippers" and were considered the pirates of modern commerce, many of whose victims were institutionalized, establishment corporations. The raiders created the suddenly announced cash takeover bid—called the "Saturday Night Special," named for a cheap handgun used by muggers—which, after the large and powerful institutionalized corporate community rallied its supporters, resulted in the passage of the relatively benign Williams Act in 1968. Nevertheless, the raiders were successful in getting shareholders of their targets to tender their shares, despite mighty efforts by target companies to persuade them not to. Institutional investors, devoted to achieving the best investment results they could, were particularly deaf to the pleas of corporate targets. In a short time, between 1963 and 1969, a new force had emerged that corporate executives would be required to deal with: the financial marketplace—one that would reward or punish companies as it saw fit, through the increasingly visible and important measure of the share price. The market would determine whether a company's prospects were worth a great deal or not. If so, a rising stock price could make investors wealthy, and if not, a lowered stock price could make a company vulnerable to a raider. Executives had to listen to the market. They had no choice.

Hard Times and New Leadership

The spirit of the 1960s, however, could not last. It survived political assassinations and urban riots. But the Vietnam War proved to be its undoing. Lyndon Johnson declined to run for reelection in 1968, but even a new president, Richard Nixon, could not end the conflict until 1973. Meanwhile, some of the economic consequences of the war were felt at home, where inflation rose into double digits, carrying interest rates with it and killing economic growth. This led the Nixon administration to embark on a series on policies that operated entirely against the free market, such as wage and price controls, capital controls, and unlinking the dollar from gold. None of them worked. To make matters worse, oil prices suddenly quadrupled after the outbreak of war between the Arabs and the Israelis in 1973, followed by Nixon's Watergate

resignation, trade disputes with Japan, the ascent of the Ayatollah Kho-
meini in Iran, more oil price rises, and the Russian invasion of Afghanistan during the ineffective Ford and Carter administrations.

American corporations were embarrassed by a variety of scandals,
ranging from illegal political contributions at home to bribing foreign
heads of state to gain export business. It was a very tough time for
American businesses—many well-known companies like the Penn
Central Railroad (the largest railway company in the U.S.), Chrysler
Corporation, and Lockheed Corporation failed or had to be rescued by
government bailouts. An investor purchasing a share of the Dow Jones
index in January 1973, just before Nixon's shortened second term,
would have to wait 11 years, until December 1983, for it to get back to
where it started. In real terms, however, after the effects of inflation
averaging about 8 percent for those 11 years, the investment would
have lost more than 40 percent of its real value. Most companies found
stock options to be of little value, and many, including IBM, were forced
to lay off workers for the first time in their corporate existence. Most
establishment companies then were being managed for survival, not
for growth or to maximize profits.

One major corporation that failed during this time was Chrysler,
and in 1978 the company endeavored to restructure itself and to renew
its future prospects. This meant new management, and Chrysler's
board selected Lee Iacocca, then president (but not CEO) of Ford Motor
Company. Iacocca had been at Ford all his business life, and had risen
to the top on the basis of the success of products and models he introduced. When he arrived at Chrysler, he found it sinking, and was able
to arrange a $1.2 billion loan guarantee provided by the U.S. Treasury
(justified at the time as being necessary to keep the American car
industry at least minimally competitive).

Iacocca cut the template for at least one style of CEO that later was
copied repeatedly—the rough-edged, results-driven, ruthless, cost-
cutting executive whose sole interest was in returning the company to
high levels of profitability so he could benefit from the generous stock
options and other compensation arrangements provided when he
agreed to take the job. The Chrysler board was desperate to get someone as experienced as Iacocca, and agreed to whatever he demanded.
Helped by lower interest rates and a turnaround in the national
economy, Iacocca did succeed in turning Chrysler around within four
years by cutting costs and reducing employment. He was extremely
well paid for his effort, and became a role model for the pay-for-
performance school of executive compensation. Iacocca himself became
a popular celebrity, by appearing in company advertisements, and on
television shows and at celebrity events, by giving interviews, and
by making news with tough talk and attitude. Iacocca was, after all,
restoring shareholder value. He was little interested in committees,
cooperation, or hobnobbing with the establishment elite. He was a

dynamic but picaresque character whose language could be foul, who drove people hard and treated them poorly, ignored good manners, and unashamedly wanted to make all the money he could. He was the first antiestablishment CEO of a major corporation in years, and the public seemed to love him for it. The more approval he received, the more outlandish he became. He remained at Chrysler until retirement in 1993.

Iacocca shook things up and got things done. Many large, institutionalized companies could see a need for an Iacocca in their own organization. Several such firms, after struggling through the 1970s, decided to make management changes to find young, dynamic, Iacocca-like figures to shake things up as well. Anthony J. F. O'Reilly, once a star rugby player for the Irish national team, took over as CEO of H. J. Heinz Company in 1979 at the age of 43. Roberto Goizueta, a Cuban-born engineer, took over as CEO of ultraestablishment Coca-Cola in 1981 at the age of 48. Jack Welch, a tough, Boston scholarship kid, took over as CEO of General Electric in 1981 at 45, and Michael Eisner became Walt Disney's CEO at 42 in 1984. By 1997 (the year Goizueta died), these four had established themselves among the most successful and most highly paid corporate executives in the United States. They were all recruited to mend troubled, but still powerful and important, American companies that had been founded generations earlier. There were many such companies among the *Fortune* 500 in the early 1980s.

THE POSTMODERN CORPORATE CEO

The 1980s were years of corporate restructuring—either by takeover, leveraged buyout, or self-imposed internal effort. Conglomerates were broken up, diversified manufacturing companies slimmed down and refocused, and many businesses were acquired by leveraged financial investor groups to operate as private companies. Investors were willing to purchase risky subordinated debt of these companies, hoping to make large gains from the reissuance of the stock in a few years' time. A merger boom developed (the first since the 1960s) to accommodate these trends, and the Dow Jones Index rose steadily, tripling from 1981 to 1989, despite a major market crash in October 1987.

The market was rewarding performance in achieving companies' basic objectives of increasing their returns on investment and market share. This performance was attributed by the market to companies' underlying strategies and executive leadership, and information about their strategies and leadership came from security analysts, press articles, and fund managers' interviews with CEOs. Companies with charismatic, results-oriented chief executives with bold strategies and good media skills were rewarded with higher stock prices, and their CEOs were in turn rewarded with more generous compensation packages. CEOs recognized the pattern, and many adapted themselves to benefit from it. They hired public relations experts to portray their actions as favorably as possible, they cultivated the analysts who reported on them, and they hired lawyers and consultants to assist in negotiating their compensation packages.

New Compensation Practices

Prior to the 1980s, most CEOs of large corporations were paid a salary, a modest cash or stock bonus, and a contribution to a retirement fund. There were perquisites as well, of course, and some had generous stock option programs. For the most part, however, stock options had been a disappointing form of compensation during the 1970s, when equity markets failed to perform well. *Forbes* published its first list of the richest 400 Americans in 1982, and no CEO who had neither founded a company nor inherited his position was on the list. At the peak of the stock market in 1999, however, several such CEOs were included on the *Forbes* 400, which then required at least $600 million in net worth to be listed, and many more had accumulated fortunes large enough to make them near-term possibilities.

The changes in compensation practices began in the early 1980s, when hostile takeover efforts began again. Boards began to provide CEOs and a few other key managers with packages that anticipated a change of control. Such a package, called a "golden parachute" in the market, provided for payments to be made to compensate the executives for their loss of office in the event of a takeover. The packages were justified by boards as being fair payment to executives to ensure that they would not unreasonably discriminate against a takeover offer by suppressing it or misrepresenting it to the board. Some boards also felt that as the payments would be made by the acquiring company, they would not cost their own shareholders anything.

In time, the definition of a change of control for compensation purposes became very soft (for example, a "change of control" event might occur if an offer for the company was made, even though it was not accepted by the board, or even when the offer was only for a modest amount of the stock, such as 25 percent). A golden parachute might be worth three or four years of future compensation, but it could be whatever the board wanted and was often more. Ross Johnson, the CEO of RJR Nabisco at the time of its LBO in 1987, had a parachute valued at $53 million.

Critics argued that the parachutes represented unreasonable pay to executives just for doing the job they were hired for—that is, to maximize shareholder value. Before long, however, the CEOs of most large corporations had been issued parachutes, partly because their boards believed that they were in the shareholders' interest and partly because so many other companies had offered them to CEOs that it became difficult to refuse.

The leveraged buyout boom in the 1980s was a temptation for many managers. In some cases, LBOs were arranged by professional firms, such as Kohlberg, Kravis and Roberts (KKR), and the firm inserted its own CEO to manage the company after the takeover. Other times, a management group, perhaps financed by KKR or other LBO operators, would arrange the deal. Those CEOs selected for such work—or inserting themselves by initiating the LBO process—could make multiples of their current compensation by the ownership and other incentives offered to managers in buyouts. The LBO business placed the pay-for-performance standard on the top of its list of ways to succeed as a CEO. And it set up a marketplace for chief executives eager to put themselves into a higher risk-reward position than they had with an establishment corporation. Lou Gerstner, for example, left a high position at American Express to become CEO of the post-LBO RJR Nabisco, succeeded in making a fortune while there, then was hired away in 1993 to successfully turn IBM around after being granted a great deal of IBM stock.

For most companies, it was easier to issue stock in the form of options because they did not have to account for the compensation expense right way, while immediately taking tax deductions for them, because for tax purposes they could recognize the expense. Options were also hard to value—many executives in the 1980s and 1990s resisted the idea that stock options could be properly valued well in advance of their being exercised—and as a result were frequently undervalued when offered by companies to employees, who therefore received more actual value from the options than the company had intended. The more options were used and the higher stock prices rose, the greater were the cumulative distortions in executive compensation, including the balance-sheet and earnings-dilution effects of compensation practices, especially among technology and other growth companies. These distortions did not favor the stockholders of the companies.

Most company boards think they have capable CEOs. It is, after all, the board's job to select someone who is highly capable. They do not relish the thought of losing a CEO to an LBO operator willing to pay him or her a great deal more than he or she was already earning. Relatively few CEOs ever received such offers, but most boards thought their CEOs were good enough to get one—and just might. So they altered compensation packages to provide munificent golden parachutes, plus stock options, just to be sure they were meeting market standards for CEOs, even though it was highly unlikely that their CEOs would actually drift away. Just to be sure they were meeting market standards, they retained compensation consultants, who conducted surveys of the compensation arrangements at comparable companies and reported back to the board. They might show the median compensation for a CEO was $4 million, the upper quartile was $6 million, but their own CEO was receiving $3.8 million, less than the median and much less than the upper quartile, where the board thought their CEO should really be ranked. So the CEO got a raise to adjust his or her compensation to where the board thought it should be, on the basis of the consultant's analysis. The adjustments raised the median for the group to, say, $4.2 million, and the consultants reported this information to other companies, and the level of compensation required to keep one's own CEO in line continued to rise—all by itself and without any direct contribution from the CEO.

If, however, a board resisted this insidious process and took the view that there were probably others in the global executive talent pool who would take the CEO job if the incumbent left, it may have been surprised when it came time to renegotiate the CEO's contract, an event that happens every three years or so. The CEO might (as many did) have retained an agent to negotiate for him or her who was well aware of the consultant's data. If the board still resisted and the CEO left, it was usually required to conduct an executive search to obtain the best person it could for the job. To do this, the company normally employed an executive recruiting firm to advise it on the compensation package needed to attract the best candidate, who in any event would appear with his or her own agent. It was very difficult to escape this process of self-reinforcing inflation in CEO compensation, and very few companies were willing to do so, for fear of appearing to be out of step with the pay-for-performance ideal.

For companies having to replace a CEO—especially those needing one for a difficult turnaround assignment (such as IBM's)—the latitude for negotiating with the candidate was often quite narrow. The candidate's agent would not only be well informed about the market for CEO talent but also would have drafted an employment contract that was very favorable to the candidate. Often these would require some sort of signing-on bonus, a guide for how the executive would be compensated once on the job, a list of perquisites, privileges, and titles, and a detailed arrangement for severance payments in the event the individual should be terminated. The board's first priority was to find the best possible candidate, and then to negotiate a contract to ensure the candidate would come on board. It was a sellers' market for CEOs in the 1980s and 1990s, and CEOs could largely write their own tickets. Often it was "golden hellos" when CEOs arrived, "golden handcuffs" while they served, and "golden goodbyes" when they resigned or were terminated. This was a far cry from the dedicated, professional managers of the establishment corporations of the past.

The executive compensation process was subject to some moderating influences, however. Pay arrangements have to be disclosed to stockholders, albeit in a format required by the SEC that misinforms the reader. This format cumulates the value of current salary and bonus payments with the value of share options from the past that were exercised in the current period and reports no value for recently issued shares or those with exercise prices below the stock price. However, annual media surveys and analyses of executive compensation data— almost invariably suggesting that compensation levels were excessive— by corporate governance commentators, academics, and regulators somewhat improved the available information about compensation. A company must report its stock market performance and contrast it to an index of share price performance for a group of comparable companies among its industry peers. Some companies have also responded to requests that compensation be tied not simply to stock price appreciation—as in the case of fixed-priced stock options whose value increases directly as the stock price rises—but to other indices that more appropriately reflect the success of the management group. Such indices, for example, may only reward stock price rises above the market index, or that of a peer group. Otherwise, a market fueled by, for example, interest-rate declines would still be the source of reward for a CEO of a company that otherwise did nothing to justify it.

The Imperial CEO   *Good of bad situation ⇒ depends on Knowledge base of CEO*

In the 1960s, the concept of the officially designated "chief executive officer," initiated by Alfred Sloan in 1937, began to spread among large corporations, though slowly at first. By designating a single individual as chief executive, it became clear that the board had vested ultimate decision-making authority in this individual. The roles of chairman, vice chairman, president, or other officers who may have shared this power were downgraded. This individual, in order to avoid any question as to who was in charge, frequently occupied the offices of chairman of the board, president, and CEO simultaneously and was given freedom to take such action as was needed to pursue opportunities without being impaired by first having to achieve an internal consensus. The idea was to give greater authority to more dynamic leaders who would accordingly produce better results for shareholders. The effect of this change was the selection and empowerment of an individual who would be charged with making the company and its stock price grow, and who therefore needed the loyalty and support of the rest of the board. This helped establish the notion that, to be worthy of selection, a CEO had to be a person with great leadership ability and charisma who could utilize the power granted to good effect. Board members, in turn, were expected to be "team players" in their support of the CEO.

The chief executive, whose de facto powers grew with this allocation

if CEO gets control of board, they become all powerful, no checks & balances

of authority, was usually able to control, directly or indirectly, all the elements of governance in the company, along with his or her own remuneration. Such elements included (1) control of the content, frequency, and information supplied at board meetings; (2) approval of nominees to the board and board committees, and of those to be re-nominated; (3) compensation, benefits, and perquisites of executives and board members; (4) selection of outside service providers, including bankers and lawyers; (5) press relations, including personal press coverage; and (6) political and charitable contributions and lobbying efforts. The CEOs would have the ultimate authority to determine how shareholder's interests were to be perceived and served. Most CEOs accepted this responsibility as a matter of course, used it appropriately, and also exercised an appropriate amount of self-restraint. But for others, it was an enormous amount of power that could be used to advance an executive's personal ambitions and avarice—transferring wealth from shareholders to management—and, when mistakes were made, to destroy shareholder value rather than enhance it.

In the 1960s, many companies that had allocated special powers to the CEO, including several companies that were admired for their aggressive, sometimes hostile acquisition practices, including the earliest "conglomerates," enjoyed strong success in creating economic value and stock price appreciation for their companies.[2] They were seen as charismatic, successful (even ideal) business leaders and were fully supported by their boards. As these companies established patterns that seemed successful, others emulated them. Even properly independent directors began to believe that they were not supposed to quibble, oppose, or openly question the CEO's actions unless drastic circumstances were involved, and usually they were not. Throughout this period and into the 1970s, however, there was one restraining element that CEOs had to face—the availability of professional legal, financial, and accounting services. Senior lawyers, commercial and investment bankers, and accountants were a conservative lot, not unduly troubled by competition for their large clients' business. They were very loyal to their clients but spoke freely to them and were uninhibited in telling them what they thought.[3] This changed dramatically in later years, as competition in the financial services, consulting, legal, and accounting businesses intensified, relationships were played off against one another, and once-exclusive relationships nearly disappeared.

Growth by Acquisition

The merger and stock market boom of the 1980s was mainly focused on restructuring and value creation from streamlining, cost-cutting, and what was then called a "return to basics." The takeover market burned out by the end of 1989, and this was followed by a recession and a bear market in stocks and in junk bonds, after the collapse of

Drexel Burnham and the arrest and trial of Michael Milken, the leading figures in the junk bond business. The slump was enough to win Bill Clinton the presidency. But Clinton did not substantially change the Reagan-Bush economic policies that had preceded him, although he did make a greater effort to reduce the national budget deficit through tax hikes, and as interest rates fell, this helped trigger a stock market recovery in 1992. From then on, throughout the Clinton presidency, the stock market powered ahead—despite corrections in 1994 and 1998—to complete the decade and the millennium at record levels. The market of the 1990s appeared to be influenced mainly by *peace* (the sudden end of the Soviet Union and the apparent end of hostilities elsewhere), *globalization* (the rise of the European Union and economic liberaliza-tion in Asia and Latin America), *technology* (the Internet, telecommu-nications and healthcare booms), and continuing economic *growth*, which in the United States had lasted even longer than in the 1960s, producing a stellar expansion pace of 108 consecutive months.

The merger market also recovered, and the 1990s saw a record level of transactions in both the United States and in Europe, where the continent's first merger boom was underway. In the 1990s, the empha-sis was on large-scale strategic acquisitions, designed to achieve strong future market positions in industries that were consolidating or oth-erwise subject to competitive reorganization. These acquisitions re-quired the cooperation of the antitrust authorities, which had backed away from preventing large mergers in the Reagan administration in the interest of deregulation. The Clinton Justice Department essentially left the Reagan position on antitrust enforcement alone, although it was tightened somewhat toward the end of the 1990s. The Europeans took a somewhat tougher approach.

Such large-scale mergers, however, were too large to be cash deals. They required a stock market that would accept huge stock-for-stock deals, and this market was prepared to do so. Mergers occurred in many industries, not just technology and telecommunications, includ-ing the financial services industry, entertainment, defense, and the pharmaceutical industries.

Merger policy was almost exclusively the domain of chief executives. For the CEO, it was a way to continue to grow the company at a pace faster than that which could be achieved internally. The higher growth would be recognized by the market as strategically important if a merger resulted in the capture of a unique brand name, offered oppor-tunities for severe cost-cutting to reduce redundancies or promote mar-ket power, and could be shown to produce accretion to earnings per share in the near future. Using stock for the acquisition usually pro-vided a favorable accounting treatment of goodwill, and there was no need to approach bankers to borrow money to finance the deal. After such a strategic combination, the firm would be very much larger, and the institutional and personal power and importance of the CEO of the acquiring company was greatly increased. Such a boost in importance was usually the occasion for compensation increases or special bonuses at the time of the deal, not necessarily after the deal had proved to be valuable to shareholders.

Still, for an acquisition to be successful, it must satisfy the investment objectives of the acquiring company and in fact be in the best interests of its shareholders. Just becoming bigger is not enough—bigness comes at a price, and the ultimate question is whether the price is worth the result achieved. Most acquirers exchange their shares for shares of a target company at a ratio that somewhat favors the target (reflecting a "merger premium"). The premium is paid for the right to control the combined postacquisition enterprise, and is roughly worth the present value of all discernible future "synergies" resulting from joining the two businesses. If the synergies are disappointing, or managerial problems from integrating two large, independent companies result, then the benefits of the acquisition may be insufficient to justify the cost, in which case the original shareholders of the acquiring company would have been better off if no deal had been made. And ill-advised acquisitions can cost shareholders twice—once through above-market prices paid to sellers and once again through above-market remuneration of deal-making top managers and their advisers.

[handwritten margin notes: 51st % costs Much more than 50th $]

Sometimes, markets detect bad marriages and sell off the stock of the acquiring company, making the economics of the transaction even more difficult. Management usually responds by saying the market is short-sighted and that the combination of businesses has great value but this will be achieved over many years in the future. Many deals, however, prove to be mistakes, and steps must be taken by boards to repair the damage once the CEO who made the deal in the first place is removed. CEOs are removed when such mistakes are recognized, but only afterward. Board members who vote to remove an offending CEO are often the same ones who enthusiastically supported the CEO when the ill-fated merger was proposed in the first place.

AGENCY CONFLICTS AND COSTS

Transferring so much managerial power to one individual, and withdrawing board restraints, has the potential to inflame agency conflicts between the interests of a corporation's manager (CEO) and its owners (shareholders). Both would like to see the share price rise, of course, but they may disagree on how much expense to incur, and how much risk to expose shareholders to, in order to achieve the desired increased share price. If a corporation pays more in managerial compensation and related expenses, for example, than an informed group of shareholders would believe to be reasonable, then the overcompensation becomes an agency cost, one that results either from error or intentional misappropriation of resources.

If the manager subjects the corporation to unusually high risks (from a faulty growth strategy, excessive leverage, or insufficient internal vigilance) in order to achieve an increase in stock price from which the manager benefits more than the shareholders, then the manager has subjected the corporation's owners to moral hazard. For example, a manager may propose a high-risk acquisition strategy to satisfy the company's growth objectives and be "incentivized" to accomplish the strategy by a generous stock option package. If (or while) the strategy works, the manager prospers more than the other shareholders (not having had to risk any capital). However, if the strategy fails, then the manager only fails to make money, while the other shareholders incur losses. The corporation experiences a drop in market value, may incur penalties and legal costs in defending itself in class action litigation, and may suffer damage to its reputation and business franchise, while the manager only loses his or her job and often is able to leave the field with substantial personal wealth intact.

Misappropriation is difficult to establish. Reasonable people can disagree over how much incentivization a particular compensation package contains, or should contain—especially when the packages have to compete in a sellers' market. Nevertheless, in the 1990s, a large number of mischievous, complicated, and obscuring compensation practices quietly worked their way into the system and were rapidly copied elsewhere in the purported interest of remaining competitive.

Many of these contained a number of overlapping compensation elements and benefits that made actual compensation totals difficult to understand, such as: (1) option programs that were created without an understanding or disclosure of their economic cost to the company; (2) the resetting of stock option exercise prices at lower levels after a major drop in the stock price; (3) allowing options to replace themselves automatically when exercised; (4) making large personal loans to CEOs to invest in company stock or homes and other noncompany assets and allowing company stock to be sold back to the firm to repay the loans;[4] (5) payment of large "special bonuses" to top executives for a one-off corporate action (such as a large merger) taken before any value to shareholders was demonstrated; and (6) and extensive postretirement consulting payments and other perquisites. Such practices received a great deal of unfavorable public attention, but there was little anyone could do about it. Shareholders were not required to vote approval of compensation plans, but even if they were, there is little evidence to suggest that they would have rejected them. The compensation practices were seen to be necessary to attract and motivate a high-powered team that would lead the company to a higher stock price.

Again, these various compensation mechanisms were said to follow the conventional wisdom of aligning manager's interests with those of

definition
when as an agent you are risking the principal more than you would your own assets

the shareholders. The more invested in the company's stock a manager was, the greater would be his or her interest in seeing the stock price rise, to the benefit of the rest of the shareholders. But the manager was not putting any money up for stock options. And if options were granted frequently, they would mature and be exercised frequently, allowing executives to take cash out of the company on a regular basis while maintaining their investment positions, something shareholders could not do. Consequently, many executives who were striving to expand their businesses and cause the stock price to rise, and who were constantly promoting the stock to analysts and employees, were at the same time hedging their bets by exercising options and selling stock on a regular basis.[5] There were a variety of options programs for compensation committees of boards to choose from, but generally they wanted "the best" for their people, even if it was very difficult for these directors to know just how much the options they were handing out were worth (see chapter 7 for a discussion of the accounting and valuation issues associated with options). Stock options were said to provide around 80 percent of the final compensation of executives during the 1990s, and because the market rose so considerably during those years, for many companies the values associated with the options soared.

During the 1990s, the reported total compensation of senior corporate executives rose by 442 percent in eight years, to an average of $10.6 million. At this level, the average CEO was being paid more than 500 times the wages of the average employee, up from 85 times at the beginning of the 1990s, and 42 times 20 years before.[6] Perhaps boards really believed that their CEOs deserved the compensation they received, even if this belief was arrived at naïvely. Or maybe they didn't care very much, but in any case, their decisions were protected by the business judgment rule in their state of incorporation (discussed in the previous chapter). In any event, the agency cost to shareholders of excessive CEO compensation was almost never more than a small part of the company's cash flow, and never more than a few tenths of a percent of the market value of the company, and consequently was usually not considered to be material, especially as compared to the far greater agency costs to which boards had exposed their shareholders through erroneous acquisition or other strategies.

CEOs, for their part, were encouraged to risk shareholders' capital aggressively, sometimes recklessly, because their diverse shareholders appeared to want them to do so. During a bull market, shareholders are not inclined to call for caution and restraint. They want the companies' boards of directors to continue to pour it on and make the most of opportunities. But with the corporate failures at the beginning of the 2000s, many such strategies were abject failures. They had catastrophic consequences for the companies involved. Most were the result of business strategies that could not or did not work (Enron, WorldCom, Global Crossing, AOL–Time Warner and many financial services companies) or involved improper or illegal efforts to rescue the situation with accounting tricks or coverups. The loss in market value alone (in stocks and bonds) from these and other disasters like them amounted to several hundreds of billions of dollars in the early 2000s.

Recent studies suggest that more than half of the large strategic mergers of the late 1990s were destructive of shareholder value in the acquiring company. Indeed, one such study concluded that acquisitions from 1998 through 2001 destroyed 12 cents of acquiring-company shareholder value for every dollar spent, or $240 billion in all, as compared to only 1.6 cents per dollar spent by acquiring firms during the 1980s.[7] A similar analysis was published by *Business Week* in 1995. Another showing even worse results was published in 2002.[8] Of 302 mergers valued in excess of $500 million from July 1, 1995, through August 31, 2001, 12 months after announcement:

- Average return for all buyers was –4.3 percent compared to the buyers' peers
- 61 percent of buyers lost shareholder value relative to their peers of an average of 25 percent
- 80 percent of these buyers continued to show negative returns relative to peers after 24 months
- Buyers paid an average premium of 19.3 percent over average return of sellers' peers
- 65 percent of buyers made acquisition with stock; their returns lagged buyers' issuing debt by 8 percent

The AOL-Time Warner combination, valued at $166 billion when announced in January 2000, was a classic example of a failed merger—and required a write-off of $54 billion on the deal two years later. Such results suggest that boards of directors were unwilling to develop an independent view of the deals proposed to them for approval, and would not or could not contain the moral hazard that the CEO's actions reflected. Evidently, moral hazard was a lot more costly to shareholders in the 1990s than excessive compensation.

As in the 1920s, the speculative market bubble of the 1990s created serious distortions in the systems of corporate governance. The Dow Jones Index increased about fivefold during the decade of the 1920s, and nearly fourfold during the 1990s. In the 1920s, much of the market's enthusiasm was justified by extraordinary new technologies (radio, electric power, automobiles), by financial engineering (pyramided utility holding companies), and by tapping into the retail investor pool (leveraged unit trusts). These themes were repeated in the 1990s, with the Internet and broadband, wireless telecommunications, and off-balance-sheet financing, and by tapping again into the retail investor pool, through both mutual funds and 401k pension investment funds.

In neither period were the regulations and governance programs in place adequate to the situation, and each ended with a crash that had lasting economic effects. But conditions in the 1990s were different from the 1920s and all other periods of American financial history in one important respect: the power of the integrated global financial marketplace—valued at more than $72 trillion ($36 trillion in equities) at the end of the 1990s, or more than seven times the GNP of the United States—had become so enormous that corporations had to recognize that their association with it had become one of, if not the most important relationship that it had to maintain. Little else would so affect their future success and value than being well regarded by the market, and this, of course, was a task assigned to the CEO.

Part III

Corporate Governance and Capital Market Institutions

Corporate management is responsible to boards of directors, and directors are responsible to shareholders. In publicly traded companies, this process functions through and within the capital markets. The owners of modern public corporations are predominantly represented by institutional investors, who act in a fiduciary capacity on behalf of their clients, a large body of individuals who own corporate shares though mutual funds, pension funds, and other money-management institutions. Over the years, the power of institutional investors has grown to control the voting rights of the bulk of all shares in public corporations. Institutional investment institutions are managed by professionals who are competing for assets and who are supervised, as corporations are, by boards of directors. However, just as there are agency conflicts between corporate managers and their owners, there are also agency conflicts between institutional financial managers and their investor clients. The capital markets also rely on experts and intermediaries for accurate information, timely dissemination of that information, and fair and efficient execution of financial transactions.

These elements—the investors and the intermediaries—represent the "external" factors affecting modern corporate governance that are as important to the enduring health of the system as the "internal" factors described in part II of this book. All of these external roles and activities are as subject to agency conflicts as are the internal roles of managers and boards.

The three chapters of this part of the book examine the modern roles and practices of institutional investors, auditors, and banks and brokerages in conducting the fiduciary and governance functions allocated to them in the capital-market system. How they monitor companies, evaluate governance issues, exercise their voting power on behalf of the ultimate owners, and act to maintain their independence so as to minimize agency conflicts is of central importance to how well the system does its job within a large and active global capital market.

We examine each of these key external agents in the governance process in turn, finding that failures of external governance have often been as serious as the failures of internal governance. Together these failures have had a compounding and corrosive effect on the modern corporate governance function as a whole and demonstrate the need for corrective action, either by the markets themselves or by sensible regulatory initiatives.

6

Institutional Investors

In 2001 more than 60 percent of all outstanding shares of U.S. publicly traded companies were owned by funds controlled by professional asset managers, a share that has been rising for years, in part as a result of growth in pension funds and, especially during the 1990s, of mutual funds. Most of the these shares are managed by a couple of hundred teams of independent professional investment managers, all of whom are sophisticated, well informed and capable—backed by access to the best of Wall Street's trading and research capabilities. The vast majority of these funds are actively managed, as opposed to being set aside for passively managed index funds or exchange-traded funds. Actively managed mutual funds and pension funds aspire to outperform market indices of one sort or another, and their managers participate in far more trading than average individual investors. Consequently, institutionally managed funds account for the vast bulk of all equity trading in the United States, and have by far the greatest influence in price-setting among all investors. In some important ways, the institutions *are* the market.

In a transparent market environment, professional investors are able to know what goes on in the companies they choose to invest in. In a liquid, orderly, and well-regulated market, these investors all have access to the same information and are able to act on it at about the same time. Informational advantages tend to be very limited, so to succeed in what they do, the managers must develop views as to which companies will perform better over time, on the basis of a variety of judgments they must make. These managers are trained and paid to detect faulty business strategies, note differences in performance versus objectives, and be able to smell out flaky schemes and concepts hyped by corporate promoters. The market, in other words, has the capacity to protect itself against the promotion of unsuitable investments. In-

121

deed, one reason pension fund trustees and individuals select these investment professionals is to do just this—to be more able to avoid foolish mistakes and capitalize on good ideas and sound business strategies than those less skilled or less well trained in investing.

During the latter years of the 1990s, it was clear that institutions on the whole were falling well short of their obligations to keep their investors out of trouble, as the asset management institutions themselves were seen to be major investors in all parts of the stock market that were subject to fraud or overvaluation. Consequently, much of the blame for the bubble, and the episode of corporate governance failures that accompanied it, can be left on the doorsteps of the institutional investors, who failed to see the dangers of the period and failed to protect their clients from them.

The fiduciary duties of asset managers are clear in both U.S. state and federal law, and have been for some time. English common law provided the concept of the "prudent man rule" as a test of satisfactory fiduciary conduct. A prudent man will manage the money of others just as he would manage his own—that is, carefully and wisely. The principal idea is that managers of other people's money must always put the interests of their clients first—ahead of their own interests—and act prudently. This often was taken to mean that fiduciaries such as pension fund trustees should seek the advice of professional investment experts, or entrust the management of the assets to the professional directly, in which case the fiduciary duties pass to the professional investor.

Professional managers not only buy and sell shares on behalf of their clients but are empowered by their clients to exercise shareholder voting powers to encourage sound corporate governance practices on the part of the companies in which they invest. Fund managers usually vote with management, with exceptions where management is clearly in the wrong. These exceptions have been increasing, but do not reflect the assertiveness expected of real owners. The law has not (yet) extended the fiduciary duties of institutional investors to their voting practices. However, their voting power—especially when acting in concert with their peers, as permitted under the law—can be considerable and influential. Institutions clearly have had the power to make a difference to companies like Enron, WorldCom, and Tyco either by not buying the stock or selling it or by voting shares against management when it was overreaching or engaging in practices that were not seen to be in the interests of long-term investors. It is not evident that institutional investors have regarded themselves as responsible for corporate governance. Yet investors whose money they manage have entrusted their voting powers to them and, it would seem, ought to be entitled to see these powers utilized in their own best interests.

Moreover, it has become clear in recent years that there are a variety of agency conflicts between institutional fund managers, for the most part operating profit-making businesses for themselves, and the interests of their fiduciary clients. Asset managers want to increase assets under management (AUM) and fee income. Their investor clients want best possible risk-adjusted investment performance and minimum fees and expenses. Are these two sets of objective compatible? Certainly the potential for conflict is apparent, and for years the institutional asset management industry persuaded the market that it was in its own self-interest to handle conflict situations responsibly. It recent years, however, it became apparent that the conflicts in fact tempted many institutional investors into abuses of clients in ways comparable to the abuses attributed to overly aggressive corporate CEOs. Indeed, as the funds ultimately supporting the equity market are owned by households and individuals, these individuals have been forced into a state of double jeopardy. They are exposed to both agency conflicts of corporate managers as well as agency conflicts of investment managers. These conflicts are not costless—to the ultimate investors, to corporations operating in the capital markets, and to the national economy as a whole.

This chapter explores the critical role of institutional investors as fiduciaries and in the governance of public companies. These institutions have more frequently encountered agency conflicts as the complexities of their businesses (managing pension funds, mutual funds, and 401ks of various types for both corporate and individual accounts) and competitive pressures have increased. They are powerful players in exercising (or failing to exercise) control rights. As an industry, they can make the difference between governance successes and failures. During the 1990s and early 2000s, excesses and misconduct on the part of institutional investors were as prevalent as they were in other vital sectors of the system. Indeed, many of the agency conflicts among professional fund managers have become embedded in the system itself, and appear to have weakened the overall ability of the market to defend against value-destroying behavior on the part of corporations.

THE ASSET MANAGEMENT BUSINESS

As of January 2004, the global total of assets under professional management worldwide was estimated at over $70 trillion, made up of some $18 trillion in pension fund assets, about $11 trillion in nonpension mutual fund assets, and another $10 trillion in fiduciary assets controlled by insurance companies, as well as some $32 trillion in assets of wealthy clients (i.e., those with more than $1 million under management). In the United States alone, there were some $7.5 trillion in fiduciary assets in the form of common stock in professionally managed portfolios that carries with it voting rights.

Assets under professional management have grown rapidly in the

United States and around the world—in the form of mutual funds and other types of collective investment vehicles—as a way of reducing transaction and information costs for the individual client, as well as improving portfolio returns and reducing risk through diversification. Portfolios have extended beyond domestic financial instruments toward a greater role for foreign asset classes, which can promise additional portfolio benefits for the investor, while extending the fiduciary role of fund managers into foreign domains.

Around 1970, the asset management business in the United States consisted of traditional fiduciaries such as individual trustees, banks, insurance companies and corporations managing assets on behalf of a great variety of different types of clients, including beneficiaries of large pension funds. Investment counselors were also becoming significant players. The passage of the Employee Retirement Income Security Act (ERISA) in 1974 raised the standards to be met by trustees of pension funds, and as a result, many corporations and government entities (pension fund sponsors) began to retain independent advisers and investment managers to assure the best risk-adjusted performance possible for the funds under their care. A whole industry developed to provide investment services to pension funds.

Investment performance was essential for most pension funds, which, at the time, usually guaranteed lifetime income and other benefits to retirees ("defined benefit" [DB] plans). If the value of the assets in the fund were less than the actuarial value of the liabilities of the fund, the pension fund sponsor was obliged to make up the shortfall. If there was a surplus, the sponsoring company or government entity was entitled to withdraw it, and many did so.

In due course, many corporations came to prefer offering to employees another type of retirement benefit in which funds would be invested in a tax-free individual account for the employee (a 401k or similarly designated account) with the entire value of the assets invested accruing to the individual, but with no outstanding liabilities to be guaranteed by the corporation. This was called a "defined contribution" (DC) plan, and by 2005 such plans amounted to about 60 percent of all pension plans in the United States. These plans rely mainly on mutual funds to manage the funds entrusted to them by employees, choosing from a company-approved list of investment alternatives. Employees check off how they want their money invested—for example, in one or more different stock or bond or money market mutual funds—and are free to change these instructions periodically. They receive a statement every so often showing the exact net asset value of the investments, which are subject to visible market appreciation or decline.

In 1974, institutional investment managers consisted of banks and insurance companies, dedicated investment management companies focused on pension funds, and mutual fund management companies.

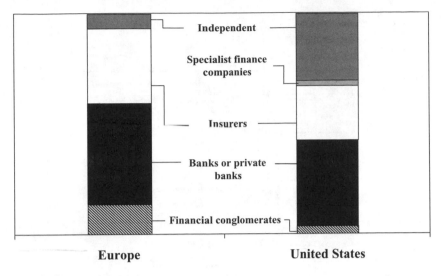

Figure 6.1. Who Owns Asset Managers? Ownership shares in percent. *Source:* Oliver, Wyman, 2002.

ERISA was intended to restrict managers to those who were entirely unconflicted. As a result, some broker-dealers who believed they might not be considered appropriate for the management of pension funds withdrew from the business. Others succeeded in staying in the business by persuading their clients that they would act in good faith.

By 2000 virtually every type of financial firm had become involved in asset management (see fig. 6.1). These include commercial and universal banks, investment banks, broker-dealers, trust companies, insurance companies, private banks, captive and independent pension fund managers, mutual fund companies, and various types of specialist firms and boutiques managing venture capital, real estate, private equity and hedge funds. Also competing for this business were "family offices" of the very wealthy, in-house fund managers at large corporations (General Electric, General Motors) and index funds. These players divided the market into four segments—pension funds, mutual funds, endowments and assests of wealthy families. The objective was to "gather" as many assets as possible to be managed by their teams of professional investors.

Industry Schematic

Figure 6.2 presents a schematic diagram covering the organization of the professional asset management industry and how it relates to the exercise of shareholder voting rights.

Various types of individual investors buy shares directly in the market (A), normally through broker-dealers (F). In the process, they may

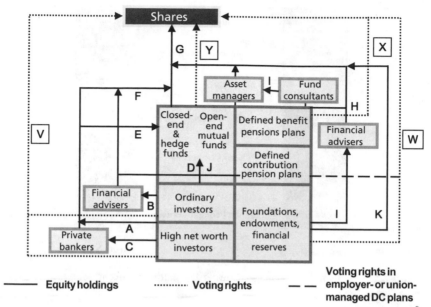

Figure 6.2. Organization of the Asset Management Industry *(Flow of money)*

obtain the advice of the brokers themselves or from independent financial advisers (B), and—if they are wealthy enough—from private bankers or high-wealth asset managers (C). Individual investors may instead purchase shares of mutual finds (D), and may use the advice of financial advisers, brokers, or bankers to do so (E). The mutual funds then purchase shares in the market (G).

Individuals may participate in pension plans sponsored by their employers, labor organizations, or governmental entities. Defined benefit pension funds may be managed in-house (H) by their corporate sponsors and trustees, or they can be managed by institutional asset managers, who in turn may be selected and tracked with the help of pension fund consultants (I). Such internally or externally managed DB pension funds will normally hold substantial amounts of equities, as well as fixed income and other assets, as part of their overall asset allocation.

Defined contribution pension assets are normally invested in a variety of approved mutual funds—usually equities (J), fixed income, and money market funds are offered—short-listed by the employer, from which the individual employee may make a choice. Mutual fund management companies may therefore combine pension assets with nonpension assets in the same equity fund.

Finally, in countries such as the United States, there are many foundations, endowments, and other financial pools (K) whose assets need to be managed either internally or by external fund managers, sometimes including large equity holdings.

he will not emphasise the right to vote on exam

Figure 6.2 also depicts the share-voting arrangements involved (dotted lines). Individuals who own shares directly have a right to vote those shares, or to designate a trustee or broker-dealer to vote them on their behalf (V). The same is true of institutional asset pools such as foundations and endowments and employer-managed DC investment plans (W), where share voting will normally be undertaken under the auspices of fund trustees, as is the case in DB plans (X). This leaves share voting by mutual funds (Y), where the right to vote is vested in the fund itself and normally executed by the fund management company. Voting practices of asset mangers are a key issue, and are discussed in depth later in this chapter.

Pension Funds

The pension fund market has become one of the most rapidly growing sectors of the global financial system, and promises—due to global aging of populations—to be dynamic in the years ahead. Pension fund and retirement assets in the United States amounted to some $12 trillion in 2003 (perhaps half the global total), of which $2.7 trillion (22 percent) were invested in mutual funds. Equity securities owned by retirement funds made up about 20 percent of all shares outstanding in the United States.

Pension funds are regulated in the United States by ERISA and enforced by the U.S. Department of Labor. DB plans are true pension funds and as such are guaranteed by the U.S. government through the Pension Benefit Guaranty Corporation (an institution somewhat similar to the Federal Deposit Insurance Corporation) to insure defined benefit plans under ERISA. The government's guarantee of DB funds clearly entitles it to a seat at the table in regulating how the funds are operated. Pension funds offering DB plans, following modern portfolio management practices, hire professional money managers to allocate portions of their portfolios. This was and is a very competitive business. So corporations, unions, and other fund sponsors apply their considerable bargaining muscle to cut fees and expenses proposed by the managers.

In contrast to DB pension plans, DC plans are essentially not pension funds at all. They are tax-deferred personal retirement accounts, creatures of the income tax code, and as such are not guaranteed by the Pension Benefit Guaranty Corporation. However, corporations have been able to offer them to their employees in lieu of true pension plans. DC plans are less complex than DB plans. They require substantial administration, they do not require corporations to stand behind the pension liabilities. DC plans arrange for asssets to be invested in one or more managed funds (or in the company's own shares), allow for changes to be made from time to time, and periodically provide information about their performance to the participants.

The growing role of DC plans has led to strong linkages between corporations and mutual funds, which seek to be selected as one of the

[handwritten margin note:] look at Chrysler's case in the late 70's

[handwritten note at bottom:] externalizing liabilities through packaging and selling off the dead wood & keeping profit making parts.

investment choices available to company employees. Some of the major equity mutual funds have benefited from large DC fund inflows. At the end of 2004, about a third of all mutual fund assets represented retirement accounts of various types, as compared to a negligible percentage in 1980. These retirement accounts were about equally divided between Individual Retirement Accounts (IRAs) and 401ks.[1]

Mutual Funds

Mutual funds are collective investment vehicles in which individual investors are invited to purchase shares to be invested in securities of various types. They are "mutual" in the sense that the investors own all of the assets in the fund, and are responsible for all of its operating costs. The funds are usually organized by a particular fund-management company that undertakes the legal registration of the fund, nominates a board of directors for the fund, and arranges for the distribution and sale of fund shares to the public. The fund's board of directors contracts with an investment adviser (usually the same fund management company) to manage the assets and to handle ongoing operational details such as marketing, administration, reporting, and compliance.

In the United States at the end of 2003, there were more than 6,000 mutual funds available to the public, with total assets of $7.4 trillion, about half the value of all mutual funds around the world. The number of U.S. equity mutual funds rose from 126 in 1951 to over 4,600 in 2003—many more than the 2,750 individual stocks listed on the New York Stock Exchange. These stock mutual funds were valued at $3.7 trillion, or 18.4 percent of all U.S. equities at the end of 2003. Mutual funds accounted for about 21 percent of U.S. household net financial wealth in 2003, more than life insurance companies and about equal to the total household deposits in commercial banks.

In the United States, mutual funds have traditionally been invested in equities—in 1975, over 82 percent of the fund assets under management were allocated to equities, with only 10 percent to bonds and 8 percent to money market instruments. By 1985, this picture had completely changed, with the equity component declining to 24 percent and money market funds capturing 49 percent—due mainly to the substitution of money market mutual funds for bank savings products by households searching for higher yields. By 2003, the pattern of mutual fund investments had shifted yet again, with equities accounting for 46 percent of the total, money market funds 31 percent, bond funds 18 percent, and hybrid funds 5 percent.

Mutual funds were created as successors to the investment "trusts" of the 1920s that suffered such great losses after the crash of 1929. They have grown in popularity ever since. The principal legislation governing the industry is the Investment Company Act of 1940. The Act covers both the qualifications and registration of management companies of

mutual funds sold to the public, and the disclosure of pertinent information to investors (as corporations are required to do by the Securities
Act of 1933 and the Securities and Exchange Act of 1934). A mutual
fund's investment adviser must also comply with terms of the Investment Advisers Act of 1940, and various state laws. The National Securities Markets Improvement Act of 1996 made the Securities and
Exchange Commission responsible for overseeing investment advisers
with over $25 million under management (accounting for about 95
percent of U.S. mutual fund assets), with state regulators responsible
for investment advisers with smaller amounts under management.
Threat of regulatory action and civil liability lawsuits are supposed to
keep the pressure on mutual fund boards to take their obligations to
investors seriously and to ensure that the fund objectives are faithfully
carried out.

Competition for asset-gathering by mutual funds can be among the
most active anywhere in the financial system, heightened by advertising efforts and intensive media coverage. Such coverage includes analytical services that track and rate performance of funds in terms of
risk and return, and against benchmarks, over different holding periods. These fund-rating services are important to fund marketing because the vast majority of new investments tend to flow into highly
rated funds. Despite clear warnings that past performance is no assurance of future results, a rise in the performance rankings often brings
in a flood of new investments and management-company revenues,
which are based on the quantity of assets under management. Star
asset managers and fund marketers are compensated commensurately,
and the more successful are sometimes recruited to move to larger and
more prestigious funds. Conversely, downgrading and serious performance slippage causes investors to withdraw funds, taking with them
a good part of the remuneration available for managers' bonuses. Mutual funds have become increasingly mass-market instruments.
"Branding" and public performance ratings are key factors in asset
gathering, which is crucial for competitive performance in the industry.
Well-known brands (Fidelity, Vanguard, and others) have always attracted funds. Investment returns matter also—they are what the rank-
ers are ranking—but many successful fund management companies
have been able to increase total assets under management on the basis
of their reputation, by aggressive advertising and by introducing new,
different, or rebranded funds even in the face of asset withdrawals due
to performance disappointments. In any event, sustained bull markets
such as existed over the 1980–2000 period provided satisfactory performance results for almost all funds, regardless of their performance-
ranked quartile, and some funds provided truly superior results.

In addition to promoting their performance, mutual fund management companies have added banking-type services such as checking
and cash-management accounts, credit cards, and overdraft lines. Se-

curities firms (broker-dealers) have also penetrated the mutual fund market, and so have insurance companies reacting to stiffer competition for their traditional annuities business. Commercial banks, watching some of their deposit clients drift off into mutual funds, have responded by launching mutual fund families of their own, or marketing those of other fund managers. Such cross-penetration among strategic groups of financial intermediaries, each approaching the business from a different direction, makes mutual fund markets highly competitive.

The management of mutual funds has been an attractive business economically for the major firms participating in both the mutual fund and the pension management parts of the business for many years. One such participant, Alliance Capital Management, noted in its annual report for 2003 that its revenues from mutual fund management, per dollar of assets under management, were 3.5 to 4.5 times larger than its revenues from management of institutional assets (pension funds; see table 6.1).

The mutual fund business, with its need for mass-marketing and distribution, was more expensive to conduct, but mutual fund investors reimbursed Alliance (from their own assets under management) for a significant portion of these expenses.

Other Institutional Investors

Pension fund and mutual fund shareholdings, between them, account for nearly 40 percent of all U.S. equity securities. Of the approximately 20 percent of institutional investor equity holdings remaining, approximately 10 percent are owned by foreign investors (mostly institutions), and the other 10 percent are divided among foundations, trust accounts, insurance companies, and hedge funds (which have experienced extraordinary growth since the late 1990s). These investors are

Table 6.1. Performance of Alliance Capital Management (assets under management and revenues)

	1999	2000	2001	2002	2003
Revenues ($billions)					
Institutional	0.409	0.514	0.669	0.628	0.65
Retail	1.334	1.744	1.598	1.364	1.277
AUM ($billions)					
Institutional	198.8	237.4	241.4	211	269.5
Retail	165.5	176.9	171.5	135.9	153.8
Revenues/AUM (basis points)					
Institutional	20.6	21.7	27.7	29.8	24.1
Retail	80.6	98.6	93.2	100.4	83.0

Source: 2003 Annual Report

similar to those who manage pension and mutual funds, but they are not subject to such high levels of regulation and scrutiny as to year-by-year (indeed, quarter-by-quarter) performance as the others.

Fund Managers in the 1990s

The fund management industry began a period of extraordinary growth early in the 1960s. By the 1980s, net assets of mutual funds alone increased more than seven times, and in the 1990s another four times. The annual rate of growth of net assets for the 20-year period from 1980 to 1999 was over 20 percent, reflecting not only the unusually large increases in stock prices during this period but also an exceptional rate of new fund sales. Individual investors did not want to be left behind when the stock market took off, and they also enjoyed the convenience of investing with funds groups that could offer stocks, bonds, hybrid (or mixed) funds, and money market funds. In 1999, stock funds accounted for 59 percent of all mutual fund assets, and money market funds were 24 percent—by the end of 2002, after several down years in the stock market and record redemptions by mutual fund investors (many to reinvest in other asset categories), stock funds made up only 42 percent of total fund assets.

INDUSTRY CHANGES

Many things about the mutual fund business changed since the 1960s. Distribution efforts became intensive, as intense competition for retail asset gathering broke out in the industry. Competition for assets expanded to include players previously content to service the pension fund market, and a variety of other newcomers to the mutual fund business, such as broker-dealers, banks, insurance companies, and other manufacturers of retirement assets. These competitors were attracted by the profile of the individual investor, with vast sums in aggregate already invested in homes, savings accounts, and pensions. By offering improved returns and the safety of a reliable brand name, these investors, it was believed, could be attracted away from the traditional banking and savings institutions. They wanted to participate reasonably closely in the strong overall stock market in order to enjoy attractive returns and were not very sophisticated about the fees, costs, and expense reimbursements that the fund management companies charged.

To succeed in the scramble for assets, fund management companies would have to offer a range of different types of funds, catering to the latest fad or style and having enough runners in the ranking tables so that at least some of their funds would be favorably ranked. To this had to be added investments in technology that would enable the administration, custody, and reporting functions of the fund to operate efficiently and in a customer-friendly manner. And new funds had to be marketed to investors as soon as they were created. Distribution was key to the industry—few funds groups had their own sales forces until the broker-dealers got into the business, and most had to rely on a network of other firms, mostly investment advisers and individual stockbrokers, to sell their funds. The major firms could also afford to spend large amounts on media advertising. Meanwhile, the professional managers of funds groups were changing as well. Skills in stock picking and analysis were no longer the most important; designing and distributing new funds were. Sales was eclipsing investment in many fund management companies.

This meant that the fund management groups were rapidly building new funds—many companies today manage 80 to 100 different funds—and other investment vehicles aimed at wealthier clients, such as hedge funds and private equity investments. By 1999, the approximately 4,000 equity funds that existed were probably managed by no more than 100 different funds groups, although competitive pressure was intense. Funds groups had to track the Dow Jones or S&P 500 indices fairly closely, or their investors might redeem their shares and buy competitors' funds. Indeed, mutual fund shareholders redeemed about 40 percent of average assets in the 1990s, as compared to only 6 percent in the 1950s. During the late 1990s, the high-tech sector and IPO activity pushed these indices into a five-year period of more than 20 percent annual growth, something that had never happened before. Mutual fund managers who feared or disdained tech stocks in the belief that they were overvalued reported annual gains during some of those years in the low single digits. To be competitive in the battle for assets, fund managers had to be where the market action was, regardless of their views about valuation.

This dynamic further eroded the role of the professional investment manager relying on basic investment principles. Many mutual fund management companies, responding to competitive pressures, thus became "momentum investors." That is, they bought what everyone else was buying, hoping to be able to get out before the others when they had to. But the good times lasted for a number of years before they had to get out, and by then they had become true believers in what they were doing and had changed the way they managed their businesses. Few avoided the massive losses that came with the end of the bubble.

Among the changes in fund management was trading activity. The median holding period of investors in mutual funds in the 1950s was 6 years; in the 1990s it was 11 months. The overall equity fund portfolio turnover in the 1950s was 17 percent per year; in 2000 it was 108 percent and averaged over 100 percent for the preceding four years. Such high turnover generated problems for investors—one was that the tax burden of fund investing rose sharply (high turnover generated regular income, not capital gains), and the other was that investment

how do you get in

managers, expecting to hold on the stocks for only a few months, had no incentive to consider corporate governance issues of the companies they invested in.

Such aggressive fund marketing catering to short-term results, of course, led to many funds that failed once the exuberant market disappeared. Failed funds were abandoned by their sponsors by either liquidating them or merging them into other funds. In the 1990s, the fund failure rate was 55 percent, as compared to 14 percent over the decade of the 1960s. Also in the 1990s, the costs to investors of owning mutual funds increased, despite the opportunities for scale economies coming from extraordinary growth in the size of the pool of assets devoted to mutual funds. The cost to investors of the average equity mutual fund rose from 1.10 percent of net assets in 1980 to 1.57 percent in 2000, a 40 percent increase.[2]

Despite these developments, the SEC as chief regulator of the industry was relaxed about mutual funds throughout the 1990s. Chairman Arthur Levitt believed the industry was respected and well behaved on the whole, and not in need of any form of special attention. Levitt did institute one reform in the industry, however, which was to insist on clearer, less legalistic language in fund prospectuses, which perhaps helped sell even more of them.

Competition

As noted, an array of financial firms emerged during the 1990s to perform asset-management functions. In broad groupings, these included domestic and international commercial banks and savings institutions, securities firms (full-service investment banks and various kinds of specialists), insurance companies, finance companies (including financial subsidiaries of nonfinancial companies, such as General Electric), investment and financial advisers, private banks, and independent mutual fund management companies. Members of each strategic group compete with each other, as well as with members of other strategic groups. Success or failure depends heavily on portfolio management skills and service quality, as well as economies of scale, capital investment, as well as transaction systems and information technologies.

Not unexpectedly, the fund management industry worldwide has seen a host of strategic initiatives among fund managers—including mergers, acquisitions, and strategic alliances—as well as between fund managers and commercial and universal banks, securities broker-dealers, and insurance companies. In general, the effect of competition in the industry has been to make it more customer-friendly, technology-sensitive, and adaptive—and more concentrated. The number of shareholder accounts in the U.S. mutual fund industry increased almost fourfold in the 1990s, to 245 million at the end of the decade, mainly due to 401ks.[3]

Criteria used by investors to select funds

The basis of competition in fund management is made up of five elements—perceived performance, management fees, expenses, direct and indirect costs of marketing and distribution, and service quality and technology.

First, investors must select from an array of investment types or styles based on asset classes (stocks, bonds, etc.). Fund managers are expected to remain true to their proclaimed investment objectives and attempt to optimize asset allocation in accordance with modern port-folio management concepts. Gathering assets to be managed is the chief marketing objective of all participants in the fund management busi-ness. Creating a "brand" and marketing it extensively, providing tele-phone and Internet-based access to the funds group, and providing assistance in fund selection and other services is a considerable expense for fund management companies. In addition, in the most competitive parts of the pension sector, access to fund trustees often relies on con-sultants. Company-sponsored retirement plans often seek advice from pension investment consultants before awarding pension mandates, or to include particular mutual funds or fund families in the menu they offer to employees in 401k plans. Fund management companies may and sometimes do provide fee or expense reimbursement to consult-ants, a practice that has increased in recent years.

Second, fund managers incur a variety of operating costs and ex-penses in running their businesses, notably for personnel and facilities, commissions, and other costs. In the case of pension funds, the invest-ment manager quotes a single, all-in expense to be charged for services that is sufficient to cover expenses and the manager's profit. The pen-sion fund, of course, is able to apply its bargaining power to the ne-gotiation process.

In the case of mutual funds, the fund management company retained by the fund enters into a contract for services in which it charges a fee for managing the assets, and its expenses, in part, are reimbursed. Combined, these fees are charged against the assets of the fund and make up the fund's "expense ratio." Fund investors may also be subject to a sales charge when they invest (a "front-end load") or at a later point when they exit (a "back-end load"), as well as a charge for mar-keting the fund to its investors—called "12b-1" fees in the United States, for the SEC rule that permits them. Marketing fees are justified on the theory that successfully increasing fund size will bring down expense ratios per dollar of fund assets, and maintaining a "stable" investor base (which may require continuous marketing) is beneficial to the fund and its shareholders.

Funds generally subject investors to higher expense ratios when the fund size is smaller, the turnover is higher, or the relative fund perfor-mance is better. Depending on tax liabilities, mutual fund investors may incur regular income or capital gains taxes when trading profits are realized—the higher the fund turnover, the higher the tax drag.

Regulations in the United States require that fees and expenses be fully disclosed, but industry practice has been allowed to obscure such disclosures by making the investor hunt for each element within the prospectus and annual reports of the funds.

Third, service quality in fund management involves ease of investment and redemptions and the quality and transparency of statements, cash management, tax computation, and investment advice. Mutual fund management companies tend to invest heavily in information technology infrastructure in order to improve service quality and cut costs—investments that are paid for in the form of fees and expenses reimbursed by the funds.

Charges, Conflicts, and Scandals

Faith in mutual funds as transparent, efficient, and fair investment vehicles was undermined with the uncovering of extensive industry scandals in 2003 and 2004, involving "late trading" and "market timing" in the shares of mutual funds, with the knowledge and sometimes active participation of the fund managers. The disclosures, legal proceedings, and settlements reached with the SEC and other regulators led to extensive further investigations of mutual fund practices and governance procedures.

Late trading allowed a favored investor to improperly execute trades at the fund's 4 p.m. daily closing net asset value (NAV) well after the closing time, sometimes as late as 9 p.m. the same evening, enabling the investor to profit from news released after the closing. Ordinary fund investors are obliged to trade at the 4 p.m. price until it is reset at 4 p.m. the following day. Such a case came to light in 2003, when N.Y. Attorney General Eliot Spitzer's office was tipped that a hedge fund called Canary Capital had been engaged in late trading with certain mutual funds in exchange for investing a sizeable sum in a hedge fund being launched by the mutual fund's management group. The practice, in effect, transferred wealth from ordinary shareholders to the sophisticated hedge fund investor so that the funds management group could benefit in launching a new fund, the earnings from which would accrue to the management group itself, not to the investors in the fund in which the late trading took place. In other words, the management company agreed secretly to skim off returns from one of its retail funds to help set up a lucrative (that is, incorporating high-performance fees for the fund manager) hedge fund of its own to be sold to sophisticated buyers. For a funds management group to allow late trading is a violation of the investment company regulations and, further, a serious breach of fiduciary duty owed to the group's investors.

The investigation by the New York State attorney general also uncovered "market-timing" trades in mutual fund shares—a practice not in itself illegal but involving rapid-fire trading by favored investors in shares of international mutual funds across time zones in order to profit from "stale" or old prices. This practice skims the returns from the mutual fund shareholders, increases mutual fund expenses, and requires them to hold large cash balances to meet withdrawals—costs that have to be borne by all investors, not just the market-timers.

The New York State attorney general alleged that there was a benefit received from the favored party that was permitted to trade this way, and that benefit offset a quid pro quo received by the fund management company that permitted the trades. What was the quid pro quo? The investors favored by the fund managers promised to park assets with the fund management companies in their own hedge funds, in effect kicking back some of their questionable market timing gains to the fund management companies, not to the shareholders of the mutual fund. And in some surprising cases, it was learned that individual fund managers engaged in these practices for their own accounts, the gains simply going into their pockets. Market timing is illegal, the SEC held, if the mutual fund's prospectus declared that they were discouraged, when in fact they were not.

The Canary Hedge fund reached a $40 million settlement with the New York State attorney general, representing a disgorgement of illicit profits from both late trading and market timing in shares of mutual funds managed by Bank of America. The investigation was extended to other fund managers, and soon included some of the better known names in the mutual fund industry: Alliance Capital Management (a subsidiary of France's Groupe AXA), FleetBoston Financial (since acquired by Bank of America), Janus Capital Group, Massachusetts Financial Services (a unit of Canada's Sun Life Financial), Putnam Investments (a subsidiary of Marsh & McLennan), Strong Capital Management, BancOne (since acquired by JP Morgan Chase), Pilgrim Baxter, Janus Capital Group, Prudential Securities (now owned by the Wachovia Group), PIMCO (a subsidiary of Germany's Allianz AG), the Invesco Fund Group, and Merrill Lynch Investment Management, among others. Altogether, the fund managers in question represented a total of 287 separate mutual funds with $227 billion in assets under management, or about 3 percent of the industry's total net assets. The damages done, however, were estimated to be rather small. One study suggested that late trading cost investors about $400 million per year, or .005 percent in annual returns for international mutual funds and 0.006 percent for domestic funds since 2001.[4] Market-timing trades, however, have had a much larger, impact. According to different study in 2002 by the same academic author, market timing cost investors about $4 billion per year and the practice was going on for at least 20 years without any intervention by regulators.[5]

In all, by July 2004 regulators and law enforcement officials prosecutors extracted over $2.5 billion in fines and penalties from some 24 mutual fund management companies in out-of-court settlements in which those charged admitted no guilt. Further settlements were expected. Over 80 fund managers were fired, and several individuals were brought up on criminal charges. Bank of America alone agreed to pay $675 million to settle charges, Alliance Capital agreed to pay $600 million, and MFS Investment Management paid $401 million. In many cases, the mutual fund firms were forced to cut future fees to clients as part of the settlements as a way of channelling some of the penalties back to those who were damaged.

For example, in the case of Putnam, the sixth largest U.S. mutual fund manager, the firm agreed to pay $110 million to settle federal and state charges. The CEO was fired, as were 15 other employees, including four fund managers who had engaged in market-timing trades for their own account. Putnam agreed to "statements of fact" that the firm knew about but failed to halt market-timing trades. Putnam lost almost $60 billion in redemptions in the fall of 2003 alone, or about 22 percent of its total assets under management, and by mid-2005 had declined to about $100 billion from a peak of $250 billion in 2000. The firm cut fees to mutual fund clients in advance of the settlement and agreed to certain management reforms. These included requiring employees to hold their investments in Putnam mutual funds for at least 90 days and fund managers for at least a year, and redemption fees were imposed to halt rapid-fire trading. Moreover, the firm agreed to subject itself to an independent compliance review every two years going forward. Some of these measures were voluntarily applied by other mutual fund families as well.

The scandals were a surprise to the investors in the industry, and many fund redemptions occurred as a result. However, the industry had in any case experienced exceptionally high levels of redemptions after 1999, following the market decline, and scandal-induced redemptions in 2004 were less than post-bubble redemptions in 2002. The funds managed by the investment groups that were named in the scandals, such as Putnam, suffered considerably more redemptions than firms that were not charged, including the industry's three largest fund managers. Indeed, a number of mutual fund investors interviewed in televised news programs expressed no concern that the industry was unsafe, and a professor of finance (not ethics) observed tolerantly that the aggregate amount of skimming from all of the cases that had surfaced amounted to well under 1 percent of the assets under management.

Some observers have argued that such conflicts between interests of managers and owners are inevitable in all but mutually owned fund managers (such as Vanguard and TIAA-CREF), and index funds, and therefore it should be seen as an unwelcome but natural friction to be endured in an industry that benefits millions of people otherwise unable to invest safely in the markets. For all profit-making fund managers, earnings are a function of the volume of assets under management, so there is relentless pressure to grow those assets by offering an increasing variety of fund products to investors who benefit from their liquidity and investment ideas.

In June 2005, a jury acquitted Theodore Sihpol, a junior executive at Bank of America engaged in facilitating the Canary hedge fund transaction, of charges of aiding illegal trading, partly on the grounds that it was unclear whether late trading was a violation of New York securities laws. This was the first case of an individual accused by Eliot Spitzer going to trial, and the acquittal was seen as casting doubt on the New York state attorney general's charges.

The late-trading and market-timing scandals were not seen to cause enough damage to inflame mutual fund investors in general, but they did raise among regulators, policy advocates, and prosecutors serious questions of conflicting interests. These questions soon embraced the larger subject of governance of the funds management companies.

Conflicts of Interest in Mutual Fund Management

The Investment Company Act of 1940 requires that mutual funds be organized as corporate entities, and that a majority of the members of fund's boards be "independent"—individuals not associated with the fund's investment adviser or management company. Indeed, most mutual funds have a "supermajority" (i.e., two-thirds) of independent directors. Directors have fiduciary duties of care and loyalty to the investors in the mutual fund, and therefore are responsible for safeguarding their interests. Inevitably, however, a variety of potential conflicts of interest face the mutual funds industry.

There are at least eight basic conflicts of interest that characterize the fund management industry:

1. Fund managers prefer independent directors who comply with the rules but are cooperative, supportive, and not difficult to work with. Investors prefer directors who will robustly perform their fiduciary duties to the mutual fund shareholders.
2. Fund managers want maximum fees and expense reimbursements. Investors want their fund directors to negotiate minimum total costs and for these costs to be fully disclosed.
3. Fund managers want to ensure that they are reappointed. Investors want boards that act vigorously in selecting the best managers they can find who are capable of top-flight, risk-adjusted performance.

Fund managers nominate directors of new mutual funds. They are subsequently elected by shareholders, and then assume the responsibility for future board nominations. Often, managers nominate the same board members to many different funds within a funds group, for each of which compensation is paid. Mutual fund directors are charged with representing the interests of their shareholders in the selection of the fund management company and in negotiating fees and expense reimbursements. If the directors are dissatisfied with a fund management company, they can pick a new one. Yet, in practice, that almost never happens (although individual portfolio managers are frequently fired to rectify deficiencies), no matter how poor the fund manager's performance or how high the fees. Partly this is out of loyalty to the fund management company that nominated the directors, and partly also because comparisons to other financial advisers or fee practices are made against peers who have very similar profiles. Such comparisons can be very complex and depend on details supplied by management. And everyone knows that a fund is part of the fund management company's group, and investors would not expect any changes, so why make an issue out of something that might be handled quietly by requesting changes in individual portfolio managers or some relief in fees or expenses? In any case, investors are always free to move their money.

Independent directors of mutual funds enjoy exceptionally lucrative conditions of employment. Directors often serve on the boards of several funds that have been batched together—sometimes involving between 100 and 200 such funds—under a common board, and the independent directors receive full directors' compensation for each fund. According to one study critical of mutual funds, the average total compensation of the directors of funds run by the major U.S. fund managers in 2000 was $386,000, as compared to $47,000 for directors of the fund management companies themselves.[6] Meantime, the workload of mutual fund directors is limited to day-long meetings several times a year, and after indemnification from the funds and director liability insurance, there is little exposure to personal liability. No wonder such plum assignments provide little incentive to rock the boat. As investor Warren Buffett has said, the reality of the independent mutual fund directorships is "a zombie-like process that makes a mockery of stewardship.... A monkey will type-out Shakespeare before an 'independent' board will vote to replace management."[7]

So it is hardly surprising that mutual fund directors have rarely made major changes in the funds they govern and have allowed expense ratios to grow, despite an extraordinary increase in assets under management in the industry. In 1978, mutual funds held $56 billion of assets, with an average expense ratio of 0.91 percent; in 2004, mutual funds had more than $7,500 billion of assets and an average expense ratio of 1.36 percent.[8] In 1978, equity funds (requiring higher expenses) represented 58 percent of total fund assets, and in 2004, they were 50 percent.

To address these issues, the SEC in 2003 proposed a series of new governance rules for mutual funds, in part based on the controversies that had surfaced in the industry over several years. The principal provisions of the new proposals were:

Not complied with by many mutual funds managers

- Seventy-five percent of mutual fund board members must be independent of the management company, up from 51 percent, as provided in the Investment Company Act of 1940, and the chair of the mutual fund board must be an independent director.
- Mutual fund boards must meet at least quarterly in the absence of nonindependent members, that is, those affiliated with the management company.
- Boards have the right (but not the obligation) to hire their own attorneys and auditors, and must have a compliance officer reporting to them, not to management.
- Boards must inform shareholders how they determine mutual fund performance and compare fees and expenses with other funds, including pension funds.

Most of the mutual funds industry was agreeable to these proposals, but there was considerable disagreement over the requirement that the chair of the mutual fund board be one of the independent directors. Overall, 80 percent of all U.S. mutual funds in 2004 were chaired by an executive of the fund management company, with Fidelity's Edward C. Johnson III chairing 292 funds, Vanguard's John Brennan chairing 126 funds, and T. Rowe Price's James Riepe chairing 57 funds.[9] In each case, as chair, the individual owed his or her undivided loyalty to both the mutual fund(s) and to the fund management company, yet with shareholders of each having incompatible objectives. Once again, Warren Buffett noted (regarding fee negotiations between the chair of a mutual fund and the chair of its management company), "negotiating with one's self seldom produces a barroom brawl."[10]

Fund management companies mounted a massive effort to resist the SEC on this issue. In a spirited defense of his role as chair of each of the Fidelity funds and chair and CEO of the management company, Ned Johnson wrote:

> I have an interest, which I am proud to disclose. I am not only chairman of Fidelity Investments' mutual funds; I'm also part owner of the management company that invests these funds' assets. In addition, my family and I have made considerable investments in these funds for over half a century. Far from constituting a conflict, these dual roles mean that my personal, professional and financial interests are directly aligned with those of Fidelity shareholders. . . . Knowing that I have a significant personal and professional stake in the company's success or failure is highly relevant to the judgment made by Fidelity's shareholders that I will devote the time and energy necessary to make sure the job is done correctly, to the best of my ability. . . . If this rule is adopted, the immediate result will be to reduce the expertise and hands-on "feel" of mutual fund board chairs across the industry,

whose long experience equips them to detect subtle nuances in
fund operations.[11]

Despite these appeals, in June 2004 the SEC narrowly voted to require all mutual fund boards to be chaired by an independent director.
In doing so, it rejected the argument that market discipline and the
reputation of the fund managers would be adequate protection against
the reduction in vigor and negotiation effort brought to bear by a board
chaired by a fund management company executive. Neither the fact
that the Johnson family holds at least $100,000 in each of the 292 Fidelity
Funds or that John Brennan's Vanguard is a mutual company (i.e., the
management company is itself owned by the mutual fund shareholders) was enough to change the SEC's resolve on the issue. The record
was too fouled by misconduct by one fund manager or another to
allow the entire industry to avoid the regulatory tightening that the
inappropriate conduct brought about—despite the fact that major fund
managers like Fidelity and Vanguard had not been caught up in the
problems and had retained their reputations for integrity and trust-
worthiness throughout the industry's scandals.

The SEC ruling prompted a lawsuit by the U.S. Chamber of Commerce claiming that the SEC did not have the authority to overrule the
Investment Company Act of 1940 by requiring 75 percent of mutual
fund directors to be independent and their chairperson to be an independent director, and had not followed its own rules in not requiring
a cost-benefit analysis of the changes and by not responding to an
alternative proposal submitted by the dissenting commissioners. A
federal appeals court in June 2005 rejected the charge of inadequate
authority but upheld the other claims, and required the SEC to conduct
a cost-benefit analysis before proceeding with the new rule. In the
meantime, the SEC chairman, William Donaldson, a Republican appointee who sided the Democratic appointees on the proposed rule,
had resigned and been replaced by a conservative republican chairman
thought to be unsympathetic to the proposed rule.[12]

4. Fund managers want to increase assets under management.
Investors want optimum investment returns, after expenses
and taxes.

When fund managers are following a strategy to keep up with the
market's momentum to protect their performance rankings, they are
not necessarily achieving optimal performance, which is the best return
over the probable life of the client's investment after expenses and
taxes. Many retail investors, however, define optimum performance
differently—to be limited to the greatest gross quarter-to-quarter increase in net asset value—and are not aware of, or are indifferent to,
fees, expenses and taxes that will have to be taken out of the returns,
they expect to earn.

John Bogle, a lifetime mutual funds manager and founder and former CEO of the Vanguard Group, which specializes in low-cost indexed funds, has been the industry's sharpest critic. As he has done for years, Bogle argues that the actively managed mutual fund industry does not offer a fair deal to its many investors. He is especially critical of the industry's high fees and high portfolio turnover, which passes high tax liabilities directly to fund investors. Bogle calculates, for example, that in the decade ending in 2003, "the stock market returned an average of 11.1 percent to investors, but the average equity mutual fund has delivered just 8.6 percent—a 2.5 percent shortfall that was roughly equal to the drain of heavy sales charges, management fees and operating expenses, and the portfolio turnover cost incurred."[13] The notorious tax inefficiency of high-turnover funds would extract several additional percentage points. The shortfall was actually another 2.4 percent worse, Bogle claims, when one calculates the actual dollar-weighted returns received by investors. Over the decade ending in 2004, the investor in the average equity mutual fund saw more than half of the gains disappear in fees, expenses, and taxes.

Still, retail investors in funds may not feel capable of managing their own small portfolios in competition with sophisticated institutions, and think their best chance to share in stock market gains is through the purchase of mutual funds. But at the very least, they certainly do not want to see their assets preyed upon by others, such as preferred investors who are making payments of one kind or another to the management company in exchange for benefits to them, or management company officials who may be tempted to overtrade or overcharge the fund for expenses.

In April 2004, the SEC adopted the first in a series of new rules for mutual funds based on the record of market-timing and late-trading abuses. Funds are now required to provide elaborate disclosure of the consequences of frequent trading in fund shares, their policies and procedures in this regard, how and when they provide fund portfolio information to individual investors, and to use "fair value" pricing to reduce the possibility of investors being able to trade at "stale" prices.

In June 2004, the SEC also began a series of investigations into payments made by mutual funds and their advisers to 401k plans they manage, wanting to know whether the lucrative DC corporate pension plans had "pay-to-play" environments in which management companies, in order to be included in a list of fund choices for employees, rebated or "kicked back" some of their fees to the pension fund sponsors. The SEC had detected that the practice existed—some fund companies helped the 401k plans offset administrative costs by sharing a portion of the management fees paid to them—and wanted to determine who got the money and why. Put another way, the fees and expense ratios for retail funds are several times greater than fees paid by corporate DB pension managers, so why should DC programs be

benefit (pensions)   ↳ contribution so much more expensive? Shouldn't corporations use their bargaining power for the benefit of their employees? Such arrangements have been described in part as a way to bid competitively for the 401k business of a corporation by offering to reimburse the company (or the fund) for some of the costs of administration.

Another issue came to light with such inquiries. When a fund manager solicits the business of a large corporation, what is expected when the business is awarded? Is there an expectation, for example, that the fund manager will not disparage or become an aggressive seller of the company's stock? Is the assumption that the fund manager will vote with the company management on important governance and compensation issues? If this is the case, how can the fund investors' interests not be compromised in the process?

5. Managers want to push their funds through brokers and financial advisers who need to be compensated by charging 12b-1 fees. Investors do not want to pay these fees if they receive no benefits from them.

12b-1 fees amounted to approximately $10 billion in 2004. These fees are to reimburse fund management companies for the costs of distributing the funds to the investors who buy them, and pay the fee. These fees appear to benefit management companies at the expense of mutual fund investors, especially in the case of those funds that have declared themselves closed to new investment and where no further distribution is occurring. Changing the regulations providing for these fees, however, could encounter substantial resistance from members of Congress lobbied by the mutual fund industry, based on the recent experience of the SEC in changing other regulations in the face of strong industry lobbying efforts.

6. Managers want to lower unreimbursed costs through soft dollar commissions from broker-dealers. Investors want best-price execution of trades and lowest commissions.

Charging "soft dollar" commissions (brokerages reimbursing various costs of fund management companies in return for their business)—notably with respect to their purpose and requiring full disclosure to investors—would encounter the same political difficulties as changing 12b-1 fees.[14] However, in 2004, the SEC proposed requiring brokers to disclose fees they are paid by mutual fund companies for distributing their funds. Given the complexity and extent of such fee arrangements between brokers and fund managers, one estimate suggested that compliance costs for new rules in the first year alone could approach $9 billion and perhaps $7 billion annually thereafter.[15] Such high compliance costs could cause some brokerages to exit the mutual fund business or restructure their fund management business to focus only on the best performers.

7. Managers want to favor their own funds by obtaining "shelf space" in distribution channels, while investors want access through brokers to the best and most appropriate funds for their own needs.

How widespread such conflicts had become was evident in an SEC investigation of mutual practices in 2003 involving 13 mutual fund management companies and eight broker-dealers who distributed them. As a result, Morgan Stanley was fined $20 million for pushing its own in-house mutual funds over third-party funds, and another $50 million for allowing advice based on hidden compensation and for selling funds carrying high fees without adequate disclosure. Both Merrill Lynch and Citigroup also became targets of class-action suits charging them with not disclosing broker's sales incentives to push selected mutual funds.

8. Managers want to be able to organize funds to assist other business interests of the firm, such as investment banking, and promoting investments in particular stocks. Investors want all investment decisions by the managers to be arm's-length and objective.

In a 2004 court case, Merrill Lynch was alleged to have omitted disclosure, in promotional materials for its Global Technology Fund, that the firm performed investment banking services for more than one-third of the companies whose stocks made up the Fund. Merrill argued that its investment banking relationships with these firms were public knowledge to which investors had access via the Internet and news reports, absolving the firm from disclosing them in mutual fund materials. Investors sued Merrill on grounds that the absence of an explicit conflict-of-interest warning represented inadequate disclosure, an argument that was rejected by the trial judge. Alarmed that this signaled a green light for future conflicts of interest regarding mutual fund disclosure, the SEC joined the plaintiffs in a friend-of-the-court brief on appeal.[16]

Institutional Investors and Corporate Governance

A key issue with respect to shareholder voting patterns is how the corporate governance role (and proxy voting process running along the designated control channels depicted in fig. 6.2) is in fact carried out. Do ordinary investors bother to understand the issues and vote proxies in an informed way? Even though they have little individual power, understanding the issues presented in proxy statements is costly, and the free-rider option beckons. It is a fair bet that shares held directly in individual portfolios are either not voted or, for convenience, voted with management. The cost of informing oneself, understanding the issues, and voting on the merits may not be worth the trouble, although this does not preclude a few active small investors—so-called corporate gadflies—from raising matters of principle in annual meetings, sometimes to the chagrin of management. Nor does it preclude individual investors participating in class-action suits against managements and boards in cases of allegedly questionable behavior. For the most part, it is likely that individual shareholders, like the nonvoting public in the political arena, are a passive lot. Such investors in the United States control about 40 percent of the outstanding shares of publicly traded companies.

How active, then, are the institutional investors in exercising their voting power? Some DB pension funds (such as the high-visibility California Public Employees Retirement System [CalPERS]) are now so large and broadly invested that they have no choice, they say, but to become active in governance matters. For others, however, it is easier to sell problem stocks than to seek redress of issues through the governance process, especially if the institutions' portfolios are subject to high levels of investment turnover, as most mutual funds have been in recent years. But if they do not participate in governance issues, are they failing to exercise their fiduciary duties to those who invest in their funds? And do fund management companies encounter conflicts of interest with the mutual fund shareholders whom they represent that may impede their exercise of an effective governance role?

If the corporate governance process runs from company management to boards of directors to shareholders, then it is of more than casual interest how the governance power vested in share ownership is in fact exercised. And it is also of more than passing interest how the 60 percent of U.S. shares whose corporate control rights are vested in institutional investors are voted. As noted, corporate board members are elected by the shareholders after being nominated by a committee of the board (which is sometimes influenced by management), and the board selects the chief executive and approves the firm's business strategy and objectives. Board members are responsible for corporate governance, and periodically present shareholders with the opportunity to vote on matters of substance proposed by management or perhaps by shareholders themselves. How shareholders actually vote therefore takes on great significance. Shareholder passivity—based on lack of information, inconvenience, or just plain lethargy and disinterest—increases the likelihood that agency problems will emerge in ways that work against their basic interests, occasionally cumulating with the kind of unsatisfactory results seen in the early 2000s. So who exactly votes the shares in public companies controlled by institutional investors, and how do they actually vote?

Institutional Voting Practices

There are several ways in which institutions exercise the voting rights of their clients and investors:

1. Voting rights of shares belonging to all mutual funds, including index funds, are delegated by the boards of the funds to their financial advisers or mutual fund management companies, which vote them.
2. Voting rights in pension funds are exercised by the trustees of the funds, who delegate them to those professional managers they have retained to manage portions of their portfolios.
3. Individuals may become owners of voting shares in public companies by participating in a DC program. The bulk of such funds are invested in mutual funds, and the mutual fund management company will normally be delegated to vote the shares. Employees may also choose to invest in the stock of their own company in a DC plan, in which case the employees are free to vote those shares themselves.
4. Shares owned by individual investors may be held in "street name"—that is, in the name of the client's brokerage firm, which must pass along company information and proxy materials. In the United States, brokerage firms have the authority under the New York Stock Exchange rules to vote customers' unvoted shares—called "broker nonvotes"—on certain "routine" matters including the election of directors, assuming proxy materials have been sent to the clients at least 15 days before the meeting. Shares represented by broker nonvotes are counted as "voted" by the brokerage firm in the election of directors, but may not be counted for other corporate matters to be voted on (such as mergers, consolidations, or other questions that may affect the rights of a stock) because these are not considered "routine" under the applicable rules.[17]
5. Shares held in trust by a bank or trust company normally are voted by the trustee.

Institutions thus vote almost all of the shares entrusted to them. Each has its own policy for determining how to vote, and these policies are sometimes disclosed. Some funds appear to follow recommendations for proxy voting prepared by Institutional Shareholder Services (ISS), a private business that maintains databanks and staff to research voting issues, and has prepared guidelines for good-governance voting. But it seems unlikely that very many mutual fund management companies or their financial advisers put a lot of expense and effort into careful monitoring of management conduct and governance issues in corporations whose stocks they hold, or into more proactively pressuring boards to avoid actions that harm investor interests. Why? Because most of the time it simply is not economically reasonable for them to do so.

A fund's success depends mainly on its net investment performance (i.e., performance after fees)—performance that is highly transparent and endlessly discussed in the media. Individual portfolio managers are expected to make the key asset allocation choices, and live or die by the results. Investors can buy or redeem funds and select others at any time. Everything is marked to market, everything is out in the open, and investors get what they see. No fund manager today claims to offer corporate monitoring or assertive governance, and if they did, it is not clear that their customers would pay much for it.

So why invest effort and expense in corporate monitoring and governance? The benefits of successful governance efforts, in any case, accrue to *all* investors (not just the firm's own clients), while the associated costs drive up expense ratios that are passed on to an individual fund's investors and thereby burden fund performance. Especially in today's competitive market, clients have become increasingly fee sensitive, and it is logical that even mutual fund investors who may benefit from monitoring and governance activity would prefer not to pay for it. It seems preferable to be a "free-rider." "Let someone else take care of the problems, and we'll enjoy the same benefits if he succeeds."

The "free-rider" issue, in combination with the basic mutual fund business model, conspires to encourage apathy in most elements of corporate governance. And to the extent that mutual funds have their own governance problems, with emphasis placed on the independence of directors who do not act independently, pressure on these same management companies from such fund directors to be more proactive in monitoring and governance matters is certain to be minimal. In the case of low-cost index or exchange-traded funds, which likewise hold shares with voting rights, there is virtually no participation in the governance system. Mutual fund investors may forsake managed equity funds for passive funds due to excessive fees or poor performance, but from a governance perspective, doing so gains nothing.

So how do the mutual fund fiduciaries, large and small, actually behave in matters of governance? In the past, few people knew— certainly not mutual fund investors, although they may not have cared much. A good guess, based on the foregoing logic, is that proxy votes have been cast with corporate management virtually all of the time. Nothing else really makes much sense, in terms of the resources that would have to be committed, investor apathy, the lack of a clear payoff to fund boards and fund management companies, and finally, the lack of transparency in how funds voted. No one would know anyway.

In 2003, the SEC promulgated a rule requiring mutual funds and other investment advisers (as defined in the Investment Advisers Act of 1940) to disclose how they voted their shares. Specifically, the rule

> requires an investment adviser that exercises voting authority over client proxies to adopt policies and procedures reasonably designed to ensure that the adviser votes proxies in the best interests of clients, to disclose to clients information about those

policies and procedures, and to disclose to clients how they may obtain information on how the adviser has voted their proxies, and to maintain records of such actions.[18]

The fund management industry fought a vigorous rear-guard action against the SEC plan, with critics' attention focused on conflicts of interest embedded in fund managers' business ties to corporations. But the real issue is probably much simpler and more fundamental than that. The industry had little to gain by disclosing its votes, and faced considerable costs to comply with the requirement. The expense was likely to be passed on the investors, which may not be seen by any of them as being a good use of their money. However, the SEC rule promised a wealth of data on the voting practices of institutional investors, and should these data—as one would suspect—show full support of management proposals, they could be embarrassing to the fund managers and require some sort of public defense or explanation. As a result of the SEC voting-disclosure initiative, future voting patterns may change to become more investor-friendly, or at least more neutral.

The new rule, which went into effect in August 2004, was called the "mutual fund equivalent of food nutrition labels." All votes are uploaded to the SEC's public website, describing each resolution voted on and whether the fund voted for or against the board's recommendations. This permits special-interest investors, such as labor unions or environmental groups, to evaluate how all funds voted on issues of concern to them. It also allows fund monitors like Morningstar, the credit rating agencies, and corporate watchdogs to score mutual funds on their diligence in governance matters. The SEC initiative soon produced parallel moves in Canada, the United Kingdom, and the Netherlands, among others.

Notwithstanding this development, our assumption, based on the evidence of past behavior of these institutions, is that corporate boards and managements will still be able to count on the great majority of votes of the trillions of dollars of shares held by mutual funds, active and passive, for most issues of importance to them. This is not about malfeasance. It is simply rational "nonfeasance," or economically imposed indifference. Whether such a position can endure against a rising concern for dutiful fiduciary conduct is yet to be seen. The experience of the late 1990s suggests that the institutions failed to exercise the powers to monitor and control that they had, and as a result they and their investors suffered losses that might have been in large part avoidable.

Given their massive market presence, the institutions collectively carry an enormous burden for shaping the governance role in corporations. To the extent that this role is not effectively carried out, beneficiary shareholders have effectively ceded their monitoring and governance rights to agents whose own interests (to gather assets and improve profits) may have been inserted ahead of those whose money

*if you are a free rider & indifferent
the*

they are managing. This results in a failure, either through market actions or voting, to impose discipline on boards, which are then vulnerable to being hijacked by dynamic, aggressive, and fully empowered corporate managers. Some of these managers have clearly operated on the principle that the only thing that matters is raising the stock price, no matter what the long-term risks to the company, and if they succeed, shareholders should have no complaints about anything else.

Institutions collectively seem to share a responsibility to their investors to preserve and apply their powers to control corporations through voting and other actions. But do individual fund management companies legally have this responsibility? It is not clear that courts have understood them to have this duty so far. But the law evolves, and if institutions persistently fail to exercise their control rights as shareholders, they may cause injury both to the capital markets (a broad social cost) and to their clients, for whom a fiduciary duty to discharge voting rights competently can be inferred.

Activism

In contrast to mutual funds, there is plenty of anecdotal evidence of other types of fiduciaries investing substantial resources in their monitoring and governance role. CalPERS and TIAA-CREF do this in the United States. Major institutional investors in the United Kingdom, and continental European banks and insurance companies that have close long-term ties to companies in which they hold stakes (and often supervisory board memberships as well), also make efforts to stay on top of things. If mutual funds have dropped the ball as effective corporate monitoring and governance agents, perhaps this is not the case for pension funds, which, in the case of U.S. defined benefit plans, have been required to vote their shares since 1988.

As noted, DB pension funds sponsored by private-sector employers, labor unions, state and local governments, and other institutions hold equities in self-managed portfolios, or they contract with external asset managers, often with the advice of pension fund consultants. If the equity portfolios are self-managed, the pension fund votes the shares, and has substantially more incentives than mutual funds to hold corporations to high standards of governance. Turnover in such funds tends to be relatively low, and fund managers have relatively long-term investment horizons.

Sometimes pension fund shareholdings are so large that they basically "hold the market," which further limits their incentive to sell shares of companies that are economically sound but whose governance problems has led to poor performance. Funds are more or less stuck with what they own, so if improved governance leads to improved performance, they ought to have a vital interest in monitoring things and exercising their control rights.

Thus DB pension funds are less susceptible to the "free-rider" problems of mutual funds, and so the asymmetry between the cost of monitoring and governance and its benefits is less—raising the incentive to perform these roles. Pension funds may also be under less quarter-to-quarter performance pressure at the plan sponsor level (but perhaps not at the manager level) and therefore have more leeway to devote significant financial and human resources to monitoring and governance issues.

For these reasons, independent pension fund trustees have an incentive to become interested in governance matters and, when appropriate, to take up direct contact with managements or boards of corporations, especially when things are not going well. Not all do this, especially corporate funds that outsource management of assets to others and where the temptation to become free-riders reasserts itself. Corporation executives, on the other hand, have an unwillingness to take public positions that may complicate important business relationships and are generally unwilling to speak out publicly on governance issues.

Some state or municipal pension executives, especially those appointed to office by politicians, are very vocal on current political or social topics that they believe are reflected in governance issues. By doing so, they may become involved in social issues, albeit with little direct, near-term economic value.

A number of U.S. state, municipal, and labor union pension funds have been especially active in exercising their governance rights. In May 2004, for example, CalPERS expressed serious concern about the governance of Safeway Stores, and joined in a vote of no confidence against the company's chairman and CEO, saying:

> Today's vote is a substantial showing of dissatisfaction by Safeway shareholders. . . . Safeway's recent corporate governance reforms are not enough. . . . Shareholders have delivered a clear message that the Board should strip [the CEO] of his chairmanship position. We will keep a close eye on how Safeway's board responds to this vote, and hope that they quickly act in the best interests of shareholders.[19]

In another high-profile case, the 2004 annual meeting of Walt Disney was marked by longstanding investor dissatisfaction with company performance, executive compensation, and governance practices, against the backdrop of an unsolicited takeover bid by Comcast. The March meeting involved a large percentage of withheld votes, signaling no confidence in management proposals on the table, including nominations of directors. In response to the vote, TIAA-CREF noted:

> During [the] shareholder meeting, TIAA-CREF withheld its support for Michael D. Eisner and the entire board of directors of Walt Disney. This vote reflects TIAA-CREF's view that corporate boards must be independent and fully accountable to meet their

fiduciary obligations to shareholders. At present, there is considerable question as to whether this is the case at Walt Disney Co. Boards of directors must play their required oversight role. To enhance shareholder value over the long term, we believe the board of Walt Disney needs to meaningfully examine and analyze its structure and board leadership to give the company the credibility it needs on issues such as CEO succession, company strategy and executive compensation. We think our vote, together with the votes of other concerned investors, sends the right message. Now that the vote is in, we urge the board at Walt Disney to incorporate legitimate shareholder concerns into their deliberations, consistent with the goals of openness and transparency.

We are pleased that the board split the positions of CEO and Chairman. It is a step in the right direction. However, it is important to note that shareholders withheld significant support from all board members, including the new chairman, [former U.S. senator] George Mitchell [who was previously lead director and himself showed an extraordinary withhold rate of 24 percent]. Going forward, it is important that George Mitchell and the board explain what these changes mean in real terms, not just formalities, and how the company expects to regain its credibility with shareholders.[20]

Two months later, Sean Harrigan, then CalPERS President, after meeting with the Disney board said:

Today's meeting was about the monumental withhold vote against [CEO] Michael Eisner and the performance of The Walt Disney Company. I think the first step was made by shareholders in March when 53 percent of shareholders, excluding the broker vote, told the Disney Board that they had no confidence in Mr. Eisner. Today was an important second step for us. Now the ball is in Disney's court.

One example of the international dimension of governance by pension funds involved Royal Dutch/Shell in 2004. The firm found itself in the center of an accounting and governance scandal that involved the overstatement of crude oil reserves by some 22 percent, which led to a massive restatement of 2002–2003 earnings and cost both the CEO and the chairman their jobs. A raft of lawsuits were filed against the firm seeking reparations for investors, as well as monetary damages from its current and past boards and senior executives and its accountants, PricewaterhouseCoopers and KPMG. A suit filed in New Jersey Superior Court on behalf of the United National Retirement Fund and the Plumbers and Pipe-Fitters National Retirement Fund charged those named with constructive fraud, abuse of control, breach of fiduciary duty, and unjust enrichment and sought monetary disgorgement and reimbursement of the company, as well as major governance changes, such as increased accountability, the right to nominate directors, and combination of the United Kingdom and Dutch boards.[21]

Problems of Institutional Investor Self-Governance

Professional investment managers compete for business on the basis of performance in making money and managing risks for their clients. But some are more exposed to competition than others. In the case of pension funds, trustees can and do get plenty of advice on the performance of a variety of fund managers, and they do change the ones they use reasonably often. Fees are kept to a minimum, and fund managers' feet are usually held firmly to the fire. By contrast, managers of mutual funds with widely dispersed share ownership enjoy greater job security and receive much higher fees.

Nonetheless, mutual funds' management feel the pressure for short-term performance. There were over 4,000 equity mutual funds in the United States in 2003, and each of these had to prove itself in a highly visible, highly regulated industry that is full of "league tables" that report performance against various benchmarks.

Managers do what they can to outperform their peers. They try to steal a march on other investment managers by obtaining sensitive information first, by insisting Wall Street analysts call their portfolio managers when new information, sometimes based on conversations with insiders, comes into the market. Such information was especially important to portfolio managers in the 1990s, focused as many were then on quarter-to-quarter performance of stocks that could rise or fall very sharply on the basis of how likely they were to meet their coming quarterly earnings expectations. This practice was substantially curtailed in 2000 by the SEC's regulation entitled "Fair Disclosure," which restricted companies from talking to favored analysts without simultaneously informing the entire market of the information passed.

Many funds followed a "market momentum" trading strategy for generating short-term profits while investing in all of the market's most active stocks so as to track the market indices closely and look good, or at least not bad, in the next quarter's mutual fund performance rankings. It was sometimes a frenetic strategy for investing—one designed perhaps to appeal to the hot-money mutual fund investors who only cared about short-term performance rankings that attracted assets to be managed albeit with high trading costs (and associated tax expenses) for investors. Such strategies showed no interest in corporate control and governance issues, unless a takeover was in process, but they were consistent with the basic mutual fund economics driven by asset growth and mass-marketing. Mutual funds' role as effective monitors and governors of corporate conduct was especially eroded during this period, and their investors, concentrating on asset growth performance and little else, did not seem to mind.

What were mutual fund management companies to do? A bubble

was on, markets were roaring, and there was a lot of money to be made. The market was irrational and causing fund managers to do things differently, but what they were doing was what their investors seemed to want. The investors were willing to pay for it, as well. Did fund management companies or mutual fund boards really have some obligation to cool off or shut down individual funds because of fiduciary obligations to investors? Both boards and fund managers took the view that they were participating in a free-market activity, only doing what others in the market did, and owed no duties to anyone beyond that.

Sensible self-governance, however, implies skirting dangerous territory, such as allowing favored clients to trade advantageously, putting corporate interests ahead of investor interests, and overcharging or concealing fees and expenses. Mutual fund boards have not developed into objective agents of self-governance, so the issue has mainly been left to the funds management companies. These companies may have been able to avoid criticism or regulatory interference because of generally good reputations and the carefully cultivated appearance of a well-ordered industry. The disclosures of many unseemly and reprehensible actions and the public furore that followed certainly changed the climate for the industry. The adverse publicity, legal penalties, new regulations, and class-action litigation have shattered the industry's reputation for effective self-governance, and it will be a long time getting it back.

Conglomeration

The agency conflicts of the asset management industry are potentially greater when mutual fund managers are part of large financial conglomerates, which have investment banking, commercial banking, or insurance relationships with corporations whose shares they hold in their mutual funds. Pressure to perform may be greater in the context of a financial conglomerate situation, in which divisions are expected to compete with each other or be subject to sanction. It may be no surprise that 7 of the 12 largest mutual fund management companies involved with market-timing abuses were parts of large financial conglomerates. Such conglomerates do most of their business with corporations or other financial institutions, and their clients are unlikely to do business with "difficult" investors who subject them to "unhelpful" governance pressure. Such clients might easily direct banking or advisory or securities business to rivals. In the highly competitive business of corporate financial services, there are plenty of fish in the sea. It is unlikely that corporate management will forego this power of coercion among financial services providers, especially in highly contested corporate actions requiring shareholder approval.

In one prominent example—the 2001–2002 Hewlett-Packard effort to acquire Compaq Computer—the merger was bitterly opposed by

William R. Hewlett, the son of one of the cofounders. Hewlett thought the merger was ill advised and had assembled sufficient shareholder backing to force a very close vote. Hewlett-Packard began to urge one of its large institutional shareholders—the investment arm of Deutsche Bank, which had opposed the merger—to change its vote. Other Deutsche Bank units, notably the corporate finance division, supported Hewlett-Packard management in the merger. But the Chinese wall between the dealmakers and the asset managers apparently held firm, and the investment managers at the bank resisted. Shortly before the proxy vote, Hewlett-Packard CEO Carly Fiorina was quoted as saying: "We need a definite answer from . . . Deutsche Bank . . . and if it's the wrong one, we need to swing into action. . . . See what we can get, but we may have to do something extraordinary to bring them over the line here."[22] Deutsche Bank, after some heated internal debate, changed its vote to favor the merger, which was approved by shareholders, although just barely. The vote switch was later investigated by the SEC and the U.S. Attorney's Office for the Southern District of New York. The SEC fined Deutsche Bank $570,000 in July 2003 for not disclosing its conflict of interest in the matter. In the event, the merger was widely regarded as a failure and Fiorina was fired as CEO in early 2005.

Mutual fund management companies can face conflicts of interest similar to those facing the accounting, banking, and securities industries. These are conflicts that threaten their ability and willingness to manage client assets carefully and loyally, the two key requirements of a fiduciary duty. Such conflicts can make it less likely that mutual fund managers will object to risky merger strategies, excessive executive compensation, or other aspects of inappropriate governance. The ordinary investor relies on the "professional" to look out for such dangers, and to respond to them when they are detected. Yet few mutual funds have exercised this role during the recent turbulence in corporate governance. Indeed, several of them were among the biggest investors in the business disasters and corporate scandals of the early 2000s.

Partly out of concern for these conflict issues, Citigroup announced in June 2005 an asset swap with Legg Mason, a broker-dealer, to exchange its Smith Barney asset management business, worth about $4 billion, for the brokerage business of Legg Mason, which would henceforth operate only as an asset manager. Citigroup would thereby forego the asset management business and concentrate instead on brokerage activities. Among other benefits, exiting the asset management business confronts Citigroup with one less conflict.

Voluntary and Involuntary Reforms

Pressure for change within the asset management business has focused on the involvement of the mutual fund industry in the pension sector and in applying appropriate standards of governance to the corporations in which they invest.

TIAA-CREF voluntarily altered its self-governance practices in 2003–2004, adopting both Sarbanes-Oxley accounting requirements for publicly traded companies and NYSE listing requirements concerning board and committee composition, although (as a mutually owned company) it was not required to do so. It appointed an independent chair for CREF (its equity investing arm) and each of its fund boards; it established annual elections for all members of TIAA-CREF boards. And it now holds regular board meetings without management present. In announcing these policies TIAA-CREF said; "We want to help lead a debate and discussion, and by applying best practices to our own environment . . . create a groundswell among other investment companies. . . . We intentionally established these principles to be aspirational. We're moving ourselves in that direction, and we hope other companies will go there too."[23]

TIAA-CREF, of course, is a noncorporate pension organization with apparently more latitude in making changes of this type. So are the large state and municipal pension funds, who have preferred to show their independence, power, and spirit by undertaking a large number of activist governance interventions. Corporate pension funds, however, are mostly unable or unwilling to make comparable changes, and they may be subject to some involuntary regulatory prodding. This is especially true of the DB funds regulated and guaranteed by the U.S. government.

At the same time, another aspect of pension fund management (under discussion since the 1970s) has again come under scrutiny—the use of "independent" pension fund advisers. Major firms include Frank Russell (owned by Washington Mutual), Mercer Investment Consulting (owned by Marsh & McLennan), Callan Associates, Wilshire Associates, and Segal Advisors. Almost half of all U.S. pension funds with more than $100 million in assets use fund consultants. Their key role is to provide pension fund trustees with recommendations on the use of fund managers, tracking performance, and investment styles and other useful services for which pension funds pay fees. At the same time, they provide fund managers with performance reporting software, marketing consulting, and conference organization, for which they also receive fees. They thus receive fees from both sides, and must report fees paid by fund managers to both their pension fund clients and to the SEC—nevertheless raising the "play to pay" issue of whether their recommendations to pension funds are tainted by compensation they receive from fund managers. In addition, pension fund consultants are sometimes in the fund management business themselves. An SEC investigation launched in 2004 focused on "practices with respect to advice regarding selection of investment advisers to manage plan assets, selection of other service providers such as custodians, investment research firms and broker-dealers, and services other than investment consulting provided to plan sponsors, investment advisers and mutual funds."[24]

In the mutual fund sector, it is now clear that the SEC has decided to take an aggressive, "show-me" position with respect to the industry. Almost all of the changes in rules governing the mutual fund industry imposed by the SEC have been resisted. In the past, the industry had great influence in both the administrative and legislative branches of government, and could hold off the SEC. However, the cascade of scandals following the collapse of the stock market in 2000, including the Enron and other corporate failures and the mutual fund late trading and market timing debacle that followed, changed the scene. Not many politicians want to step out to oppose calls for reforms and punishment. True, this particular moment in mutual fund history will pass, and the industry will revert to normal. But for now, many regulators, enforcers and public critics are not wasting the benefits of the "crisis" in order to make durable changes in the industry.

Lasting Improvements

Lasting improvements will require regulators to continue to point the tips of their spears at fund management concerns, which are not very disposed to voluntary efforts to clean up their own houses. Rather than opposing reforms, they should understand that clearing out malignant agency conflicts may be the best thing they can do to protect their own interests. Few are willing to do more than they consider necessary, so progress requires the regulators to establish appropriate changes in what is necessary.

The SEC's 2000–2004 regulations for mutual funds are steps in the right direction, but no one should believe that director independence, as defined by regulators, even now, means anything of the sort. Beyond these regulations, large fund groups and multibusiness financial conglomerates should recognize that Chinese walls between potentially conflicting areas need to be hardened. If this is impossible, they should make them unnecessary by selling those businesses that present residually dangerous conflicts. Relations between corporations and fund management companies also need to be examined, preferably by influential people unaffected by business relations with either of them. And, for their own benefit, fund managers can make an effort to educate investors to avoid overly speculative short-term behavior in favor of solid longer term (and hence lower cost) holdings, to reveal all costs and charges in a user-friendly manner and support that effort by advertising and promotion, and by being willing to turn away quick infusions of hot money that might contradict these efforts. In the end, actions like these will be most likely to accelerate the road to recovery of the reputations of the entire industry, following a particularly unattractive time in its history—one that is not unlike the experience of the 1930s.

Following the 1930s, a tidal wave of financial regulation occurred that changed the fund management industry forever, making it both more expensive to operate and more trustworthy (because of the government's regulatory role) than ever. Recapturing of trust enabled the industry to grow, indeed to explode with opportunity. Today, the government has intervened extensively in the industry, adding expense and inconvenience to operational tasks. Aside from individuals like John Bogle, few mutual fund leaders have stepped forward to act as change agents. That is probably normal. The danger is that regulatory cost can be a great burden to the industry and its investors. Unnecessary or duplicative regulation wastes resources. If industry leaders participate more actively to put in place long-lasting changes in the way funds work—lowering agency conflicts, despite the fact that some revenues may have to be sacrificed to do so—then the whole industry will be better off than if the government believes it must keep things tight in order to keep them safe.

ASSET MANAGEMENT AND MARKET DISCIPLINE   *read all 6*

We believe there are at least six conclusions that can be drawn from the discussion presented in this chapter.

1. The asset management industry has been one of America's great financial achievements. Half of all U.S. households now participate in the stock market, mainly through retirement and mutual funds, the largest proportion ever. Ordinary individual investors are able to invest with results, and at costs, not greatly different from what wealthy investors experience. The industry itself has attracted a vast amount of capital, and is likely to grow substantially in the years ahead. Institutional investors increasingly *are* the market and, accordingly, have potential to be major factors for the imposition of market discipline on corporate management and boards. However, they also have the ability to allow the markets to drift away from rational valuation of companies by introducing or tolerating distortions caused by an accumulation of significant agency conflicts. Major players in the industry have shown that they have been reluctant, unwilling, or unable to discipline themselves to ameliorate these conflicts.

2. The structure of the asset management industry reflects a high degree of competition among traditional and new players. On the one hand, this should bring lower costs and greater value to investors, especially if the players begin to respond to stiffer regulatory pressure to provide greater transparency in fees, costs, and after-tax results. On the other hand, the industry already has hundreds of competitors, and these have apparently preferred to continue practices that have enabled them to keep fees and investor costs higher than they were 20 years earlier. The SEC now seems to recognize that part of its duty is to pressure the industry with new rules to remove these practices and tip it toward competition based mainly on greater value for investors.

3. The mutual fund industry, in particular, is vulnerable to regulatory and legal action to suppress agency conflicts, of which many have

been identified but largely explained away by the industry. After years of tranquility with respect to fiduciary duties, the industry has headed into a stormy and dangerous time, which can continue unless the basic agency conflicts are persuasively removed.

4. The fund management industry is in the process of being required to deal with governance issues of its own. These include the independence, leadership, and functioning of fund boards, how funds are marketed, the transparency and level and nature of fees, and its increasing complex relationships with corporations and consultants. The industry has resisted almost all of these changes. But since about 2003, the SEC, taking advantage of a crisis-induced, proreform environment, has persistently pressed for changes without being fatally challenged by politicians sympathetic to the fund management firms.

5. Self-improvement can make a difference. Mutual funds have a lot to clean up, and they should be able (and incentivized) to get on with it. All institutional investors can become more proactive about corporate governance issues and, if they fail, may be pressured by regulators and litigators to do so. Pension funds, especially corporate pension funds, need to become more active (or at least supportive) of governance issues.

6. There is a strong likelihood that unless the industry reforms itself, it will be vulnerable to substantial change. New competition may enter the business and displace those of yesteryear unwilling to admit the need for change. Already, indexed funds have taken away about 20 percent of the market from actively managed funds. Competition from new players, such as those with trusted brand names like WalMart, Costco, Microsoft, or General Electric, could set up funds groups owned by investors and pledged to total transparency and avoidance of conflicts. Such new sponsors would find ways to benefit from money flows and economies of scale and scope. Their job would be to evaluate, monitor, and employ the best active money managers, to lower costs, and to remove any conflicts of interest that might affect investor returns, fully exploiting the sponsor's marketing capability and bargaining power. Most of today's big mutual fund managers are likely to have too much riding on the old business model to offer anything like this. Some of the big consumer marketers are already in the mutual fund business, and they too may not be quite as committed to the old models.

Financial history is replete with new models. Money market funds developed because banks and their regulators exploited the retail deposit market, opening the door to new competitors from the securities industry. Index funds developed as a more cost-effective way than actively managed funds to invest in broad market aggregates. This is the way free markets are supposed to work, after all. When leaders remain mired in the status quo, innovators find a better way.

7

The Auditors

The free-market-based economic system is heavily reliant on transparency. Bad information and bad dissemination can distort capital markets and lead to bad investment decisions. Distorted information can allow capital to flow to the real underperformers that ought to be subject to market discipline and forced to adjust. Equally, healthy corporations under such circumstances can find access to capital more difficult and expensive than it should be. The aggregate impact of such distortions of the efficiency of the market economy as a whole can be significant.

Accounting firms and auditors play a critical role in delivering transparency to capital allocation decisions involving public corporations. Indeed, although the source of financial information is the company itself, in the United States, a public company is required under federal securities laws to retain an *independent* accounting firm to audit (i.e., to examine) its accounts, and to certify that the company's financial statements "present *fairly*, in all *material* respects, the financial position of the company in accordance with *generally accepted accounting principles* applied in the United States of America."[1] The appointment of auditors must now be approved every year by the audit committee of the board of directors and by a majority vote of shareholders at the annual meeting.

The operative words in the regulatory requirements are "independent," "fairly," "material," and "generally accepted accounting principles" (GAAP).

- "Independence" suggests that the auditor's objectivity in rendering an opinion is not compromised by conflicts of interest—a condition that did *not* prevail in all of the large auditing firms in the 1990s.

- The notion of "fairness" suggests a financial report that is fair in the overall context, not one that is only technically fair in the sense that items on the checklist have been ticked off, while nevertheless the resulting report may be not-fair in the context of the business as a whole.
- The word "material" is not precisely defined—it is generally thought to mean that deviations in reporting individual items should not change overall results by more than, say, 5 or 10 percent (i.e., an amount that should not change the minds of interested parties).
- GAAP represent a set of accounting principles and standards adopted by the profession and updated periodically to represent best practices.

Although the authority for setting accounting principles and standards was vested in the SEC by the Securities and Exchange Act of 1934, the SEC has for many years allowed the accounting profession to self-regulate principles and standards, subject to its oversight, and the industry has long maintained a board of standards staffed and directed by senior accounting professionals and more recently by the Federal Accounting Standards Board (FASB), which includes public members. The FASB proposes updates and changes in accounting practices, airs them for public comment and then, after any revisions, adopts them as requirements going forward.

The standard-setting process, however, is subject to pressures and resistance from the business community and through it from the accounting industry itself. Sometimes opposition to accounting changes is so severe as to involve intensive lobbying (even at the SEC level and through members of Congress) and political campaign contributions. Controversial accounting changes, such as off-balance-sheet accounting, accounting for derivatives and corporate stock options, have generated sufficient opposition to delay the adoption of new accounting rules by as much as a decade, during which time the industry could report financial data in any of a variety of ways.

Recent history has shown that there have been widespread failures in the auditing function, leading to substantial amounts of wrong information being used in financial analysis and investment decisions. These failures have included the evolution of such severe conflicts of interest in the auditing profession as to render the term "independent" questionable. There have also been abuses in assessing fairness and materiality, and out-of-date accounting principles and standards have been used to formulate audit opinions, contributing significantly to some of the corporate governance disasters of the early 2000s.

This chapter traces how the accounting industry has evolved, how the accounting profession operated in the late twentieth century, leading to its virtual collapse in the early 2000s, and the regulatory reforms and measures aimed at assuring its recovery.

HOW THE INDUSTRY EVOLVED

Auditing has been in existence almost as long as accounting itself. Ancient clay tokens found in the region known as Mesopotamia (today mostly contained within the country of Iraq) attest to a viable system of recordkeeping.[2] In ancient Egypt, bookkeepers were motivated to maintain accurate records for fear of punishment by fine, mutilation, or even death during the royal audit.[3] Greece in the fifth century B.C. had its official "public accountants," citizens who maintained control over government finances. In Rome, the *quaestors*, who managed the treasury, were regularly examined by an audit staff and were required to account to their successors and the Roman senate when they left office.[4]

The principles of modern accounting were established with the publication of a treatise dating back to 1495, *Summa de Arithmetica, Geometria, Proportioni et Proportionalita* (Everything about Arithmetic, Geometry and Proportions), by the Italian monk Fra Luca Pacioli. In 36 short chapters, the treatise explained the system of double-entry bookkeeping, "in order that the subjects of the most gracious Duke of Urbino may have complete instructions in the conduct of business."[5] The book was immensely popular, and few of the basic principles were changed dramatically over the next 500 years.

Today's professional accountants evolved from the "chartered" (licensed) government accountants practicing in Scotland in the midnineteenth century. Early accountants often worked in law offices. Indeed, typical assignments of a Glasgow accountant might include serving as a factor, or trustee, in sequestered estates, managing property, and making statements and reports to file legal claims in court, in addition to typical accounting and auditing work.[6] The first accounting bodies were regional in nature—in 1854, the Institute of Accountants in Edinburgh was the first to be granted a royal charter.[7] Over the next few years, accounting bodies proliferated—in London, Liverpool, Manchester, and Sheffield. The latter half of the nineteenth century saw the rapid growth of auditing work in Britain, as more companies came to be traded on stock exchanges.

There are varying theories that attempt to explain the emergence of the professional auditor in Britain. One theory suggests that there has always been a demand for auditors as long as there has been a separation of ownership and control, since the auditor brings the solution of an honest intermediary to the agency problem. During the nineteenth century, this demand developed rapidly, and soon there was a supply of suitable professionals, along with chartered accounting bodies. Firms with chartered professional accountants could offer their clients the benefit of economies of scale, and this encouraged other firms to use chartered accountants as auditors as well.[8]

Another argument suggests that the growth of the chartered auditor was shaped by the economic and legal climate of nineteenth-century business and by the self-promotion strategies of the profession itself.

Toward the end of the nineteenth century, the profile of shareholders of firms began to change from wealthy investors, with insider knowledge and contacts, to public shareholders concerned about reporting and distribution of profits. At the time, the law was largely ineffective in resolving corporate disputes, especially those related to dividend payouts. So directors preferred not to appeal to the law to settle conflicts with shareholders about such matters. Instead, the chartered, independent auditors stepped in as key players in the determination of solutions to issues of corporate governance.

Chartered accountants seized an opportunity and gradually began to take over the profession. They became involved in new-company formation, and in advising managements. They touted the benefits of the chartered accountants as professionals whose specialized expertise could be invaluable in such thorny matters as the distribution of profit in comparison to the amateur, nonchartered accountant. Thus, accounting firms began to dominate auditing and, in turn, transformed their main source of business from handling insolvencies as representatives of creditors into public company auditing.[9] The auditing profession received institutional sanction and legitimacy slowly—in 1900, the Companies Act was passed in the United Kingdom, which required the presentation of an audited balance sheet. But the Companies Act did not stipulate that the auditor had to be a chartered accountant until 1947.

In the United States, the auditing profession was led by the migration of Scottish and British accountants to the New World to audit accounts of American enterprises in which British investors had exposure. In 1890, for example, the British firm of Price Waterhouse established its first office in the United States, in New York, to audit American breweries. Accounting firms banded quickly to form an accounting body, the American Association of Public Accountants, in 1887, and New York State in 1896 passed the first law to recognize the qualification of Certified Public Accountant (CPA), the approximate equivalent of the British chartered accountant.[10]

As in the United Kingdom, professional auditing developed informally faster than did legislative actions requiring it—by 1926, more than 90 percent of industrial corporations listed on the NYSE were already being audited,[11] although there was no formal requirement for doing so. The big thrust for the accounting profession came in the aftermath of the Great Depression, when President Franklin D. Roosevelt signed into law the Securities Act of 1933 and the Securities

Exchange Act of 1934. The 1933 Act provided for registration of new issues of securities, and the 1934 Act provided for the formation of the SEC and annual reporting requirements of public companies.

The SEC was empowered to set financial disclosure and accounting and auditing standards in the United States, which were required to be followed by all corporations using public securities markets. The key accounting feature of these laws was that *all* public companies had to retain professional accountants as auditors to certify their financial statements, and that these auditors had to be independent of the companies being audited. Subsequent to the Securities Act of 1933 and the Securities Exchange Act of 1934, financial disclosure in the United States became extensive, detailed, routine, and periodic, and was tied to common national accounting and auditing standards. Such disclosure provided the necessary transparency required for a fair and free market in securities trading. The Acts also paved the way for the rise of professional accounting firms in the United States, and their subsequent spread globally.

Setting the Standards

The accounting profession today follows two broad sets of standards, those related to auditing (or examining of information) and those related to accounting (organizing information into financial statements).

Audit Standards. Issuance of exacting auditing standards was precipitated in the United States in 1937 by a massive auditing scandal at McKesson & Robbins, a wholesale drug company with sales at the time of $174 million and assets of $87 million.[12] The firm had inflated receivables and merchandise inventory by creating a fictitious Canadian subsidiary. The firm's auditors, Price Waterhouse—then the largest organization of public accountants in the world—had signed off on the accounts without inspecting the Canadian subsidiaries. The event led to an SEC inquiry in which the commissioners concluded that while Price Waterhouse's audit procedures had conformed to what was mandatory, "they failed to employ that degree of vigilance, inquisitiveness and analysis of evidence available that is necessary."[13] Prompted by the scandal, the American Institute of Accountants (the predecessor of the American Institute of Certified Public Accountants [AICPA]) in 1939 created a standing committee to develop audit procedures. Over the next few years, the committee published several independent pronouncements, which were consolidated in 1972 into a single document. The standing committee was renamed the Auditing Standard Executive Committee (AudSEC) in 1972 and once again renamed in 1978 as the Auditing Standards Board (ASB).[14] The ASB is the entity within the AICPA that until recently set the standards by which auditors determine how the information reported in financial statements is to be accurately collected and verified—recognizing that the auditors are not expected to duplicate the financial books and records of companies but rather to set up procedures for systematically determining that the information being used in the financial statements is fairly stated in all material respects in accordance with generally accepted accounting principles. As for the auditing standards themselves, they have their origin in various sources—through members of the ASB, through other divisions of the AICPA, through initiatives outside the profession, and through litigation.[15] Today, in accordance with the Sarbanes-Oxley Act, such standards are determined by the Public Company Accounting Oversight Board.

Accounting Standards. The development of accounting standards—GAAP in the United States for the private sector—has followed a similar path. The creation of the SEC in 1934 gave it the power to establish accounting standards in the United States that had to be followed by public corporations. The SEC chose instead to delegate this function to the accounting profession, in particular to the AICPA's Committee on Accounting Procedure (CAP). In 1938, the CAP issued an initial 51 proclamations—the so-called Accounting Research Bulletins—that formed the basis of GAAP. The CAP was replaced in 1959 by the Accounting Principles Board (APB), which issued 31 additional principles over the next 14 years, with a mandate to attack some of the more controversial accounting issues. In 1972, the Financial Accounting Standards Board (FASB) replaced the APB, and the term "accounting principles" was replaced by "accounting standards," to reflect the new role of FASB as the system's committed independent accounting *standard* setter.

Today, the FASB has seven full-time members and operates under the Financial Accounting Foundation (FAF), which funds it. The FAF is made up of a number of sponsoring organizations, among them the AICPA, the Securities Industry Association, and the Institute of Management Accountants.[16] The problematic issues of FASB dependence for funding on the accounting firms themselves, and on sponsoring financial intermediaries and corporations, long remained below the surface. During the 1990s, it became clear that accounting principles (and standards) involved significant economic interests, especially to corporate managers attempting to legitimize certain otherwise problematic transactions by fitting them under the benign umbrella of GAAP. Such managers, especially when they operated collectively, had great influence on their auditing firms, on other intermediaries and on legislators and regulators through the power of the purse to direct business and to make political contributions.

International Standards. The development of international accounting standards is less clear. Every nation has its own accounting conventions. The International Accounting Standards Board (IASB) was formed only in 1972 and, with 140 professional accounting bodies in

101 nations, has an arguably tougher task, in terms of harmonizing and issuing accounting standards worldwide. There are 13 member countries on the Board, as well as the Nordic Foundation, Swiss companies, and financial analysts. Also on the Board is the International Organization of Securities Commissions (IOSCO), of which the SEC is a member.

The first 10 years of the IASB's history were devoted to codifying best practices. Accounting principles were "descriptive, rather than prescriptive," and member countries could use one of many accepted practices. For example, inventory could be accounted for under "Last in First Out" (LIFO), "First In First Out" (FIFO), or any of the other principles used by member countries. During its initial decade of activity, the IASB worked on strengthening the original standards and, like FASB, addressed an array of difficult and contentious issues. The IASB today identifies its mission as gaining recognition in the key capital markets, working on an interpretation program of accounting standards, and establishing working relationships with national standard setters. It has amended a number of its own international accounting standards and issued some standards where none existed before.

Harmonization of Standards

With the globalization of capital markets, the issue of harmonization of accounting standards has become important. Harmonization, in an accounting context, can be defined as the "process of increasing comparison of accounting practices by setting bounds to their degree of variation."[17] It is widely acknowledged that harmonization of accounting standards can play a key role in reducing capital costs and costs of preparation of financial statements for multinational companies and in enhancing capital flows by improving international comparability in financial statements.[18] Recognizing the importance of harmonization, both FASB and IASB in April 2001 announced a short-term convergence project aimed at ensuring a "single set of quality, understandable and enforceable global accounting standards."

It remains to be seen whether full harmonization, in the form of a single set of global accounting standards, can indeed be implemented. Many barriers stand in the way of full harmonization—economic, cultural, and political forces within each country, together with the lack of enforcement authority surrounding the "official" international standard setter (the IASB), as well as continuing differences between the IASB and the FASB, the other powerful standard setter.

Economic, political, and national factors make harmonization not so much an accounting process as a cultural and political process. In continental European countries such as France and Germany, for example, accounting has tax and commercial implications, and French and German commercial and tax laws contain detailed accounting rules. Legislators and governments in these countries thus retain control of the accounting standards.[19] In addition, political factors, such as the strength of user interest groups (foreign versus domestic users of financial statements, for example), and economic factors (such as the country's reliance on international capital markets) can also have a profound effect on national accounting issues.[20]

A key conflict in harmonization is that while the beneficiaries tend to be international firms, the cost is borne mainly by local players, adding to the political ramifications of harmonizing accounting standards.

In this context, unless the standard setter has the recognition and compliance authority that, for example, the FASB has in the United States, ensuring compliance with a set of international standards is a nearly impossible task. For example, French banks in 2003 lobbied furiously to oppose the new IASB standard on financial instruments and hedging, designed to provide greater transparency in accounting for structured and derivative transactions. The argument was that the new standards would increase the volatility of bank earnings, and thereby threaten both share prices and the stability of the French financial system. Counterarguments focused on the need for up-to-date values of financial contracts, with the implied conclusion that if standards failed to provide an adequate level of transparency, an increasing number of banks and corporations would opt for conversion to GAAP, which would then become the de facto global accounting standard.[21] An alternative would be for firms to adhere to market value accounting for derivatives, even if not required to do so. The improved transparency, it was argued, would boost share prices and lower the cost of capital of such firms, ultimately encouraging the recalcitrant firms to go along.

There are also potential areas of conflict between the IASB and the FASB, reflecting differences in their approach to accounting standards. The corporate scandals of the early 2000s reignited a longstanding debate about "rules-based" versus "principles-based" accounting. The U.S. rules-based approach reflected in GAAP seems to have provided little protection to investors in light of the myriad ways for smart managers, lawyers, and accountants to evade them in substance while remaining technically in compliance. GAAP accounting has been characterized by detailed checklists and high levels of precision that some times, taken together, yielded misleading financial information. At the same time, defining compliance with principles-based accounting rules is often difficult and subjective, as appealing as these principles may be.

What the market really requires is a full and fair portrayal of the financial condition of companies. This may mean starting from a GAAP base with a "comply or explain" or "true and fair override" provision. That is, in cases where GAAP results may fail to provide a true and fair picture of the condition of the business, or of the economic substance of transactions, management would be required to explain the use of alternative approaches taken to make the presentation true and fair. Such a requirement, however, would undoubtedly introduce a wealth of subjective judgments and complications, and may become the sources for exploitation by aggressive litigators. Efforts to minimize damages in class-action suits have indeed led U.S. auditors to rely on checklist approaches, and although shifting to a more principles-oriented form of accounting might prove to be theoretically desirable, doing so may be impracticable for those operating within the U.S. legal system.

The current status on harmonization is not promising. In December 2003, the FASB proposed changes to bring American rules nearer to international norms, while the IASB in turn presented rules of accounting more in line with American practice.[22] The proposals met with resistance on both sides. One of the new proposals of the FASB requires firms to restate earnings for prior years after any accounting changes, rather than have the traditional one-time adjustment. Businesses say that in the wake of several scandals and restatements, investors are wary of even innocent earnings revisions. In Europe, the new accounting rule for derivatives proposed by the IASB met with aforementioned resistance from European banks and insurance companies, who complained that the new rules would make their earnings too volatile. Even more resistance was expected as the FASB and the IASB move on other subjects, such as revenue recognition or treatment of mergers and acquisitions.[23]

The Business Model

Prior to the 1980s there were eight large, international auditing firms, and 10 to 12 firms with an important national or regional presence. In addition, there were hundreds of small public accounting firms specializing in accounting and auditing services for midsize and small businesses. In order to sell new issues of securities, underwriters would require companies to secure the services either of one of the "Big Eight" or a respected and known member of the next tier.

Emphasis on Auditing

An SEC audit was a much more expensive service than an ordinary audit, because of the more extensive disclosures and higher standards required. As every publicly traded company had to supply an SEC audit once a year, plus unaudited quarterly reports—whether or not the firm undertook to sell securities in the market—the auditing business was oligopolistic (the Big Eight firms audited more than 90 percent of all public companies) and quite profitable. The firms also offered some additional services, such as management consulting (mostly related to IT systems such as payroll, inventory, and bookkeeping) and tax advice. But the basic accounting work was the bread and butter of these firms, amounting to 89 percent of revenues for the Big Eight in

1975. Globalization helped expand the businesses the firms audited or advised, and by the late 1970s half of Arthur Andersen's offices, for example, were located abroad.

Most firms were organized as professional partnerships, as required by the SEC in 1934, when it declared that independent auditing firms could not have outside investors, and because of a long tradition of having partners stand accountable for the firm's work as a whole. To maintain independence, the partners of auditing firms were expected not to own any securities issued by clients of the firm. International associations, mergers, and other combinations were complicated for partnerships, and the usual solution was to join separate partnerships of each national entity under an international umbrella structure that would to provide global direction, marketing, and controls.

During this period, accounting firms strongly believed that their respected names conveyed reliability and integrity to the companies they audited. This was a benefit for which they should be paid in the form of higher fees. To assure that their "brand names" were protected by stellar reputations, the partners established procedures for ensuring high-quality professional standards in their auditing practices. In each firm, there was a senior partner assigned to chairing a technical group or "practice committee" that would have to approve any deviation from the standard accounting principles and auditing practices used by the firm. A different way to recognize income or to treat a new financial instrument had to be presented to the firms' practice committees and, so it was believed, the auditors would pronounce their decisions without regard to client economics or other issues. The practice committees were willing to hear arguments, but they were generally regarded as very difficult to convince—none more so, during this time, than Arthur Andersen's practice committee.

Industry Consolidation

A factor that was important in driving growth in the accounting industry prior to 1990—closely related to the transition of accounting firms to full-service professional organizations—was the consolidation wave within the industry. At the start of the 1980s, the Big Eight firms consisted of Arthur Young, Price Waterhouse, Coopers & Lybrand, Arthur Andersen, Deloitte, Haskins & Sells, Peat Marwick Mitchell, and Ernst & Whinney.

The consolidation drive began in the 1980s with the merger of Peat Marwick Mitchell and KMG Main Hurdman, the U.S. affiliate of the European firm Klynveld Main Goerdeler, in 1987. This resulted in the creation of KPMG Peat Marwick, and the merged entity became the second-largest U.S. firm until 1989, when fourth-ranked Ernst & Whinney and sixth-ranked Arthur Young formed Ernst & Young, which became the largest accounting firm in the United States. In the same year, seventh-ranked Deloitte Haskins & Sells and eighth-ranked Touche Ross merged to form Deloitte & Touche, then the third-largest firm in the United States. At the end of the decade, the "Big Eight" had shrunk to the "Big Six"—KPMG, Price Waterhouse, Coopers & Lybrand, Arthur Andersen, Deloitte & Touche, and Ernst & Young.[24] In 1998, sixth-ranked Price Waterhouse merged with fifth-ranked Coopers & Lybrand to become the second-largest firm, called Pricewaterhouse-Coopers. The Big Eight had been reduced to the Big Five.

The consolidation drive was the result of multiple factors that can be broadly divided into economies of scale and economies of scope. Economies of scale refer to the notion that the average cost of production decreases as a result of increasing production volume. Economies of scope refers to the notion that average total cost of production decreases as a result of increasing the number of different products or services, and that cross-selling these products or services generates higher volumes or prices.

Audit firms established economies of scale and scope through international consolidation. In doing so, they were driven by their clients' own growth. Some of the aforementioned mergers were motivated by region-specific strengths. For example, in the late 1980s, Ernst & Whinney had an established network in the Pacific Rim countries, while Arthur Young did not. Similarly, Price Waterhouse had a network in South America, while Coopers & Lybrand's principal network was in Europe.[25] As they consolidated, the firms gained access to a larger capital base, a critical ingredient to growth, since they were limited in raising capital by virtue of their partnership structures. A larger capital base attributable to mergers gave the firms the resources to expand in staff training and development and to bring down costs, thus improving operating efficiencies to offset declining margins, as auditing fees remained flat or decreased (in inflation-adjusted terms) in the late 1980s and 1990s.[26]

Consolidation led to further economies of scope, as firms expanded into new areas of industry-specific and technical expertise in audit services, and into nonaudit services—especially management consulting. The Ernst & Young merger brought together two firms that specialized in health care (Ernst & Whinney) and technology (Arthur Young). Similarly, the Price Waterhouse and Coopers & Lybrand merger brought together two firms that dominated the market for audit services in utilities and telecommunications, respectively. In addition to gaining specific industry expertise in audit, some mergers also helped firms to build nonaudit services in management consulting. For example, the Deloitte Haskins & Sells-Touche Ross merger brought together a firm with a substantial audit and tax consulting practice and a firm with a strong management consulting business.[27]

THE AUDITING PROFESSION IN THE 1990S

The business models of the auditing firms were affected by several new but very powerful market forces during the 1990s. There was an explosion in the use of corporate information technology, which greatly expanded demand for the kind of IT systems consulting work done for clients by the auditors. Before long the consulting businesses became as important, then more important, than the auditing business. There was an equally dramatic explosion in new forms of financial securities, practices, instruments, and derivatives (and their tax treatment) and in financial services regulation—all requiring rapid development of new accounting principles and standards. Financial markets boomed in the 1980s and 1990s as never before, but they also went through several corrections, market reversals and bankruptcies that inevitably resulted in litigation aimed at auditors, which the auditing firms were often compelled to settle for large sums. By the end of the 1990s, all auditing firms were continuously involved in class-action litigation for alleged violation of professional or fiduciary standards. However, the combination of auditing and consulting revenues was growing rapidly, and the associated profits available to accounting professionals became very tempting. The firms themselves began to feel the need for greater scale and scope, as well as better management to take advantage of these developments.

Each, by then, was a vast, multinational organization (most operating as a collection of national partnerships) serving thousands of clients all over the world. The increasing complexity and competitiveness caused serious quality control issues to emerge. By the end of the 1990s, market failures attributed to faulty auditing and accounting had become commonplace, and all major U.S. firms suffered considerable loss of reputation and prestige. One, Arthur Andersen, was forced into liquidation.

The State of Independence

The growth of nonaudit revenues began to conflict with the auditing firm's core attribute—their independence. Over the decades after 1975, accounting firms steadily began to increase the provision of nonaudit services, and by 1998 revenues from management consulting had grown to an average of 45 percent of revenues, ranging among the major firms from 34 to 70 percent.[28] A study of more than 4,000 proxy statements on the SEC's EDGAR database filed between February and June 2001 showed that nonaudit fees averaged two-thirds of total fees billed by the Big Five auditors, as compared with less than half for non-Big Five auditors. The purchase of nonaudit services was widespread—96 percent of audit clients in 2001 had contracted for nonaudit services. However, a relatively small number of clients accounted for a disproportionate amount of nonaudit fees.[29]

There was also a growing tendency for nonaudit fees to exceed audit fees—in 2001, at least half the Big Five firms' clients paid nonaudit fees in excess of audit fees.[30] Anecdotal evidence brings these numbers into sharper focus. One of the most striking examples is the case of Enron, which in its SEC filings indicated that it paid Arthur Andersen (its auditors) a total of $52 million in one year, of which $25 million was in the form of audit fees. This number was contested by Andersen's CEO in testimony declaring that the audit fees were in fact $13 million and the nonaudit fees approximately $34 million, with another $4 million going to the firm's consulting arm.[31] Whatever the exact number, there is no doubt that Enron paid its auditor exceptional amounts in fees for nonaudit services. In another case, a 2001 filing showed that Walt Disney had paid PricewaterhouseCoopers, its auditors, $8.7 million in auditing fees and $32 million in nonaudit fees.[32]

Not surprisingly, the growth of nonaudit services changed the business models of many accounting firms. Audit services, by the late 1970s, had become commoditized. The liberalization of the accounting industry by order of the Federal Trade Commission (removing restrictions on advertising and solicitation of business), and competitive bidding increased competition in the accounting industry and served to drive down prices. Audit services became loss leaders used, in some cases, to gain entry to more lucrative nonaudit opportunities. Suspicions of competitive "low balling"—offering deliberately underpriced audit fees in order to obtain a new client, from which additional fees might be generated from nonaudit services—became widespread. Cuts in audit fees of between 25 and 50 percent were widely reported in the industry.[33]

With the traditional professional accounting business becoming more competitive than ever before, and the competition being driven by opportunities to perform in the lucrative consulting business, the classic business model of the accounting industry was transformed. The firms adapted by reorganizing themselves into two generally separate parts—accounting and consulting—operating under a worldwide parent organization. The two groups often clashed over management issues and division of profits, but the reality emerged that the auditors were used as marketers of consulting services, and their compensation and promotion opportunities reflected their success in doing so.

In line with this dynamic, Arthur Andersen established its Andersen Consulting subsidiary to become the consulting division of the group. It was so successful that by 1983, Andersen Consulting was the leader among all U.S. consulting companies in terms of revenues.[34] By then, the revenues from Andersen's consulting business began to catch up with its accounting arm, and surpassed them for the first time in 1984. By 1988, Andersen Consulting was generating 40 percent of the entire firm's profits. In 1989, as part of a restructuring process, Arthur Andersen and Andersen Consulting were set up as two stand-alone business units, charged with providing separate and complementary services. Arthur Andersen supplied tax and audit services, while Andersen Consulting provided management and technology consulting services. The two business units were linked by a parent organization, Andersen Worldwide, whose mission it was to ensure that the two entities performed compatibly. In July 2001, after an acrimonious divorce, Andersen Worldwide spun off Andersen Consulting (as Accenture) in an initial public offering of shares.

The move toward nonaudit services increasingly raised the question of auditor independence. The SEC defined independence not just as "independence in fact"—the state of mind that permits performing of an audit service without being affected by external influences—but also "independence in appearance," the avoidance of circumstances that would cause a reasonable third party to conclude that the firms' integrity or independence has been compromised.[35] This definition takes into account that over the years, there had been persistent debate about whether auditor independence was *in fact* compromised by provision of nonaudit services, or whether there was only the *appearance* of auditor independence that was being compromised by nonaudit services.

Research and public opinion focused on whether audit quality had in fact been affected by auditor independence issues. Audit quality is defined as the "probability that the financial statements are free of material errors."[36] If they are (free of material errors), then independence no longer has the importance it once had; it doesn't really matter, appearances notwithstanding. Competing arguments over this issue have been heated for many years.

On the one hand, there were academic studies suggesting that there was no evidence that provision of nonaudit services impaired auditor independence. In one study, in only 3 of 610 claims against auditors was there an allegation that independence had been impaired.[37] Another study of 944 firms that issued proxy statements and that disclosed audit fees for 2000 found that issuing "going-concern" opinions (a sign that a company may not remain in business; issuing such an opinion would suggest auditor independence) *increased* as audit fees increased.[38] Such findings can perhaps be explained by assigning importance to the reputational capital that an auditor builds. Although it would seem that auditors have an economic incentive to accede to their client's wishes by not reporting errors, there is a counterincentive for auditors to maintain high levels of quality—a lower quality audit may be discovered, and this could drive away clients who value higher quality.[39] The auditor, in becoming more dependent on *all* its clients, becomes more independent of *any* one.[40]

At least one study concluded that provision of nonaudit services can actually increase the quality of audit, due to productive economies of scope (economies of scope arising from the fact that both types of service need to utilize the same set of information and professional qualification) and contractual economies of scope (the economies connected with the fact that cross-selling of professional services involves high transaction costs, and therefore it becomes worthwhile to make use of safeguards, such as brand name, reputation, and client confidence, already developed, when contracting for new services).[41]

Accounting firms, of course, strongly attempted to justify the provision of nonaudit services by maintaining that these actually enhanced audit quality. One such study, conducted by the Panel of Auditing Effectiveness, indicated that in no instance did the panel find that provision of nonaudit services reduced quality, and that in a quarter of the cases, it actually enhanced audit quality.[42] Such studies were typical of those commissioned on behalf of an industry by its lobbyists.

On the other hand, studies in the accounting literature suggested that provision of nonaudit services increased the auditors' incentive to acquiesce to client pressure.[43] Such studies seemed to indicate that the more the firms paid their auditors for nonaudit services, the more likely they were to engage in "earnings management"—that is, in meeting or beating Wall Street analysts' forecasted earnings per share.[44] Another study, commissioned by Congress in the late 1970s (and never acted upon), noted that an auditor's ability to remain independent was diminished when the firm provided both consulting and audit services to the same client.[45] In 1987, the *Journal of Corporation Law* observed that "as accountants today are expanding into business and investment consulting and tax planning areas, questions of independence can arise."[46] Academic inquiries usually presumed that if a conflict can be proven to exist, then it is likely that the parties involved will succumb to its temptations, regardless of the concurrent need for the parties concerned to maintain reputational capital and abide by high professional standards that would provide an effective safeguard against exploitation of conflicts of interest.

In a 1994 review, the SEC concluded that its staff should continue to be "aware of problems" of independence that might be caused by nonaudit services. The Special Committee on Financial Reporting (the Jenkins Commission) noted that

> users [of financial statements] are concerned about current pressures on auditor independence. They also are concerned that auditors may accept audit engagements at marginal profits to obtain more profitable consulting engagements. These engagements could motivate auditors to reduce the amount of audit work and to be reluctant to irritate management to protect the consulting relationship.[47]

Despite these studies, and conviction by the then SEC Chairman Arthur Levitt that conflicts were threatening auditing and reporting accuracy, the SEC was unable or unwilling to act meaningfully on auditor independence issue at the time.

Through the end of the 1990s, the debates on auditor independence were largely held to be academic, although the arguments persisted—despite increasing numbers of accounting failures, evidenced by the restatement of audited financial statements (over 500 cases from 1997 to 2000) and hundreds of regulatory and class-action suits aimed at the major auditing firms. The SEC, empowered by the 1934 Act to refuse to accept certifications provided by auditors deemed not to be independent, made various pronouncements about the independence of auditors but actually did little or nothing to assure it. It took the spectacular collapse on Enron in 2001 and WorldCom in 2002 to focus public attention on the issue. In both cases, Arthur Andersen was the failed company's auditor and provided substantial consulting services. Andersen would not survive the aftermath of these events.

The State of the Standards

Meanwhile, if the auditors were less independent than people expected, there had to be a mechanism to transmit their willingness to please their clients that would not at the same time place the auditors in jeopardy for fraud or misrepresentation. The auditors were willing, as a matter of policy, to be client friendly, but not that friendly.

The mechanism that emerged was the capacity to interpret GAAP in a manner that would be favorable to the company. Generally this seemed difficult to do. GAAP was well established, and there were hundreds of bulletins, research studies, and other documentation of what generally accepted accounting principles were and how they were to be applied. Still, there were a number of loopholes in GAAP, caused by changing business practices and technologies that introduced new factors that had to be rendered into acceptable accounting. And the process of finalizing a new accounting principle could be extremely long while argumentation, foot-dragging, and strenuous lobbying efforts played out. In the interim, ersatz forms of accounting treatment were applied, often inappropriately or carelessly, because there were as yet no hard-and-fast rules.

The FASB was charged with keeping accounting principles up to date, but it was limited in what it could do in the face of opposition from its own industry (FASB members were seconded to the Board by the accounting firms themselves), or from the FAF's corporate sponsors, or from the business community at large, which could mount public relations efforts and lobby for support among politicians whose campaigns they helped finance.

In the late 1990s, the biggest unresolved issues relating to accounting principles were (1) the treatment of off-balance-sheet liabilities for "special purpose entities," or SPEs, (2) the valuation and accounting for financial derivatives, and (3) the accounting for the issuance of employee stock options by corporations. These issues were all awaiting action by the FASB to establish standards. There were other unclear issues as well, related to revenue recognition (rules establishing proper treatment already existed, although they were always susceptible to imaginative or novel approaches to evade them) and the reporting of "pro forma" earnings in company financial statements to reflect the effects of mergers, reorganizations and other "one time" events.

In short, during the 1990s there were many companies that operated aggressively to exploit opportunities in financial and merger markets that needed favorable accounting treatment of their actions to make the most of them, and these corporations were accommodated by their auditor/consultants and strongly urged them to be more "creative" and "responsive." Some companies projected themselves as "new economy" corporations that were doing things that were unprecedented, claiming that therefore newer and more tailored accounting methods had to be developed to give investors a true picture of their efforts. Certainly Enron and WorldCom, and many others, were among these companies, and used their considerable leverage with the accounting firms to persuade auditors to find a way to go along. There were four domains that covered most of the problems.

First was the accounting treatment of SPEs. In Enron's case, what was demanded of the auditors was favorable treatment of off-balance-sheet SPEs, of which the company had created more than 800. It needed to exploit a loophole in the ersatz accounting treatment of such transactions—which enabled off-balance-sheet treatment for liabilities of an SPE if only 3 percent of the equity and debt of that SPE was owned by an independent third party—and to provide a source of new ideas for similar treatment of more and larger transactions. Enron also wanted broad tolerance of issues of "materiality," in which, for example, a transaction that failed to qualify for off-balance-sheet treatment might be overlooked because it was not itself "material" in the context of Enron's overall financial position.

A second issue related to accounting for derivatives—an issue that raged on for years during the 1990s, especially in the financial services industry. These issues migrated to the telecom industry late in the decade, when "swaps" of capacity were made between two fiber-optic cable operators (Enron and Global Crossing, among others) that placed unrealistic values on the properties.

Revenue recognition issues resulted in many cases of earnings restatement by corporations in the late 1990s. GAAP provided that companies could book expected revenues on certain long-term contracts before the revenues were realized under specific circumstances. This not only helped offset high front-end costs associated with such contracts but also allowed substantial leeway in earnings reporting. In one example, Electronic Data Systems Corporation (EDS) signed a $9 billion contract with the U.S. navy and booked a substantial portion as up-front revenue. When subsequent political delays raised questions about when the cash flows would actually be received, EDS had to take a

$2.2 billion charge in the third quarter of 2003 and wait for the funds to actually arrive.

Such practices clearly reduced the transparency of company accounts for investors, which probably more than offset the benefits to companies in smoothing earnings.[48] Revenue recognition usually required the consent of the auditor, as it was difficult to conceal such information. And auditors were frequently cooperative in setting up "creative" ways to treat revenue-recognition issues during the latter 1990s. Often these resulted in later financial restatements that shocked the markets, as occurred among such major corporations as Lucent and Xerox and later AIG. Expense recognition became a testing ground for the human imagination. For example, WorldCom managed to persuade its auditor, Arthur Andersen, that a portion of its operating expenses were in fact eligible to be capitalized as long-term assets.

A third issue involved employee stock options, which under GAAP were not required to be expensed when granted, so long as they were executable at market value at issuance. Economic understanding of options was poorly developed when their accounting treatment was initially adopted, but at the time employee stock option grants were very modest in relation to most companies' capitalizations. During the 1990s, both of these factors changed. It was widely accepted among financial academics that options had determinable, underlying fair value when granted, and that this value necessarily represented a cost to the firm's shareholders. And the relative importance of employee stock options ballooned to hundreds of times what it had been. A Federal Reserve study at the time indicated that U.S. corporate earnings per share as a whole were significantly overstated, perhaps in the range of 2 to 4 percent, as a result of the failure to expense stock options when granted. Another study in 2003 suggested that the cost of stock option grants at Cisco Systems (a major issuer) was likely to be as much as 20 percent of the company's earnings per share in the 2004 and 2005 fiscal years.[49]

The FASB attempted to reform the treatment of such options but was prevented from doing so by very determined lobbying efforts on the part of corporations and their accounting firms. The SEC opposed the lobbying effort initially, but Chairman Arthur Levitt noted that he was compelled by members of Congress to drop his resistance or see the SEC's operating budget drastically reduced.

A fourth issue was the use of "pro forma" earnings, which became widespread during the stock market bubble and merger boom of the 1990s—and did a great deal to camouflage what was actually going on within corporations. Often derided as "earnings before the bad stuff," pro forma numbers generally exclude such costs as restructuring expenses, which often appeared later as special one-time charges, resulting in earnings restatements. With investors focusing on price-earnings ratios, comparisons were obviously highly sensitive to earnings definitions. One study calculated that the S&P 500 index in April 2003 was trading at around 32 times GAAP earnings, but only 19 times "operating earnings"—a difference explained by costs that are ordinary business expenses under GAAP but treated as nonrecurring extraordinary items under "operating earnings" that were often restated later.[50] Another study by security analysts at UBS traced the difference between pro forma earnings and GAAP earnings and showed them to be 19 percent higher during the 1991–2001 period, and almost 50 percent higher in 2001 alone. The largest differences between pro forma earnings and GAAP earnings were among companies being investigated for accounting irregularities by the regulators.

In sum, by the end of the 1990s it was clear that the major accounting firms had lost their ability to affect accounting discipline among their clients. The internal accounting practice groups were becoming toothless. In many cases, the economic interests of the firm (and the compensation and promotion opportunities of certain partners) were weighed alongside the firm's reputation for professional integrity—and the economic interests prevailed. The consequence was the gradual contamination of the markets by incorrect or misrepresented financial information on corporations whose securities were, accordingly, misvalued. Because of the massive size and trading volume in the equity markets during the late 1990s, the quantity of misvalued securities was vastly greater than ever before. So a very important degree of responsibility for the bubble and the damages associated with its subsequent collapse may be attributed not only to management but also to the auditing profession, which contributed significantly to the market failures.

Some, however, claim that the more sophisticated financial analysts actually knew of the distortions when they occurred and never did rely excessively on the auditors for what they needed to know. If this is the case, then the responsibility associated with the market failures of the late 1990s spreads to other parts of the system, to the intermediaries and investors whose activities are discussed in the previous chapter of this book. And it raises the question whether, in a world dominated by highly knowledgeable and sophisticated financial intermediaries, audited financial statements of corporations are needed at all.

Litigation Explosion

Through the 1990s and early 2000s, auditors' liabilities related to professional conduct became very large, expensive, and contentious. Partly this is a result of the increase scope of the class-action lawsuit and greater enforcement efforts by regulators, but it is also evidence of a lowering of standards in the industry.

Many accounting industry professionals believe that their exposure to lawsuits has expanded to insufferable levels because of tricks and manipulations available to skilled trial lawyers. Whenever there is a sizeable bankruptcy or significant restatement of corporate earnings, lawsuits alleging responsibilities of auditors are a near certainty, they believe, regardless of fault. Some in the accounting industry have argued that accountability and responsibility can go too far. To quote one such view:

> The Big Four accounting firms are asked to take responsibility for all the failings of public companies around the world. The system ought to be like a shop—if there is a problem you get your money back. If you buy a television and it doesn't work no one suggests you should get back 400 times the price [through lawsuits].[51]

Others, including their pursuers in the law firms, claim that the accountants have made themselves vulnerable by unacceptably lowering professional standards and failing to enforce quality controls.

Either way, the reality has been that accounting firms and their insurers have participated in a constant and extensive transfer of wealth to trial lawyers and their collective clients for at least a decade. The cost of insuring against such expenses and losses became a part of doing business, most of which was passed on to clients. This resulted in increased audit fees, and a system for forecasting litigation risk, which enables firms to charge higher fees to clients thought to be high risk, if indeed such clients are retained at all. Enron, for example, was classified as a high risk by Arthur Andersen, and accordingly, the audit fees charged to Enron were materially higher than to lower risk clients. Once the risks were covered by differential fees, however, the temptation on Andersen's side may have been to become indifferent to them.

Whereas class-action suits have been the most expensive form of litigation, actions brought by regulators such as the SEC have grown as well, and they have indeed been fatal. The U.S. Justice Department was outraged that Arthur Andersen—under a restraining order from a prior case—had continued to engage in practices that were supposed to be prohibited. So it brought criminal charges against the firm for obstruction of justice. These charges resulted in a conviction, and the almost instantaneous bankruptcy and liquidation of the firm in 2002.

QUESTIONS OF LIABILITY

Two main questions are associated with auditor liability: (1) *who the auditor is liable to*, and (2) *what the auditor is liable for*. In the United States, three broad standards are commonly applied by the courts to decide who the auditor is liable to, although no one standard is uniformly applied: (1) the *privity* standard, (2) the *known and intended* class of beneficiaries (also called the near-privity standard), and (3) the *reasonably foreseeable* standard.[52]

The privity standard is the narrowest standard, holding that the accountant should not be held liable to third parties for mere negligence in civil suits that do not involve gross negligence or fraud. Over the years, accountants' liability has been extended, and now some states in the United States adopt the "reasonably foreseeable" standard for third-party liability. This extends liability to reasonably foreseeable third party users of financial statements.[53] (Third-party liability is relatively recent in other countries—it emerged in the United Kingdom, Canada, Australia, and New Zealand only during the 1960s.)[54]

Accounting firms argue that third-party liability leads to a large number of frivolous or weak-claim lawsuits against them that are nonetheless long and expensive to settle. Research on litigation in the 1990s against U.S. accountants showed that around 40 to 50 percent of cases involved weak claims, but that these cases nevertheless took an average of 3.7 years to settle.[55] There is also the danger that with the existence of third-party liability, persons who used a variety of risk assessment tools before deciding whether to transact now claim to rely exclusively on audited financial statements.[56] All this, accountancy firms argue, makes it increasingly difficult and expensive for them to procure liability insurance.

Not surprisingly, the accountancy profession has lobbied strongly for a narrowing of liability, as well as other measures, to ensure that auditors are not the only ones held responsible. In the United Kingdom, for example, the profession has pressed for director liability insurance, capping of auditor liability and proportionate rather than "joint and several" liability.[57] In countries such as the United Kingdom, Canada, New Zealand, and Australia, these efforts (other than for the capping of liability) have been fairly successful—there has been a consistent narrowing of the "duty of care" definition back to privity or near-privity standards. Court judgment in the United Kingdom have held, for example, that in general, auditors only owe a "duty of care" to their corporate client (as a legal person) rather than to any individual shareholder.[58]

The second area of auditor liability deals with what the auditor can be sued for. Auditors can be sued for: (1) breach of contract, (2) ordinary negligence by their clients, and (3) gross negligence, constructive fraud, and fraud by third-party users of the financial statements. Breach of contract is defined as the failure to provide contractual duty, such as the failure to produce an audit report on time, failure to discover a material error or irregularity, or withdrawal without justification from an engagement. Negligence involves the failure to exercise due care and is distinguished from gross negligence or constructive fraud, which involves the failure to exercise even minimal care. Fraud involves the intentional misrepresentation of facts. The definitions make it clear that it is difficult to draw the line between what constitutes negligence and what constitutes fraud.

The audit industry claims that increased litigation is due to an audit "expectations gap," the gap between the auditors' required standards

of performance and public expectations of their standards of performance. The auditors have a responsibility to search for errors that may
have a material effect on financial statements, but the auditor is not the
guarantor or ensurer of the accuracy of the statements. On the investors' side, it is often difficult to distinguish between auditing failures
and business failures, so auditors may be taken to task when the firms
they audit run into business trouble. A study of 472 cases involving
the 15 largest public accounting firms in the United States showed that
156 suits were brought against accounting firms during the period from
1970 to 1974, while 133 were brought from 1980 to 1984—both periods
corresponding to major business slumps.[59]

Not all legal action against auditors is brought by the investing
public. In the United Kingdom, for example, where class-action suits
are not permitted, some of the largest lawsuits involve accountancy
firms: one firm, in its capacity as a trustee in bankruptcy, taking action
against another, in its capacity as auditor. For example, Touche Ross
initiated a legal action involving an $8 billion claim in 1993 against
Price Waterhouse,[60] the auditors of the failed Bank of Credit and Commerce International (BCCI). Price Waterhouse launched a £1 billion
lawsuit against Touche Ross over the collapse of Atlantic Computers
in 1994.[61] In the same year, Coopers & Lybrand launched a £400 million
lawsuit against BDO Stoy Hayward, the auditors of Polly Peck.[62] Coopers & Lybrand, in turn, was sued by Price Waterhouse, the liquidator
of the failed merchant bank Barings, in 1996.[63] Yet another accounting
firm, KPMG, sued Coopers & Lybrand in 1997 for £120 million over
alleged audit failures at Wallace Smith Trust.[64]

Besides lobbying for measures to reduce auditor liability, accounting
firms use a number of mechanisms to minimize litigation costs. Mechanisms can: (1) Be preventive or defensive—such as peer reviews or
defensive auditing; (2) Be risk-protection oriented—usually involving
liability insurance; or (3) Involve out-of-court settlements. Self-
regulatory bodies such as the AICPA have long held to a tradition of
elaborate peer reviews and quality control mechanisms aimed at ensuring audit quality. The auditing industry has evolved its own system
of defensive auditing, which includes use of carefully worded engagement letters, client acceptance policies, and risk assessment of client
firms.

Auditing firms also routinely get liability insurance, although they
claim that insurance premiums are excessive. Moreover, accounting
firms actively pursue out-of-court settlements, which reduce litigation
costs through quicker settlement and often cut the original litigation
amount. For example, in the United Kingdom, Ernst & Young faced
lawsuits of $10 billion over its involvement in BCCI, but various court
judgments reduced the damages, and it is estimated that the actual
settlement has been a fraction of the original amount, in the area of $2
billion.[65]

Triggered by the Arthur Andersen meltdown, the accounting industry reopened the lobbying for reform in two key areas: (1) a return to proportionate liability from joint and several liability, and (2) a cap on auditor liability. Joint and several liability statues say that damages are to be awarded in the proportion to the amount of injury caused. When the client firm is in bankruptcy, the audit firm—as the remaining entity with financial resources—can be held liable for the entire penalty assigned to the bankrupt firm, as well as that assigned to the auditor. Accounting firms claim that they have neither the capital nor the insurance coverage to protect against joint and several liability. This could prevent them from taking on audit assignments, leaving whole sectors of the economy unable to obtain appropriate auditors.[66] The accountancy profession has also lobbied for capping auditor liability at some multiple of audit fees.

These proposals have met with mixed success. While there has been a positive reaction to joint and several liability proposals, there has been far less sympathy for a cap on auditor liability. Countries such as Australia introduced proportionate liability in 2002 while rejecting calls for cap on auditor liability.[67]

THE SYSTEM BUCKLES

In 1984, the Supreme Court, in *United States v. Arthur Young & Co.*, assigned to the accountant the role of a "public watchdog" who owes "ultimate allegiance" to the corporation's creditors and stockholders, as well as to the investing public.[68] Such a role is more in line with the public's perception of the auditor as a sentinel to detect fraud and malpractice than it is with auditors' own perceptions of their role. In either case, during the 1990s, there was very little barking by watchdogs.

As noted, it was a decade marked by large-scale bankruptcies such as those of Enron and WorldCom, and more earnings restatements than ever before. So the auditor's role was called into question fundamentally. Especially the years 1997–2001 saw an avalanche of financial restatements due to accounting irregularities—an increase of 145 percent during the period, with the sharpest growth occurring post-1999. The proportion of listed companies on the NYSE, the American Stock Exchange, and NASDAQ identified as restating their earnings reports tripled from less than 1 percent in 1997 to around 2.5 percent in 2001 and around 3 percent in 2002.[69] Another study identified 523 restatements from 1997 to 2000, with a significant increase in restatements from 1997 to 1998 and continuing increases in 1999 and 2000.[70]

Enron and Andersen—The Catalyst for Change?

One of the most significant and high-profile accounting cases involved Enron, which filed for bankruptcy on December 2, 2001. The Enron story had begun to unravel publicly less than two months earlier, when, on October 16, 2001, the company issued a press release announcing a $618 million third-quarter loss because of a $1.01 billion write-off on various investments related to Enron's broadband, telecommunications, and other businesses. That same day, although it was not part of the press release, the company announced a reduction in shareholder equity by approximately $1.2 billion. Less than a month later, on November 8, 2001, the company issued a restatement of earnings for 1997 to 2001, following a retroactive consolidation of some of its special-purpose entities. Enron indicated that there would be a reduction in reported net income of more than $580 million for the years 1997–2001 and increases in the company's debt of $711 million in 1997, $561 million in 1998, $685 million in 1999, and $628 million in 2000.

Enron's stock already had been under pressure and in decline since May 2001. Following the October announcement, in the next three weeks, Enron's stock price fell from over $33 per share to $9 by November 2001,[71] the day before management announced that the firm would restate earnings. The stock had been at more than $80 only six months earlier. The shares lost 85 percent of their remaining value over the next three weeks, after a buyout offer by an industry rival fell through.[72] As the value of its stock fell, rating agencies downgraded Enron's debt, which triggered additional major liabilities and led to a bankruptcy filing in December 2001—the largest since Texaco's bankruptcy filing in 1987.

Arthur Andersen had been Enron's independent auditor for 16 years, and after Enron's bankruptcy, public scrutiny fell on the auditors. Several charges were levied against Andersen related to the quality of its Enron audit. These centered around the fact that the firm had taken no action on Enron's questionable accounting practices, especially those related to its SPEs, even after being warned by employees at Enron and Andersen's own professional standards group.

The Andersen case took on an entirely different life when the Department of Justice alleged that Andersen's Enron team began the wholesale destruction of documents relating to Enron in October 2001, under orders from Andersen partners. So in March 2002, the Justice Department charged Andersen with deliberately destroying evidence related to its audit of Enron while an investigation was already underway, and in May 2002, the trial began. Although Andersen argued that the shredding of documents was part of a routine document retention policy, the firm was found guilty, less than a month later, of criminal obstruction of justice by shredding evidence related to the Enron affair. That same day, the firm notified regulators that it would cease to practice before the SEC, and on September 2, 2002, Andersen announced that it had surrendered to state regulators all licenses to "practice public accountancy" and was out of business. Nevertheless, Andersen appealed the conviction and the case was ultimately accepted by the U.S.

Supreme Court which unanimously overturned the judgment in May 2005 because of unclear jury instructions as to what constituted guilt. The reversal was a technical victory for Andersen, but of no practical value to the firm which by then was defunct.

The Enron and Andersen cases brought out some of the issues that had long been building in the auditing industry. First, they highlighted the issue of compromised auditor independence. Enron's SEC filings indicated that Andersen had been paid large fees for nonaudit services, in addition to its significant audit fee. Andersen also took on (outsourced) internal audit work for Enron. In addition, the relationship between Enron and Andersen was seen as a revolving door, leading to several Andersen employees crossing over to Enron to work in key positions. Although Andersen denied that provision of nonaudit services had affected the quality of its audit and indicated that it had repeatedly warned Enron's board that its accounting practices were high risk, Andersen had not documented its objections.

Andersen's own collapse also raised important issues of auditor liability, especially how it should be determined what liabilities large accounting firms have when clients go bankrupt, and whether these should be proportionately allocated among various parties to prevent firms from collapsing under the weight of class-action liabilities. And the breakup of Andersen indicated how much the major accounting firms had changed over the years.

Andersen to the end remained one of the champions of central control and had retained the motto "One firm." When trouble came, however, it found that its divided and self-interested partners could not agree on appropriate actions, and the firm became helpless to keep the worst from happening. Subsequently, its international partners across the world sold their individual practices separately to Andersen's competitors.

Auditor malfeasance at Andersen, although under intense scrutiny in the Enron debacle, was not a new phenomenon. At least two other cases were cited in court as evidence of a pattern in Andersen's history—Sunbeam and Waste Management. Sunbeam Corporation was a consumer appliance manufacturer marketing such brands as Mr. Coffee, Mixmaster, and Powermate. In the 1990s, the Sunbeam CEO, "Chainsaw" Al Dunlap, used accounting tricks such as recording contingent earnings and booking revenue months ahead of actual shipping. In 1998, Sunbeam announced that its audit committee had determined that Sunbeam was required to restate its financial statements for previous years, and that the adjustments would be material.[73] A few months later, in October 1998, Sunbeam announced a restatement of its financial results for a six-quarter period from the fourth quarter of 1996 to the first quarter of 1998, and dismissed its CEO. In February 2001, the corporation filed for bankruptcy. In 1999, a consolidated class-action suit was filed against Sunbeam, Arthur Andersen, and certain

Sunbeam principals.[74] The total settlement was $141 million, and Andersen paid $110 million of this amount—an action that surely encouraged further accounting industry class-action suits. The SEC charged the Andersen engagement partner with aiding and abetting violations at Sunbeam[75] but later dropped the fraud charges, and allowed him to settle with the SEC without admitting guilt, although he was barred from practicing accounting for three years.[76]

The second Andersen case involved Waste Management, which in 1998 issued the largest corporate restatement prior to Enron. The SEC charged Waste Management with perpetrating a massive fraud for five years. Andersen was named in the case for aiding the fraud by issuing unqualified approvals on materially misleading financial statements, which exaggerated earnings by $1.7 billion. The SEC fined Andersen $7 million in June 2001, and the firm settled with Waste Management shareholders for $220 million. Andersen was forced to promise not to sign off on spurious financial statements in the future, or be barred from practicing before the SEC. Its failure to do so in the Enron context prompted the Justice Department to charge Andersen with criminal—rather than civil—offenses, which, upon conviction, led to its instant liquidation.

Following Enron were two more large accounting scandals involving Andersen: the largest nonprofit bankruptcy in U.S. history—the Baptist Foundation of Arizona (BFA)—and the largest commercial bankruptcy, WorldCom. Both suggested that Andersen's reputation as a serial perpetrator of auditing malfeasance had continued right up until its demise. The BFA was formed in 1948 to raise funds for the church. It had invested heavily in real estate, and when the market took a downturn in Arizona, its managers remained under pressure to produce profits. Foundation officials allegedly took money from new investors to pay off existing investors in order to keep the cash flow going. As the story began to unravel, the BFA filed for bankruptcy, with debts of around $640 million against assets of around $240 million. Investors took Andersen to court, alleging that the firm had approved the false financial statements that perpetuated the fraud. Andersen stood by its audit and blamed BFA management for providing misleading information. In May 2002, after two years of investigative activity showed that Andersen had been repeatedly warned of the fraud by BFA employees, the firm agreed to pay a $217 million settlement to the foundation and its creditors.

In the same year, Andersen's largest client, WorldCom, announced that it had wrongly accounted for nearly $3.9 billion of expenses and had overstated earnings for 2001 and the first part of 2002, and that earnings would be restated. The WorldCom stock price plummeted, and the firm fell into bankruptcy, one that was twice as large as Enron's. Andersen blamed WorldCom management for the irregularities, while WorldCom's bankruptcy trustees and its new board faulted Andersen for not finding the misbehavior that it claimed had been perpetrated by previous management right under Andersen's nose.

Other Andersen clients also ended the 1990s in serious trouble, including Global Crossing, which filed for bankruptcy, and Qwest Communications, which admitted that it had used improper accounting methods and indicated that it would have to restate earnings for 1999, 2000, and 2001. Lawsuits were filed against Andersen in those cases as well, which maintained that it had conducted its audits properly. But by the time these cases came to court, Andersen was gone.

Other Audit Problems

There were many other instances of auditor malfeasance against the Big Five. In the 1980s, KPMG gave Penn Square Bank in Oklahoma a clean bill of health just before it collapsed under the weight of bad energy loans that helped take down Continental Illinois as well, America's largest bank failure. It turned out that the firm had audited only 15 percent of the banks' portfolio. KPMG also paid $75 million in 1998 to settle a group of lawsuits charging that its audits of bankrupted Orange County, California, had failed to warn about the dangers of risky investments. And in 2003, the SEC charged KPMG and its partners with allowing Xerox to manipulate its accounting to close a $3 billion gap between actual and reported results. Ernst & Young was one of the chief accounting firms embroiled in the collapse of savings-and-loan associations in the 1980s, and paid a settlement in 1992 of $400 million in connection with a dozen failed S&Ls. Ernst & Young was also embroiled in litigation over financial fraud at Cendant Corporation. In July 2002, the SEC announced action against PricewaterhouseCoopers and its broker-dealer affiliate PWC Securities for violations of auditor independence rules.

Meanwhile, in Europe, the accounting firm of Grant Thornton came in for heavy criticism in the 2004 Parmalat financial fraud in Italy. The Parmalat case came on top of two other major bankruptcies in Europe— Royal Ahold in the Netherlands and Adecco in Switzerland. Grant Thornton was the Parmalat auditor for eight years, until the firm was replaced by Deloitte & Touche in 1999, as per Italy's auditor-rotation requirement. But Grant Thornton continued to audit Parmalat's offshore financial activities in the Cayman Islands. The Parmalat fraud surfaced after revelation of a fictitious $4 billion deposit with Bank of America, and the head of Grant Thornton's Italian business and a partner were arrested and charged with falsifying the Cayman audits. As Deloitte had relied on Grant Thornton's subsidiary audits for its own audit of Parmalat, its audit unintentionally perpetuated the fraud. Given Parmalat's use of complex SPEs to disguise its true condition—evidently structured by aggressive banks and securities firms—the similarity to the Enron, WorldCom, and other major failures in the United States might have been picked up by the auditors. But this was not the case.

The financial market participants compounded the failures of the auditors—banks, securities firms, credit rating agencies, and institutional investors. Why a company such as Parmalat that claimed to have massive cash reserves would undertake large successive bond issues was never properly explored, nor, apparently, was the required due diligence performed by underwriters of the bonds, who were subsequently sued in both Italy and the United States.

Signs of regulator crackdown on accounting firms began to appear early in the new century. In April 2004, Ernst & Young, one of the (now) Big Four, was temporarily banned by the SEC from taking on new public audit clients in the United States due to issues of auditor independence. Ernst & Young had to pay $1.7 million and to "cease and desist" from future regulatory violations. The ban related to Ernst & Young's work with PeopleSoft, where it was auditor from the mid-1990s to 2000, while it had at the same time a business agreement involving software and consultancy that compromised the independence of its audit work. More damning were the words of Judge Brenda Murray, who wrote: "Despite Ernst &Young's strong denials, the evidence shows that the firm paid only perfunctory attention to the rules on auditor independence in business dealing with a client."[77]

THE SYSTEM STABILIZES

Prior to the Arthur Andersen indictment, the firm retained former Federal Reserve Board chairman Paul Volcker to attempt to mediate with the Justice Department to avoid criminal charges. Volcker immediately took the position that the string of accounting failures associated with Andersen was principally the result of the serious conflicts of interest that developed when audit firms compromised their independence by conducting a large nonaudit consulting business. He proposed that Andersen should voluntarily agree to withdraw from the consulting and to focus only, as it had in its earlier days, on auditing. The Justice Department did not commit to anything, but was thought to be amenable to discussions.

The partners of Andersen, however, were unwilling or unable to follow the Volcker course of action—thinking it inappropriate, uneconomic, and unnecessary—and instead followed a course that went right over the cliff. This may have been a poor call by the Andersen partners, but the issue of conflicting interests in the auditing profession that was once again highlighted by Volcker received much attention, including in Congress, where testimony was being taken by several committees seeking to redress the wrongs exposed by Enron's collapse. Within six months of Enron's bankruptcy came WorldCom's collapse, and the conflicts of interest in that case mirrored those exhibited in Enron and indeed extended them further. These events combined to give an impetus to efforts in Congress to pass new legislation that would reform corporate accounting, finance, and governance to prevent similar abuses in the future.

Sarbanes-Oxley on Accounting

The Sarbanes-Oxley Act of 2002, the result of this effort (the Act is examined in greater detail in chapter 10), was allowed to run its course unimpeded by the usual frictions and delays in passing controversial laws. There was overwhelmingly public support for Congress to insert itself into the picture, which was portrayed as one of corruption, greed, and exploitation of little people by corporate giants. The Act, which was pulled together in less than six months, was the most important piece of legislation to affect public securities markets since 1934. It contained 11 "titles" (sections). The most important of these dealt with the auditing and accounting issues and with broad corporate responsibilities for enhanced governance practices by boards of directors.

The accounting issues included in Sarbanes-Oxley were essentially two. First, a new Public Company Accounting Oversight Board would be formed under the direction of the SEC to establish auditing, quality control, and independence standards for the public accounting industry and to supervise and discipline firms in the industry, and there was a requirement that auditors reestablish independence by withdrawing from (most) nonaudit services businesses. So, with a single piece of legislation, a set of embedded conflicts of interest that had been growing for a least a decade and thought to be out of control was remedied. Auditors could not be significant consultants to their audit clients. Period. And they would be watched and checked closely by the new Oversight Board.

These constraints on the accounting industry, it is worth pointing out, were well within the existing powers of the SEC. The Securities Act of 1933 and the Securities Exchange Act of 1934 gave the SEC the authority to require and accept audited statements, which it could have refused to do if these did not meet its standards. But the de facto powers of the SEC had been weakened considerably over the years, and it was not (according to Arthur Levitt) able to withstand concentrated efforts to lobby Congress to threaten the SEC if it acted too powerfully or arbitrarily. So, although the new law was not really required to achieve the necessary accounting reforms, the realities of government were such that the new law was in fact needed to enforce powers already in the hands of the SEC.

Accounting Industry Regulation after Sarbanes-Oxley

The Sarbanes-Oxley Act essentially signaled that the self-regulation of the U.S. accounting industry was over.

Before, the trade organization of accountants, the AICPA, had used its own system of peer reviews, quality control procedures, and an oversight board—the Public Oversight Board (POB)—to regulate the accounting profession. The POB was set up to be an independent body—but in reality it was funded by the AICPA, thus raising questions of objectivity and independence. With the collapse of Enron and Andersen in 2001–2002 and the wave of accounting scandals, the SEC proposed moving away from self-regulation, specifically replacing peer review with independent scrutiny of standards and replacing the POB with an independent public board. Sarbanes-Oxley adopted this proposal in its requirements for the Public Company Accounting Oversight Board.

According to the Sarbanes-Oxley Act, the five members of the Public Company Accounting Oversight Board are appointed by the SEC (after consultation with the Federal Reserve and the Treasury) for five-year terms, serve on a full-time basis, and are supposed to be "financially literate." Two of the members must be (or must have been) certified public accountants (CPAs), and the remaining three must not be (and cannot have been) CPAs. The chair may be held by one of the CPA members, provided that he or she has not been engaged as a practicing CPA for five years. None of the members can "share in any of the profits of, or receive payments from, a public accounting firm," other than "fixed continuing payments" such as retirement benefits.

The Board's mandate is to (1) register public accounting firms; (2) establish or adopt "auditing, quality control, ethics, independence, and other standards relating to the preparation of audit reports for issuers"; (3) conduct inspections of accounting firms; (4) conduct investigations and disciplinary proceedings, and impose appropriate sanctions; (5) perform such other duties or functions as necessary or appropriate; (6) enforce compliance with the Act, the rules of the Board, professional standards, and the securities laws relating to the preparation and issuance of audit reports and the obligations and liabilities of accountants with respect thereto; and (7) set the budget and manage the operations of the Board and the staff of the Board. The mandate covers both U.S. and foreign accounting firms auditing U.S. companies. It is required to cooperate with professional accounting bodies such as the FASB and may adopt or reject accounting standards adopted by such bodies. The budget of the Board is covered by registration fees paid by public accounting firms.

With respect to company audits, the Board must require second-partner reviews (with both the lead and reviewing partner required to rotate every five years), must require record retention for not less than seven years, and

> must require the auditor evaluate whether the internal control structure and procedures include records that accurately and fairly reflect the transactions of the issuer, provide reasonable assurance that the transactions are recorded in a manner that will

permit the preparation of financial statements in accordance with GAAP, and a description of any material weaknesses in the internal controls.

The Board functions as a self-regulatory organization (SRO), under the auspices (and sharing the statutory authority of) the SEC. Any accounting rule changes accepted by the Board must be approved by the SEC, which also has the power to review sanctions imposed by the Board on accounting firms.

Board-supervised entities such as the FASB (previously an SRO) must (1) be a private entity; (2) be governed by a board of trustees (or equivalent body), the majority of whom are not or have not been associated persons with a public accounting firm for the previous two years; (3) be funded in a manner similar to the Board; (4) have adopted procedures to ensure prompt consideration of changes to accounting principles by a majority vote; and (5) consider, when adopting standards, "the need to keep them current and the extent to which international convergence of standards is necessary or appropriate."

Audit firms must be engaged by and be accountable to audit committees of clients' boards of directors (not just to management) and must report to the boards' audit committees all "critical accounting policies and practices to be used . . . all alternative treatments of financial information [within GAAP] that have been discussed with management . . . ramifications of the use of such alternative disclosures and treatments, and the treatment preferred by the firm."

The Sarbanes-Oxley Act requires only periodic *auditor* rotation, not rotation of *audit firms*, as in the case of Italy. This suggests that it is *individuals* who need to maintain independence, not entire firms, but ignores the fact that dysfunctional incentive structures and management practices were at the root of the Andersen debacle. This is a key issue. There is a great deal riding on auditor independence, notably the honesty of information upon which investors most rely in global financial markets.

Internationalizing the Sarbanes-Oxley Provisions

In the wake of the Enron scandal and the U.S. response to ending the era of self-regulation of the accountancy profession, other countries took a hard look at their own accounting bodies. It has been argued that the increased scrutiny attributable to the Sarbanes-Oxley Act may have led auditors to apply greater scrutiny that brought to the surface severe financial problems at various firms. As one observer noted, "these scandals serve to underline the way that the culture of the accountancy profession and the techniques of modern investment management have not helped the auditor's role as a guarantor of the integrity of the numbers on which the capitalist system relies."[78]

Europe's accounting industry has been largely self-regulated—a

1988 study showed that countries followed a broad spectrum of regulation in the accounting industry: self-assessment by firms (Austria,
Italy), peer review by a panel of auditors (Belgium), peer review on a
firm-on-firm basis (Denmark), monitoring of individual auditors
(France, Norway), external regulation (Germany, Czech Republic) and
self-regulation by the accountancy bodies (Spain, Finland, and the
United Kingdom).[79]

The United Kingdom accounting industry maintains that its self-
regulation is more robust than in the United States. The director of the
Accountancy Foundation Review Board cited several provisions of the
Sarbanes-Oxley Act as mirroring those already existing in the United
Kingdom—the need for working papers to be retained for seven years
(the United Kingdom already requires papers to be retained for six
years) and the need for second partner reviews (already required in
the United Kingdom), among others. He also argued that the United
Kingdom already goes further than the rigorous clauses of the
Sarbanes-Oxley Act. For example, while the Sarbanes-Oxley Act requires that firms with more than 100 audit clients be examined annually
(a figure he believed would cover only five such firms in the United
Kingdom), the Joint Monitoring Unit (Britain's oversight board) in-
spects the top 20 auditing firms, which cover 95 percent of the listed
companies, on an annual basis.[80]

Despite such sentiments, the fallout of the Sarbanes-Oxley Act in
terms of ending the self-regulation of the accountancy profession can
be seen in the United Kingdom as well. A poll conducted in July 2002
by the Co-ordinating Group on Audit and Accounting Issues (CGAA)
showed that auditors were split down the middle in terms of whether
monitoring of auditors should remain with the accounting bodies or
transferred to an independent regulator.[81] In 2003, the CGAA recommended the creation of a single, authoritative regulator responsible for
setting, enforcing, and monitoring accounting and auditing standards.[82]

Other countries are following suit. In Australia, the profession itself
has come up with a proposal for external oversight through a separate
unit overseen by the Financial Reporting Council (FRC).[83] The German
audit profession envisages a more ambitious, pan-European version of
the U.S. Public Company Accounting Oversight Board, with five members registered by the European Commission and all European auditing
firms to be registered.[84] In March 2004, the European Commission proposed that individual countries set up regulators similar to the U.S.
PCAOB.[85]

Long-Lasting Measures

Sarbanes-Oxley will force many changes in the public accounting system in the United States and other developed countries, removing toxic
conflicts of interest that had become embedded in the fabric of financial

markets and removing the powers of self-regulation from this important industry. It will add considerably to the expense of maintaining public financial markets, force new duties and responsibilities on various participants, and resolve yet another issue of market failure by increasing the depth and breadth of government regulation—which has rarely been seen as the sharpest and least expensive method of maintaining free markets. In the long run, the costs of Sarbanes-Oxley relative to the value of improved market efficiency will have to be assessed. This cannot be done now. But what is clear is that one of the single most important causes of market failure—false, misleading, or unclear accounting information—has been substantially removed from the system. Other matters await resolution, such as how effectively the FASB will be able to operate in determining and updating GAAP, and how much interference by corporations and legislators sympathetic to them on accounting issues will be allowed in setting accounting standards. But for now, the profession appears to have been reset to its default position, in which fair and accurate financial reporting is expected and provided.

8

The Bankers

Monitoring and influencing the way companies are governed in a market economy assigns an important role to financial intermediaries—firms that function as the "middlemen of finance." They are agents for investors and corporations using the markets, and they sometimes act as principals (using their own money) to facilitate short-term trades between clients, or to make speculative investments of their own. They are not asset holders so much as asset users in the pursuit of financial transactions. They are paid in commissions or spreads between the buy-and-sell prices on trades.

Intermediaries are proactive. They are supposed to stimulate trading and investing by their clients, and do so as best they can. They represent both sides of the capital market, the users of capital and those who supply the funds. Intermediaries operate in both retail and wholesale markets (the latter being the kinds of operations with which this study is concerned).

Prior to 1933, most large, money-center banks had subsidiaries that acted as intermediaries in wholesale finance. They acted as underwriters of new issues for corporations and (foreign) governments and engaged in brokerage and trading generally with large, wholesale market players. These banks competed with specialist securities firms ("investment banks") that avoided the banking business as being too cumbersome and capital intensive for them. After the stock market crash of 1929 and allegations of serious (but not illegal) financial market misconduct by banks, followed by massive bank failures and the onset of the Great Depression, Congress was induced to pass the Banking Act of 1933, which incorporated many banking industry reforms and included the Glass-Steagall provisions, which required banks to divest most of their securities operations to avoid risk and conflicts of interest.

After 1933, the U.S. securities industry emerged as distinctly separate from banking. Banks were to act in the financial system as deposit takers and commercial lenders, and investment banks were to act as advisers, underwriters, and traders. This functional division remained that way until the 1990s.

INDUSTRY CHANGES

The securities markets were relatively inactive until the 1950s, after which a steady increase in volume of trades developed. There was a stock market boom in the 1960s, followed by a slump in the 1970s, mainly caused by the inflationary effect of the Vietnam War, the collapse of the international monetary system, two oil crises, and years of political turmoil. The 1980s saw another stock market recovery, together with a merger boom, as overdue corporate restructuring occurred through market transactions plus two important elements of change affecting financial intermediaries. One was the boom in securities trading that resulted from the dramatic increase in the supply of government bonds during the Reagan Administration. The other was the collapse of savings-and-loans and numerous commercial banks because of market-risk mismatches between loans and deposits and overeager lending practices that produced major write-offs. The collapse required the U.S. government to intervene as a guarantor of deposits, which cost the public about $300 billion before recoveries. The commercial banks that failed and had to be sold or rescued by the Federal Deposit Insurance Corporation. Others that did not fail were deemed to be so weak as to be placed on a special watch-list and restricted from doing anything that might make their financial conditions worse.

The Banks Decline

Major banks such as Citibank, Chase Manhattan, and Bank of America were on this list during the 1980s, and essentially prevented from expanding or exploiting new business opportunities during what was otherwise a market boom. The investment banks benefited greatly from the condition of the banks during this time. Deposits were drawn away to money market mutual funds, which invested the proceeds in treasury bills and commercial paper and which constrained the banks in an important line of business—short-term working capital loans. Term loans were replaced by lower cost bond issues or medium-term notes in the markets. Lucrative merger and restructuring transactions had little room for banks, except as providers of lines of credit and high-risk leveraged buyout loans. Hemmed in by government restrictions on their activities, banks watched helplessly as much of their business disappeared into the capital markets. The investment banks, fattened

by profits from trading, mergers, equity issues, and restructuring transactions, rolled their operations overseas and began to invest their capital in new ways, including in making loans to corporations.

THE BANKS RECOVER

In the 1990s, the banks had worked their way out of their "penalty
box." They were recapitalized and streamlined under new and more
rigorous management. They merged and acquired each other at a rapid
pace—more banking acquisitions occurred in the 1990s than in any
other industry—consolidating some of the major players into much
larger entities. The distress of the 1980s allowed many banks to get
around legal restrictions on interstate banking that had existed since
the 1920s (and have since been repealed), so many banks decided to
stick to consumer and regional banking, which they understood, as
opposed to following the wholesale business into the capital markets,
which they did not. Still, a few banks, the largest, chose to try to
compete for leadership positions in the wholesale finance sector as well,
which meant that they had to devise strategies to enable them to do
so.
    There were three legs to these strategies. First, the Glass-Steagall
restrictions had to be reduced or eliminated so these banks could legally
enter the business. The large banks lobbied hard for this, claiming that
they were being prevented from offering competition in a market dominated by a handful of investment banks, and that foreign banks were
not similarly restricted. They also challenged the complex regulatory
limits and found a number of loopholes. Most important was Section
20 of the Glass-Steagall provisions of the 1933 Banking Act, which
allowed the Federal Reserve to permit a limited amount of otherwise
prohibited transactions to occur. The Fed gradually opened the door
to banking participation in the capital markets in the early 1990s, and
several banks set up special Section 20 subsidiaries to function as investment banks.
    The second leg was to hire experienced teams of investment bankers
and have them effect the culture changes necessary to enable their
Section 20 subsidiaries to compete effectively. This approach was found
to be difficult, and produced mixed results whenever it was tried. So
the third approach was attempted—to acquire investment banks and
let them compete from the powerful platform of a financial conglomerate. This strategy was seen most dramatically in the acquisition by
Travelers Group of Citicorp in 1998—despite the fact that combining
of banking, insurance, asset management, and broker-dealer businesses
was prohibited at the time. The transaction turned out to be a catalyst
for the ultimate repeal in 1999 of Glass-Steagall and the Bank Holding
Company Act, which had been working its way through Congress for
years, in the form of the Gramm-Leach-Bliley Act.

This regulatory liberalization triggered a number of other securities firm acquisitions by banks, especially by Chase Manhattan (which had itself been acquired by Chemical Bank in 1996 and acquired JP Morgan in 2001 and Bank One in 2004), Bank of America, Bankers Trust (acquired by Deutsche Bank in 1999), First Union (now Wachovia), UBS, and Crédit Suisse. These acquisitions usually resulted in a form of integration between the bank's corporate lending business and its investment banking activities, and at the end of the 1990s (the height of the bubble), the new banks were aggressive in lending money to clients whose investment banking business they coveted. They promoted themselves as "multiline" financial service firms with a lot more to offer clients than "monoline" investment banks because of their "big balance sheet" capabilities. This strategy required finding companies that needed bank financing and at the same time were generating substantial investment banking business. Such companies included the "new economy" firms of the bubble period, including the technology, telecommunications, and restructured "old" economy giants that were aggressively auctioning off their businesses to the highest bidders. Once in the door with these companies, the banks hoped there would be a great deal of investment banking fee business to pick up—merger advisory, stock underwriting, brokerage, and one of the banks' specialties, organizing "special purpose entities" and structured (off-balance-sheet) financing, using aggressive and innovative new ideas.

INVESTMENT BANKING IN THE 1990s

Meanwhile, the clients for wholesale financial services were enjoying a buyers' market. There were always several contenders for every large transaction, and rates and commissions began to show the effects of more vigorous competition, some of which was supplied by the newly enabled commercial banks. Corporate clients began to auction their business. Some insisted that, if the banks and investment banks wanted their fee business, they should extend credit to them, and in addition should be shown favorable treatment by banks' research analysts and stock traders, and by its most creative corporate finance thinkers. The firms did want the business, and did aim to please. Competition was intense. Corporations were not loyal to their bankers if they could find a better deal, and the big-balance-sheet strategies put pressure of the less heavily capitalized investment banks. Business volume was high and the fees to be earned potentially enormous. In the process, the banks lost whatever ability they once had had to discipline their clients. Someone else would do the deal if they criticized too much. As the bubble inflated, these issues became ever more compelling.

By the end of the 1990s, some of the larger banks had acquired significant securities and insurance business capacity. They had become multiple business platforms, often by acquiring other, low-growth financial businesses at high prices, and hoped to recover their invest-ments by cross-selling the new services to both old and new customers. They were not only lenders but market-makers, principal investors, underwriters, advisers, brokers, asset managers, insurance underwrit-ers, and sometimes also private bankers to members of corporate man-agement. They were involved in selling many services and products to many different types of customers in many different roles. The tradi-tional, stand-alone investment banks were not quite so complex, but they likewise offered many types of services to a variety of customers in different roles, all of this under unusually stiff competitive condi-tions.

Competition was often imposed by clients hoping to squeeze sup-pliers as much as possible. "Your competitor offered me X, so you should too." In time, X came to include, implicitly, analyst "buy" rec-ommendations on the company's stock, help in organizing tricky off-balance-sheet deals in which the bank took a piece itself, margin loans and allocations of hot IPOs to top management, and, perhaps most important, showing the good sense not to raise objections or ask too many questions. Existing regulations and laws did not appear at the time to preclude these competitive responses, as long as the bank itself was not deliberately engaging in fraud or deception. Indeed, the gov-ernment had just deregulated the banking industry to increase com-petition in finance, bankers may have thought at the time, so the ad-ditional competition was just what was wanted and expected.

The 1990s were active for investment bankers in all parts of their domain, but after 1995 (the year Netscape went public), the technology sector began to dominate and caught the imagination of investors like nothing since the Tulip Bubble centuries earlier. Far more important technologies—electric power, the telephone, the automobile, the air-plane, and television—had been introduced without a comparable re-action by the stock market. But this time heads were turned as never before. Institutional demand for Internet-related securities (i.e., hard-ware, software, and applications) became intense—no fund manager wanted to miss this thing—and this demand passed through the in-vestment bankers to the companies themselves, many of them just a few years old (if that) with hardly any revenues and large operating losses.

Before the mid-1990s, major investment banks would have rejected any request to take such companies public. After all, the firms had standards for initial public offerings that they would manage, including that the companies must have had at least a few years of profitable operations.

The New World of Wholesale Banking

The larger and more traditional banks hung back, while some of the smaller, more technology-oriented investment banks jumped in to make large profits on late-stage private equity investments and bridge loans, IPOs, follow-on equity issues, and merger-and-acquisition advisory work, as the companies followed their natural maturation and progression. It became clear that there was a lot of money involved in such progressions, so the major firms began to rethink their positions. The business would make sense, they thought, if banks could identify very good companies early on, take a supportive and sponsoring stake, and then manage all their subsequent financing requirements.

The key to this business lay with finding the very good companies early, and wrapping them up. Neither was easy. Internet technology was new, amorphous, and sometimes hard to see in terms of the commercial possibilities. The companies themselves were often organized by peculiar young computer "nerds" with no business experience or leadership qualities. They usually had some venture capital backing, but even this was often from newcomers to the startup business who seemed to be willing to bet on anything. No one employed at major investment banks in the early 1990s had any idea about the Internet. So the search began for Internet "experts," who were usually supplied by the banks by converting equity analysts who volunteered. A few were solicited from Silicon Valley businesses, but for the most part, Wall Street trained its own research analysts, who were then encouraged to go bounty-hunting for Internet companies. And, since almost any company that made it to market did well during the euphoria, it was hard to find an Internet company the analysts did not like.

One reason was that analysts were paid for any business they discovered or helped to bring in. This followed a longstanding Wall Street practice—one that had never produced significant problems before— of paying analysts a "teamwork bonus" for services rendered to other departments or divisions of the firm. An analyst in the forest products industry might come across a privately owned timber company and refer it to the firm's investment bankers. Or, in order to evaluate a potential timber company stock issue, the investment bankers might ask the opinion of the experienced forest products analyst, who would thereafter be restricted from writing about or recommending the stock for a considerable period of time, to his or her professional disadvantage, which required that a bonus be awarded. After all, no Wall Street research department directly contributed any revenues to the firm at all, so everything the analysts did was seen as contributing to revenues at units elsewhere in the firm. It seemed natural to reward contributions for what they were, although prior to 1990 the contributions of other business units to analyst compensation were comparatively modest.

Once a promising Internet company was identified, the firm had to get itself retained. In the beginning, the bankers were shown prospective Internet issuers by venture capitalists or other advisers, who valued the sponsorship role to be played by the banker. But after a few issues soared to extraordinary post-offering price levels, and institutional demand filtered in, the banks started to look for companies earlier in their development. But even then, they often found several other banks already on the scene. The companies were frequently advised by sophisticated investors or advisers who knew which banks would be good sponsors, and what to press these banks for: (1) A strong institutional commitment to achieve broad distribution of the issue and to keep the aftermarket from skyrocketing and then plunging; (2) Favorable after-offering research coverage by a respected analyst, which was critical in maintaining institutional interest; (3) Market-making, to provide liquidity for investors going forward; and (4) The ability to assist the company in the merger market later on. Sometimes the bank would be allowed to buy some stock in the company six months or so before an IPO was decided. There were many tests to pass to be selected as manager of an IPO. And even then, the banks aspired to be appointed as "lead" or "bookrunning" manager in order to control the highly lucrative distribution and sales of the issue and the allocation of shares to investors.

Most of the firms believed they had established a rational process to pursue this business. They would hire and appropriately compensate good people to find the top companies. Then, already convinced of a company's potential, they would readily sponsor and recommend the company to investors, and become a loyal part of its advisory team for the future. This is the way business had been done with IPOs before the bubble—although the companies were never quite so undeveloped and fragile, nor was there such an inexplicable demand for their shares from institutional investors. Those investors were assumed to know what they were doing and to be able to look after themselves.

Once selected as lead manager, the bank would begin the process of bringing the company to market. This involved solid due diligence to be sure the prospectus information was accurate. Indeed, prospectuses were written in a highly conservative manner, listing every conceivable thing that could go wrong with the company in the future, such that they would have been a great discouragement to marketing had anyone read them or took their warnings seriously. Under the securities laws, underwriters share prospectus liability equally with issuers. But in the 1990s, very few cases were brought against underwriters for this reason, despite the technology mania and the long period during which it lasted.

Pricing an IPO was complex; there was no market price to base it on, nor could the companies be easily valued, because they had no earnings and no immediate prospect of earnings. In most cases, the companies were selling new stock (not stock owned by insiders) in the IPO to raise additional capital. Sales of insider stock could occur in follow-on offerings at what was expected to be a significantly higher price. A sharp first-day boost in price was seen to favor the insiders as much as the investors, so "underpricing" was usually not resisted too much. Underwriters knew, however, that the issue would have to be approved by state securities regulators in order to be sold to the investing public, and some of the regulators were skeptical of prices that did not seem justified by the facts, and this also contributed to IPO underpricing. Arguably, the toughest state securities regulators had more to do with setting the price than did the salespeople and bankers managing the issue. The higher the price, of course, the greater the underwriting risk that attends an unsold issue. Bankers looked to the precedent of other issues to set their initial price thinking, and refined it as purchase orders came in.

Finally came the task of allocating a finite number of shares in a hot IPO to the many investors who wanted them. In an underwriting, by agreement, the underwriters as a group purchase the shares from the company at a price and commission (for arranging and distributing the issue) fixed just before the offering. The shares then belong to the underwriters, to do with as they see fit, while abiding by securities laws that require, among many other things, that the underwriters sell all the shares (and not retain any for themselves) and do so only at the price agreed in the underwriting agreement. If the issue rises in price right away, the underwriters benefit only to the extent that their holding (at risk) period is shorter. The investors clamoring for shares, however, benefit greatly—especially if they choose to "flip" the stock as soon as they get it after the initial price "pop" has occurred. If they do flip the stock, then the shares have to be sold again to another investor, and so on, until the issue comes to rest at some price and some sort of ultimate distribution has been achieved. Underwriters do their best to affect a sensible final distribution, but this can be difficult in hot markets with many flippers.

To illustrate the economics of an IPO allocation, assume a company issues 1,000,000 shares at $20 per share for $20,000,000. For transactions of this size, underwriters usually charge 7 percent for their work ($1,400,000), half of which is paid as sales commissions and the other half is divided—although not equally, since it is the lead manager who does all the work—among all members of the underwriting syndicate. An investor receiving an allocation of, say, 5,000 shares (0.5 percent of the deal) may sell it later the same day at $100 if the deal is very hot, for a one-day profit of $400,000. The first-day seller (the "flipper") probably does not have to put up any money, because both trades occur and are settled at the same time a few days later. Needless to say, in the late 1990s, when the average IPO was valued at much more than $20 million, and there were many IPOs each year, everyone wanted to be a flipper, though some thoughtful institutional investors wanted to accumulate shares for the long term. To do this, they often had to acquire additional shares in the aftermarket (not having been allocated their requested amount in the initial offering). Bankers knew who they were and tried to get shares to them. But sometimes getting a large

Laddering

IPO allocation meant that the institutional investor was required by the banker to make several additional purchases at rising prices in the aftermarket. This is a process called "laddering," which may be interpreted as a market-rigging violation of securities laws, since the investing public is unaware of the private aftermarket purchase agreements.

The IPO lead managers (of which Crédit Suisse First Boston was the technology market leader) were under great pressure to accommodate investors' demand for IPO allocations. Some investors were grateful for what they received, appreciating the underwriters' problems in trying to effect a broad distribution of the shares. Many, however, were not at all grateful, and inferred that they would cut off commissions or other business with the underwriter unless they were allocated more shares. Some of these, notably hedge funds and big mutual funds, were important customers of the investment banks. Some were wealthy families who had entrusted the firms to manage their money for them. Some offered inducements to the investment bank to accommodate them, some cajoled and pleaded, others threatened. The firms wanted to do right by their important customers and resist being bullied, but it usually meant that no one would be happy with the bank's IPO allocation performance. Of course, if the bank had a pre-IPO equity stake in the firm and expected to do other business for the issuing company in the future, it would stand to make quite a bit more than its share of the 7 percent underwriting commission.

Telecommunications

The telecommunications industry was likewise experiencing enormous upheaval during the 1990s as a result of deregulation, new technologies, and large mergers, acquisitions, and divestitures. A new set of entrepreneurs had risen to the top of the industry, and they were in a race with each other to secure a dominant share of the market. There were many different types of players, from very different domains (land-line telephone, cellular, cable, Internet, and satellite). The largest merger-and-acquisition deals of the decade were all done in this sector—AOL's acquisition of Time Warner ($165 billion), Vodafone's acquisition of Mannesmann ($180 billion), MCI-WorldCom ($133 billion), and Olivetti-Telecom Italia ($60 billion). The industry is very capital intensive, which is ideal for large banks seeking to secure investment banking mandates by aggressively offering bank credit. Many telecom companies saw themselves as the "new economy" firms because they had taken tired old businesses and converted them into high-growth, entrepreneurially driven companies that were capitalizing on massive restructuring of the telecommunications industry. The CEOs of the leading telecom companies were well known for being aggressive and hard-driving and demanding a lot from bankers. The CEOs wanted three things from the bankers: (1) Help with achieving a high stock price with which to be able to acquire other companies; (2) Favorable access to debt capital markets; and (3) Assistance with "structured" (or off-balance-sheet) financing that would preserve their credit standing in the capital markets. They expected loyalty and company support, quality service at short notice, and creative thinking and innovation to enable them to do new things differently.

Jack Grubman, at Citigroup's Salomon Smith Barney investment bank, was an experienced telecommunications industry analyst who had converted enthusiastically to "new telecom." He could offer companies like WorldCom what it needed most, an endorsement of their strategies and activities to boost the stock price, which would in turn validate these strategies and activities. Grubman also had influence with the bankers who controlled Citibank's balance sheet, and he became a favorite of WorldCom CEO Bernie Ebbers.

Because of the business he brought in, Grubman quickly became a star at Salomon Smith Barney, and began to exercise some of a star's prerogatives. As a valuable employee, he became known to Citigroup's CEO, Sandy Weill, and they exchanged favors with each other. Grubman played a much bigger role in the relationship with WorldCom than a security analyst normally would. He was entrusted with confidential information, he attended board meetings as a friend and adviser of the company, and he continued to write up the company favorably. Such relationships are not necessarily illegal or inappropriate—it all depends on what the analyst does with the information made available by the firm.

Meanwhile, Citigroup was busy lending money to the telecommunications industry and assisting its leading players. Citibank made a personal loan to WorldCom CEO Bernie Ebbers to buy a $60 million property in Canada and funded a $500 million loan to a company controlled by Ebbers to buy timberland, along with margin loans to buy additional WorldCom stock. Citibank syndicated other WorldCom loans, and sold its bonds to investors, while promoting its stock activities, which continued until not long before the largest corporate bankruptcy in American history.

Other firms in the banking industry preferred to emphasize ingenious transactions that would enable telecommunications companies to remove or revalue assets on their balance sheets. For example, two companies might swap holdings of "dark fiber"—unleased fiber-optic cable—at an arbitrarily established price that was reported as a profitable sale of the asset by one company to the other. Banks, after all, were supposed to be competing aggressively to acquire investment banking market share by using their big-balance-sheet strategies. As they operated multiple lines of business with many different types of customers and counterparties, they were performing multiple transactions that involved potential conflicts.

Structured Finance   *made up*

Banks began to offer "structured finance" in the 1980s to assist LBO transactions and to create "synthetic securities" through the use of swaps and other derivatives contracts. Before that time, banks had long helped organize sale-lease transactions of various sorts to take advantage of tax and accounting wrinkles that would, for example, enable a corporation to exchange on-balance-sheet debt for off-balance-sheet lease obligations, or to create a new security that would have the tax advantages of debt while retaining the balance sheet advantages of equity. Such highly technical transactions are dependent on current interpretation of accounting principles and on tax rulings or opinion letters. The rules changed continually, as tax and accounting positions changed, but corporations believed that they had the right to use whatever favorable tax and accounting treatments were legal at the time. Bankers, of course, could earn large fees by arranging such transactions. They could earn an even larger fee if they were able to invent the new way to do things. And they could earn still more by directly providing the funding for such deals.

Many large corporations engaged in some form of structured finance. Such deals were common in highly leveraged and capital-intensive industries such as energy. Enron, of course, was a chronic user of structured finance deals, having set up several hundred SPEs. If handled strictly by the rules, these transactions were legitimate, even if poorly understood by shareholders. The stock analysts and rating agencies did understand them, when they were properly disclosed, so that the information about them did reach the market, even if all market participants did not necessarily follow the details.

Some deals were made overly tempting. For example, Merrill Lynch was actively involved in structuring and financing an SPE for Enron called LJM2, which conducted energy trades with Enron (and whose CEO was simultaneously Enron's CFO). Merrill, perhaps inappropriately, was both a lender to and an investor in LJM2—as were, no less inappropriately, a number of senior Merrill executives and unaffiliated private and institutional investors advised by the firm. Merrill also structured a repurchase transaction for Enron involving a number of power-generation barges in Nigeria. Allegedly, the sole purpose of the LJM2 and Nigerian barge transactions was to enable them to be treated as off-balance-sheet transactions, and thus potentially misrepresent Enron's financials to the market.[1] At the same time, Merrill performed a range of other advisory and underwriting services for Enron, provided equity analyst coverage, and was one of Enron's principal derivatives trading counterparties. Merrill's relationship with Enron provided an array of incentives for the firm to make money from the company by going along with questionable transactions or arrangements promoted by the corporation, all at the expense of investors in various Enron securities. Eventually, four Merrill bankers were convicted on conspiracy and fraud charges in the case, while Merrill paid an $80 million fine on Enron-related transactions.

Conflicts of Interest

Potential conflicts of interest are and long have been a fact of life among the financial firms that help direct the many-faceted flow of capital in the modern economy. Most firms endeavor to ensure that the conflicts that arise in their business are not exploited or otherwise allowed to endanger clients. They can do this by withdrawing from transactions, by waiting until the conflict has been resolved before proceeding in the pursuit of their own interests, and by being very careful to gather all information about the existence of conflicts so that potentially damaging transactions are not taken on inadvertently. Firms routinely take legal advice on potential conflicts, and act to ensure that confidentiality of all client information is maintained.

Nevertheless, conflicts of interest emerged in the banking and brokerage industries in the 1990s with greater frequency and complexity than ever before. This is partly because of the massive increase in market volume in the 1990s, and because of a far greater tendency than in the past for banking firms to act in the market with their own money as market-makers, proprietary traders, and lenders. In addition, as noted, the deregulation of the banking industry prompted several large commercial banks to engage vigorously in the securities business, arguably without building into the system adequate safeguards against abuse of conflicts caused by combining banking and securities activities—that is, the very conflicts that helped give rise to the 1933 Glass-Steagall provisions in the first place. As consolidation occurred in financial services, almost all of the leading investment banks became publicly traded businesses as well—Goldman Sachs went public in 1999, the last major investment bank to do so. The banks had access to inexpensive public-market capital, but this invariably came with performance expectations. Meeting those expectations often meant taking more risk; accordingly, some of the risk was taken by permitting the magnitude of conflicts to grow and become more complex, which they did throughout the 1990s, until they reached levels that were nearly impossible to control. In a pay-for-performance environment as intense as it was in the late 1990s, even when conflicts were known, they were frequently ignored or skirted.

THE SYSTEM RESPONDS

In December 2001, Enron filed for bankruptcy under Chapter 11, declaring on- and off-balance-sheet liabilities of more than $60 billion.[2] As a consequence, the banks and securities firms that had helped design and execute some of the structured finance transactions (and in some cases marketed them to other clients) were charged with assisting Enron in committing securities fraud. In July 2003, JP Morgan Chase and Citigroup agreed to pay $193 million and $127 million, respectively, in fines and penalties (without admitting or denying guilt) to settle SEC and New York State charges of financial fraud, which in turn encouraged civil suits and risked some of the banks' loans being exposed to "equitable subordination" (to other lenders) in the Enron bankruptcy proceedings.[3] According to the report of the Enron bankruptcy examiner, Citigroup alone was associated with over $3.83 billion in Enron financing. The report concluded that both Citigroup and JP Morgan "had actual knowledge of the wrongful conduct of these transactions, helped structure, promote, fund and implement transactions designed solely to materially misrepresent Enron's financials, and caused significant harm to other creditors of Enron."[4]

Bankruptcy Liabilities

In the $103 billion WorldCom bankruptcy in 2002, Citigroup was identified as having had many roles and relationships with the company. It was serving simultaneously as research analyst recommending purchase of the stock, it advised WorldCom management on strategic and financial matters, it maintained an active lending and underwriting relationship (including making large loans to the CEO), and it served as exclusive pension fund adviser to WorldCom. It executed significant stock option trades for WorldCom executives as the options vested, while at the same time conducting proprietary trading for its own account in WorldCom stock. All at the same time, Citigroup was representing the company, independent investors, and the bank itself in transactions that generated substantial earnings for the firm.

The broader the range of services that a financial firm provides to an individual client, the greater the possibility that conflicts of interest will compound in any given case, and the more they compound, the more likely they are to damage the firm. This is particularly so in the wholesale banking industry, which is both heavily regulated and subject to civil litigation, and where transactions are large and highly visible. The agency costs generated by such exposure to conflicts are ultimately paid for by the firm's shareholders.

Certainly Citigroup, and JP Morgan Chase, the country's two largest banking groups in 2000 and the most active banking competitors in the investment banking business, paid a heavy price for their activities in the late 1990s. These banks had roles in almost all of the major corporate bankruptcies of the period, and most of the other corporate scandals. They were sued by regulators, by law enforcement officials, by other banks, by major debt holders, and by stock investors. Citigroup announced a $5 billion after-tax write-off in the second quarter of 2004, related to settlements of WorldCom and other litigation. This followed a $1.3 billion after-tax write-off in 2002. Similarly, JP Morgan Chase set aside $2.3 billion for litigation reserves in 2004, following a $1.3 billion write-off in 2002. Citigroup alone was estimated at the time to be likely to experience pretax loan losses, fees, fines, and expenses related to defending itself against alleged regulatory, criminal, and civil infractions in excess of $10 billion in total. These charges are not a large cost relative to the banks' net worth or market capitalizations, but it is about half of what they earned from their investment banking activities during the years 1998–2001, when most of the damage was actually done. This must be viewed as a major setback to the big-balance-sheet, full-service strategies espoused by both banks during the late 1990s.

In the postbubble period, there were many similar efforts to extract fines and penalties from those thought to have shared in the responsibility for investor losses from corporate bankruptcies or other failures. It is understandable that investors with claims to make will bring them to those who still have money—which bankrupt companies and their managements do not. In the case of WorldCom and Enron (and there were a great many more bankruptcies in this period), the big losers were invariably the lenders and bond investors as well as the equity holders.

Among the losers were numerous public institutions, such as the University of California and other institutional investors, who were prepared to organize class-action suits against the banks involved. Such suits are commonplace in American finance and, once vetted by a judge and allowed to proceed to trial, are usually settled privately out of court. But there has to be merit to the cases for the settlements to be large, or indeed for them to be brought at all. In the years after the bubble, billions of dollars of financial class-action suits were settled, with each bank standing on its own record. Some paid a lot, some very little, depending on individual circumstances. Those paying the most were the most deeply committed to multiline business platforms and strategies, from which the banks had developed seriously conflicting interests with their clients and counterparties.

Internationally as well, the role of the major banks came into question. In the Parmalat case, for example, the company's bankruptcy administrator in 2004 filed suit in New Jersey (where both Parmalat and the banks had substantial business interests) against Citigroup for helping the Italian dairy group to obscure the company's financials through structured transactions, while helping to sell its bonds and channeling company funds to executives through its private banking relationships. The suit was filed one day after Parmalat settled an SEC suit that did not fine the company but required it to institute far-reaching governance reforms after it emerged from bankruptcy in 2005. Parmalat's suit argued that its $10 billion in losses were a "direct result" of activities in which Citigroup participated by "knowingly structuring financing . . . with the intentional purpose of disguising Parmalat's debt and artificially increasing its cash flow from operations."[5] The suit was thought to be the forerunner of additional suits against Bank of America, UBS, Crédit Suisse First Boston, Morgan Stanley, Deutsche Bank, and Banca Intesa, among others.

Public Prosecutions

The market failures after the 1990s were so substantial that they inflamed the public—at least as expressed in the media. The inflamation was such that politics necessarily got involved—terrible things had happened, and somebody had to pay. The Justice Department appointed a special high-level Enron task force to bring charges against corporate executives, which later changed direction and evolved into a more generalized task force on corporate crime. Ultimately, federal prosecutors brought charges of "obstruction of justice" (not fraud) against Arthur Andersen, Frank Quattrone of CSFB, and (unrelatedly) Martha Stewart. These cases were all largely circumstantial, but they resulted in convictions by juries and, for the latter two, jail time. Criminal charges of fraud were subsequently brought against some of the most visible corporate executives of the time, including the CEOs and other top executives of WorldCom, Enron, Tyco, Adelphia, and HealthSouth. By June 2005, criminal convictions had been obtained of the CEOs of WorldCom, Tyco, and Adelphia; one CEO, Richard Scrushy of HealthSouth, was acquitted of all charges.

The SEC has the power to bring civil charges against any corporation, accounting firm, or bank that it believes may have violated federal securities laws. These laws (which include SEC "rules" issued by its staff) are extensive and complex, and are generally thought to require a good understanding of the securities business and the industry concerned in order to investigate allegations comprehensively, and to bring charges fairly. The federal laws operate alongside state securities laws, which are usually not involved with major financial market matters, and state corporation laws that address the duties of officers and directors. Securities law is a special subset of the corporate legal profession. In 2002, the SEC was headed by Harvey Pitt, a distinguished securities lawyer who had, however, represented accounting and banking firms before being appointed to the SEC. Pitt was inclined to stick to the laws and regulations at his disposal, and was seen by some at the time as being too methodical and studied to respond with the urgency demanded by the public—and maybe too tied-in with the accounting and securities industries from his previous career to pursue them appropriately.

Nevertheless, the enforcement division of the SEC had been active all along. In late 2001, it received a tip that IPO allocations managed by Crédit Suisse First Boston were improperly conducted. Newspaper reports followed that CSFB, the leading manager of technology IPOs during the late 1990s, had taken kickbacks from investors begging to be allocated shares in the issues. It was said that CSFB had asked some investors—hedge funds, apparently—to return a portion (between a third and two-thirds) of the profits that had been made on the IPOs through overpriced brokerage transactions in other securities, or by purchasing more of the IPO in the rising aftermarket through laddered transactions to "support" the deal. Later it was suggested that CSFB may have used the power of allocating the IPOs to reward corporate clients and potential clients with generous grants at the offering price, hoping for and expecting investment banking business in return. This process was called "spinning."

In January 2002, the SEC announced a settlement with CSFB of kick-back and related charges associated with its IPO business, in which the bank would pay a fine of $100 million. The full details of CSFB's conduct, and any defense it might have, were not released. CSFB, by then under a new CEO, agreed—without admitting guilt—to pay the fine in order to settle the issue, and the SEC was happy to avoid a trial in which it would have to prove that what CSFB did was actually illegal. Since underwriters have a great deal of leeway in allocating shares in an IPO, and since damages are hard to assess, the case might have been difficult for the SEC to win. The settlement, however, triggered an avalanche of class-action litigation against underwriters of IPOs, with over 300 such suits being filed. In June 2003, the lawyers involved in these class actions reached a proposed settlement between the issuer-defendants (and their officers and directors) and the plaintiffs that would guarantee at least $1 billion in payments to investors. The case against 55 investment bankers was subject to continuation without settlements.

In early 2002, a new party entered the lists on behalf of those allegedly victimized by bank actions. Eliot Spitzer, attorney general of the state of New York, was armed with a state statute dating back to 1921, the Martin Act, which provided extraordinary powers to state officers prosecuting a criminal or civil case of securities fraud, the essence of which was that motivation did not have to be proved, only that there were damages. (By contrast, the SEC could not bring criminal charges. Only the Justice Department could do that under federal law, and it had to establish a motive or purpose.) Under the Martin Act, the simple fact that something had happened could be enough to bring a case, even a criminal case, to trial. Any financial services firm charged with a criminal offense could suffer devastating consequences, as was demonstrated by Arthur Andersen's experience. Even a criminal indictment could be seriously and possibly fatally damaging to a financial firm, which could expect instantly to lose both clients and credit facilities as a result.

Spitzer announced that he was investigating the high-tech research recommendations of several broker-dealers, looking for cases in which analysts falsely promoted stocks in exchange for investment banking business. He began by issuing subpoenas for all of the e-mail files of several firms. Then he put these through a search process that was programmed to look for key words. Through this, he was able to review many thousands of e-mails quickly, and harvest those of relevance to his investigation. Some were leaked to the press. Henry Blodgett of Merrill Lynch was embarrassed by comments that revealed in salty language that some of the stocks he recommended were not worthy of his own recommendations. Jack Grubman, of Citigroup's Salomon Smith Barney, was surprised to find his deep involvement with WorldCom's CEO and his relationship with Citigroup's chairman, Sanford Weill, fully revealed. This relationship was described by Grubman to suggest that Weill, a director of AT&T, wanted him to revise his negative stock rating on AT&T so as to enable Citigroup to receive a mandate for a coming stock issue. Spitzer then began investigating Weill, and although no charges were brought, Weill abruptly resigned in 2003 as Citigroup CEO while remaining as chairman.

Spitzer's information set off a furore of press commentary about the insincerity of Wall Street analysts, and in turn a number of legal actions against analysts and their firms were filed. In July 2003, however, two federal judges in New York dismissed suits against several major firms, noting that investors eager to take on risks of investing in technology stocks were responsible for their own investment losses. These cases were the first in which the tide against Wall Street was rolled back.

However, Spitzer's bold and dramatic actions quickly seized control of the headlines and made him appear to be the voice of government in bringing justice to the badlands of the securities markets. Harvey Pitt of the SEC, himself already under pressure for appearing less active than Spitzer, was taken aback. The SEC, not New York State, had jurisdiction over the federal securities markets. Spitzer's actions were not only interfering but also were making the SEC look ineffective. To the public, Spitzer seemed like a courageous public servant protecting the small investor. To the industry, Spitzer seemed to be an unpredictable demagogue, willing to do anything that worked for the headline value (he soon became a candidate for governor), who was seeking to blame Wall Street because the market went down and people had lost enormous amounts of money. Spitzer, especially with the Martin Act, was far more dangerous to the industry than Pitt, who in any event was replaced by the Bush administration in 2003 by William Donaldson, a former Wall Street executive.

In early 2003, Spitzer, surrounded by SEC officials and other regulatory figures, announced an agreement in principle between regulators and the investment banks to resolve conflicts of interest in their research activities. There were many details to be worked out, and it was not until late April 2003 that Spitzer and his cohort of other regulators announced that a "global" settlement had been reached with the 10 largest securities firms for $1.4 billion, part to be fines and penalties, part to be set aside for shareholder claims, and part to fund reforms in Wall Street research.

This was the largest such settlement in the history of Wall Street, and in some ways the least likely. Conspiracy is always hard to prove, especially when the conspirators are vigorous competitors for every scrap of business that comes along, and no individual executives were named as having conspired or otherwise committed fraud. For all the research complaints published in the media and mentioned in press conferences, only two out of thousands of industry analysts—Blodgett and Grubman—were identified and sanctioned, while several other high-profile high-tech analysts of the period were never criticized. Conduct related to IPOs was also singled out, but again with no specific individuals mentioned or charges brought.

Citigroup, burdened with Grubman and the legacy of WorldCom, had the biggest share ($400 million) of the fines, followed by Merrill Lynch and CSFB ($200 million each), but all of the top firms paid a share of the settlement. The settlement also required that the industry accept 10 structural reforms in their business practices, provide enhanced disclosure, and agree to contract with independent research providers to deliver alternative research opinions to the banks' clients for five years, and that $80 million of the settlement to used for "investor education." Apparently, the idea of integrating reforms with penalties was Spitzer's, and, contrary to prior experience, the SEC and the others went along.

The industry's view of the settlement was that it was bludgeoned through unfairly and without much due process, by the threat of criminal charges under the Martin Act. Going to trial in New York state against Eliot Spitzer, where the verdict might be unfavorable no matter what defense was presented, was not attractive to any of the firms. Agreeing to the settlement, however, allowed all of the firms to admit no guilt (helpful in the inevitable class-action litigation to come) and to close the books on the matter and get on with business.

The media and the public in general seemed to believe that justice had been done. Maybe the firms did not conspire or commit fraud according to the technicalities of the law, some said, but the popular view seemed to be that the firms had made unconscionable amounts of money during the bubble period, when they were really just out for themselves, not their clients: "It is only $1.4 billion divided up among the lot of them, so they can certainly afford it." For legal experts and scholars, this settlement would have to be regarded as a form of regulation by threat of prosecution, or as application of "public justice," or trial by the press, without regard to niceties of the law.

There was little time or interest in the spring of 2003 to consider the legal principles and philosophies of the global settlement. The public was satisfied, and Spitzer and the others were ready to move on, and began next to investigate the spinning of IPOs to favored customers or prospects. In June of 2003, the regulators questioned more than 50 CEOs and investment banking executives. In September 2003, Eliot

Spitzer filed a civil lawsuit demanding that five officials of telecommunications companies return the profits they had made in IPO shares allocated to them by Citigroup Salomon Smith Barney. Spitzer accused them, including billionaire Phillip Anschutz, of commercial bribery.

In October 2003, the House Financial Services Committee, which was also interested in spinning, released a list of executives at 21 companies who were allocated IPO shares by Goldman Sachs (including shares of its own IPO). Anschutz settled with Spitzer by agreeing to donate $4.4 million in IPO profits to charity. William Ford, then chairman of Ford Motor Company, also agreed to donate $4.7 million of IPO profits to charity, although no charges were brought against him or Goldman Sachs.[6] Ford and others on the House Committee's list were longstanding, important clients of Goldman Sachs who occasionally received allocations or similar benefits in recognition of their relationship to the firm. In 1999, however, the gains from IPOs were exceptionally large, and favored clients made large profits. Spitzer was not impressed with Wall Street's past practices, and proceeded with his charges, which were also settled without a trial, usually involving contributions to charity to affect at least a symbolic disgorgement of profits.

Spitzer was able to move on after the Wall Street research settlement (two more firms accepted the terms of the settlement later) to pursuing mutual fund misconduct (discussed in chapter 6), and the former chairman of the New York Stock Exchange, Richard Grasso, for allegedly defrauding the Exchange by manipulating its board into overcompensating him. Grasso claimed that his compensation, which involved approximately $190 million over several years, was not inappropriate under the circumstances of his employment, and that the board of directors of the exchange (which included CEOs of several Wall Street firms) knew all about it and had authorized it.

The NYSE is authorized by the SEC to act as a self-regulatory organization, and as such is entrusted with regulatory powers over key operations of the exchange and its member firms. Several of the NYSE board members were senior officers of member firms, subject to NYSE regulation. Other board members were officers of listed companies or distinguished public figures, neither of which could be very familiar with the complex and arcane operating practices of the Exchange. Grasso, who had been at the Exchange for more than 30 years, was an operations expert. He had been paid large bonuses in the midst of the market bubble, when stock prices and volumes were soaring and competitive electronic exchanges were hiring capable executives for large sums. Grasso's board believed he was an excellent manager and wanted to keep him at the Exchange—a nonprofit organization with no stock options to grant—and paid him accordingly, some board members argued. Once the bubble burst, however, and the compensation details were released, the contract seemed absurd and possibly criminal.

Some observers argued that the board was really paying him to fight a rear-guard battle against change—against encroachment by NASDAQ and upstart electronic exchanges that would erode the value of entrenched NYSE floor brokers and specialists—while others turned the argument around, suggesting that Grasso used his power to keep technology at bay to bludgeon their board representatives to go along with his compensation package.

Whatever the case, the issue became a public relations disaster, and in September 2003 the board decided that Grasso had to go. He was replaced by a retired CEO of Citicorp, John Reed, who reorganized the board and governance structure of the Exchange, recruited a permanent chief executive, and took legal steps to recover for the Exchange some of the "excess" compensation paid to Grasso. Although normally such a dispute would be addressed by the parties directly, in this case Spitzer intervened on behalf of the NYSE to press its claims. And in the end, the underlying market economics reasserted themselves for the good of the Exchange when John Thain, the new CEO, announced major technology initiatives that would improve efficiency and immediacy in trading and encroach on the NYSE's legacy trading platform.

This initiative was probably helped along by a NYSE investigation, in consultation with the SEC, of the five leading "specialist" firms (floor-traders) for improper trading, three of which were owned by large financial firms. A newspaper report in early 2003 suggested that the specialists had systematically overcharged NYSE customers for trades to the extent of $155 million over three years. The activities of specialists are subject to complex rules of the Exchange, and are difficult for outsiders to understand. The specialists denied the claims, but the appearance of the charge in the press, particularly under the circumstances of financial scandals elsewhere in the system, more or less forced the issue to a settlement. In October 2003, the firms settled with the NYSE for $150 million. However, the matter did not end there, because class-action suits against the firms were being readied, as they had in 1996 when NASDAQ—the national over-the-counter equities market—agreed to a $26 million settlement with the SEC and its regulator, the National Association of Securities Dealers. This settlement became the basis for class-action litigation against NASDAQ that involved another settlement in 1998, this time for nearly $1 billion. In April 2005 15 NYSE specialists were charged with fraud by the SEC for manipulating orders and illegally pocketing $19 million in profits over 4 years, while 20 specialists were cited for front-running their customers. The NYSE itself was censured for failing to police its members, fined $20 million, and subjected to external supervision for the first time in its 213-year history.

Selling before your client insider trading

The Dust Settles

In the 1930s, when the aftermath of the soaring markets and crash in 1929 was being sorted out, a number of figures were charged with federal offenses. A high-profile case, noted in chapter 1, involved Samuel Insull, CEO of a vast public utilities group that failed (the Enron of its day), who was tried three times for securities fraud and acquitted each time. The bankers and investment pool operators were not tried at all—there were no laws yet in place prohibiting what they had done, although their conduct proved to be the inspiration for the Securities Act of 1933 and the Securities Exchange Act of 1934 that followed, the real watershed of that period.

The bubble of the 1960s did not involve much regulatory reform or litigation at all. And in the 1980s, a number of Wall Street bankers and lawyers were found to be guilty of insider trading or market manipulation, a major investment bank (Drexel Burnham Lambert) was forced into liquidation, and several highly visible players of the period went to jail. All were events that were sobering to bankers at the time, and caused the firms to be much more careful with price-sensitive information and banking and trading relationships. Significant compliance efforts were applied to controlling the risks associated with insider trading, and have been kept in place ever since.

The postbubble events in the early 2000s, reflecting the relative magnitude of market losses of the time, resulted in an extensive set of regulatory and legal interventions affecting financial intermediaries. There were three main reactions: criminal prosecutions of Arthur Andersen and about 25 senior corporate executives and bankers; the passage of the Sarbanes-Oxley Act to tighten regulations related to accounting and governance of corporations; and the Global Settlement orchestrated by Eliot Spitzer.

The Global Settlement was not only aimed at punishing the whole industry for the faults of some firms and individuals, but it was also meant to reform it. For over 70 years, reforms had been left to the SEC to effect through rules, which it published routinely. This time, because of the unusual powers of the Martin Act (uncontested as a constitutional matter) and the aggressive role played by Spitzer, the relative influence of the SEC diminished. By his intervention, the New York state attorney general had politicized securities regulation, possibly setting a very awkward precedent. This time, reforms were incorporated into the settlement, but did not reflect a keen understanding of how the securities industry really worked. To the industry, a $1.4 billion settlement was expensive but affordable. Still, the new rules—requiring separation of research and investment banking and disclosure of any contacts between bankers and analysts, and the provision of independent third-party research to clients—would involve considerable additional cost to implement and maintain. Ongoing compliance costs would add to these, but the benefits to be derived from them would be modest, at best. Added to this was the potential for class-action liabilities—the harvest of plaintiff victories would encourage other suits to the filed, and the plaintiffs would have longer checklists of compliance items to find defective. Thus, the financial market had probably experienced a net increase in regulatory costs, which ultimately would be reflected as a higher cost of capital, or lower returns for investors.

After the settlement, Wall Street banks set about doing what they had to. Few doubted that they could comply with the requirements and still handle the mergers, underwriting, and brokerage business they had been doing. But the economics of investment banking would undergo change. The implementation and compliance costs would be about the same for all firms, regardless of size and market share. The smaller firms would be harder pressed, and might decide to abandon parts of the securities business to their larger competitors, further increasing concentration in the industry. There were also questions as to whether firms not included in the settlement would have significant competitive advantages over those who were, or whether markets in Europe unaffected by the settlement (or Sarbanes-Oxley) might become more attractive to clients than they had been before and cause a shift of business into less heavily regulated markets. Accommodating or even arranging such shifts would not be difficult for the largest American firms, which were already extensively global.

There was also concern that the cost of research, including the need to provide third-party research, might become prohibitive relative to the solely commission revenues it could generate, and the benefits of research to the marketplace might be lower. True, Wall Street had been known to generate large volumes of research that often went unread, but the availability of research in general added to market transparency, even through the 1990s, judging from the small number of analysts actually sanctioned. Many midsized and smaller companies believed after the Global Settlement that they might be denied research coverage altogether if the economics made it unattractive for the banks. By mid-2003, a year of market recovery, one major Wall Street firm said it had reduced the number of U.S. companies receiving research coverage by about 20 percent, and was then covering only 800 out of about 7,500 listed public companies. Most other firms made similar adjustments. In the end, the direct and indirect costs of the underlying research reforms would be paid by the market and its users.

There was also the long chain of expensive civil litigation and class actions that would consume a large portion of the industry's earnings from the associated transactions. The litigation affected mainly banks and other intermediaries and would take several years to resolve. The litigation experience of the banks would not only considerably raise the costs but also bear on the stock prices of many banks that were believed, given the nature of the business, to be unavoidably exposed to it. The firms would also begin to realize that class-action suits were increasingly hard to defend against, and strict compliance with the letter of the law would not necessarily be enough—especially if a sudden market collapse caused widespread losses among investors. This would make managing a large investment banking business and training new employees very difficult: What should they be told when merely following the rules may not be enough?

In retrospect, however, there can be no doubt that Wall Street bankers frequently and carelessly exposed themselves to situations in which conflicts of interests were tilted to be resolved in their own favor. Clients were denied nothing, even if what they wanted was unwise or dangerous. Loans and advice were provided that jeopardized the interests of other market participants. Research was tainted to curry favor. Techniques were improvised to transfer value in IPOs back to the firms underwriting them. Practices that in ordinary markets are acceptable may not be when markets overheat. In too many situations, senior executives did not restrain their paid-for-performance employees from reaching for the easy money by putting the firm's reputation for integrity at risk, to the point where the costs of settling charges and class actions could threaten some firms' solvency. The bubble distorted judgments, but even without the bubble, other forces had led the largest financial intermediaries into believing that multiline platforms and big balance sheets were strategic necessities, even if the banks' executives could not convincingly demonstrate that they could consistently manage the business safely for their own shareholders.

Banks and brokers may have been clobbered with a blunt instrument by Spitzer and the SEC and a battery of plaintiff's lawyers during the period, and suffered considerable costs and damages, but few tears are shed for them by knowledgeable observers or by the public at large. Their reputations have been so damaged by revelations of exploitative conduct and unfair play that few outside the industry appear to care very much. The market, of course, needs financial intermediaries to make it function effectively at low agency cost. But it may not need firms, however sizeable and powerfully connected, that impose high agency costs on their clients. Such firms cannot function successfully for their own shareholders without public support and confidence. If they choose instead to rely on invisibility, complexity, or technical compliance as necessary with the rules and regulations to justify their conduct in pursuit of profits, they will ultimately lose.

Such revelations today lead immediately to adverse publicity, which now quickly exposes a firm to harsh and arbitrary regulatory settlements that are followed by expensive class actions, and these costs in aggregate can be enough to drive firms from the business altogether. Wall Street history is rich with such examples—Drexel Burnham in 1990, Salomon Brothers in 1994, Kidder Peabody in 1994, Bankers Trust in 1996—all firms that did not survive as independent concerns once they were caught up in questionable activities.

A financial system that depends on market discipline to help ensure appropriate corporate governance relies on the institutions active at the interface between the firm and its ultimate owners (accountants, asset managers, and financial services firms) to transmit that discipline. The previous two chapters have suggested that accountants and institutional investors have been found wanting, and that regulatory change has been underway that may help improve their performance. We have suggested in this chapter that financial intermediaries have likewise dropped the ball, assuring a regulatory response. Indeed, they have proven to be poor monitors, purveyors of misinformation, and designers and facilitators of corporate transactions ultimately damaging to shareholders. As in the other domains, the pendulum has swung back, and financial intermediaries will have to live with the consequences and try to avoid the next area of excess, when the process is likely to repeat itself.

Part IV

Governance, Restraints, and Conflicts of Interest

In the corporate marketplace envisioned by the authors of the new financial regulatory regime enacted in the 1930s, great reliance was placed on the power of a marketplace of independent investors and their advisers and intermediaries to restrain corporations from undertaking actions that the market might perceive to be contrary to its interests. But to be sure that corporate officials and market professionals did not attempt to hijack the system, they established and empowered the SEC to become the principal on-field referee. This approach worked well for a great many years, during which people have diverted a substantial portion of their savings to the capital markets, and the development of these markets has become an important national resource, lowering the cost of capital to corporations and providing a safe, efficient, and creative venue for both individual and institutional investors.

So it was thought, until 2000 and the great unraveling that followed. Much of the failure was blamed on inappropriate, exploitative activity by corporations, encouraged or at least unrestrained by boards of directors. Much of the blame, too, was directed to the market institutions, both investors and intermediaries. And indeed, a significant share of the blame has been placed on the regulators themselves for inattention and inaction.

This part of the book addresses the evolution of the legal and regulatory system supporting the markets, and focuses on its troubling impotence as a consequence of modern political realities. It then takes up the principal malady of the system—conflicts of interest—and analyzes how these have become a more serious threat to the well-being of the market system than before.

The common thread in failures of corporate governance, both internal and external to the business firm, is indeed the issue of conflicts of interest. Some of these conflicts are fairly easy to monitor and resolve, while others require either the application of powerful market discipline (often aided by aggressive media reporting) or effective regulatory intervention. We contend that conflicts of interest in the *external* domain of corporate monitoring, as exercised by institutional investors and financial intermediaries, have become the most important governance problem that still needs to be addressed. The reason is that the dynamics of competition in their own industry has the potential to push them in the direction of tolerance of questionable actions by clients, or even malfeasance in aiding and abetting serious corporate misconduct.

Conflicts of interest between owners and managers have been well understood for many years. A transparent marketplace should automatically adjust prices to reflect dangerous conflicts where they exist, and to force changes. Markets, however, are neither moral institutions or necessarily efficient in exercising such discipline. They can be indifferent to agency conflicts in some cases and punitive in others. Even in the broadest and deepest of today's capital markets, scrutiny of agency conflicts may merit only a passing glance—at least while things are on the way up—and the markets' own institutions may suffer from agency conflicts as severe that those of corporations.

In the late 1990s and early 2000s, rapidly expanding capital markets were exceptionally permissive of agency conflicts. As long as stock prices were rising, the conflicts didn't matter very much. Inevitably, of course, a correction would have to be made. Some of the agency problems identified in this book have since been addressed. Some have not. As the storm recedes, so will the preoccupation with governance issues. Yet there is a residue of important blemishes that remain unattended and that may reappear with a vengeance down the road.

In the final chapter, on the future of governance, we offer an analysis of, and a prescription for, addressing these as yet untreated issues that uphold an "uneven" or "tilted" system of responsibility for the proper discharge of fiduciary duties that all agents in the financial system bear. The "tilt" to the system has emerged over the last 20 years or so—as a result of legal constraints, passive regulatory enforcement, and the common American practice of indemnification and insurance of officers and directors for all but "gross negligence." We believe this troublesome tilt can be removed, but first it needs to be recognized and understood.

9

Government Regulation and Corporate Governance

Some 200 years after his death, Adam Smith's ideas today dominate the organization of economic activity more strongly than ever. Markets emerge to allocate labor, capital, intellectual, and natural resources in the most efficient possible way—if they are allowed to do so by keeping them free of influences that distort them, such as monopolies, government interference, and excessive regulation. Free markets are guided by an "invisible hand" that takes into account all the forces acting in the market at the time and creates a balanced outcome that produces the greatest good for the greatest number.

Adam Smith predicated his views on the idea of free markets and perfect competition in which lots of self-interested players interact, with none sufficiently powerful to affect prices and competition. He acknowledged that markets were not free in the Britain of which he wrote in 1776, because of royal prerogatives, ancient practices that interfered with the mobility of labor and flexibility of wages, and because of parliamentary actions taken to protect special interests. A key theme was to clear out all these interferences in the market, to make it freer, and the result would be a large increase in British "opulence," or national wealth. Smith's belief that the market would regulate itself, together with similar thoughts by French economic theorists of the time, gave usage to the term "laissez-faire."

The world described by Smith and his laissez-faire disciples, such as Walter Bagheot, Alfred Marshall, Joseph Schumpeter, Friedrich Hayek, and Milton Friedman, has been remarkably robust, repeatedly beating back challenges from alternative visions of economic society, ranging from the Fabian socialists of the nineteenth century to the Marxists and fascists in the twentieth century. Even milder forms of centralized government planning and control, such as those employed by the French, the Swedes, and the Indians have had to be bolstered by a shot of free-market capitalism from time to time, by allowing a robust private sector to develop and periodically using it to "privatize" unwieldy state-controlled businesses.

Even when an alternative system is imposed for a very long time, as Marxism-Leninism was over a good part of the world for well over half a century, the invisible hand creeps in again through black markets, minicapitalism, work-minimizing behavior, and a host of other ways now thoroughly familiar in the history of Soviet-style command economies. The success of "emerging markets" in Asia, Latin America, and eastern Europe really reflects little more than Smith's invisible hand being allowed more room to apply its touch.

If the invisible hand so dominates the landscape of economic ideas, then laissez-faire must certainly be the essential anchor of national and international policy toward the business sector. Market-users should be left to their own devices, to do what they perceive is best for themselves, and to create the kinds of organizations that hold the best promise of moving in that direction. Measures that distort markets should be absent altogether, or at least be as nonintrusive as possible. In any case, if governments are too intrusive, human ingenuity will find ways around them. Certainly government intervention should be calibrated against its market impact in the cold light of how people are most likely to respond, not according to some theoretical view as to how they *ought to* respond. Any such intervention needs to be tested as to whether it is effective in making the market work more efficiently, and then, if it is not, whether it works *with* market incentives or *against* them, and ultimately whether the social gains achieved by the intervention outweigh the cost—that is, the loss in market efficiency. Where free markets have been permitted, they have usually left powerful performance benchmarks behind, and recent history certainly suggests that policies that deviate too far from them are doomed to eventual collapse.

Periodic market failures—which are to be expected in an essentially laissez-faire system—are a means to punish error and reward caution, both necessary ingredients of a self-regulatory mechanism. Investors who risk their wealth should be careful and demand information sufficient to evaluate adequately the progress of the investment. If they fail, they will presumably be more careful in the future. They will learn whom to trust and rely upon, and whom not to. In the long run, the market adapts to its own experience, and as the Romans said, "caveat emptor" (let the buyer beware).

Laissez-faire notwithstanding, markets must operate within a society that appreciates their value and safeguards their freedom. The more democratic the society, the greater will be the demand for the assurance of orderliness, equal access, and fair play. Too free a market, some argue, produces excessive swings and cycles, which can imperil the public welfare. Too exclusive a market keeps ordinary citizens from benefiting from the opportunities. And markets that are widely considered "unfair" or "exploitative" eventually give rise to rules and standards to deal with the issues.

Adam Smith's notions of efficient markets have been subjected over the last 230-odd years to the claims of a politicized society that insists on a stable set of rules of conduct. Indeed, when such rules are absent, as in the "Wild West" of yesteryear, or the roaring 1920s, and in some of the "transition economies" of the 1990s, the market is clearly subject to distortions of lawlessness. When there is a lack of law and order, when sanctity of contracts and private property are called into question and there is no recourse to courts of law and no protection from extortion, the functioning of free and fair markets collapse. Institutions to provide such protection eventually must be created in order to achieve a high level of sustainable economic performance. The process of creating such institutions may itself go through phases of vigilantism, self-regulation, and informal market rules before arriving at its destination. Even then, once regulatory and enforcement institutions have been created and allowed to function, they remain subject to further regulatory enhancement as citizens exercise their rights of protest and their votes.

THE ECLECTIC REGULATORY FRAMEWORK

The American economic system was conceived not long after Adam Smith's work *The Wealth of Nations* was published in London, a work destined to ensure his celebration as one of the leading figures of the Enlightenment and the founding father of economics. The work was meant to offer suggestions to the rich and powerful in England as to how the national prosperity—already one of the highest in the world— could be improved further. The rich and powerful benefited from many of the economic restrictions on market freedom of the time, and therefore ignored much of what Smith had to say. But some of America's founding fathers had read the book and were ready to create a new society across the ocean that would be free of the prerogatives, restrictions, and customs that prevented Britain, according to Smith, from achieving maximum economic performance. So the American markets began as free institutions, although they were hemmed in by trade practices of other countries and by protectionist ideas to encourage local manufacturing. The American government would stay out of the private sector (other than occasionally financing necessary public utilities to get them going), would provide no monopolies or land grants to favorites, and would rely on the states to regulate corporations, with the federal government retaining the right to regulate only interstate commerce. These were favorable conditions for entrepreneurs and investors at the time. The New York Stock Exchange was established as a private-sector initiative in 1792 to provide a venue (and some rules) for trading in securities, mainly government bonds and the paper issued by banks, public utilities, and a few other corporations.

From the beginning, there was a great appetite to create new corporations to operate toll roads, canals, insurance companies, banks, and similar institutions. When the railroads emerged, vast quantities of new securities were offered to finance them, and the federal government established interstate regulations to promote them. Until 1930, however, government regulation of economic activity had been concerned with public utilities, interstate commerce, monopolies, labor, and public safety. Even Adam Smith recognized that there were times when the government had to intervene in the economy in the public interest (e.g., for national defense), and it is possible he would have agreed that much of the regulation that occurred in the first 150 years of the United States could be justified as being necessary.

Federal regulation of financial markets did not develop until the early 1930s, after the experience of massive market failures in banking and securities markets. But when it came, it was profound. Publicly traded corporations had to register with the government, providing voluminous information that had to be truthful, with serious consequences for noncompliance or misstatements. Soon all financial intermediaries had to be similarly registered with federal or state authorities—banks, brokers, traders, investment advisers, accountants, and exchanges. The cost of this regulation was considerable, and much objected to by the participants. One consequence, however, was that in time, public confidence in banking and financial markets was not only restored but enhanced, and public participation in those markets expanded well beyond levels that might have been imagined at the time the regulations were adopted. More participation in the markets made them more robust and efficient, perhaps a fair price to pay for the cost of regulation that was passed on to market users.

Since the 1930s, the regulatory framework in the United States has evolved and sought to fulfill a new purpose. No longer will the public be endangered by seasoned professionals operating in the markets in the spirit of buyer-beware. Instead, the regulatory umbrella was for the first time opened to protect the public from abuse and exploitation. Protecting the investor became a new purpose of federal financial regulation, and this required more regulation. This regulation, however, could only restrict specific, identified transactions and practices. If not so restricted, a business practice was considered permissible. Every few years, however, a dynamic market environment will tend to produce new practices and transactions, and in time the regulatory machinery catches up and declares some of them impermissible. When a major episode of misconduct occurs (one so described by the public and their politicians), the regulatory machine accelerates and catches up quickly. And when this happens, sudden and sometimes retroactive changes in the "ground rules" are declared that inevitably catch a number of practitioners off guard.

WHY REGULATE?

Even the most free-market-oriented countries have chains of social and economic policies that constrain exploitative market behavior. In this sense, the *political* process invariably guides the *economic* process in directions that depart (sometimes significantly) from what would happen under totally free-market conditions. The need for such forms of guidance is to assure that market mechanisms produce socially acceptable results. There are several reasons why.

Adam Smith's approach to resource allocation via the free market may well be the most efficient from an economics perspective, but not necessarily from the perspective of politicians who have extensive non-economic agendas. In a totally free market, some get rich and some get poor. It all depends on your natural endowments, your investment in skills, your saving and spending patterns, your entrepreneurship and ingenuity, your level of effort, and your luck. It's all up to you.

But democratic society doesn't see it quite that way. For every perceived success, there may be many failures, too many for a full-fledged democracy in which every voice can be heard. So in a democracy, some (perhaps a majority) will advocate assistance and protection be offered to diminish the consequences of being a loser. The poor are to be lifted to a tolerable standard of living by means of social safety nets. The unemployed are taken care of for a while, often for quite a long while, and sometimes (especially in Europe) at incomes not too far from what they earned when they were working.

Meanwhile, the winners are taxed more aggressively than the rest, usually in ways that likewise promote social concepts of fairness. There are progressive income taxes, which take proportionately more from those who are better off than those less fortunate, but there are also sales taxes, real estate taxes, excise taxes, estate taxes at time of death, "sin" taxes on tobacco and alcohol, and more, each reflecting prevailing concepts of "fairness" as much as the need for revenues. In federal countries like the United States, tax fairness is fine-tuned at the state and local level as well. You are taxed progressively on your income from work both at the federal, state, and sometimes even municipal level. You are taxed on your income from interest and dividends (which have already been taxed at the corporate level), assets accumulated from income *already* taxed once, and when those assets appreciate and are sold they are taxed yet *again* as capital gains, if even those gains may only be due to inflation. Then, when you die, most of these assets are taxed one last time before they pass on to heirs. All the while, however, you can deduct from taxable income mortgage interest, sometimes property taxes, and medical bills and claim various other tax breaks considered by politicians to have socially redeeming value. And the wealthy strive to convince politicians to provide tax breaks for them to offset the burdens that they must endure.

The result is a transfer of income and wealth from the richer to the poorer members of democratic society, as a measure of moral justice by the peoples' representatives, the politicians. The privileged should be forced to assist the needy. Most members of the privileged classes believe that to be an acceptable trade-off. The important middle classes are built up, and the economic safety net that such policies create may shield the economy from extreme unemployment and depressed markets for all kinds of goods and services. It may also address a society's need to treat its citizens humanely, and to redress various aspects of inequality of opportunity and access to wealth. All well-developed societies have this system of transfer payments to some extent. But it comes at a price of reducing freedom in the markets, economic efficiency, and often higher unemployment and less attractive prospects for future economic growth.

Normally, one would expect politicians to recognize the value of preserving the market system, and not to damage it excessively by yielding to the temptations of populism. More or less free markets can survive in such climates very well. But what they cannot do is tolerate extreme inefficiencies in resource allocation. When the pendulum swings too far in one direction, the economy sustains critical damage that can take a long time to repair.

Public Goods

There are certain things the free market is not good at providing—those things whose value is hard to identify and to allocate among beneficiaries in rough proportion to the benefits received, even as others (as *free-riders*) are able to enjoy them without sharing in their cost. National defense, parks, and public safety are obvious examples. Others, ranging from public schools and hospitals to airports, highways, and postal services, are often subject to debate. Some of these have been privatized successfully to let market-based actions increase the quality of services and reduce their cost of delivery.

Vigorous discussion has developed in many countries about the efficacy of market-based solutions to such problems as environmental pollution and maintenance of fisheries—solutions that are "incentive compatible" and vest resource users with ownership rights that make it clearly in their own interests to maintain that resource on a sustainable basis. So even though the market demonstrates some weaknesses when costs and benefits cannot easily be allocated, it can nevertheless be used to provide cost-effective solutions to social problems involving public goods. On the whole, however, "public goods" provide a durable rationale for government intervention to allocate costs and benefits of shared resources effectively. But only, of course, to a point beyond which economic efficiency will suffer unacceptably.

Negative Externalities

In a classic essay published almost a half century ago,[1] Nobel Prize–winning economist Ronald Coase asked a simple question: Suppose a doctor examining his patients is interfered with by a candy-maker next door who is operating noisy equipment. In pursuing his own interests, the candy-maker is interfering with the doctor. His noise pollution damages the neighbor—pollution from which he derives benefits (being able to make candy at a profit) but for which the victim receives no compensation. Economists call this type of interference a "negative externality." The conventional solution to this externality problem is for the candy-maker himself to be restrained, maybe even put out of business. Coase pointed out that this completely overlooks the damage such restraint would do to the candy-maker, who is only making noise in the pursuit of his own livelihood with no intent of harming the doctor.

There are two possible outcomes: The doctor's business continues to suffer, or the candy-maker is forced to shut down. Which causes the greater harm? Coase demonstrated that forcing the candy-maker to shut down may be an inferior solution compared to a freely negotiated arrangement between the two parties whereby the doctor is compensated by the noisy candy-maker or the doctor compensates the candy-maker to quiet down—the eventual solution depending on the relative size of gains and losses faced by the two parties. That is, negative externalities can be dealt with most efficiently by means of costlessly negotiated arrangements between parties, regardless of whether the law makes people liable for the consequences of their own actions.

The law should place the burden of avoiding harmful effects on the party that can accomplish it at lowest cost, and leave the rest to private negotiation. This is the famous "Coase theorem." The best legal solutions to social issues and conflicting property rights are those that mimic most closely what people would come up with if they were free to negotiate them. This goes for all kinds of rights, ranging from free speech to aircraft overflights, from air pollution to clean streets.[2] And even when negotiations between parties are costly (for example, due to poor information, difficulties in identifying injured parties, etc.), governmental or private institutions tend to develop over time to mitigate these costs. So, when social costs arise, public policy and institutional arrangements tend to be called into action to deal with them, but their design can lead to more or less efficient results depending on how closely they align to freely negotiated outcomes.

Negative externalities have historically played a big part in financial markets, with crises (and costly crisis prevention) and questionable practices regularly visiting losses on innocent parties. Finance is and always will be a highly "pollution-intensive" industry, one requiring active and considered public policies to deal with the many forms of interference that affect it.

Contestable Markets and Competition

Adam Smith predicated his description of the remarkable operation of free markets on perfect competition, that is, large numbers of small suppliers incapable of affecting prices, perfect information, zero transactions costs, and the like—conditions painfully familiar to any beginning student of economics. In the real world, of course, perfect competition rarely exists for many reasons, such as economies of large-scale production, differentiated products, and "natural" monopolies such as electricity supply to homeowners. And there is the fact that producers detest perfect competition and having to sell in "commodity" markets where the sole determinant of success is price. So they busy themselves trying to escape it, sometimes constructively and sometimes not so constructively. People enroll in training programs and graduate schools trying to differentiate themselves from others in order to command higher compensation. Sometimes, when they are talented enough, they do very well indeed in creating a virtually unique presence in the marketplace, as do media and sports stars. For their part, companies try to invent better mousetraps and advertise the extraordinary quality of their products to command higher prices and larger market shares. Success stories abound. All of this is a vital part of the market-driven system of economic organization, especially when *economies of scale* and *economies of scope* are important aspects of the production process— effective competition and the vigorous contesting for market position has to hold out the hope of a pot of gold at the end of the rainbow.

Corporations sometimes try to exploit the market by effectively blocking out rivals in inappropriate ways, shifting economic benefits from others to themselves—what economists call "rent-seeking." Examples include creation of monopolies and producer cartels, collusion in pricing designed to drive prices far above costs, pleading for protection against imports at the expense of the consumer, and predatory dumping intended to drive weaker players from the market and subsequently permit monopoly pricing. In such cases, governments usually step in either to regulate prices, break up the monopolies and collusive practices, or otherwise improve the functioning and contestability of the market. Competition policy itself is almost always imperfect, however. How do we best identify the existence of a monopoly? What is "collusion"? What is a "cartel"? How do we define "predatory"? What happens when the apparent benefits of cooperation among suppliers seems to exceed by far the dangers of market exploitation? How do we avoid competition-regulation aimed at yesterday's problems? What about anticompetitive practices that occur abroad, outside national jurisdiction, yet have significant impacts on the local market? Many of these questions have been answered only imperfectly, although recent advances in the economics of industrial organization probably have contributed to more efficient regulatory policies. But still, the less competition there is in a market system, the more likely it is that the market will be unable to work its magic.

Information and Transactions Costs

Information is often expensive. It has to be created, absorbed, processed, and acted upon in order to be effectively applied in the market. Sometimes this is not a big problem. In the foreign exchange market, perhaps the most perfect in the world, dealers can check rates on screens, with brokers and other dealers in whichever markets are open on a 24-hour basis virtually year-round. All major players have almost the same information almost all the time, as well as essentially the same costs of doing transactions. So success or failure in this virtually seamless market depends mainly on the dealer's *interpretation* of whatever information is available at the moment. Compare this with the hapless American tourist in France, wandering into a *bureau de change* on a cathedral square 40 miles outside Paris, staring blankly at the extortionate posted rates, armed with little or no information and few immediate alternatives.

The fact is that information has value. Those who have it can charge for it through fees, spreads, and other means. Those who don't have it must pay for it, either by incurring the costs of obtaining it for themselves or by meeting the seller's price. The same thing applies to transaction costs, including the cost of taking business elsewhere, which may be quite easy and cheap in come cases, but in others may well involve establishing entirely new relationships with new suppliers— what economists call *recontracting costs.*

Information and transaction costs are fairly easy to deal with in interprofessional, or wholesale, markets, where solutions can be left to the interplay of competitive forces. Exceptions arise when information is stolen. Proprietary information is embedded in the value of a firm. When it is misappropriated, there are clear victims, principally the owners of the firm. Stealing information is not a victimless crime. Some people (those who wouldn't buy or sell if they were privy to the same information) are injured in the process. Consequently, coming down hard on those who steal information may well be justified—quite apart from the fact that information theft disadvantages honest participants and compromises the integrity of the market, encouraging them to take their business elsewhere.

Information and transaction costs tend to be far more serious when it comes to doing business with unsophisticated retail customers, who may be poorly informed or find it difficult to shop around, making them ripe for picking by unscrupulous operators. This goes for any market, but it applies especially to financial markets. *Buyer beware* is a good rule, but people who find financial affairs difficult to understand

and far removed from their expertise and everyday life tend to be the
least capable of making complex decisions that are truly in their own
interests. For this reason, they may have to be protected by society—
protection that may in the end be in the public interest—by forcing
adequate disclosure in language that ordinary people can understand,
limiting access to certain risky financial products, specifying in detail
how certain financial services may be sold, and cracking down on
various kinds of abuses.

Finally, while free-market activities may be efficient in the long run,
they can cause extreme harshness in the short run for a great many
people. So political pressures develop to interfere in the market—to
have government regulation overrule market forces, so that a more
benign environment may develop in its place.

To summarize, the main reasons for intervening in markets are the
following five: (1) fairness issues, defined in the social and political
domain; (2) achieving and paying for the benefits of public goods and
services; (3) resolving issues of external interference with the rights of
others; (4) the extent to which competition really exists; and (5) the
costs and access to information. These things have to be balanced
against society's need for an efficient, growing economy that is best
achieved by letting markets work.

LAYERS OF SOCIAL CONTROL

Thinking about all of these issues makes it clear that allowing control
of economic outcomes to be entirely left to the actions of a free market
is probably not feasible in any democracy that tries to create the maximum level of welfare for the maximum number of people. Since this
is more or less the professed goal of virtually every political system
that exists today, constraints on firms, labor unions, individuals, and
other economic actors are ever present—and probably always will be.
These constraints constitute a "web of social control."

As depicted in figure 9.1, the business firm itself, whose managers
are supposed to be intent on maximizing long-term shareholder wealth,
is at the center of the web.

If managers and owners are different, as in a corporation whose
shares are publicly traded, then agency conflicts can arise, leading to a
situation where shareholder wealth may not be maximized. Conflicts
may arise on retained earnings—with managers opting to retain earnings rather than distributing them to shareholders, even though shareholders' welfare may be better served with cash distribution in the
absence of projects providing high investment returns. Managers may
also be more risk averse than investors if much of their own capital—
whether financial or human—is tied up with the firm, whereas investors can afford a more diversified portfolio.

Market forces governing corporate control and shareholder value

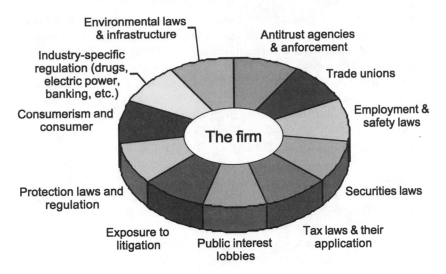

Figure 9.1. The Web of Social Control.

are supposed to make sure that such agency conflicts (or costs) are kept in check. Waste, inefficiency, and bad management are reflected in share prices, and if the stock price drops low enough, it will trigger takeover action by investors or other companies who think they can do better after ousting current management. In short, market-imposed discipline is supposed to govern the destiny of the firm—its overall performance in the market for goods and services, for labor, raw materials, and other resources, as well as for capital, and ultimately for corporate control. The firm is the source of economic energy for the system, the goose that lays the golden eggs.

But suppose, for example, that—intent on the pursuit of maximum shareholder wealth—management fails to deal with environmental pollution and so imposes serious costs on others in society. This may create a response among the victims that will ultimately find resonance in the political arena. It could trigger legislation to address the problem, possibly through taxation, prohibitions, fines, or other enforcement actions. In United States environmental policy, for example, the critical point probably came with Earth Day demonstrations in the late 1960s and the publication of Rachel Carson's *Silent Spring*. This was followed in short order by the National Environmental Quality Act and later federal air and water quality legislation and the establishment of a large bureaucracy, the Environmental Protection Agency, in 1969 to ensure enforcement at the national level and to promote consistent enforcement at the state and local levels as well.

Within only a few years, the United States had created a control process to try to deal with the problem of environmental protection. A new layer of social control had been imposed on corporations. Firms had to conform, and their costs rose; they had to come to grips with efficiency in pollution control as yet another competitive element. Their relative product prices reflected the whole process and accordingly influenced consumer behavior. The environment, a public good that previously had been "unpriced," in short order had to be factored into market decisions and became an important element of economic life.

Or take product safety. Firms in pursuit of free-market objectives may well be tempted to cut corners in product design, placing at risk consumers who lack pertinent information when they make their buying decisions. So a host of federal legislative initiatives has evolved over the years to protect consumers, including the Fair Packaging and Labeling Act of 1969 and creation of the Consumer Product Safety Commission and various consumer safety initiatives at the state and local levels. Most affected in this regard were the food and pharmaceuticals industries, and in response, the Food and Drug Administration (FDA) was established (tracing its roots to the Pure Food Act of 1906), a government agency that is responsible for rigorous testing and product approvals in advance of broad-scale availability in the market. Again, firms in the affected industries have had to adapt in ways that have raised costs and prices, influenced product availability and time-to-market, and affected shareholder values. While there is plenty of controversy about *how* the regulatory system works or *what* ought to be regulated—such as the FDA's efforts to classify cigarettes as addictive and subject to its control (which finally succeeded in 2004), while making no similar move on alcoholic beverages, for example—few people today would argue for scrapping the FDA.

Such initiatives have dealt not only with health and safety but also with general product quality and sales techniques. Efforts by corporations to skimp on product quality are usually reflected in market forces, with consumers soon defecting to buy from competitors who do better. Even here, however, there have been many consumer protection initiatives, including legislation leading to the creation of the Federal Trade Commission in 1914, and a broad range of state and local measures such as "lemon laws" for automobiles, taxi commissions, and the like. The area of consumer protection has been especially targeted by nongovernmental organizations such as Consumers Union, as well as consumer activists of virtually every stripe. Producers may not like it, but they have to deal with it.

In matters of labor, the dynamics of corporate relations with their employees gave rise to organized labor in the nineteenth century and collective bargaining over compensation, job classifications, working conditions, and job rules. Normally, collective bargaining would be left to negotiators to settle these issues, but again, government bodies have been created in the political environment to affect the process, notably the National Labor Relations Board (1935) and much later the Occupational Safety and Health Administration (1971).

In various industries, problems at the interface between the market and society have given rise to further constraints on business in the form of very specific controls. In transportation, for example, the Interstate Commerce Commission was initially given the task of regulating the U.S. railroads in 1887 in response to farmers' complaints about high freight rates, as well as railroads' complaints about predatory pricing by their competitors, a regulatory mandate later extended to other forms of transportation. In air transport the Civil Aeronautics Board (CAB) was originally created to allocate routes, fix prices, and designate services in what was regarded as a unique industry. Although the CAB was scrapped during the Carter administration, many of its functions were assumed by the Department of Transportation. In all, hundreds of federal and state regulatory agencies have been created to regulate commerce and industry in the United States, powers originally granted to Congress under the Constitution and put to use ever since.

In short, we know that virtually all forms of economic life are limited, restrained, or explicitly controlled by government regulation of one form or another. Layers of social control affect all industries. All pay greater or lesser amounts of taxes, all are subject to environmental, labor, consumer health and safety, and antitrust statues. All are subject to federal and state securities laws. And all are exposed to fines and penalties under these laws, and to civil litigation based upon them. The idea is that these various layers of restraint, like the thin threads used by the Lilliputians to hold down the giant Gulliver, will balance the uneven distribution of power between corporations and their customers, employees, and other constituents in the marketplace.

Periodically the balance of power shifts. Too little external restraint permits exploitative behavior on the part of corporations. During 2001 and 2002, governance failures in the United States led to the massive bankruptcies discussed earlier in this book. Although the number of such incidents was small (in actual terms only about 20 out of the more than 15,000 companies that file annual reports with the SEC),[3] the impact they had was substantial. Four of the ten largest bankruptcies from 1980 to 2004 occurred in less than a year—Enron in December 2001, Global Crossing in January 2002, Adelphia in June 2002, and the largest, WorldCom, in July 2002. The bankruptcies and ensuing scandals helped push stock prices down further in a period already depressed by the bursting of the technology bubble and the aftermath of the terrorist attacks of September 11, 2001.[4]

That the cases were all different only served to highlight the common problem of inadequate external restraint. On the surface, it appeared that proper governance mechanisms were in place at these firms. They were audited by the then "Big Five" accounting firms. Their boards appeared to follow sound principles. John Duncan, former chairman of the Enron Executive Committee, described his fellow Enron board members as "experts in the area of finance and accounting."[5] Board members were ostensibly independent—at Enron, only two members represented management. Boards held regular meetings. The trouble seemed to be that governance mechanisms did not function properly or were inherently flawed. At Enron, for example, strong financial ties weakened the independence of the board members. Several board members had lucrative consulting contracts—one earned almost $500,000 for consulting work during 1991–2002. Others encouraged substantial donations by Enron or the Lay Foundation to charitable organizations they presided over, or benefited from sales to Enron subsidiaries.[6] In contrast, the Adelphia board made no pretense of independence, with five of nine directors being members of the founding Rigas family. Auditor and banker independence and objectivity may also have been compromised by business interests of clients like Enron, as discussed in previous chapters. Such internal and external governance failures and the economic losses they helped bring about triggered calls for new regulation to control excesses.

The presuppositions of corporate monitoring, governance, and control in a market-driven system of economic organization, both internally and externally to the business firm, can be listed as follows.

Internal Corporate Governance

- Incentive-compatible management contracts
- Appropriate board structure and conduct
- Full and fair disclosure of material information
- Exercise of fiduciary role of boards members

External Monitoring and Control

- Independent audits and rigorous accounting standards
- Independent stock analysts—and efficient equity pricing
- Institutionalization of equity holdings—pension funds and mutual funds
- Professional credit assessment and commercial bank lending
- Objective investment banking advice and underwriting
- Objective legal advice: management and boards
- Strong debt monitoring by independent rating agencies
- A powerful market regulatory infrastructure (governmental and SROs)

Each element in the control chain is supposed to function as we have described in this book, so that this inventory can be used as a benchmark to calibrate how the control process actually works, as opposed to how it is supposed to work. Undertaking this exercise for WorldCom, Adelphia, Parmalat, or any of the other corporate disasters of the early 2000s suggests that the problem is hardly one of "a few bad apples." Rather, the problem in the control system is systemic and suggests that market discipline has failed to provide consistency and durability to corporate governance. Consequently, as in other domains of market failure, discipline shifts from economics to politics, and the system reacts.

Still, even as calls go out for more regulation and reinforcing the web of social control, too much restraint leads to corporate impotence and weak economic performance. Under such circumstances, the regulatory burden may be lifted (as began to occur in the United States in the late 1970s) in a gradual process of deregulation. It can also, of course, lead to vigorous efforts to avoid the regulatory burden by shifting business activities abroad, or migrate to black market or "underground" economic activities.

Setting the Performance Benchmarks

The conduct of any business firm today is calibrated against two different sets of benchmarks, (a) its performance in the competitive marketplace; and (b) its performance against the changing standards of social control.

Management must work to optimize between both sets of benchmarks. If it strays too far in the direction meeting the demands of social and regulatory controls, it runs the risk of poor performance in the market, severe punishment by shareholders, and possibly even the firm's takeover. If it strays toward unrestrained market performance or sails too close to the wind in terms of acceptable market conduct, its behavior may have disastrous results for the firm, its managers, its employees, and its shareholders.

These are the rules of the game, and firms have to live with them. But they are not immutable. There is constant bickering between firms and regulators about the details of external constraints on corporate conduct. Sometimes firms win battles (and even wars), leading to impressive periods of deregulation. Sometimes it's possible to convince the public that self-regulation or the reputation-effects of misconduct are powerful enough to obviate the need for external control. Sometimes the regulators can be convinced, one way or another, to go easy. Then along comes another big transgression, and the system constricts again and creates a spate of new regulations. Everyone gets into the act in this constant battle to define the rules under which business gets done—managers, politicians, the media, activists, investors, lawyers, accountants—and eventually a new equilibrium is established that will define the rules of conduct for the period ahead.

Between Values and Expectations

There are some more fundamental things at work as well. Laws and regulations governing the market conduct of firms are hardly created in a vacuum. They are rooted in social expectations as to what is appropriate and inappropriate, which in turn are driven by values imbedded in society. These values are pretty basic. They deal with lying, cheating and stealing, with trust and honor, with what is right and what is wrong. These are the *ultimate* benchmarks against which conduct is measured and can be found, for example, in the Ten Commandments, embedded in Judeo-Christian values, and most other major religions as well.

But fundamental values that appear in society may or may not be reflected in people's *expectations* as to how a firm's conduct is assessed. As everyone knows from Hollywood, business people are stereotyped as unattractive—usually greedy, aggressive, unsympathetic individuals only interested in their own success. John Wayne never played a banker on the way to foreclose a mortgage. Certainly the image of Wall Street professionals in the 1980s, when Ivan Boesky and Michael Milken ruled the headlines, was not very favorable. Movies such as *Wall Street* or *The Smartest Guys in the Room* and bestselling books like *Bonfire of the Vanities, Den of Thieves,* and *Barbarians at the Gate* hardly pictured Wall Street at its best. Considering the events of the day (mainly the 1980s), one can see why. So there may be a good deal of slippage between practical social values and how these are reflected in the public expectations of business conduct. Such expectations, however, are important, and managers ignore at their own peril the buildup of adverse opinion in the media, the formation of special-interest lobbies and pressure groups, and the general tide of public opinion with respect to one or another aspect of market conduct.

Moreover, neither values nor expectations are static in time. Both change. But values seem to change much more gradually than expectations. Indeed, fundamental values such as those identified here are probably as close as one comes to "constants" in assessing business conduct. But even in this domain, things do change. As society becomes more diverse and mobile, for example, values almost certainly evolve. Values in Victorian England were very different from those a century before and after. They also differ across cultures. Nor are they easy to interpret. Is lying wrong? What's the difference between lying and bluffing? Is it only the *context* that determines how behavior is assessed? The same conduct may be in fact interpreted differently under different circumstances, interpretation that may change significantly over time and differ widely across cultures.

Between Expectations and Public Policy

There is yet further slippage between society's expectations and the formation of public policy, and the attitudes of public interest groups. Things may go on as usual for a while, despite occasional mutterings from religious or other organizations or the media about inappropriate behavior of a firm or an industry in the marketplace. Then the fateful day comes. Some sort of social tolerance limit is reached. A firm goes too far. A confluence of interest emerges among various groups concerned with the issue. The system squeezes, and another set of constraints on firm behavior emerges, perhaps complete with implementing legislation, regulation, and bureaucracy. Or maybe the firm is hauled into court to face a massive lawsuit. Or its reputation is seriously compromised, and its share price drops sharply.

The reality is that the value of the firm suffers from these uncertain conditions. Since maintaining (indeed, maximizing) the value of the firm is the ultimate duty of management, it is management's job to learn how to run the firm so that it optimizes the long-term trade-offs between profits and external control. It does no good to plead unfair treatment—the task is for management to learn to live with it, and to make the most of the variables it can control.

The Politics of Regulation

The fine regulatory balance just described can be tilted by the political nature of the process—through lobbying that distorts regulatory structures in favor of well-organized, politically powerful groups in society. Individuals may not challenge regulation if this involves significant costs or if they feel they can free-ride on the efforts of others. Meanwhile, powerful interest groups have much to gain from new regulations and may therefore actively lobby to ensure that it is in their favor—"rent-seeking" behavior.[7]

Lobbying involves spending (often heavily) to persuade legislators or regulators to support particular policy measures, perhaps by "educating" legislators, entertaining them, or supporting their reelection through campaign contributions. While lobbying is often vilified for its less savory characteristics, its supporters claim it helps elected representatives understand the complexities of issues and the opinion of the electorate. Lobbying has certainly been used effectively by powerful industry groups to influence regulation that, in hindsight, may have facilitated serious governance problems. Prominent examples cited in previous chapters include stock option expensing, tort reform and auditor independence.

The expensing of employee stock options has been an ongoing accounting issue since the 1990s. Twice in the 1990s, the FASB tried to close loopholes in stock option reporting that helped companies to avoid recording the cost of stock option awards in their financial statements. Especially technology companies able to benefit from high stock prices in the late 1990s lobbied strenuously against an accounting treatment that required the expensing of new stock options when they are granted, preferring to ignore the cost to shareholders of granting options and deferring expense recognition until the options are exercised some time in the future. During the 1990s, corporate America opposed new accounting treatment to expense stock options—and was supported by the accounting industry. The lobbying had its effect. In 1994, Congress passed a resolution to condemn the FASB expensing proposal, and the FASB dropped its plan to force companies to account for stock options when granted as a measurable cost to shareholders. A compromise was worked out in 1995 whereby companies had to disclose liabilities for future stock options in a footnote to the financial statements. As a result, in the late stages of the 1995–2000 bubble, many corporate executives were gorging on stock options that were appreciating rapidly, with the result that corporate profits were greatly overstated.

A second, highly publicized example of lobbying and its impact on regulatory structures was the suppression of shareholder derivative and class-action lawsuits for securities fraud. A wave of such suits struck California in the second half of the 1990s, charging that executives of companies whose stock prices had risen sharply had sold shares at the peak of the market before some sort of bad news was released. Plaintiffs were shareholders who participated in the ensuing losses, and who wanted to be reimbursed by executives who bailed themselves out before any warning to public shareholders. The Private Securities and Litigation Reform Act of 1995, which made it much harder for investors to sue companies, was strongly supported by accounting firms, high-tech firms, and venture capitalists. The accounting firms had quickly organized themselves to form an effective lobbying group, the Accountants Coalition, and lobbied hard for the Act. The efforts were successful. In December 1995, Congress overturned President Clinton's veto and passed the Act, protecting the three interest groups.

A third example of lobbying to influence legislation was the SEC proposal in 2000 to force the separation of nonaudit practices from auditing practices of accounting firms in an effort to assure auditor independence. The accounting industry, led by the then Big Five and the AICPA, strongly lobbied against this initiative. In 2000, the "Big Five" lobbying expenditure amounted to $9 million, up 50 percent from the previous year.[8] Intense pressure was put on the SEC and its chairman, Arthur Levitt, to rescind the proposal—with Congress threatening to reduce the SEC's budget if it did not. In November 2001, the SEC agreed to a compromise solution requiring firms to at least disclose how much they were paying for nonauditing services of their audit clients.

REGULATORY BALANCE AND CORPORATE CONDUCT

Given the political nature of regulation and the regulatory balance, how should regulation of corporate conduct proceed? What distinguishes "good" regulation from "bad" regulation? What is the balance between self-regulatory codes of practice and formal statutory rules? What kind of regulatory structure could support the appropriate regulatory mix?

A difficult set of policy trade-offs invariably confront those charged with designing and implementing governance regulation. On the one hand, they must strive to achieve economic efficiency and protect the competitive viability of the business firms that are subject to regulation. On the other hand, they must safeguard the stability of economic institutions and the integrity of markets, sometimes by protecting themselves against their own mistakes. In addition to encouraging acceptable market conduct—including the politically sensitive implied social contract between business and financial institutions and small, unsophisticated customers—they must also protect against problems of contagion and systemic risk. And the need to maintain an adequate safety net is beset with difficulties such as moral hazard and adverse selection.

Regulators constantly face the possibility that inadequate regulation will result in costly failures, as against the possibility that over-regulation will result in opportunity costs in the form of economic efficiencies not achieved, or in the relocation of firms to other, more friendly regulatory regimes. Since any improvements in economic stability can only be measured in terms of damage that *did not occur* and costs that were successfully *avoided*, the argumentation is invariably based on "what if" hypotheticals. Consequently, there are no definitive answers with respect to optimum regulatory structures with respect to corporate governance. There are only "better" and "worse" solutions, as perceived by those to whom the regulators are ultimately responsible, in light of their collective risk-aversion and reaction to past regulatory failures.

Some of the principal options that regulators have at their disposal range from "fitness and properness" criteria, under which corporations may be established, continue to operate, or be shut down; line-of-business regulation as to what specific types of activities companies may undertake; and regulations applying to a range of management practices. Regulatory initiatives, however, can have their own distortive impact on firms and markets, and regulation becomes especially difficult when those markets evolve rapidly and the regulator can easily get one or two steps behind—and also when there is jurisdictional conflicts or overlaps between different corporate regulators.

The regulatory vehicles that may be used for implementation (the "delivery system") range from reliance on self-restraint on the part of boards and senior managements of business firms concerned with the market value of their own franchises, to industry self-regulation, to public oversight by regulators with teeth, including the possibility of criminal prosecution.

There has been lively debate about the effectiveness of firm self-regulation, since business firms continue to suffer from incidents of misconduct and misgovernance, despite the often devastating effects on the value of their franchises. Control through industry self-regulation is likewise subject to substantial controversy, as discussed hereafter.

But reliance on public oversight for governance regulation has its own problems, since virtually any regulatory initiative is likely to run up against powerful vested interests that would like nothing better than to bend the rules in their favor, as we discussed earlier in connection with lobbying.[9] Even the judicial process that is supposed to arbitrate or adjudicate matters of regulatory policy may not always be entirely free of political influence or popular opinion. Moreover, some of the regulatory options are fairly easy to supervise but potentially distortive, due to their broad-gauge nature. Others (e.g., fit and proper criteria) are possibly highly cost-effective but devilishly difficult to supervise, even as some supervisory techniques are far more costly for industry to comply with than others.

Finally, regulatory intervention in routine operations of business firms is common. This intervention reflects a dynamic that exists between regulators and the regulated, and often results in a healthy and constructive nonlegislative remedy to a newly perceived problem. It is sometimes occasioned by a perceived failure in the marketplace, or because public attention has been drawn to a particular incident and a regulatory response is politically unavoidable. However, some interventions result in redundancies or costs and are of little value. But they nevertheless reflect the reality of the regulatory give-and-take in the economic and political marketplace.

A good regulatory structure targeted on corporate governance issues should satisfy four criteria: (1) proportionality, (2) consistency, (3) flexibility, and (4) accountability.

First, regulation is meant to correct market failure, but care must be taken that the cure is not worse than the disease. Excessive regulation can lead to an increase in both direct and indirect costs, possibly reaching a stage where the marginal social costs vastly exceed marginal social benefits. Costs of regulation include not only direct administrative costs but also indirect compliance costs.[10] Furthermore, opportunity costs of reduced innovation and higher inefficiency need to be included for a full assessment of regulatory costs and burdens. Indirect costs can often outweigh the direct costs—for example, the direct regulatory costs associated with federal agencies in the United States is around \$25 billion;[11] but the estimated compliance costs appear to be in the region of around \$600–700 billion annually.[12]

Second, good regulation attempts to ensure trust between the regulator and the regulated to ensure good compliance, and this can be achieved by applying uniform and consistent procedures in an impartial way.

Third, good regulation calls for flexibility—a principle strongly championed by countries such as the United Kingdom, which tries to operate on a "principles" basis. Flexibility covers both flexibility in devising regulations and flexibility in their implementation. It supports a "lean" regulatory structure and a relatively adaptable approach on the part of the regulators.

Finally, regulators must be accountable, with performance metrics set to evaluate how much regulation is achieving in relation to its costs, in order to prevent regulation from descending into bureaucracy. This requires that the regulatory process be transparent—that is, that all parties are included in the regulatory process and the way in which regulatory decisions are made is well known to those involved.

Codes of Practice

These are stiff criteria to meet, and no single regulatory system can claim superiority across a regulatory spectrum that encompasses both codes of practice and statutory rules.

Codes of good corporate practice are part of the regulatory system in many countries, perhaps led by the United Kingdom, which has a long tradition of developing codes of corporate governance. In 1991, the Cadbury Committee's report on corporate governance was a reaction to large number of corporate governance failures and an important attempt to formalize recommendations on good corporate governance. Various other governance codes followed the Cadbury report—collectively covering all aspects of governance, including functioning of boards of directors and auditors, management remuneration, and public disclosure of information. Such codes of governance typically contain principles or guidelines, rather than precise rules, and tend to be voluntary in nature—using a "comply or explain" approach that does not require the regulated firms to comply with the code, but rather to provide information on the state of compliance and reasons for noncompliance. Codes of practice can transition from informal self-regulation to the application of institutional authority, as has developed in the United Kingdom and Switzerland through the listing rules of the stock exchanges. As guidelines and principles, codes of good practice satisfy the criteria of flexibility, proportionality, and market discipline. Through their "comply or explain" approach, they avoid the problem of creative compliance, in which companies jockey to find ways to comply with the letter but not the spirit of the rules.

But codes of compliance can suffer from drawbacks, such as a lack of transparency in drafting precise rules, leaving open the potential for abuse by regulatory agencies in interpretation, and by the regulated in achieving compliance. There is also a real possibility of noncompliance—a study in the United Kingdom found that only 17 percent of 500 firms making up the Financial Times All Share Index fully complied with the recommended code.[13]

Statutory rules, on the other hand, embody the advantages of reducing indirect costs and transparency. Thanks to their statutory nature, they have to be complied with. But because of their specificity and lack of flexibility, there is a persistent danger of over- or underregulation. And there is a strong possibility that loopholes in regulation are exploited and a mere "box-checking" occurs, defeating the purpose of the regulation.

Given the advantages and drawbacks of both systems, a regulatory approach relying on one of these extremes is unlikely to be optimal. The key question is how the mix should evolve.

Forcing Compliance

Apart from the content of corporate governance regulation, an appropriate regulatory structure must also provide for the promulgation of rules and their enforcement. The 1934 Securities and Exchange Act establishing the SEC gave that agency full powers to enforce federal securities laws in the United States, including powers to deny access to public markets, set accounting and auditing standards, authorize exchanges, approve broker-dealers, and certify employees. This concentrated a great deal of power in the executive branch of government, and before long, Congress and others became concerned that it could be abused in some way. The SEC's budget became the subject of Congressional negotiation, and in time the SEC found it politically propitious to delegate some of its statutory powers to other bodies like the FASB, the NYSE, and the NASD. The SEC retained oversight over these other institutions, but as time passed its ability to force them to do things gradually weakened, arguably setting the stage for the governance abuses that followed.

Regulatory structures can also be highly fragmented. For example, regulation of financial firms in the United States is shared between the Federal Reserve System, the Comptroller of the Currency, state banking departments, the Office of Thrift Supervision and the Federal Deposit Insurance Corporation (FDIC); of securities markets by the SEC; insurance by state commissioners; pensions by the Labor Department and the Pension Benefit Guaranty Corporation; and commodities and financial futures by the Commodities Futures Trading Commission (CFTC). Such a widespread regulatory network is awkward in cases of companies that may be able, through mergers of other strategic initiatives, to engage in all kinds of financial businesses under a single roof.

REGULATING THE KEY GOVERNANCE DOMAINS

Until 1930, financial markets in the United States were characterized by little regulation. Corporations were subject to no governance requirements as we know them, but they were subject to market and competitive pressures. Boards were protected by the "business judgment doctrine" sacred in most state courts, which allowed the courts to side with boards of directors if the boards had acted in good faith. Corporations were expected to operate as profit-making entities without much concern for the impact of their activities on others. That changed with Roosevelt's New Deal in 1932, which called for a more regulated economy to help end the Great Depression, and with it came the foundation of securities and banking regulation that has been sequentially extended and occasionally liberalized over the years.

After World War II, government's efforts were focused on controlling corporate power through antitrust actions and labor policies. The recovery of securities markets in the 1960s was welcomed, and with a few important exceptions, regulation bearing on corporate governance was not greatly changed. The 1970s were years of considerable distress in financial markets and in American corporations, with numerous corporate scandals, causing the SEC to become more actively engaged in looking for problems and in investigating reports of misconduct. The 1980s gave us the insider trading scandals on Wall Street and the collapse of the savings-and-loan industry, as well as many commercial banks. It was this period that reinvigorated the concept of "corporate governance," mainly in the form of a series of self-restraining steps that boards of directors took to meet their responsibilities to a growing number of "stakeholders," or constituencies of the corporation. These ranged from making directors more independent, to greater openness to takeover proposals (in shareholders' interests) and to meeting social obligations of various kinds. An era of wise, ethically driven corporate statesmanship seemed to be taking hold.

On the other hand, U.S. corporate economic performance in the 1980s was as unsatisfactory as it had been for decades—after having survived the 1970s by defensive measures—and an extended period of restructuring to increase "shareholder value" ensued. The wise, ethical corporate statesman was being pushed aside by the dynamic, shareholder-value-enhancing CEO who did everything possible to make the stock price rise. As discussed in chapter 5, in the 1990s many of these CEOs became national celebrities, admired for their leadership and the achievements of their corporations, however

rough these had been in terms of layoffs, downsizing, and outsourcing.

Indeed, the last two decades of the twentieth century saw a trend
toward deregulation in many industries. 1980 was somewhat of a
benchmark year for deregulation—the Regulatory Flexibility Act and
the Paperwork Reduction Act were enacted that year. Ronald Reagan,
in keeping with his electoral promises, issued a key executive order
requiring cost-benefit analysis of all regulation. A high-level Regulatory Relief Task Force was established. No new regulatory agency
was established, and no existing regulatory program was significantly expanded during this period.[14] As noted earlier, the Public Securities Litigation Reform Act was passed in 1995 and was strengthened three years later, providing increased protection to accounting
firms from class-action lawsuits. Deregulation continued in 1999, in
the waning days of the Clinton era, as Congress voted to remove the
walls separating banks and other financial institutions that had been
set up under the Banking Act of 1933 and the Bank Holding Company Act of 1956. A review of regulation during this period proclaimed that "proponents of regulation now feel obliged to talk about
costs as well as benefits, private as well as public sector alternatives,
incentives and disincentives, and thus to consider the advantages as
well as the disadvantages of this form of government intervention in
the larger society."[15]

After the stresses following the collapse of Enron and the other
large companies, the search was on to rediscover the precepts of
good corporate governance of 20 years before. They were hard to
find, having evaporated in the supercharged atmosphere of the 1990s.
But with the serial revelations of corporate misconduct, the news media and elected officials focused intensively on the issue for a year or
two, and the notion of appropriate corporate governance made a
comeback. Here again were proposals for improved accounting,
greater director independence, and more honest markets. In short order, all three were subjected to legislative actions requiring a new set
of rules, compliance standards, and legal settlements that were supposed to right the wrongs of an era when few paid much attention to
such issues.

The Sarbanes-Oxley Act

The events of 2001–2002 called for new regulation to bring the large
American corporation under control. The Sarbanes-Oxley Act of 2002
was a very significant piece of legislation, the most important federal
set of regulations related to corporate activities since the 1930s. It was
a response in part to an angry cry to reform abuses that had been in
the headlines for months (although these focused on not many more
than a dozen companies), and in part to a need by serious legislators

to block some of the abuses that large corporations were able to get away with through intimidation, lobbying, and other efforts to lighten their regulatory burden. The Sarbanes-Oxley Act of 2002 marked yet another swing of the regulatory pendulum. The basic provisions of the Act are as follows.

- Creates a new accounting oversight panel—a regulatory board with investigative and enforcement powers to oversee the industry and discipline auditors. The SEC appoints members (only two may be accountants) and will oversee the board. Funded by all public companies by a charge based on market capitalization. Foreign accountants are subject to Board oversight if clients do business in the United States.
- Prohibits auditing firms from offering a broad range of consulting services to publicly traded companies that they audit.
- Requires accounting firms to change the lead or coordinating partners for a company every five years.
- Requires auditors to report to audit committees of Boards, which must be given the means to access independent counsel and auditors.
- Requires enhanced financial disclosure and the certification of the information by the CEO and CFO of public companies.
- Establishes rules pertaining to corporate fraud and accountability.

The Act was introduced as a post-Enron bill, where it wallowed in an uncertain Congress. The final vote on the bill and its signing into law by President Bush were triggered by yet another and even larger scandal—the collapse of WorldCom. The Act is sometimes seen as a mandatory equivalent of corporate governance codes in other countries. It explicitly states investor protection as its aim, citing its objective "to protect investors by improving the accuracy and reliability of corporate disclosures made pursuant to the securities laws, and for other purposes." The 11 sections of the Act cover a broad range of activities and agencies, including auditors, accountants, corporate officers, lawyers, securities analysts, credit rating agencies, investment banks and financial advisers, and state corporate lawmakers.

The Act calls for the creation of a Public Accounting Oversight Board (discussed in chapter 7). The duties of the Board are broadly similar to the existing AICPA board and include registration of public accounting firms, inspection of such firms, and ensuring compliance with the Act on the part of public accounting firms. The Board has the authority to modify or alter auditing and related attestation criteria, quality control, and ethics standards.

A second main area the Act tackles is auditor independence, setting

out an array of activities—including bookkeeping, financial information systems design and implementation, management functions and
human resources, internal audit outsourcing services, and legal or
expert services unrelated to the audit—as "prohibited" activities. Most
management consulting activities conducted by accounting firms in the
past, which were major profit centers for them, are now disallowed. In
addition, the list will include in future any activity the Board determines by regulation to be not permissible. While the aforementioned
services are prohibited, audit firms can engage in other nonaudit services only with the permission of a corporation's audit committee. And
the Act spells out principles of auditor independence, including audit
partner rotation, banning the "revolving door," whereby auditors move
from the audit firm into CFO or other senior management positions
with their audit clients.

The Act makes audit committee independence mandatory. The
CEO and CFO must certify that, to the best of their knowledge, the
financial statements do not contain untrue statements of material fact
and must ensure and report on the integrity of internal controls. The
Act penalizes improper disclosures by ruling that the CEO and CFO
must forfeit their bonuses, incentive pay, or equity options, should
the earnings of the company be restated within 12 months. They also
stand to lose profits on the sale of securities during this 12-month
period.

As a direct response to Enron, the Act bars any director or executive
officer from conducting trading in his or her company's equity during
any blackout period, and indicates that the pension plan administrators
must notify participants and beneficiaries who are affected by any such
trades in advance. In response to the WorldCom, Tyco, Adelphia, and
other scandals, the law prohibits personal loans to executives and directors. Other areas of the Act include significant increases in penalties
covering white-collar crime, and providing protection for employees
of publicly traded companies who provide evidence of fraud—
"whistle-blowers."

Finally, the Act calls for eight broad-ranging industry studies that
could have far-reaching implications for business and the accounting
industry: (1) a review of the potential effects of requiring mandatory
rotation of registered public accounting firms; (2) a GAO study on
consolidation of public accounting firms; (3) an SEC study and report
regarding credit rating agencies; (4) a study and report on violators
and violations of the Act's provisions; (5) a study of enforcement actions; (6) a study of investment banks; (7) a study by the Commission
on the adoption of a principles-based accounting system; and (8) a
study and report on special-purpose entities. What the Congress would
do with these studies remained unclear.

The Sarbanes-Oxley Act has been called a "sweeping reform" by its supporters as well as its critics. President Bush praised it as representing "the most far-reaching reforms of American business practice since Franklin Delano Roosevelt." Some even likened its influence to that wielded by RICO (the Racketeer Influenced and Corrupt Organizations Act of 1970), which focused on organized criminal activity and has been applied by prosecutors to corporate crime with the aim of striking fear into the hearts of "corporate crooks." Detractors criticized the Act for being "more sweep than reform," claiming that it simply put together a variety of existing federal regulations, state laws, stock exchange and securities laws, accounting practices, and corporate governance practices, rather than representing any new legislative departure.

Some who have studied the accounting and corporate requirements of the Act believe that no new powers were created that were not otherwise held by the SEC—although the SEC may have weakened these powers over a long period of delegation to the accounting industry's professional association, and to exchanges such as the NYSE and NASDAQ. But to comply with the detailed requirements of the Act constituted a very large task that promised to cost a great deal. One large *Fortune* 100 company announced that compliance with the Act would cost the firm $40 million in the first year, and a significant portion of that every year thereafter. Unfortunately, much of the compliance costs are the same whether a company is large or small, and the Act applies to all 15,000 publicly traded companies in the United States. Even if the compliance cost were only $5 million per company on average, the initial total cost would be $75 billion, with perhaps half of that amount annually going forward. AMR Research estimated that the *Fortune* 1000 companies would spend approximately $2.5 trillion on Sarbanes-Oxley compliance over the years, and that audit firms could increase their fees by as much as 30 percent in the wake of the Act, partly triggered by increased training for their professionals. Chief executive officers, board members, and other executives could also demand higher remuneration packages to compensate them for the higher personal risk attributable to the Act. Other countries with firms whose securities are listed in the United States have also reacted adversely to costs imposed on them by the Act. And there were concerns in countries such as Switzerland that Sarbanes-Oxley clashed with national laws of their own.

The cost of Sarbanes-Oxley—as well as the mutual fund reforms (chapter 6), additional accounting reforms (chapter 7), and securities industry reforms (chapter 8)—has to be borne by domestic and foreign users of U.S. financial markets: corporations, governments, and investors. Some may decide that they can acquire the financial services that they need in other less expensive marketplaces. Others may decide that liquidity, transparency, and a level playing field is worth

paying for—that optimum regulation is not the same thing as minimum regulation.

LIVING WITH REGULATION

Regulation is a fact of life for the modern corporation. It is accompanied
by nefarious civil litigation that can turn modest regulatory defeats
into massive class-action settlements. Market actions punish most corporate misconduct as soon as it is known. Regulatory action against
even a failed corporation can be excruciating and ruinous, as many
executives of major bankrupted companies in the early 2000s discovered. Class-action suits can sweep up whatever is left, and stick financial intermediaries and advisers with much of the bill. The risk of
running afoul of regulators is a serious one to the modern corporation,
one that public shareholders should more carefully bear in mind in the
future than perhaps they did in the recent past.

Regulators, however, are shown in times of market failure and scandal to be creatures of the political world that created them. Headlines
are sometimes more important than using regulatory power to prod
and inspire a market structure to clean and protect itself. By the time
a market failure reaches a reform measure, the danger is great that the
value of reform will fall short of the cost of achieving it. Hotheaded,
grandstanding politicians do not concern themselves much with unintended consequences of regulation on competitive performance in
the long term.

Yet regulators must try to keep up, by spotting the problems and
acting on them when they can, not letting themselves get too far behind.
But markets sometimes move faster than they do, and too often the
abuse for which an expensive new law or regulation has been created
will have disappeared with the particular market conditions of the day,
to be replaced by something else. But the cost of compliance remains
behind. This is a sign of the imperfect world of attempting to regulate
in a free marketplace.

In the end, financial regulators are looking to fulfill a public duty,
to protect retail investors—however limited their individual participation in the market may be—from abuses by either corporate or institutional agency conflicts. Legislating away agency conflict will not
succeed. It is too idiosyncratic, too changeable, and too opaque to be
generalized into a tight little package that can be controlled by a well-
drafted law. Better to let well-informed regulators like the SEC craft a
series of inconspicuous rules that address problems as they come up,
shutting the gates to this or that shortcut triggered by unpredictable
and unpredicted market opportunity. For this to work, regulators have
to be strong enough to do the jobs they are assigned, They cannot back
away from overlobbied members of Congress seeking to protect con-
tributors at the cost of the SEC's budget. But the SEC lives in the same

world of political *Realpolitik* that Congress does. All are affected in one way or another by the political climate in which they must work. That being the case, expectations must be kept in check. Regulators can help. They can get things right. But equally they can fail, just as corporations, accountants, bankers, and fund advisers will also fail from time to time. Nirvana is too expensive.

10

248-269

Conflicts of Interest

In 2001 the Department of Trade and Industry of the United Kingdom (DTI) released its final report on one of that country's most dramatic financial scandals, the looting of almost $600 million in pension funds belonging to employees of the late Robert Maxwell's Maxwell Communications Corporation and Mirror Group Newspapers PLC. The theft had come to light 10 years before, and blame was placed squarely on CEO Robert Maxwell (who apparently committed suicide) and on his son, Kevin. Indeed, the events had vindicated the DTI's own judgment in having censured Maxwell, as far back as 1971, as being "unfit to run a public company." Particularly shocking to many observers was the DTI's conclusion, reached in a deliberate and thoughtful way and including phrases like "cliquishness, greed and amateurism," that the crime could not have been committed without the active participation of lawyers, accountants, and financial intermediaries. Maxwell's accountants (Coopers & Lybrand Deloitte) had not noticed the missing pension assets, his law firm and financial adviser (Clifford Chance and Samuel Montagu) suppressed their legal and due diligence judgment to avoid jeopardizing fee income, and his broker-dealers (Goldman Sachs and Lehman Brothers) helped support the Maxwell Communications share price using third parties as a front. Despite a shabby track record—both in terms of the man's character and his business practices—each of these reputable firms evidently chose to overlook major flaws to align themselves with Maxwell's own interests in return for the fees he paid them. Others were left to fend for themselves.

Meanwhile, across the Atlantic, there was the final report of Enron's bankruptcy examiner, released in the summer of 2003, entitled "A Culture of Greed and Corruption." Besides outlining the internal governance failures centered on Enron's management and its board, the examiner's report singled out lawyers, accountants, and financial intermediaries, without whom the then largest bankruptcy in U.S. history (exceeded only by the WorldCom bankruptcy shortly thereafter) could not have occurred. Arthur Andersen was cited for aiding and abetting financial fraud, failures in audit integrity, and conflicts of interest, quite apart from the firm's subsequent guilty plea to obstruction-of-justice charges. Vinson & Elkins, Enron's Houston law firm, was cited for legal advice clouded by business interests. Enron's commercial banks were faulted for lack of credit judgment. And the investment banks and investment banking divisions of financial conglomerates were alleged to have aided and abetted fraud by creating financial vehicles having no commercial purpose, designed solely to misrepresent Enron's financial condition and deceive investors. According to the report, they were not merely facilitators but were active initiators and participants—suppressing their obligations to all other constituencies in the pursuit of fees from the Enron relationship.

Shortly after the Enron report, the Italian dairy products company Parmalat discovered some $12.5 billion in "missing" company funds. The SEC later termed the episode "one of the most brazen financial frauds in history," which was the result of hiding operating losses and financial transfers to the personal accounts of CEO Calisto Tanzi by accounting manipulations and offshore vehicles. Parmalat carried large amounts of debt on its books, made up of both bank loans and bonds placed with institutional investors and Italian retail investors. The scandal came to a head in 2003, with the improbable discovery of some $4 billion in nonexistent deposits with Bank of America.

A 2004 report by Enrico Bondi, the bankruptcy administrator appointed by the Italian government under special legislation to deal with the scandal, noted that Parmalat's auditor, Grant Thornton, lacked competence and was too close to the client, and that its audit work continued to contaminate the audits of its successor, Deloitte & Touche, under Italy's mandatory auditor rotation rules. He found that Parmalat's lead law firm was actively involved in structuring offshore entities in the Cayman Islands that helped perpetuate the fraud. And he found that "banks and investment banks directly supplied financial products that contributed to the false representation of the economic and financial situation of the Group's accounts."[1] Among those named were Citigroup, Deutsche Bank, Morgan Stanley, Crédit Suisse First Boston, and UBS, along with the leading Italian banks. According to one observer at the time, "they are thinking very seriously about going for advisers and for those banks which were writing debt that helped Parmalat carry on for so long."[2] A month later, a suit by the administrator, seeking to recover company funds from the banks (just as the Maxwell administrators had done successfully a decade earlier), was filed against them in New Jersey and in Italy.

These three reports, covering events spread out over a decade in three different countries, are all about fraud and criminal conduct by corporate executives. But they also focus attention on another key issue—the frauds could not have occurred without the participation of willing or naïve financial intermediaries, all of whom experienced conflicts between their own interests (to generate fees from their corporate clients) and those of investors whose money was committed to the corporations' securities. In each case, the conflicts were resolved by the intermediaries in favor of their own interests, despite all of the regulatory, managerial, and market-discipline constraints designed to protect investors.

Not only did these intermediary firms fail to carry out effectively their external monitoring and control functions, through which they might have detected the frauds, but they also failed in their fiduciary duties to their investing clients. As we know, in the late 1990s and early 2000s, a dozen or more cases of financial intermediaries caught up in corporate failures came to light.

How could these frauds be perpetrated—repeatedly—in a presumably well-regulated and relatively efficient marketplace made up of many sophisticated institutional investors and corporations, most of them with histories of at least a decade of sound "corporate governance?" To what extent were the frauds aided by powerful, highly skilled financial intermediaries with strong motivations to look after their own revenue growth and earnings? Can such intermediaries be trusted with the critical role of external monitoring and control agents in the free-market system? Is it possible that financial firms have conflicts of interest and governance problems of their own as serious as— or perhaps even more serious than—those of their clients?

In earlier chapters we have identified well-known agency conflicts between the owners and managers of public corporations, and between the owners and managers of public investment vehicles. These conflicts, of course, involve potential agency costs, which investors rely upon boards of directors and public regulation to minimize—or at least to keep within tolerable bounds. But there is another set of agency conflicts in the system—those related to intermediaries representing both corporations and their various transactions in the financial markets, and investors who purchase the securities or loans generated by the transactions.

In principle, financial intermediaries serve both suppliers and users of capital in the markets and must be seen as evenhanded between the two if they hope to remain in business. In reality, the scene is somewhat different. Intermediaries are not just "honest brokers." They are often very active principals investing their own money (in underwriting, trading positions, and bridge loans), and facilitating transactions (new issues of securities, mergers, restructuring, and off-balance-sheet finan-

Role Conflict

of intermediaries

cial vehicles) on the interface between buying and selling clients, for which their fees and returns on their own investments can be considerable. Today, all of these financial intermediaries are publicly traded entities with share prices to support by meeting profit forecasts and achieving market-share improvements. The most important financial intermediaries that together dominate wholesale and investment banking consist of fewer than a dozen firms, operating in almost all product and business areas with impressive financial and human resources at their disposal.

Potential conflicts of interest are, therefore, a fact of life among the financial firms that help direct the flow of capital in the modern market-oriented economy. Normally they are managed by the intermediary firms so as to minimize agency costs (e.g., by withdrawing from or postponing participation in a conflicted transaction). When conflicts of interest are exploited, however, agency costs are imposed on all users of financial markets, from the smallest retail investor to the largest corporation—and sometimes multiple agency costs are involved. As a result, both efficiency and fairness in financial markets suffer, and so does the effectiveness with which financial intermediaries engage in their role as objective monitors of corporations and their governance processes.

When competition is perfect and when markets are fully transparent, exploitation of conflicts of interest cannot take place—everything is known. So the necessary condition for agency costs attributable to conflicts of interest is market and information imperfections. The role of banks, securities firms, insurance companies and asset managers— market operators and purveyors of information—in repeated episodes of conflict of interest exploitation suggests that the underlying market imperfections are systemic, even in highly developed financial systems like that of the United States. And, judged by their appearance in lawsuits by regulators and private plaintiffs, the bigger and broader the financial intermediaries, the greater seem to be the agency problems associated with them.

[margin note: there are Market imperfection give rise to agency cost]

IDENTIFYING CONFLICTS OF INTEREST

There are essentially two types of conflicts of interest that face intermediary firms: *Type 1 conflicts* arise between a firm's own economic interests and the interests of its clients, usually reflected in the misappropriation of economic gains or mispriced transfers of risk; *Type 2 conflicts* develop between clients, placing the firm in a position of favoring one at the expense of another—bankers who systematically favor corporate clients over investing clients would be an example of this type of conflict.

Both types of conflicts can arise either from interprofessional trans-

[margin note: 2 types of conflicts]

actions carried out in wholesale financial markets, or in activities involving retail clients. The distinction between these two market "domains" is important because of the key role of information and transactions costs, which differ substantially between these two broad types of market participants. Their vulnerability to conflict exploitation differs accordingly, and measures designed to remedy the problem in one domain may be inappropriate in the other. In addition, there are "transition" conflicts of interest, which run between the two domains—and whose impact can be particularly troublesome. The following classification shows the principal conflicts of interest encountered in financial services firms by *type* and by *domain*.

Wholesale Domain

Type-1:

   Firm-client conflicts

   Principal transactions

   Tying

   Board memberships

   Spinning

   Investor loans

   Self-dealing

   Front-running

Type-2:

   Inter-client conflicts

   Misuse of private information

   Client interest incompatibility

Retail Domain

Type-1:

   Firm-client conflicts

   Biased client advice

   Involuntary cross-selling

   Churning

   Inappropriate margin lending

   Failure to execute

Misleading disclosure and reporting

Privacy-related conflicts

Domain-Transition Conflicts

Type-1:

Firm-client conflicts

Suitability

Stuffing

Conflicted research

Misuse of fiduciary role

Laddering

Bankruptcy-risk shifting

Conflicts of Interest in Wholesale Financial Markets

In wholesale financial markets involving professional transaction counterparties, corporations, and sophisticated institutional investors, the
asymmetric information and competitive "frictions" necessary for conflicts of interest to be exploited are usually limited. *Caveat emptor* and
limited fiduciary obligations rule, in a game that all parties fully understand. Nevertheless, several types of conflicts of interest do seem to
be exploited even in the most sophisticated markets, as follows:

Principal transactions. A financial intermediary may be involved as a
principal with a stake in a transaction in which it is also serving as
market-maker, adviser, lender, or underwriter, creating an incentive to
put its own interest ahead of those of its clients or trading counterparties. Or the firm may engage in misrepresentation beyond the ability
of even highly capable clients to uncover. One of the classic examples
involved complex Bankers Trust derivative transactions with Procter
& Gamble and Gibson Greetings in 1995, which, when revealed, caused
major damage to the Bank's franchise, brought key executive changes,
and ultimately led to the Bank's takeover by Deutsche Bank in 1999.

"Tying." A financial intermediary may "tie" its lending power to
influence a client to employ its securities or advisory services as well—
or the reverse, denying credit to clients that refuse to use these other
services. For example, a 2002 survey of corporations with more than
$1 billion in annual sales found that 56 percent of firms that refused to
buy fee-based bank services had their credit restricted or lending terms
altered adversely, and 83 percent of the surveyed CFOs expected adverse consequences should they refuse to buy noncredit services.[3] In
2003, for example, the Federal Reserve imposed a fine of $3 million on
WestLB, a German bank, for violating antitying regulations.[4] That is,

costs may be imposed on such clients, as a result of banks' market power, in the form of higher priced or lower quality services or possibly denial of services altogether. This differs from cross-subsidization, in which a bank engages in lending on concessionary terms (i.e., below market) in order to be considered for securities or advisory services. There may be good economic reasons for such cross-selling initiatives, the costs of which are borne by the bank's own shareholders. The line between tying (which is a violation of banking regulations under some circumstances) and cross-selling is often blurred—and its effectiveness is debatable.[5]

Board interlocks. The presence of bankers on boards of directors of nonfinancial companies may cause various bank functions such as underwriting or equity research to differ from arms-length practice. A high-profile case emerged in 2002, when a member of the AT&T board, Citigroup chairman and CEO Sanford Weil, allegedly urged the firm's telecom analyst, Jack Grubman, to rethink his negative views on the company's stock. AT&T's CEO, Michael Armstrong, also served on the Citigroup Board. AT&T shares were subsequently up-rated by Grubman, and Citigroup coincidentally was mandated to comanage a major issue of AT&T Mobile tracking stock. Grubman down-rated AT&T again not long thereafter, and Weill himself narrowly averted being implicated in subsequent regulatory sanctions.[6] Although constrained by legal liability issues, director interlocks can compound other potential sources of conflicts of interest, such as simultaneous lending and advisory and fiduciary relationships.[7] Such conflicts may impose costs on the bank's shareholders and on clients.[8]

Spinning. Securities firms involved in initial public offerings may allocate shares to officers or directors of client firms on the understanding of obtaining future business, creating a transfer of wealth to those individuals at the expense of other investors. Such issues were prominent in the 2003 Wall Street settlement arranged by New York state attorney general Eliot Spitzer (see the discussion in chapter 8).

Self-dealing. A financial firm may act as trading counterparty for its own fiduciary clients, as when the firm's asset management unit sells or buys securities for a fiduciary client while its affiliated broker-dealer is on the other side of the trade. In the United States, the 1974 Employee Retirement Income Security Act (ERISA) bars transactions between asset management units of financial firms that are fiduciaries for defined-benefit pension plans and their affiliated broker-dealers, despite possible costs of this prohibition in terms of inferior execution of trades.[9] Transactions involving principal positions of securities firms with investing customers must be disclosed at the time of the trade. However, in some markets, especially those involving managed accounts in Europe and Asia, disclosures required in the United States or the United Kingdom may be neglected or otherwise performed after the fact.

Front-running. Financial firms may exploit institutional, corporate, or other wholesale clients by executing proprietary trades in advance of client trades that may move the market. For example, in 2003 investigations by the SEC and the NYSE were aimed at floor specialists allegedly violating their "negative obligation" or "affirmative obligation" to assure orderly markets in listed securities, and instead "trading ahead" of customer orders—evidently confirming longstanding rumors of suspicious specialist behavior. Included in the 2003 investigation were specialist affiliates of major financial firms, including FleetBoston Financial Group (now Bank of America), Goldman Sachs Group, and Bear Stearns. A total of 15 NYSE specialists were charged in April 2005 by the SEC for illegally pocketing $19 million at clients' expense, and another 20 specialists were accused of front-running their clients, while the NYSE itself was fined $20 million for regulatory failures and forced to submit to external monitoring for the first time in its history.[10]

All of the foregoing are examples of exploitations of type 1 conflicts, which set the firm's own interest against those of its clients in wholesale, interprofessional transactions. Type 2 conflicts, dealing with differences in the interests of multiple wholesale clients, mainly seem to center on the following two issues.

Misuse of private information. As a lender, a bank may obtain certain private information about a client, which can be used in ways that harm the client's interests. For instance, it may be used by the bank's investment banking unit in pricing and distributing securities for another client, or in advising another client in a contested acquisition.

Client interest incompatibility. A financial firm may have a relationship with two or more clients who are themselves in conflict. For example, a firm may be asked to represent the bondholders of a distressed company and subsequently be offered a mandate to represent a prospective acquirer of that corporation. Or two rival corporate clients may seek to use their leverage with bankers or institutional investors to impede each other's competitive strategies. Or firms may underprice IPOs to the detriment of a corporate client in order to create gains for institutional investor clients from whom they hope to obtain future trading business. In 2003, for example, some investor clients were alleged to have kicked back a significant part of their gains to the underwriting firms in the form of excessive commissions on unrelated trades during the IPO boom of the late 1990s and 2000.

Conflicts of Interest in Retail Financial Services

As noted, asymmetric information is a much more important driver of conflict-of-interest exploitation in retail financial services than in "interprofessional" wholesale financial markets. Assuming that financial institutions scrupulously honor client confidentiality, retail conflicts of interest issues appear to involve primarily *type 1 conflicts*, setting the interests of the financial firm against those of its clients.

Biased client advice. When financial firms have the power to sell affiliates' products, managers may fail to dispense impartial advice to clients, because they have a financial stake in promoting high-margin "house" products. Sales incentives may also encourage promotion of high-margin, third-party products—to the ultimate disadvantage of the customer. The incentive structures that underlie such practices are rarely transparent to the retail client. Even when the firm purports to follow a so-called "open architecture" approach to best-in-class product selection, such arrangements normally will be confined to suppliers of financial services with whom it has distribution agreements that may not be fully apparent to the clients. "Know your customer" rules are supposed to assure the appropriateness of client advice.

Involuntary cross-selling. Retail clients may be pressured to acquire additional financial services on unfavorable terms in order to access a particular product, such as the purchase of credit insurance tied to consumer or mortgage loans. Or financial firms with discretionary authority over client accounts may substitute more profitable services, such as low-interest deposit accounts, for less profitable services, such as higher interest money market accounts, without the client's consent.

Churning. A financial firm that is managing assets for retail or private clients may exploit its agency relationship by engaging in excessive trading, which creates higher costs and may lead to less efficient investment portfolios. Commission-based compensation of brokers is the usual cause of churning behavior.

Inappropriate margin lending. Clients may be encouraged to leverage their investment positions through margin loans from broker-dealers, exposing them to potentially unsuitable levels of market risk and high credit costs. Broker incentives tied to stock margining are usually the reason behind exploitation of this conflict of interest.

Failure to execute. Financial firms may fail to follow client instructions on market transactions if doing so benefits the firm. Or payments may be delayed to increase the float. Regulatory enforcement in the brokerage industry is supposed to tightly circumscribe failure to execute.

Misleading disclosure and reporting. Financial firms may be reluctant to report unfavorable investment performance to clients if doing so threatens to induce outflows of assets under management. Whereas a certain degree of puffery in asset management performance reviews is normal and expected, there is undoubtedly a "breaking point" where it becomes exploitive.

Violation of privacy. The complete and efficient use of internal information is central to the operation of financial services firms, including such functions as cross-selling and effective risk assessment. This may impinge on client privacy or regulatory constraints on misuse of personal information, and raises potentially serious conflict-of-interest issues, which tend to be increasingly problematic as the activity lines of a particular bank or financial firm become broader.[11]

Wholesale–Retail Conflicts

Conflicts of interest between the wholesale and retail domains—characterized by very different information asymmetries—can be either type 1 or type 2, and sometimes both at the same time.

Suitability. A classic domain-transition conflict of interest exists between a firm's "promotional role" in raising capital for clients in the financial markets and its obligation to provide suitable investments for retail clients. Since the bulk of compensation usually comes from capital-raising side, and given the information asymmetries that exist, exploiting such conflicts can have adverse consequences for retail investors.

Stuffing. A financial firm that is acting as an underwriter and is unable to place the securities profitably in a public offering may seek to cut its exposure to loss by allocating unwanted securities to accounts over which it has discretionary authority. This conflict of interest is unlikely to be exploited in the case of closely monitored institutional portfolios in the wholesale domain. But in the absence of effective legal and regulatory safeguards, it could be a problem in the case of discretionary trust accounts in the retail domain.

all unbought securities

Conflicted research. Analysts working for "multiline" financial firms wear several hats and are subject to multiple conflicts of interest. In such firms, the researcher may be required to: (1) provide unbiased information and interpretation to investors, both directly and through retail brokers and institutional sales forces; (2) assist in raising capital for clients in the securities origination and distribution process; (3) help in soliciting and supporting financial and strategic advisory activities centered in their firms' corporate finance departments; and (4) support various management and proprietary functions of the firm. Several of these diverse roles are fundamentally incompatible, and raise intractable agency problems at the level of the individual analyst, the research function, the business unit, and the financial firm as a whole.

The extent of this incompatibility has been reflected, for example, in the post-IPO performance of recommended stocks;[12] contradictory internal communications released in connection with regulatory investigations; evidence on researcher compensation; and the underlying economics of the equity research function in securities firms. In their defense, banks and securities firms have argued that expensive research functions cannot be paid for by attracting investor deal-flow and brokerage commissions, so that corporate finance and other functions must cover much of the cost. This has been reflected in eye-popping researcher compensation levels that have been far in excess of anything that could possibly be explained by incremental buy-side revenues at prevailing, highly competitive commission rates. These issues, of course, came to a head during the "bubble" years of the late 1990s and early 2000s.

Some recent evidence seems to suggest that efforts to exploit this conflict of interest are generally unsuccessful in terms of investment banking market share and profitability.[13] Nevertheless, it is argued that equity research conflicts are among the most intractable. Researchers cannot serve the interests of buyers and sellers at the same time. No matter how strong the firewalls, as long as research is not profitable purely on the basis of the buy-side (e.g., by subscription or pay-per-view), the conflict can only be constrained but never eliminated, as long as sell-side functions are carried out in the same organization. And even if research is purchased from independent organizations, those organizations face the same inherent conflicts if they expect to develop further business commissioned by their financial intermediary clients.

Misuse of fiduciary role. Mutual fund managers who are also competing for pension fund mandates from corporations may be hesitant to vote fiduciary shares against the management of those companies, to the possible detriment of their own mutual fund shareholders. Or the asset management unit of a financial institution may be pressured by a corporate banking client into voting shares in that company for management's position in a contested corporate action such as a proxy battle. In such cases, the potential gain (or avoidance of loss) in banking business comes at the potential cost of inferior investment performance for its fiduciary clients, and may violate its duty of loyalty to these clients. These issues were discussed in chapter 6.

Market timing and late trading. Important clients tend to receive better service than others, in the financial services sector as in most others. When such discrimination materially damages one client segment to benefit another, however, a conflict-of-interest threshold may be breached and the financial firm's actions may be considered unethical or possibly illegal, with potentially serious consequences for the value of its business franchise. This issue has been discussed in more detail in chapter 6, in connection with mutual funds and other institutional investors, notably insurance companies' variable annuities.

Laddering. Banks involved in initial public offerings may allocate shares to institutional investors who agree to purchase additional shares in the secondary market, thereby promoting artificial prices, intended to attract additional (usually retail) buyers who are unaware of these private commitments.

Shifting bankruptcy risk. A bank with credit exposure to a client whose bankruptcy risk has increased, to the private knowledge of the banker, may have an incentive to assist the corporation in issuing bonds or equities to the general public, with the proceeds used to pay down the bank debt. Such behavior can also serve to redistribute wealth between different classes of bondholders and equity investors, and represents one of the "classic" conflicts of interest targeted by the 1933 separation of commercial and investment banking in the United States that lasted until 1999.

Historically, there appears to be little evidence that this potential conflict of interest has in fact been exploited, at least in the United States. During the 1927–1929 period, investors actually paid higher prices for bonds underwritten by commercial banks that were subject to this conflict of interest than for bonds from independent securities firms that were not, and these bonds also had lower default rates.[14] The same finding appeared in the 1990s, when commercial bank affiliates were permitted to underwrite corporate bonds under Section 20 of the Glass-Steagall Act prior to its 1999 repeal. The reason may be that information emanating from the credit relationship allows more accurate bond pricing, less costly underwriting, and reinforced investor confidence.

CONFLICTS OF INTEREST AND STRATEGIC PROFILES OF FINANCIAL FIRMS

In chapter 8, we discussed the consolidation and conglomeration of the financial services industry during the latter 1990s in some detail. Many large banks have placed their bets on "big balance sheet" strategies as a means of creating economies of scope from cross-selling products to clients, often acquired through mergers—and by lowering the unit costs of managing the combined bank's infrastructure. Such strategies also require the banks to move into the higher margin areas of business, away from the intensely competitive, commoditized activities. But higher margin businesses also tend to be riskier—often involving innovations not yet fully tested or requiring the bank to take on considerable market or credit risk as a part of the transaction—than their more traditional businesses. But the higher margin businesses is where all the major intermediaries logically want to be, and so the competition for large mandates for corporations doing multiple financial and strategic transactions is intense, and involves aggressive marketing to win assignments. Aggressive marketing usually means being willing to do whatever the corporation asks to get the assignment. Frequently what is asked, in essence, is a commitment to favor the corporation's objectives over those of investors. In an important way, this involves using the intermediaries' influence in the market to promote and advocate the interests of the corporation.

The more the financial firm moves in this strategic direction—that bigger and broader is better—utilizing the full range of its activities, the greater will be the likelihood that the firm will encounter troublesome conflicts of interest with the potential to impose agency costs on clients. Sooner or later, however, the conflicts inevitably become known, and the "bill" is presented to the firm in the form of legal settlements, loss of reputation and client defections, increased compliance costs, and the like. If complexity leads to conflicts of interest, then their exploitation will tend to offset scope-related gains (e.g., cross-selling) realized by the multiline financial services firm. The firm may initially enjoy revenue and profitability gains, at the expense of clients, but subsequent costs of legal, regulatory, and reputational consequences—along with the necessary managerial and operational cost of compliance with new or imposed control requirements—can be considered "diseconomies of scope." It has not yet been established that any financial firm that has engaged in a strategy of acquisitions leading to multiline megabusinesses has been able to achieve positive net economies of scope through a four- or five-year market cycle. Such evidence may indeed exist, but it is certainly elusive.

The potential for conflict-of-interest exploitation in financial firms can be depicted in a matrix such as figure 10.1, listing on each axis the main types of retail and wholesale financial services, as well as infrastructure services such as clearance, settlement, and custody. Cells in the matrix represent potential conflicts of interest. Some of these conflicts are basically intractable, and remediation may require changes in organizational structure. Others can be managed by appropriate changes in incentives, functional separation of business lines, or internal compliance initiatives. Still others may not be sufficiently serious

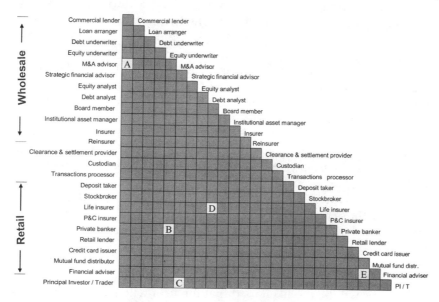

Figure 10.1. Indicative Financial Services Conflict Matrix

to worry about. And in some cases it is difficult to imagine conflicts of interest arising at all.

For example, cell D in figure 10.1 is unlikely to be made up of activities that pose serious conflicts of interest. Other cells, such as C, have traditionally been ring-fenced using internal compliance systems. Still others, such as B and E, can be handled by assuring adequate transparency. But there are some, such as A, that have created major difficulties in particular circumstances (such as advising on a hostile takeover when the target is a banking client), and for these, easy answers seem elusive.

Potential Conflicts of Interest in Multifunctional Client Relationships

The foregoing discussion suggests that conflicts of interest are essentially two-dimensional—either between the interests of the firm and those of its client (type 1), or between clients in conflict with one another (type 2). They can also be multidimensional, however, spanning a number of different stakeholders and conflicts at the same time. Figures 10.2 and 10.3 provide two examples from the rich array of corporate scandals that emerged during 2001–2004.

In the Merrill Lynch–Enron case (fig. 10.2), a broker-dealer was actively involved in structuring and financing an off-balance-sheet special-purpose entity (LJM2), which conducted energy trades with

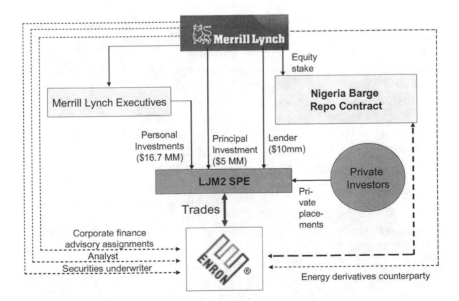

Figure 10.2. Multilateral Conflicts of Interest: Merrill Lynch-Enron. Fees 1999–2001: Underwriting $20 million; Advisory $18 million; Fund raising $265 million.

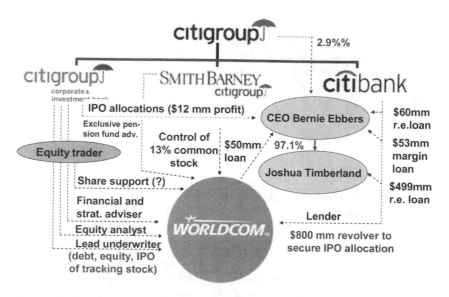

Figure 10.3. Multifunctional Client Linkages and Conflicts of Interest

Enron and whose CEO was simultaneously Enron's CFO. Merrill was both a lender to and an investor in LJM2—as were a number of senior Merrill executives and unaffiliated private and institutional investors advised by the firm. Merrill also structured a repurchase transaction for Enron involving a number of barges in Nigeria. Allegedly, the sole purpose of the LJM2 and Nigerian barge transactions was to misrepresent Enron's financials to the market.[15] At the same time, Merrill performed a range of advisory and underwriting services for Enron, provided equity analyst coverage, and was one of Enron's principal derivatives-trading counterparties. Conflicts of interest in this case involved Merrill and Enron shareholders, investors in Enron and LJM2 debt, Merrill executives, as well as unaffiliated institutional and private shareholders in the LJM2 limited partnership.

In the Citigroup–WorldCom case (fig. 10.3), a multiline global financial conglomerate was serving simultaneously as equity analyst supplying assessments of WorldCom to institutional and retail clients, while advising WorldCom management on strategic and financial matters. As a major telecommunications-sector commercial and investment banking client, WorldCom maintained an active credit relationship with Citigroup and provided substantial securities underwriting business. Citigroup also served as the exclusive pension fund adviser to WorldCom and executed significant stock option trades for WorldCom executives as the options vested. It also conducted proprietary trading in WorldCom stock. Citigroup was closely allied with WorldCom CEO Bernie Ebbers—an alliance that involved personal and business loans, as well as an investment in one of his private business ventures. Simultaneous conflict-of-interest vectors in this instance involve retail investors, institutional fund managers, WorldCom executives, and WorldCom shareholders, as well as Citigroup's own positions in WorldCom lending exposure and stock trades prior to its bankruptcy in 2002.

Such examples suggest that the broader the range of services that a financial firm provides to an individual client in the market, the greater is the possibility that conflicts of interest will be compounded in any given case, and (arguably) the more likely they are to damage the market value of the financial firm's business franchise once they come to light.

Conflicts of Interest and the Corporate Governance Function

This chapter began with three examples—one British, one American, and one Italian—of how conflicts of interest can undermine the monitoring and control of corporations even in highly developed financial systems where transparency, a level playing field, and fair dealing are assumed to dominate. Today's global capital markets are not supposed to contain murky corners rife with financial skulduggery and exploitive behavior. Yet the endemic nature of conflicts of interest experienced by financial intermediaries seems to assure that bad things that can happen will happen (especially in overheated market conditions), reflecting the incompleteness of whatever constraints are supposed to exist and the persistence of market imperfections and information asymmetries.

One recent study suggests that conflicts of interest can indeed impede the monitoring and control function of financial intermediaries. The study examines the relation between institutional investor involvement in and the operating performance of large firms, and confirms a statistically significant relation between a corporation's operating cash flow returns and both the percent of institutional stock ownership and the number of institutional stockholders. This result would be expected. However, this relationship is found only for institutional investors with no potential business relationship with the firm, suggesting that institutional investors with potential business relations with the firms in which they invest are compromised as monitors of the firm.[16]

As in the 1980s, when many American banks and thrifts failed, banks in expansive phases can become sloppy in their lending—and subordinate credit decisions and loan monitoring to other profit and growth objectives. In their eagerness to ring the cash register, financial firms may reduce due diligence standards or the objectivity and incisiveness of research in order to keep the advisory revenues flowing, corrupting the signals to the market that ought to trigger corrective action on the part of investors, and ultimately by management and boards of directors. Bankers, who ought to be objective, no-nonsense telegraphers of market information and currents, and catalysts seeking the alignment of management actions with the interests of shareholders, have instead pursued other agendas, violating one of key roles of financial intermediaries as external agents of corporate governance. Restoration and strengthening of this role depends in good part on effective constraints bearing on conflict of interest exploitation.

CONSTRAINING EXPLOITATION OF CONFLICTS OF INTEREST

From a public policy perspective, efforts to address exploitation of conflicts of interest in the financial services sector should logically focus first and foremost on improving market efficiency and transparency. There are, of course, regulatory penalties and exposures to class-action litigation that are thought to act as deterrents. Nonetheless, over the past 20 years, during which time both market transparency and the deterrents were functioning as well as at any time in the past, there was widespread conflict-of-interest exploitation involving all of the major-bracket U.S. investment banks, all of the multiline financial conglomerates, four of the top six United Kingdom merchant banks (prior to their acquisition by larger financial firms), all of the major Japanese securities houses, and most of Japan's commercial banks. It is discouraging that, even under today's intense free-market competition, supported by considerable regulatory oversight across multiple jurisdictions, there still appears to be plenty of scope for conflict exploitation on the part of financial intermediaries.

There is also some contrary evidence, however. In corporate actions that lead to changes of control, banks are active in collecting borrower information and facilitating the transmission of this information to potential acquirers. Focusing on hostile takeovers between 1992 and 2003, one study shows that bank lending intensity has a significant and positive effect on the probability of a firm becoming a target, that this probability is enhanced in cases where the target and acquirer have a relationship with the same bank, that the importance of bank lending intensity in predicting takeovers rises with the number of firms the bank deals with, and that takeover completion rates are positively related to bank lending intensity. Indeed, where both the target and the acquirer deal with the same bank, the equity market responds more favorably than it does to deals where no banks are involved, suggesting that banks perhaps do play a disciplining role in the control process.[17]

Still, with the consolidation of the financial services sector, auction-like competition for lucrative fee paying assignments, and the emergence of multiline financial conglomerates, some would argue that exploitation of conflicts of interest has become endemic to the industry. Conflict exploitation—what some financial firms might call "aggressively pursuing opportunities for market-share penetration and enhancement through cross-selling"—has become part of the "business model" for some of them. In fact, the banks have become so large and are so committed to their business models that hefty fines and legal settlements may not be effective deterrents. Even litigation reserves in the billions may just be "water off a duck's back" as a percentage of earnings. Since conflicts of interest seem to be linked to high-margin market opportunities, as opposed to low-margin, conflict-free commodity businesses, the expression "No conflict, no interest" rings uncomfortably true.

Market-Discipline Constraints

Chapter 9 outlined the main regulatory dimensions involved in controlling conflicts of interest in financial firms, and thereby reinforcing their critical role in the governance process. That chapter concludes that the regulatory process is often imperfect, politicized, and sometimes susceptible to "capture" by those it is supposed to regulate. External regulatory constraints applied to conflict-of-interest exploitation tend to be blunt instruments, difficult to devise, calibrate, and bring to bear on specific problems without creating unintended collateral damage. So if financial regulation to address conflict of interest exploitation is bound to be imperfect, then what is the alternative?

Conflicts of interest are often extremely granular and sometimes involve conduct that is "inappropriate" or "unethical" rather than "illegal." So the external impact of conflict exploitation on the "franchise value" of a financial firm may provide a more durable basis for defenses against exploitation of conflicts of interest than regulation. This means, in effect, that the market would evaluate the extent to which a financial firm is likely to become involved in conflict situations that result in higher costs, penalties, settlements and related sanctions, and tangible reputation losses that sends clients fleeing. Such developments will be valued by the market and a multiplier applied, and the stock price adjusted accordingly. Once the adjustment is made, a board sensitive to its stock price (as they all are) will make governance changes to reduce the franchise discount, and corrective action will be taken.

Of course, it doesn't always work that way—sometimes the market sees an aggressive financial firm plowing into rich territory as being worth a higher franchise value because it is more willing to take risks and act opportunistically. In the longer run, however, the market adjusts to reality, and if aggressive conduct results in a serious offset in enterprise value because of conflict exploitation, it will apply market sanctions. Otherwise, it won't. To the financial firm, the incentive is to avoid the offsets cause by conflict exploitation, which usually means avoiding the conflicts or dealing with them in ways that minimize damage to the franchise. But sometimes it just means keeping the conflicts from being known, at least for a while longer.

How these factors may come together to damage a firm's market value can be illustrated by a case involving J. P. Morgan (well before its acquisition by Chase Manhattan), illustrated in figure 10.4. Simultaneously acting as commercial banker, investment banker, and adviser to Banco Español de Crédito (Banesto) in Spain, as well as serving as an equity investor and fund manager for coinvestors in a limited partnership (the Corsair Fund, L.P.) holding shares in the Banesto. In addition, Morgan's vice chairman served on Banesto's board. There were many overlapping conflicts of interest in the Banesto relationship between Morgan and its other clients, which became especially problematic when Banesto collapsed in December 1993. Banesto's CEO, Mario Condé, was later convicted on charges of financial fraud and imprisoned. Morgan was embarrassed by the event, but managed to work itself out of the spotlight at a relatively minor financial cost. However, the market reduced the Morgan share price by about 10 percent of its market capitalization at the time, a drop of approximately $1.5 billion, as against an accounting after-tax loss from the affair of perhaps $10 million.[18] This fifteenfold market reaction is consistent with the findings of an earlier event study involving Salomon Brothers' involvement in a Treasury bond auction scandal in 1991, in which market capitalization of the firm dropped by about one-third, and ultimately contributed to Salomon's acquisition by Travelers, Inc. a few years later. Such evidence seems to suggest that market discipline can in fact work, and can send the right signals.

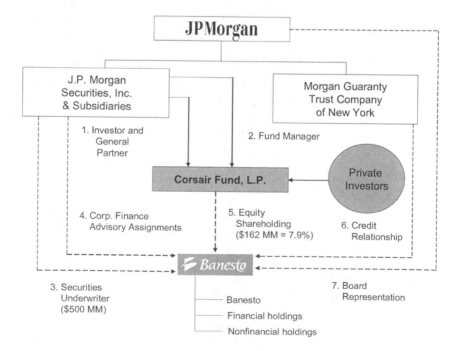

Figure 10.4. Measuring the Stock Price-Effects of Conflicts of Interest

Exploitation of conflicts of interest, whether or not they violate legal and regulatory constraints, can have even more severe consequences. In the case of Bankers Trust's aforementioned 1995 derivatives trading with Procter & Gamble and Gibson Greetings, in which the bank was alleged to have exploited its two clients, the negative publicity nearly killed Bankers Trust. The bank always claimed it was innocent of charges against it, that the two firms were sophisticated trading counterparties, not retail clients, and that they were perfectly capable of looking after themselves. The two companies, the bank claimed, made risky bets on currency movements that, when they went wrong, resulted in large losses and complaints to try to get their money back. But no one seemed to believe the bank, because published excerpts from its traders' conversations revealed coarse locker-room talk of how the traders were setting up the companies to exploit their ignorance of the complex derivatives market. Subsequent revenue losses from client defections dwarfed the $300 million in restitution the bank agreed to pay the two companies. The bank's board of directors changed the CEO and various senior managers and agreed to discontinue derivatives trading, one of its most profitable businesses. Shortly thereafter, the new CEO sold Bankers Trust to Deutsche Bank for $8.7 billion in 1999, earning himself a nifty $140 million bonus in the process.

Increased regulatory pressure on conflict exploitation, particularly since 2000, has required a major increase in the compliance infrastructure of financial firms that has reduced operating margins. The $1.4 billion securities industry settlement with regulators in 2003 applied large mandatory direct and indirect costs to the business that will have to be maintained for years. These included forced organizational changes and separation of functions, which, among other things, impair realization of economies of scope. Compliance with regulations intended to protect against conflict exploitation adds a major expense to the financial intermediary businesses.

REGULATION AND MARKET-BASED CONSTRAINTS

One can argue that regulation-based and market-based *external* controls of conflict exploitation create the basis for *internal* controls that can be either *prohibitive* (as reflected in imposed Chinese walls and compliance systems) or *affirmative*, involving the behavioral "tone" and incentives set by senior management relying on the loyalty and professional conduct of employees. The more complex the financial services organization—especially in the case of massive, global financial conglomerates built by acquisitions of dissimilar businesses—the less likely it is for such an *affirmative* culture to emerge, suggesting greater reliance on prohibitive internal controls and the external role of market discipline. External regulation of conflicts, however, has shown itself to be complex and difficult to implement effectively. But, supported by market discipline, regulatory actions (usually after the fact) can perhaps make a lasting difference.

First, when such actions are announced—and especially when they are amplified by reporting in the media—they can expose the financial firm (whether provably guilty or not) to serious adverse effects on its stock and debt prices. In turn, this affects its access to and cost of capital (essential for financial intermediaries), its ability to make strategic acquisitions, its vulnerability to takeover, and other issues affecting its viability as an independent concern. Such effects reflect the market's response to the impact of regulatory actions on prospective revenues, costs (including derivative civil litigation), and exposure to risk.[19] Boards and managements are presumably sensitive to posttraumatic market reactions, in which the punishment extracted by market realities may end up being worth many times the economic value of the cause.

Second, even in the absence of explicit regulatory constraints, actions that are widely considered to be "unfair" or "unethical" or that otherwise violate accepted behavioral norms can trigger disproportionate market discipline. In a competitive context, this will affect firm valuation through revenue and risk dimensions in particular, with situations, for example, in which one unit of revenue may be worth two of risk. So avoiding conflict-of-interest exploitation is likely to reinforce the value of the firm as a going concern and, with properly structured incentives, management's own compensation. In a firm well known for tying managers' remuneration closely to the share price, former Citigroup CEO Sanford Weill noted in a message to employees: "There are industry practices that we should all be concerned about, and although we have found nothing illegal, looking back, we can see that certain of our activities do not reflect the way we believe business should be done. That should never be the case, and I'm sorry for that."[20]

Third, since they tend to provide constant reinforcement in metrics that managers can understand (market share, profitability, the stock price), market discipline constraints can reach the more opaque areas of conflict-of-interest exploitation, and deal with those issues as they occur in real time, which external regulation normally cannot do.

Fourth, since external regulation bearing on conflicts of interest tends to be linked to information asymmetries and transaction costs, it should logically differentiate between the wholesale and retail domains discussed earlier. Often this is not possible, so there is overregulation in some areas and underregulation in others. Market discipline–based constraints can help alleviate this problem by permitting lower overall levels of regulation and bridging fault-lines between wholesale and retail financial market segments. And just as market discipline can reinforce the effectiveness of regulation, it can also serve as a precursor of sensible regulatory change.

Finally, market structure and competition across strategic groups can help reinforce the effectiveness of market discipline. For example, inside information accessible to a bank as lender to a target firm would almost certainly preclude its affiliated investment banking unit from acting as an adviser to a potential acquirer. An entrepreneur may not want his or her private banking affairs handled by a bank that also controls his or her business financing. A broker may be encouraged by a firm's compensation arrangements to sell in-house mutual funds or externally managed funds with high fees under "revenue-sharing" arrangements, as opposed to funds that would better suit the client's needs.[21] Market discipline that helps avoid exploitation of such conflicts may be weak if most of the competition is coming from a monoculture of similarly structured multiline firms that face precisely the same issues. But if the playing field is also populated by a mixed bag of aggressive insurance companies, commercial banks, thrifts, broker-dealers, independent fund managers, and other "monoline" specialists, market discipline may be much more effective—assuming competitors can break through the fog of asymmetric information.

We conclude that because of the asymmetry between risks and rewards to financial firms of exploitation of conflicts of interest, the conflicts should be seen by managers and directors of the financial firms themselves as potentially very dangerous, and thus they should regulate themselves in a disciplined way to avoid them. We thus rely on Adam Smith's wisdom in believing that informed self-interest determines market actions and outcomes, and that such motivation (based on market discipline) is the best natural cure for chronic conflicts of interest.

But it may be that the financial firms themselves can be blinded to this reality by the need to produce quarterly results consistent with their professed business strategies. Most financial firms are now publicly traded, and must meet the demands of the market or suffer the consequences. Managers of firms need to avoid the consequences and therefore favor aggressive actions ("You eat what you kill" is a favorite Wall Street motivational phrase), pursuing innovation and risk-taking to put the firms into the center of the high-margin arenas, which are often loaded with ambiguities that do not appear until a market break or scandal erupts. So a natural cure may not be sufficient for an industry that has become intimately tied to market hot spots, personal performance measures, and short-term time horizons.

11

The Future of Governance

After the disaster of the early 1930s, a new financial regulatory system was devised as part of a broader effort to stabilize the economy and set the stage for recovery. The failures in banking and finance had ended the country's faith in and reliance on a self-regulated financial marketplace. Those who constructed the new rules of the game evidently felt that the economy was too large, complex, and dynamic to accommodate any uniform system that depended on on-the-spot policing to be effective. They also knew that regulation imposed costs that had to be paid by users of banking and financial markets that could impair economic efficiency and growth, so they wanted to avoid a system that would be excessively comprehensive, cumbersome, or demanding. They sought the right balance between free markets and public-interest regulation, but where that balance was to be struck would be left to experience—by trial and error.

They probably knew they would make some mistakes. But doing nothing was not an option. What they did agree on in the 1930s was that good disclosure and transparency on the part of corporations, banks, broker-dealers, and investment managers would help the market to make well-informed choices based on economic performance. If all the participants in the market were striving to maximize economic performance, they would allocate investments to reward success and punish failure, thereby promoting both efficiency and growth.

The early reformers also knew that agents controlling corporations, banks and other financial intermediaries, and institutional investors— that is, their professional managers—might be tempted to operate the enterprises in their care more for their own benefit than for that of their distant, uncomplaining, and unempowered public investors. They recognized that, like regulatory costs, conflicts of interest can get in the way of optimal economic performance, acting as a friction in the economic system. So they provided for a federal government agency (the SEC) to make rules for the financial markets and all those who use them. If necessary, the SEC could go to court to bring civil charges against offenders, and the Justice Department could prosecute criminal offenders under federal law. Private lawsuits also could bring complaints against corporate managers or investors under state or federal laws, so a potential offender would know that violation of the law could mean legal trouble from any of several quarters. But at least equally important was the idea that the market itself would detect wrongdoing and would discipline those engaging in it through the share price. Professional investors were numerous, independent of each other, highly sophisticated, and well informed. They could smell misconduct or faulty conduct at a distance, and shed any security holdings in suspect companies. A sharp-eyed market was the most difficult adversary to fool, especially over an extended time period, so as a check on rapacious managers, the market itself was to be the first line of defense. The system worked without serious setback for more than 70 years, only to lose its bearings in the late 1990s.

THE DULLING OF THE MARKET

What changed toward the end of this period was an apparent dulling of the market's instincts to perform its disciplinary function. Many factors played a role, perhaps the most important being the widespread acceptance of significant conflicts of interest on the part of many market participants that affected their willingness to act appropriately in the interests of those to whom they had fiduciary obligations. Some of these conflicts have since been reduced or eliminated by regulatory actions, such as the Sarbanes-Oxley Act, which includes requiring accounting firms to separate themselves from management consulting businesses to help assure audit independence. But, as noted in the previous chapter, many embedded conflicts have not been eliminated. Indeed, some of them may have become even more deeply institutionalized by deregulatory actions in recent years, or have been allowed to fester because of political influence that has suppressed efforts by regulators to force changes to either disallow conflicts or to force their public disclosure.

Just as Berle and Means called attention to the dangers of agency conflicts in "modern" publicly owned corporations in the 1930s, we suggest that the "postmodern" public corporation of today—one that exists within a vast, liquid, volatile financial marketplace in which expectations are set and ruthlessly enforced—is likewise confronted by serious agency conflicts. But these are much more extensive and elusive than simple owner-manager conflicts. The conflicts have spread to affect the market's most powerful originators, its monitors, its gatekeepers, and its important end-users, the institutional investors. These conflicts have the potential, as in the late 1990s, to be highly destructive if they are not neutralized or well marked for the unwary.

The natural remedies for market inefficiencies extended by agency conflicts is to find ways for the market to cure itself at relatively low cost in ways that would avoid the permanent structural impediments associated with heavy regulation. The traditional way to do this is to require greater and more timely disclosure, so that the market would know what to embrace or avoid, and to provide greater reliance on self-regulatory efforts to control market abuses.

Reliance on disclosure, however, has often been neutered by the poor reading habits of most investors, and by the fact that many professionals already know the information to be disclosed but may have no interest in acting on it. Mutual fund managers operating a so-called momentum fund (to ride current market trends wherever they go) may be uninterested in disclosures of situations like the excessive management compensation at companies such as Tyco that were performing well at the time. Equally, managers of such funds are unlikely to call attention to high management fees charged by competitors if they too think they can get away with them. Self-regulatory organizations have repeatedly lacked forcefulness and perseverance in addressing conflict issues. For example, the FASB could not restrain or discipline the leading firms of the accounting profession, and both the NASDAQ (then an SRO) and the NYSE (currently an SRO) were ineffective in spotting and controlling excessive trading margins by its member firms. And the Investment Company Institute did nothing to combat late trading and market timing in mutual funds, nor did the Securities Industry Association flag any of the abuses that involved its member firms, despite widespread rumors about what was happening.

If reliance on the classic measure of transparency fails to work, critics point out, then the government is obliged to step in to enforce standards more rigorously. This may be unfortunate, but it is necessary. As we have emphasized, this regulatory dynamic has occurred at regular internals in American financial history, as reflected in tens of thousands of pages of regulations that now try to assure participants that the market for financial instruments is fair and efficient. Had regulators been more alert and intervened more forcefully, perhaps the exceptional events of market failure of the late 1990s would not have happened, even despite the disorienting investment bubble of the time. So the government's motivation and ability to intervene when necessary in order to better regulate markets remains suspect; there were five prominent government impediments to effective regulation that came to light during the early 2000s.

First, federal and state laws covering fiduciary conduct were shown to be dysfunctional—business incorporation and many fiduciary functions are state matters, although securities laws are principally enforced by the federal government, and securities class-action suits must be brought in federal (not state) courts.

Second, the SEC, as the principal regulator of securities markets, has been stripped of many of its powers by delegation to SROs, by the lobbying efforts of interest groups, and by a lack of desire on the part of politically appointed officials to allow the Commission free rein to discipline well-connected corporations. The SEC and other regulators are subject to budgetary constraints, which can be used to thwart regulatory initiatives and reforms.

Third, ineffective regulation of the accounting industry by the SEC has resulted in unreliable financial information penetrating the markets on a large scale. This important industry has since been diminished by the sudden liquidation of one of its major firms, leaving it to rediscover a healthy and viable economic strategy for the future, something the industry has not yet been able to achieve.

Fourth, state and federal banking, securities, insurance, and commodities regulators and designated SROs are numerous, overlapping, and often conflicting. They are organized exclusively along functional lines, and do not come together at the top to consider the broader regulatory picture. A major flaw is that most of the powerful financial firms operate in many or all of these different functional areas simultaneously, without being regulated or governed as a single entity. The system of specific "regulation by function" has come about as far as it can from the more general "fitness and properness" of institutions and their governance.

Fifth, powerful financial firms have been allowed through deregulation over several decades to set aside past regulatory considerations— investor responsibilities, market consolidation, fiduciary obligations, and conflicts of interest—in order to evolve into a more competitive financial services industry. The more concentrated and powerful the firms become—each of the three largest such U.S. firms now controls assets of well over $1 trillion—the greater becomes their political and lobbying capacity, as well as their ability to absorb regulatory penalties without having to alter their course.

A major legislative effort was expended on Sarbanes-Oxley (like the banking and securities regulation of the 1930s, also initiated under intense political pressure), and an equally massive enforcement effort was undertaken by the Justice Department, the SEC, and the state of New York, in order to "restore confidence" in financial markets. These efforts have addressed some of the conflicts in the financial system and have had effects that may help improve confidence in the markets. But a great many other issues (including those just enumerated) have not been addressed, and much of the area of agency conflict identified in chapter 10 of this study has not been addressed by these reform and enforcement measures.

The dilemma, therefore comes down to this: If better disclosure doesn't really matter, if SROs don't work, and if the federal government is unable to address the serious dysfunctional elements of the legal and regulatory framework of the market, what hope is there that the integrity of the system (upon which economic growth and prosperity much depends) can be improved over what it was during a time of some of its worst failures? Are we destined to live with the status quo ante, even after the lessons and correctives of the early 2000s?

Finding the Fault-Lines

One response might be that all real-world economic and financial systems suffer from similar problems that in the end do impose a significant costs, but that these costs ought to be minimized in a free-market system by its natural checks and balances, particularly the discipline of the market itself. Most of the time, it is fair to say, the markets do their job tolerably well. As the perils of risk from conflicts of interest or misconduct become evident, the market has every incentive to shift in favor of managers who can inspire greater confidence in their abilities to serve investors and clients effectively and fairly. Market forces do punish wrongdoers, and the system tends to clean itself.

Still, serious fault-lines in market discipline remain, these are sufficient to sorely test the faith that free-market adherents have in the system. Indeed, sometimes even widely accepted elements of the system can become corrupted, and unless this corruption is effectively addressed there may be little hope that the invisible hand will reappear anytime soon to restore fairness and efficiency. If the balance is not periodically reset to where it needs to be for optimum performance, then the system has developed a serious tilt, a flaw that in time can grind away much of its value. Observers have long pointed to such flaws in emerging markets as serious obstacles to economic performance and growth. But no markets are immune; all markets demand constant renewal and defensive investment.

This leaves us searching for some of the most serious fault-lines in the market-driven system, the ones that are powerful enough to create long-duration distortions that are embedded deeply enough to be considered the way things are really done. As we have structured the discussion in this book, these fault-lines appear both within the governance of modern corporations and in the monitoring and control system that lies between the firm and its ultimate shareholders.

Internal Flaws in the Governance Process

Four more-or-less distinct issues can be identified as persistent problems in the internal governance of the modern corporation.

The first is cheating and fraud, for which laws and punishments exist and to some extent have been enhanced. These include accounting and disclosure fraud, concealment, and sleights of hand that ought to be harder to perform in the future. Not many companies out of the more than 7,000 corporations listed on U.S. stock exchanges have been alleged to have committed such offenses, and the ones that did have largely been dealt with. The aggregate cost to the entire system from cheating and fraud is probably not serious enough to constitute a debilitating flaw in the system. But this is hardly a reason to avoid aggressive enforcement and signaling—even small tumors have a dangerous tendency to spread.

Second is the imbalance of power between the board and the chief executive, which can lead to major corporate mistakes, including unsuccessful mergers and faulty corporate strategies that remain uncorrected for far too long. These issues are up to boards of directors to control, and the evidence seems to be that the overwhelming majority of boards eventually do in fact redress such power imbalances. Those needing help will benefit from a new, much higher profile of corporate governance practices and a plethora of reform proposals. But, all things considered (and despite all the attention given to this), current board practices do not appear to constitute a debilitating flaw in the system.

A third issue is moral hazard, brought about by misaligned compensation practices that encourage managers to misallocate and take excessive risks with shareholder's money. Such moral hazard has led to serious costs, and opportunity costs, borne by shareholders, not managers. This can be a serious risk for a single corporation, and compensation misalignments are widespread among many of them, but the flaw itself is not systematically dangerous and ultimately is likely to be addressed by market discipline—although it can reach serious proportions and can persist for extended periods of time.

A fourth issue is the minimal consequences borne by directors for failures of fiduciary duties owed to the shareholders they serve. Such fiduciary duties long have been treated under state law, and most states employ the "business judgment rule," which protects directors from responsibility for errors made in good faith. Moreover, directors are invariably indemnified by their corporations against all directors' liabilities and associated legal expenses (except for those due to "gross negligence"), and this indemnification in turn is usually insured. Such extremely limited liability allows directors to serve in a benign or passive capacity—to subordinate themselves to the idea of "supporting management"—and therefore to refrain from loyal opposition, criticism, or questioning. If directors' exposure to liability were higher (as intended by the authors of state incorporation laws), directors would exercise greater independence, diligence, and caution. The absence of really meaningful levels of fiduciary liability for corporate directors (including corporations or partnerships that manage money and operate banks, brokerage, insurance, and accounting businesses) is a serious flaw in the system, one that is deeply embedded and difficult to change.

Of these four internal fault-lines of effective corporate governance, we believe the first three are amenable to either existing regulation or market discipline, or both working together. However, the effective exercise of board power in the face of limited liability for individual consequences of malfeasance or nonfeasance remains a serious flaw in the system that needs to be corrected.

External Flaws in the Governance Process:
The Institutional Investors

If the key internal governance fault-line resides in the real-world conduct of boards of directors, then some people are failing to hold them to account. Key among these are the fund managers who today control the majority voting share of most of the large publicly traded corporations, and thus represent the market as a whole. There are three issues affecting these fund managers that are not dissimilar from those just noted.

First, once again, is cheating and fraud committed against their investor clients. In the early 2000s, a few managers (among a great many) were alleged to have engaged in fraudulent activity—such as late trading and undisclosed market-timing trades—sometimes even for their own accounts. The revelations were surprising because they involved two of the most trusted kinds of institutions, mutual funds and insurance companies. But, as in the case of corporate cheating and fraud, laws and penalties exist, and enforcement after detection has been vigorous. It is doubtful that this is a serious flaw in the system, except for the governance of the involved firms themselves—although it does illustrate the double jeopardy to which ordinary investors can be exposed through malfeasance of their investment fund managers and of the corporations in which they invest.

Second is inadequate independence of board members of mutual funds and other investment institutions. As a safeguard to investors, mutual funds are required to have board members, and at least half of these are required to be independent of, or unconnected to, any members of the fund's management or advisory company. Governance practices of these boards have been left mainly to self-supervision and the self-restraint associated with the protection of the good names of the directors individually and collectively. In reality, even independent board members of investment funds, like many corporate board members, do not forcefully challenge the management companies that initially nominated them and provide generous compensation for little work. Whether or not the chair of the board is also independent may not make much difference in this context. Equally, whether or not board members are independent would seem to make little difference if they are passive and uncritical. The reputation of asset management companies depends almost entirely on the enforcement of high standards of integrity adhered to by the management company, something many were able to maintain during the bubble years of the late 1990s. Board performance in asset management is certainly a flaw, and one that affects the whole industry, but perhaps it is one that does not rise to the level of being dangerous to the market system as a whole, especially after regulatory reforms and improved transparency.

A third possible fault-line is conflicts of interest between owners and managers of asset-gathering institutions and the investors they represent. Most mutual funds retain one or more separate advisory firms to manage their portfolios. In a small number of cases, the advisory firm is owned by the investing entity (e.g., Vanguard, TIAA-CREF), so that gains to the adviser are retained by fund investors. In most cases, however, the advisory firm is distinctly separate from the fund, and its profits are retained by its owners. These profits are derived from fees paid by investors for assets-under-management, and the principal business objective of managers is to gather as many assets as possible. This is done by manufacturing and distributing mutual funds and by soliciting pension fund management assignments as well as by increasing the value of assets-under-management through investment results.

The fiduciary liabilities associated with investment management, especially in mutual funds, require the performance of duties of care, candor, and loyalty to investors. To satisfy reasonable standards of duty of care, for example, fund managers would have to be familiar with and diligently exercise voting rights of the shares held in their portfolios with respect to corporate strategy and governance issues. Candor would at least require full and accessible disclosure of fees and expenses, and the tax consequences of the funds' trading practices. Duties of loyalty would include avoiding transactions that benefit the manager at the expense of the investor. These fiduciary duties have been neglected by decades of lax regulation by the SEC and affiliated SROs. Such conflicts of interest have long been embedded in the mutual fund industry, and represent a serious flaw that needs to be addressed.

External Flaws in the Governance Process: The Auditors

In the external environment, institutional investors have a key role in corporate governance of companies in which they invest, in deciding what to buy or sell, and in voting the shares they hold and thereby influencing the internal governance process. Both functions depend on the availability of timely and complete financial information, so those charged with this function—auditing and accounting—have a key role in the system. There are three main issues.

First, auditors developed major lines of nonaudit business to sell to clients that compromised their objectivity. All of the major auditing firms created new business lines (business and technology consulting, tax advisory work, etc.) that became more important to the firms, in aggregate, than the auditing business. Firms began to market these new business services aggressively, and to support particular lobbying and related interests of clients. In some cases, questionable business practices were devised by an accounting firm's consulting division and later approved by the same firm's audit division, sometimes evidently against the specific advice of the firm's business practices watchdogs. Such actions, in clear violation of the required independence of auditing firms, long evaded market discipline and begged for a regulatory approach, and so were largely addressed in the Sarbanes-Oxley Act. Presumably they can no longer be considered a serious flaw in the system.

Second, the accounting industry was able to undermine the spirit, if perhaps not the letter, of the U.S. GAAP, so as to be able to meet corporation demands for changes in accounting treatment. As delegated by the SEC, accounting principles are the responsibility of the FASB, which is an industry-sponsored association, and is subject to accounting industry pressure, as well as pressure from corporate clients. In the early 2000s, it became apparent in a variety of cases that serious flaws in the process of maintaining appropriate accounting principles had developed, especially in the areas of accounting for derivatives, off-balance-sheet liabilities, and employee stock options, all of which were blocked or delayed by special interests. The accounting industry itself mounted intensive Congressional lobbying efforts, usually on issues related to accounting principles and their supervision by the SEC. The Sarbanes-Oxley Act, which authorized the creation of a new Public Company Accounting Oversight Board, did not directly address the flaws in accounting principles. Some of the accounting principles mentioned, in the light of scandals and public attention, have since evolved in the right direction, but there is no assurance that the matter will not revert to what it was in the past, and therefore represents a serious remaining fault-line in the system.

Third, the public accounting industry may have become too weak to survive in its current form. After the failure of Arthur Andersen, the U.S. accounting industry is down to only four firms large enough to handle audits of major corporations, most of which are also multinationals. These four firms have been subjected to heavy economic blows; forced separation of their profitable consulting businesses, exposure to continuous streams of class-action litigation and settlements following corporate and other scandals, and increased compliance costs are some of these. Some have also lost their most experienced partners, who have chosen to retire and take what they have invested in their firms before it is too late. Yet the entire free-market system depends upon accurate accounting information, through the publication of audited financial statements. If one or more of these major firms should go on to fail, the ability to provide adequate auditing coverage may fall into doubt. This risk has to be considered a serious potential flaw, and may require a fundamental restructuring of the public accounting industry worldwide.

External Flaws in the Governance Process: The Banks

In addition to external monitoring and governance fault-lines related to the role of institutional investors and auditors, a final set of problems involved the role of bankers and advisers. There are again three specific issues involved.

First, conglomeration and concentration in the financial services industry seem to have encouraged conflicts between the interests of managers of financial firms and their corporate clients and their shareholders. In the late 1990s and early 2000s, financial service providers have been drawn into conglomeration (different businesses) and concentration (bigger in size and market share) that have proven to be fertile ground for of conflicts of interest. Large banks and financial firms are now engaged in all kinds of activities, retail and wholesale, and function in these businesses as both agents and principals. The remedy for abuse of such conflicts increasingly has taken the form of civil litigation, which can impose significant settlement costs and be costly to the firm in terms of a resulting stock price decline. But some of the financial conglomerates have become so large and diverse that they may be impervious to financial punishment—even large settlements may affect earnings by only a few cents per share. Further, such firms are required to demonstrate to their investors that they are growth enterprises, worthy of a high price-earnings ratio. These firms are under intense competitive pressure to demonstrate that they can grow faster than the national economy by increasing market shares through aggressive business development and innovation, suggesting that the pressures that generate these conflicts will continue despite settlements here and there. This suggests a serious flaw in the system, but probably not yet among those of highest concern, since current levels of concentration are not very substantial—even in the most concentrated financial businesses, the top firms have only slightly over 10 percent market share—and competitive and regulatory disciplines are keen. But this may change in the years ahead.

A second issue concerns ambiguity as to what bankers' responsibilities are in corporate failures. In all large corporate bankruptcies, after the corporation has lost its ability to repay creditors, investors or creditors can be expected to sue the bankers who organized the deals for breach of fiduciary duties to them or for other offenses. Such litigation is usually settled for a monetary amount, which the organizing bank pays to end the matter without admitting or denying responsibility for anything. Generally, the settlement is a small portion of the amount originally demanded, and is often covered by insurance. In most cases the banks can shrug it off and move on. In the rounds of litigation following the 2000–2003 corporate failures, some very large settlements occurred, but the banks (because they had become so large through mergers) were able to walk away without serious financial damage, despite charge-offs in the billions. In effect, banks may have become too big to reprimand. The ambiguity of this issue has been reinforced by the failure of Congress to pass legislation defining what the responsibilities of banks acting as advisers and arrangers are when there is fraud or other forms of malfeasance. The Supreme Court failed to rule on such an issue (*U.S. v. Bank of Denver*, involving charges of a bank aiding and abetting fraud) until Congress made these responsibilities clear, which it has not done.

Third, some have argued that the government has begun to lose control over the banking system. Many Americans know that the Federal Deposit Insurance Company is obligated to guarantee bank deposits up to $100,000 per qualified account. Others know that institutional holders of deposits far in excess of $100,000 are not insured. But almost everyone believes that, given what happened after the S&L and banking crises of the 1980s that cost the taxpayers some $150 billion after recoveries, all deposits in all large U.S. banks are, in effect, guaranteed in full by the government. This is technically incorrect, but nonetheless may be necessary to avoid the risk of a system-wide banking collapse. Banks have always been regulated as instruments of monetary policy and as indispensable conduits of payments and credit throughout the economy.

In the past, the government (through the Federal Reserve, the Comptroller of the currency, and the FDIC) regulated everything from interest rates to capital adequacy, to permitted deposit-taking locations, to corporate activities (including mergers with other banks or with nonbanks) under comprehensive regulations that restricted which lines of business they could engage in. The simple idea was that if banks are likely to be guaranteed by the taxpayer—they become different from other businesses and are offered relatively cheap capital because of it— then the government is entitled to regulate the insurance risks that it implicitly assumes. However, in recent years most of the controls to which banks were subject in the past have been repealed—banks are now sometimes parts of multiline conglomerates that are free to do more or less what they want, and most of the old rules restricting mergers or business expansion have been removed. The government, in the spirit of deregulation and liberal economic thinking, went along with this willingly, after much lobbying and many generous political campaign contributions. If it could be established that a laissez-faire financial system is in the country's best interest, then the issue is moot and would not present a serious flaw in the financial system. This point of view has not been established, however, so an unintended erosion of government control of banks may be just such a flaw.

These various internal and external flaws in the governance chain, all of them important but some more so than others, have perhaps interfered with the quick, corrective resilience of the free market upon which the system for decades has come to rely. At its best, the market will sense problems well before they reach crisis proportions, and alter the outcome by market discipline. It is a wonderful system when it works, even if it never works perfectly. But it is up to those who use and understand the market to protect it by removing the toxic elements that inevitably creep in from time to time.

PROTECTING THE MARKET

In our view, the two most serious and potentially dangerous fault-lines in the corporate governance chain that leads from the management of public companies to the ultimate investors are (1) uncertainties about how fiduciary duties of officers and directors of corporations, institutional investors, and financial intermediaries are to be maintained and enforced, and (2) persistent gaps in the regulation of both the accounting and financial services industries. The key objective is to close these fault-lines in the system as simply and effectively as possible, working alongside market discipline and minimizing any efficiency losses that might result.

Agency Costs and Uncertain Fiduciary Duties

We have emphasized in this book that agency problems can seriously increase the cost of using the capital markets and impose an unfair "tilt" that favors those who are aggressive and connected over the interests of ordinary investors—a tilt that can damage confidence in the financial markets as a repository for the wealth and savings of ordinary people. It is easy to forget that the financial markets are in the end a tool for social welfare, and must earn and maintain their legitimacy in that context—quite apart from the notion that rigged markets usually turn out to be inefficient, illiquid, and uncompetitive as well.

Agency costs in the governance chain are high when there is a poisonous confluence of (1) weak boards of directors and (2) institutional investors basically uninterested in the long-term development of companies whose shares they control on behalf of their own investor clients. They are also high in financial management companies that are unable to resist the temptation to put their own interests ahead of those to whom they have long-recognized fiduciary obligations.

The market-driven system has generally relied on self-restraint by principals whose reputations and exposure to regulatory and legal sanctions are at stake. When this self-restraint was found to be insufficient to prevent abusive behavior in the 1920s, a new regulatory regime was imposed to level the playing field. In the 1990s, competitive complexities, deregulation, innovation, and market ebullience appeared to throw these leveling effects seriously off balance.

Whereas the incentives and means to compete in business have been enhanced over the past decades, the incentives and means to satisfy fiduciary duties have been diminished. These duties have largely been muddled by separate federal and state legal systems, and left unclear by out-of-court settlements that involve affordable fines and penalties but are made without any admission or denial of responsibility or disclosure of the details of the case. Officers, directors, and principals have likewise been insulated from direct responsibility for violations of fiduciary duties by indemnification and insurance. In short, the importance of fiduciary duties has been diminished at the expense of the competitive dictates of the market—if companies and their officers and directors cannot be meaningfully sanctioned, then how can the governance fault-lines be addressed?

Meanwhile, those responsible for proper fiduciary conduct—corporate officers and directors, fund managers and intermediaries who owe duties of care and loyalty to investors—have been compromised by the desire to pursue their corporate and individual financial interests. Although compromised, they continue to be well protected against the claims of those to whom their duties are owed. This clearly tilts the market to favor the powerful and better informed. Such a tilted market is hardly a free market.

If fiduciary duties were taken more seriously, then those who bear them would adjust their behavior and take the tilt (or much of it) out of the market. This sounds simple, but it is not. Financial institutions' resistance to acknowledging anything to do with an alleged tilt, or to changing anything having to do with the status quo as it pertains to fiduciary duties (from which they are well insulated), suggests serious opposition to meaningful changes of any sort.

For meaningful changes to occur, jurisdictional issues will have to be resolved or clarified, and a clearer idea will have to be developed as to what fiduciary duties actually are, as well as what it takes to breach them. Remedies too will have to be established.

Jurisdiction. Because fiduciary duties to corporate shareholders are matters of state law, the SEC has preferred to avoid them, although the U.S. Constitution allocates powers to the federal government to regulate interstate commerce, of which national securities markets can be considered a part. The SEC could point out that the 1933 Act (related to underwriting of new issues of securities) attaches fiduciary duties to corporate officers and directors and to underwriters, bankers, and advisers. Therefore, it can claim that the 1934 Act implies similar powers to apply fiduciary laws to protect a large interstate community of investors. Had these principles been established at the time, the SEC might have brought federal charges against the board of Enron for having breached their duties of care and loyalty to shareholders. Apparently, the SEC considered doing this and decided not to proceed because of the state-federal conflict-of-law issue, and expectation of major difficulties in bringing and in being able to win such a case. If charges had been brought, however, and if the case had gone to trial and been successful, then the SEC could claim to have established valuable new case law that would govern fiduciary duties of boards for years to come—just as the federal *BarChris* case defined necessary standards of due diligence in underwriting in 1968 (see chapter 2). None of the state and federal settlements of 2001–2004 broke any new ground in determining what is inside or outside legal boundaries, and the territory remained as uncharted as ever.

One can appreciate that the issue of director liability is itself important enough to justify going to some trouble to establish a better legal framework for it, but the chances of such a case being thrown out or successfully defended probably diminished the appetite for such a case by the hard-pressed SEC. But the Commission cannot afford to waste a good series of scandals—one that weakens conventional wisdom sufficiently to enable legal reforms to be considered that might otherwise have little chance, and enables the SEC to find a way to assert itself constructively into places where it properly ought to be, for example, defining corporate fiduciary issues. In any case, the SEC also has the option to try to persuade Congress to enact legislation that would establish federal access to the fiduciary arena under appropriate conditions.

Another possibility open to the SEC is to declare a clear position on fiduciary duties, provide some benchmarks on what it means, and offer guidelines as to what standards of conduct would afford a "safe harbor" against prosecution. It may be that claiming state fiduciary law unto itself could be challenged in court—and even lost—but the system might benefit nonetheless. Attention would be drawn to the importance of enforcing fiduciary duties, and would (if not successfully challenged) become the common practice. If challenged, some other remedy might emerge by legislative action or by working out what powers the SEC might be able to retain. The SEC has acted in a similar way—promulgating rules that later could be subject to legal challenge—in the sale of unregistered securities, or "private placements" (rule 144 and others), and in establishing standards for dealing with insider trading cases (rule 10b5-1 and others). In the latter case, the SEC took positions that were challenged in court, and ultimately overturned by the Supreme Court, but the process resulted in decisions as to what the standards should be for the future.

Defining the duties. What is needed is a generalized understanding that *all* who bear fiduciary responsibilities will be treated in the same manner. This brings corporate officers and directors, investment managers and intermediaries into the same arena, where they should be judged by common, long-established standards. Under English common law, generally held to be applicable today, fiduciary duties apply to those acting as agents on behalf of others who entrust the care of property them. The fiduciary can be held to a standard of a "prudent man" caring for his own property, who owes particular duties of care, candor, and loyalty to his client. However, in most jurisdictions, an officer or director or other fiduciary is entitled to the protection of the "business judgment rule," which, in the absence of any clear violation of his or her fiduciary duties, affirms that courts will not impose their own ideas of what a good business decision might have been. So fiduciaries are protected from legal actions that are directed toward alleged business mistakes if they were made in good faith.

Breaching the duties. Breaching fiduciary duties is a matter of material violation of duties of care, candor, and loyalty, with the burden of proof being placed on the plaintiffs. The natural defense against such charges is that the accused did all he or she could reasonably have done to render fair and appropriate decisions, but was forced to rely on inaccurate information provided by managers. In *BarChris,* the federal judge deciding the case determined that defendants must be able to demonstrate that they had done all they reasonably could to conduct independent inquiries and to act diligently in trying to determine the true story before they made their decisions or provided their consent. The defendants, in short, had to be able to prove that they were not relying totally on what they were told but were actively making an effort to challenge and investigate it. This is now known as the "due diligence" defense that all financial intermediaries recognize may be required if they are accused of wrongdoing, aiding or abetting, or simply being asleep at the switch. But *BarChris* has generally not been applicable to corporate directors when not involved with public offerings or to directors of investment management companies. Moreover, these directors are already indemnified and insured against legal judgments and expenses applied to them personally—except in cases of "gross negligence," which is a very difficult condition to establish in court. As we have shown, for most corporate and financial directors, the due diligence test that might have been applied has been pushed aside for a much more difficult standard of gross negligence.

In the past, the SEC has offered "safe-harbor" guidelines as to what does *not* constitute a breach of its rules. For example, the complex issue of safe-harbor guidelines related to the sale of unregistered securities, once published, made it clear that if the guidelines are followed, the SEC would not prosecute. Similarly, with respect to fiduciary duties, the SEC might determine that it would not bring actions against any fiduciary who could demonstrate that he or she had acted diligently to assure that duties of care, candor, and loyalty were carried out. Guidelines would have to specify the details, but one can assume that, based on other safe-harbor guidelines, the principal quality to be demonstrated is independence of directors in both gathering information about issues and deciding them. Directors under the burden of having to meet a higher standard would have to be more careful. Nonmanagement directors might wish to retain independent legal counsel and perhaps financial expertise to guide them in their efforts to be appropriately diligent in their duties. This process of legitimatizing the independence of nonmanagement directors occurred in the 1980s during a period of heightened activity involving hostile takeovers. Using case law developed in the Delaware Chancery Court, nonmanagement directors were encouraged to separate themselves from management and to take charge of the board's decision-making related to takeover proposals if management was thought to be conflicted. To do this, the Court virtually required that independent professional advice be obtained. The case involved with this decision, *Smith v. Van Gorkom* (Delaware Supreme Court, 1985) was highly controversial, but the ruling has stood ever since, resulting in a major change in conduct by boards of directors in takeover situations as compared to what it had been before.

Legal remedies. Following the scandals of 2001–2004 (including the mutual fund and insurance industry scandals that followed the corporate, accounting, and investment banking scandals), there was a great effort in the heated spirit of the moment to raise the threshold of punishment for white-collar offenders. Sarbanes-Oxley provided many such sanctions. Congress increased punishments to be rendered by federal judges through further revisions of the federal sentencing guidelines. And public prosecutors and juries hearing class-action suits were aggressive in seeking suitable punishment for those held before the public as perpetrators of fraud and deception. So it seems unnecessary to suggest further legal remedies for offenses that appear to have already been well provided for, although such measures are subject to change over time and are likely to be softened as public anger recedes.

However, the effort to tidy up fiduciary responsibilities to make them *equal* in importance to the opportunity for corporations to pursue profits needs one more step. There should be a dismantling of the blanket, all-purpose immunization of corporate directors and officers from fiduciary responsibility by indemnification and insurance.

After all, the original concept of corporate directors was not to exonerate them from anything they might do that was not grossly negligent. Directors are supposed to be fiduciaries, and most people who have not read the terms of the corporate indemnification agreements and directors and officers insurance policies no doubt still think they are. It is true that many worthy directors might choose to resign rather than risk their own unsheltered fortunes to the vicissitudes of politically overactive prosecutors or class-action suits. However, the period since Sarbanes-Oxley—with its higher standards for CEOs, CFOs, and corporate directors—has not resulted in a great shortage of willing, qualified officers or directors, in spite of dire predictions to the contrary when the Act was passed. Presumably, some high-quality individuals have accepted that to be a director requires at least being able to satisfy a due diligence defense that they have met their basic duties appropriately. It is also worth noting that for many years, general partnerships operated in the United States with unlimited personal liability of partners, and these firms managed to prosper in business nonetheless. And it should be remembered that in the *Smith v. Van Gorkom* case referred to earlier, the court took the position that the directors had to feel their responsibilities personally for them to feel them at all; it disallowed the usual corporate indemnification and insurance and held them to be personally liable for the plaintiff's claims. This certainly shocked the world of corporate directors at the time. But the world recovered, adjusted to the new realities, and moved on. Since then, nonexecutive directors of WorldCom agreed to bear personally a share of the settlement cost in a class action suit.

To apply these lessons to the present, the SEC might announce, for example, that it would not interfere with any officers' and directors' indemnification or insurance plans, except where individual directors could not satisfactorily demonstrate due diligence defenses in the case of the exercise of fiduciary duties. In such cases, the SEC would be prepared to petition courts to withhold protection. If a director cannot demonstrate such a defense, he or she would have to stand the consequences personally. Nothing, it would seem, would motivate directors to upgrade their independence and openmindedness more effectively than making them truly responsible for duties that they accepted when signing on as directors. The SEC may not have to do more than to state its intent to proceed down this road—the message would get through to individual directors very quickly. They would not want to take the chance of continuing with inadequate performance if the consequences might possibly be what the SEC suggests. Some directors, being unwilling or unable to change, might resign. But if so, public shareholders might ask what good such a director is to them in the first place.

Addressing Institutional Deficiencies

In addition to the revelation of inadequate exercise of fiduciary responsibilities, the events of 2001–2004 have revealed some institutional deficiencies that need attention. The first of these is the unreliability of GAAP, which is of great importance to the effectiveness of capital markets. These have been shown to be subject to manipulation by interested parties, including the accounting industry leaders, seeking to ingratiate themselves with large corporate clients. The second deficiency relates to the long-term viability of the accounting industry, and the third relates to whether, in pursuit of an ill-defined objective, Congress did not in fact imperil the financial system it was hoping to protect by far-reaching deregulation.

Reasserting Control of Accounting Principles. It was clear in the late 1990s that the SEC had lost much of its ability to impose strict controls and conditions on the accounting industry. Arthur Levitt's explanation of his difficulty with Congress over the SEC's efforts to insist on accounting independence, and on accounting principles related to employee stock options, tells us all we need to know—that the political pressures deflected a serious effort by the SEC to exercise its statutory powers on an industry under its supervision. Perhaps Levitt should have resisted more than he did, but the SEC chair is a presidential appointee and therefore never very far from the political realities of the day. It is discouraging to think that GAAP, the financial language that supports and maintains free markets in the United States, may be subject to manipulation given the political realities. Indeed, in the spring of 2004, two years after the passage of Sarbanes-Oxley, efforts were made by members of Congress to propose legislation that would effectively overturn a recently decided (and long overdue) FASB rule requiring that employee stock options be expensed by companies granting them.

Indeed, Sarbanes-Oxley provides a section under provisions establishing the Public Company Accounting Oversight Board that deals with accounting standards. This section affirms the SEC's authority to set and approve GAAP, although it permits the agency to rely on a private entity such as FASB, which in turn must meet numerous governance standards provided by the Act. It also requires a *study* of "principles-based accounting standards" (such as exist in the United Kingdom) as contrasted with "rules-based standards" such as prevail in the United States. Otherwise, accounting principles are left as they were. The question is whether the affirmed authority of the SEC over accounting practices may be no more a reality than it was before the scandals of the early 2000s. Time will tell.

But the Congress did create in the Public Company Accounting Oversight Board a new regulatory creature that reports to—but is one political degree removed from—the SEC. The Oversight Board is to have very strict standards for objectivity and integrity and has initially been filled with a distinguished group of independent-minded members. While it is true that the Oversight Board is meant to focus on auditing standards and procedures, and to certify auditors of public companies, its duties easily can be construed to cover anything related to accounting. This could include enforcement of independence standards and signing-off on changes to GAAP. The Oversight Board has the potential to assert itself as an authoritative and independent source (similar to the Federal Reserve Board) of standard-making that would be difficult for politicians to undermine in the future. If so, this may be the single most important achievement of the Sarbanes-Oxley Act. But again, time will tell.

Support of the Accounting Industry. By 2004, the U.S. accounting industry had endured such traumatic change, controversy, and instability that its future was in doubt. Less than two years earlier, the firms in the industry had been allowed to consolidate themselves into five enormous limited partnerships, and along the way had altered their economic base so dramatically as to be unable to satisfy their basic obligations as independent auditors. Arthur Andersen's subsequent demise left a big hole in the industry and sent a dismal message to partners and principals of all the other firms—many of whom were seeking ways to leave the industry, for fear that something similar might happen to them. Then the economics of the business was again altered drastically when the firms were required by Sarbanes-Oxley (and prior enforcement measures) to separate themselves from their various management consultancy businesses. Meanwhile, the litigation threshold for other alleged audit failures was lowered, and the number and size of potential lawsuits facing them became very significant. The industry was extremely discouraged, but it was also attempting as best it could to rebuild itself.

The Public Accounting Oversight Board can be helpful in this process. It must certify accountants, and to do so must get to know them and to have important influence over them. It should indicate clear guidelines for certification, assert leadership in advancing and resolving issues of accounting principles, and encourage smaller firms to expand to meet the demand for more competent auditing firms capable of operating on a large enough scale to handle audits of major corporations. Four major global auditing firms, as a permanent condition, is unlikely to satisfy basic market discipline requirements in the accounting industry, nor be enough to meet the needs of the system. The Public Accounting Oversight Board cannot see itself as presiding only over the strict disciplining of accounting firms; it must also see itself as being responsible for the recovery and sustainable health of the industry.

Control of Banks. In November 1999, Congress passed the Gramm-Leach-Bliley Act, which repealed the Glass-Steagall provisions of the Banking Act of 1933 requiring separation of commercial and investment banking. This Act followed an earlier action that repealed federal laws restricting banks to branches in their own states (the McFadden Act of 1927). To most observers, the Gramm-Leach-Bliley Act acknowledged a decade of step-by-step deregulation of banking to eliminate competitive restrictions that were no longer considered necessary. Large banks had argued that, in order to be able to keep up with powerful European "universal" banks (that could engage in both securities and banking businesses), these legacy restrictions should be set aside. Otherwise, U.S. banks would be incapable of competing effectively in global financial markets. Although this argument had broad support in academic and regulatory circles, one key element of the argument—that unrestricted universal banks are a successful and sustainable business model—has never been demonstrated. Among European universal banks (of which fewer than 10 compete meaningfully in global wholesale financial markets), only three (UBS, Crédit Suisse, and Deutsche Bank) have so far risen to be serious contenders (see chapter 8). Indeed, many traditional nonbanking securities firms (notably Merrill Lynch, Morgan Stanley, and Goldman Sachs) have been able to retain investment banking leadership positions both before and after the repeal of Glass Steagall. Nonetheless, at least two American multiline financial conglomerates (Citigroup and JP Morgan Chase) have entered the list of top players.

Despite laws and regulations designed to prohibit "tied lending" activities, in which bank loans are directly connected to mandates to lead securities issues or mergers, it is well understood that exactly this now occurs as a result of the Gramm-Leach-Bliley Act. Numerous studies have demonstrated that the ability to offer (or to deny) important credit facilities can determine whether a bank is assigned an investment banking mandate. The large banks speak of their "big balance sheet," multiple-line-of-business strategies that are intended to increase their market share through cross-selling to corporate and institutional clients. As a result of this additional competition, some evidence exists that banking fees have been lowered and that competition has increased, despite the fact that the same five or six players have controlled more than half of all the investment banking business worldwide for several years. Two issues emerge, however, from acknowledgment of the major banks' and financial conglomerates' success in increasing competition.

The first is what price banking conglomerates have been paying to "buy" the business they have been adding. Each of the leading U.S. banks has been involved in each of the largest corporate bankruptcies (see chapter 10) and has been charged with a wide range of offenses, from disregarding fiduciary responsibilities to participating in or tolerating fraudulent conduct by their clients (including Enron, WorldCom, and Parmalat) and allowing employees to falsify research and engage in improper procedures related to IPOs. Ultimately, well over $10 billion is likely to be paid in fines, settlements, and private litigation by the three largest banks alone in the United States, before these matters are finally settled.

Certainly such problems demonstrate that the ability to regulate and restrain the actions of such enormous banks is limited at best. Each conglomerate business entity tends to be regulated separately by one or more financial regulators, none of which sees beyond the checklist information that it requires to conform to its narrow regulatory interest. Clearly, this did not work well in the 1990s, when the banks were themselves able to tear down the walls separating banking and securities well before Gramm-Leach-Bliley was actually passed. And one could ask whether the increased competition has come at the cost of reduced professional standards, tolerating conflicts, and ignoring fiduciary responsibilities for fraudsters and marginal companies. Increased competition is good for customers and for the efficiency and creativity of the financial system, but the organizational structures that accompany it can create a partial offset in the form of elevated agency costs.

As troubling as these issues may be, however, a still larger one resides in the shadows. American banks and investment banks, as a result of mergers and aggressive growth strategies, have become concentrated in a relatively small cohort—perhaps a dozen—firms that are indeed now "too big to fail." The government cannot allow them to collapse (arguably, these include some of the stand-alone investment banks) for fear of the consequences to the global financial system as a whole. This means that in the event of failure, panic, or malfeasance, the government must become the lender of last resort to rescue these giant financial institutions from whatever fate awaits them. Judging by the number of fines, prosecutions, legal settlements, and loan write-offs, the banks do not believe that they can fail economically, no matter what their managers do. With banks' principal officers compensated according to generous programs to reward (mainly) growth in shareholder value, there is the danger that the interests of creditors, guarantors of deposits, and lenders of last resort will be jeopardized. The possibility of another banking crisis like the savings-and-loan and banking industry crises of the 1980s cannot be ignored. Privatization of returns and socialization of risks is always a questionable proposition and usually is a recipe for disaster.

It would be appropriate for financial regulators in the United States to agree to a multiagency oversight body to review the actions of the megabanks and to apply meaningful regulatory initiatives that cover whole firms, not just individual financial functions. This is unlikely to happen, as most politicians dread concentrating such large powers in a single regulatory body. Even if it did, it would not be immune from political pressure, lobbying, and the corrosive effects of campaign contributions.

It seems more likely that investors will come to recognize the perils that go along with megabanks, as well as their advantages, and put market prices on these organizations that reflect the long-term realities of the strategies they are attempting to execute. If a better understanding of the strategies results in repricing the megabanks at a lower level, then perhaps they will react in such a way as to influence the pricing in the other direction. This might mean being less aggressive, or less committed to the big-balance-sheet strategy, or becoming more skillful and diligent in managing their conflicts and fiduciary responsibilities. They may also be constrained by the higher fiduciary standards mentioned in the preceding section.

THE FUTURE OF GOVERNANCE

Repairing latent problems in the financial system is unlikely to be addressed by regulators until some catastrophe occurs, after which (as in the 1980s) it will be done in haste and at considerable public cost. And, our confidence in a resurgent SEC, or new oversight boards to reform the industries for which they are responsible, may be misplaced. Regulators, operating as they must in the political arena, have rarely stepped in to avert looming disasters. We believe that there are some important things that regulators could do to utilize their powers more effectively, but we know that it is difficult for them to do them. So, we must rely first on an enhanced sense of market discipline to encourage reforms that are needed. But, for market discipline to function as well as it can, we need appropriate regulation and transparency to clean out the conflicts of interest that have worked their way into the system over many years.

To remove the conflicts first requires their recognition. As these conflicts are better understood, they are likely to be less extensively tolerated. For identification, we must look to the most unconflicted parts of the system—independent research analysts, rating agencies, financial journalists, and active investors—and listen to them when they speak. As we understand the conflicts better, the market can react to them, and its influence, once awakened, can be powerful. But we have also suggested that important parts of the market itself have become conflicted, and may not contribute meaningfully to the deconflicting process. To get as much support as possible, others have to become involved—corporate directors overseeing their own futures, directors of investment companies, and litigants of all sorts, who, despite much criticism, persist in bringing landmark cases that catch the attention of market forces and of the regulators themselves. The market must follow its own self-interest, not the interests of it agents.

The future of governance lies more in getting the market forces back to full potential than it does in regulatory reforms or in the politically correct effort to impose standards of economic self-restraint on corporate directors, or to make them technically more independent or require them to attend longer meetings of board committees. The essence of governance in the modern economy that is dominated by vast capital market operations is to use the market's own forces to govern the players. This is best done by addressing head-on the conflict of interest issues that are this book's principal theme. The conflicts are hurting the markets, and have given it a tilt that is potentially harmful. We can resolve the tilt by insisting that key fiduciary responsibilities, already in place in our legal system, be taken as seriously as they deserve to be.

Notes

Chapter 1

1. This chapter relies extensively on Roy C. Smith, "The Investors," chapter 3 of *The Wealth Creators* (New York: St. Martin's Press, 2001).

2. The change in market capitalization reflects factors other than price increases. During the 1990s, for example, $470 billion of new issues of stock (IPOs) were offset by approximately the same amount of corporate share repurchases, but there were also $5.2 trillion of mergers, of which approximately $1.8 trillion were in cash. The net effect of these transactions actually reduced the number of shares outstanding in the market by a considerable extent, suggesting that the price increases experienced during the period were greater than 14 percent.

3. Karen Lowry Miller, "Too Much Money," *Newsweek*, August 18, 2003, quoting Robert Hormats of Goldman, Sachs & Co.

4. The first Amerian industrial revolution was in the early 1800s, and the second, often called the "rise of big business," was from 1870 to 1930.

5. Richard Sylla, "The New Media Boom in Historical Perspective," *Prometheus* 19, 1 (2001): 17–26.

6. Barrie Wigmore, "What Is the Real Outlook for the S&P 500,"unpublished paper, July 1998.

7. Dennis Berman, "Telecom Investors See Big Potential in Failed Networks," *Wall Street Journal*, August 14, 2003.

8. With assets of $63 billion, Enron's bankruptcy in December 2001 was the largest ever recorded until WorldCom, with assets of $104 billion, was filed in July 2002.

9. Andersen's conviction was overturned in 2005 because of the peculiar method used by the jury to determine guilt. Even if it had not been convicted, however, a mere indictment on criminal charges would have perhaps have been fatal to the firm. Very few financial services firms have ever survived a criminal indictment, as clients, employees, creditors, and service providers all abandon the firm at once. In any event, Andersen also had many other claims against it to resolve even before addressing the potentially enormous cost to it of settling claims related to Enron and WorldCom.

10. The *Financial Times* reported (July 31, 2002) that among America's top 25 bankruptcies since 1999, involving more than $200 billion of lost market value, executive compensation totaled nearly $3.3 billion.

11. Edward Altman, "Bankruptcy and Default Statistics," working paper, New York University Stern School, Salomon Center, August 31, 2002. The bankruptcies include only those with liabilities of $100 million or more.

12. Min Wu, "Earnings Restatements: A Capital Market Perspective," working paper, New York University Stern School, Accounting Department, January 2002.

13. Source: available online at the website of Stanford Law School, Securities Class Action Clearing House, Federal Class Actions, March 7, 2005.

14. Arthur Levitt, testimony to Senate Committee on Government Affairs, January 24, 2002.

15. Frank Partnoy, a professor of law at the University of San Diego, testified before the Senate Governmental Affairs Committee in January 2002 that he had conducted his own investigation of Enron using only published data filed with the SEC and other sources and was able to construct a good understanding of what the company was endeavoring to do with its off-balance-sheet transactions, a process Partnoy maintains could equally have been performed by stock market or credit market analysts.

Chapter 2

1. A study by McKinsey Global Institute in January 2005 reported that global finanacial assets were $118 trillion in 2003, up from $12 trillion in 1980, of which bank deposits represented 30 percent and 45 percent, respectively.

2. This chapter draws heavily on two works previously published by the authors: Roy C. Smith, *Comeback* (Boston: Harvard Business School Press, 1993), and Ingo Walter and Roy Smith, *High Finance in the Eurozone* (London: Prentice-Hall, 2000).

3. Michael C. Jensen, statement before the House Ways and Means Committee of the U.S. Congress, February 1, 1989.

4. The method used for determining merger intensity is to divide the value of completed domestic and U.S. cross-border transactions for the five-year period by the midyear nominal GDP of the United States. In 1898–1902, based on data complied by Ralph Nelson, the volume of mergers was $6.3 billion, which, divided by the 1900 U.S. GDP of $18.7 billion, was 33.7 percent. The five-year total of mergers done in the United States in 1994–1998 was $2.64 trillion, based on data supplied by Securities Data Corp. This, divided by the 1996 nominal GDP of $7.67 trillion, was 34.4 percent.

5. Abraham Bleiberg, "Tech M & A, Size Does Matter," *Goldman Sachs Investment Research Report*, June 1998.

Chapter 3

1. Stuart Bruchey, *The Roots of American Economic Growth 1607–1861* (New York: Harper and Row, 1965), pp. 143–148.

2. Roy C. Smith, *Money Wars* (New York: Dutton, 1990), pp. 24–28.

3. Thomas K. McCraw, *Prophets of Regulation* (Cambridge, Mass.: Harvard University Press, 1984), p. 64.

4. Frederick Lewis Allen, *The Great Pierpont Morgan* (New York: Harper and Row, 1948), pp. 145–146.

5. McCraw, *Prophets of Regulation*, p. 64.

6. McCraw, *Prophets of Regulation*, p. 62.

7. McCraw, *Prophets of Regulation*, p. 79.

8. Roy C. Smith, *Money Wars* (New York: Dutton, 1990), pp. 46–47.

9. John K. Galbraith, *The Great Crash* (Boston: Houghton-Miflin, 1988), p. 112.

10. J. Bradford deLong, "Did J. P. Morgan's Men Add Value?" in *Inside the Enterprise: Historical Perspectives on the Use of Information*, edited by Peter Temin (Chicago: University of Chicago Press, 1991), pp. 205–236.

11. McCraw, *Prophets of Regulation*, pp. 59–60.

12. Adolph A. Berle, Jr., and Gardiner C. Means, *The Modern Corporation and Private Property* (New York: Macmillan, 1932), pp. 19–33.

13. Berle and Means, *The Modern Corporation and Private Property*, p. 1.

14. This essay is included in Alfred Chandler, *The Essential Alfred Chandler*, edited by Thomas McCaw (Boston: Harvard Business School Press, 1988).

15. Adoph A. Berle, Jr., foreword to *The Corporation in Modern Society*, edited by Edward Mason (Cambridge, Mass.: Harvard University Press, 1959).

Chapter 4

1. *Escott v. BarChris Construction Corp.*, U.S. District Court, Southern District of New York, 1968F. Suppl. 643.

2. Originally devised in 1984, the shareholders' rights plan issued rights to purchase new shares at a steep discount to all shareholders, except the purchaser of more than a specified percent of the company's shares. Such a purchaser's position would, therefore, be substantially diluted by the exercise of the rights, and the purchaser would therefore be forced instead to negotiate with the board to be able to buy the shares in exchange for the board's disabling the rights plan. These plans were upheld by most state courts in which they were contested, though the courts could disallow them under certain conditions. Most companies listed on the NYSE had adopted such plans by the end of the 1980s, believing they gave shareholders time to consider the proposed offer before reacting to it. Critics of the plans have asserted that the poison pills only increased the price that an acquirer had to pay for corporate control, and thus was an inappropriate form of market intervention.

3. Roy C. Smith, *The Money Wars* (New York: Dutton, 1990), pp. 150–155.

4. Smith, *Money Wars*, pp. 150–155.

5. *Smith v. Van Gorkom*, 488 A.2d 858, Delaware Supreme Court, 1985.

6. William T. Allen, "Our Schizophrenic Conception of the Business Corporation," in *Corporate Governance* (New York: New York University Center for Law and Business, 1992).

7. Cornerstone Research, Press Release, March 2, 2005.

8. Investor Responsibility Research Center, *Board Practices/Board Pay 2002: The Structure and Compensation of Boards of Directors at S & P 1,500 Companies* (November 2002).

9. Sarbanes-Oxley requires that any such civil penalties be turned over and added to the disgorgement funds that are now to be available for the relief of victims. According to the General Accounting Office, the SEC only collected about 14% of all awards made to it in the period 1999–2001—it was too expensive and labor intensive to do more, apparently. Now, however, the SEC will be accountable to the public, i.e., to victims (for no fee), to secure recovery of disgorgements and collection of penalties accessed. Now that the SEC has been more abundantly funded (by Sarbanes-Oxley) it will be able to increase its collections, but, ironically, in doing so, it is placed in a position similar to a plaintiff's lawyers in trying to find and collect money for victims.

10. L. William Seidman, "How Can the U.S. Experience in Removing Bank Bad Debts Be Useful in Japan?" address made in Japan, Resolution Trust Company, Sept. 25, 2001.

11. Greg Hitt, "SEC Chief Says Worst of Fraud Is Likely Past," *Wall Street Journal*, July 23, 2003.

12. Michael Schroeder, "Cleaner Living, No Easy Riches," *Wall Street Journal*, July 22, 2003.

Chapter 5

1. David Farber, *Sloan Rules* (Chicago: University of Chicago Press, 2002), pp. 74–240.

2. Roy C. Smith, *Money Wars* (New York: Dutton, 1990), pp. 84–89.

3. In the 1950s and 1960s, bankers and investment bankers frequently sat on the boards of their clients. Sidney J. Weinberg, senior partner of Goldman Sachs from 1930 to 1969, sat on more than 30 corporate boards during his career. In the mid–1960s, the approximately 40 partners of Goldman Sachs sat on approximately 85 different corporate boards. Mr. Weinberg was fiercely loyal to his clients but believed he had a duty to guide them well and not to flinch from confrontation when necessary.

4. In one particularly egregious example, Enron CEO Ken Lay allegedly borrowed $77.5 million from the company and subsequently repaid the loans with Enron stock in installments every few days in 2001—without disclosure to shareholders. In this way, according to a civil suit, he could talk up Enron shares to investors and purchase additional stock with full disclosure to demonstrate his confidence in the company, while at the same time unloading far more shares through the loan repayments, which were not disclosed. See "The SEC to Top Execs: Read the Fine Print," *Business Week*, July 26, 2004.

5. Some CEOs, however, even made money when their stocks declined sharply by resetting option strike prices or selling the company and collecting on golden parachutes.

6. Joseph E. Stiglitz, *The Roaring Nineties* (New York: Norton, 2003), p. 124.

7. Sara Moeller, Frederick Schlingemann, and Rene Stulz, *Wealth Destruction on a Massive Scale: A Study of Acquiring-Firm Returns in the Recent Merger Wave* (Dice Center working paper no. 2003–28, Fisher College of Business, Ohio State University, August 2003).

8. "Mergers: Why Most Big Deals Don't Pay Off," *Business Week*, October 14, 2002 (based on a study by Mark L. Sirower, Boston Consulting Group).

Chapter 6

1. *Mutual Fund Fact Book* (Washington, D.C.: Investment Company Institute, 2004).

2. John Bogle, *John Bogle on Investing* (New York: McGraw Hill, 2000), p. 163.

3. *Mutual Fund Fact Book*, 2004.

4. Eric Zitzewitx, *How Widespread Is Late Trading in Mutual Funds?* Stanford Business School research paper (Stanford, Calif.: Stanford Business School, September 2003).

5. Eric Zitzewitz, *Who Cares about Shareholders? Arbitrage Proofing Mutual Funds,* Stanford Business School research paper (Stanford, Calif.: Stanford Business School, March 2002).

6. John C. Bogle, "Mutual Fund Directors: The Dog That Didn't Bark," *Vanguard,* January 28, 2001.

7. Berkshire Hathaway Inc., *2000 Annual Letter to Shareholders.*

8. The industry's trade association, the Investment Company Institute, has argued that the "cost of ownership" of mutual funds actually declined during this period. But this seems largely to be the result of investors substituting cheaper funds (including index funds) for more expensive ones.

9. "Governance: Who's Right, the SEC or Ned Johnson?" *Business Week,* June 28, 2004.

10. Berkshire Hathaway Inc., Chairman's Letter, 1985.

11. "Why I Share the Shareholder's Interest," *Wall Street Journal,* February 17, 2004.

12. Jenny Anderson, "Appeals Court Tells SEC Director Rule Needs Review," *New York Times,* June 25, 2005.

13. Bogle, 2000, op. cit., p. 199.

14. Karen Damato and Judith Burns, "Cleaning Up the Fund Industry," *Wall Street Journal,* April 5, 2004.

15. Emily Thornton, "Mutual Funds: The Cost of Full Disclosure," *Business Week,* June 28, 2004.

16. Tom Lauticells, "U.S.'s SEC Asks Courts to Tighten Disclosure Edicts," *Wall Street Journal,* July 1, 2004.

17. See also Robin Sidel, "Shareholders Say: Not My Vote!" *Wall Street Journal,* April 4, 2004.

18. Securities and Exchange Commission, "Final Rule: Proxy Voting by Investment Advisers," rule 206(4)-6[17 CFR 275.206(4)-6 and amendments to the Investment Advisers Act of 1940 (February 2003).

19. CalPERS press release, May 20, 2004.

20. TIA-CREF press release, March 4, 2004.

21. Sheila McNulty, "U.S. Pension Funds File Suit on Behalf of Shell," *Financial Times,* June 26, 2004.

22. See Peter Burrows, *Backfire: Carly Fiorina's High-Stakes Battle for the Soul of Hewlett-Packard* (New York: Wiley, 2003). See also Deborah Solomon and Pui-Wing Tam, "Deutsche Bank Unit Is Fined Over H-P," *Wall Street Journal,* August 19, 2003.

23. TIAA-CREF, *Statement Regarding Fund Governance Practices,* June 2, 2004.

24. Arden Dale, "SEC Looks at Pension-Fund Advisers," *Wall Street Journal,* February 11, 2004.

Chapter 7

1. Patrick R. Delaney, Barry Epstein, Ralph Nach, and Susan Budak, *Interpretation and Appliation of Generally Accepted Accounting Principles 2005* (New York: John Wiley & Sons, 2005).

2. Denise Schmandt-Besserat, "Accounting with Tokens in the Ancient Near East," available online at the website of the University of Texas.

3. Alexander, "History of Accounting."

4. Alexander, "History of Accounting."

5. Alexander, "History of Accounting." Quotation from "Ancient Double Entry Bookkeeping: Lucas Pacioli's Treatise 1914," R. Emmett Taylor, *No Royal Road: Luca Pacioli and His Times* (Chapel Hill: The University of North Carolina Press, 1942), p. 241.

6. Alexander, "History of Accounting."

7. Website of the Institute of Chartered Accountants of England and Wales (ICAEW), Library and Information, available online at: www.icaew.co.uk/library/index.cfm?AUB=TB2I_54923,MNXI_59423. Accessed September 23, 2004.

8. R. L. Watts and J. L. Zimmerman, "Agency Problems, Auditing and the Theory of the Firm: Some Evidence," *Journal of Law and Economics*, vol. 17 (1983), as cited in Josephine Maltby, " 'A Sort of Guide, Philosopher and Friend': The Rise of the Professional Auditor in Britain," *Accounting, Business and Financial History* 9, 1 (March 1999): 141.

9. Josephine Maltby, "Sort of Guide, Philosopher and Friend," available online at http://econpapers.repec.org/article/tafacbsfi/v_3A9_3A9_3A1999_3Ai_3A1_3Ap_3A29-50.htm, April 8, 2005.

10. Stephen A. Zeff, "How the U.S. Accounting Profession Got Where It Is Today," pt. 1, *Accounting Horizons* 17, 3 (September 2003): 189–205.

11. Zeff, "How the U.S. Accounting Profession Got Where It Is Today," 189–205.

12. W. T. Baxter, "McKesson & Robbins: A Milestone in Auditing," *Accounting, Business and Financial History* 9, 2 (July 1999): 124.

13. Securities and Exchange Commission, *In the Matter of McKesson and Robbins Inc.* (Washington, D.C., 1940; reprint, New York: Garland, 1982), as cited in Baxter, "McKesson & Robbins," pp. 121–125.

14. "A Brief History of Self-Regulation," available online at the website of the AICPA: www.aicpa.org/info/regulation02.htm.

15. David Solomons, "Setting Auditing Standards: Whose Responsibilty?" Saxe Lectures in Accounting, held at Baruch College, CUNY, April 1978, available online at http://newman.baruch.cuny.edu/digital/saxe/saxe_1977/solomons_78.htm, April 2004.

16. "A Brief History of Self-Regulation."

17. Qingliang Tang, "Economic Consequence of the International Harmonization of Accounting Standards: Theory and Its Chinese Application," *International Journal of Accounting* 17 (1994): 268–270.

18. A. Carey, "Harmonization: Europe Moves Forward," *Accountancy* 19 (March 1990): 21–28, and F.D.S. Choi and G. G. Mueller, *International Accounting* (Englewood Cliffs: Prentice-Hall, 1992), both as cited in Asheq Rahman, Hector Perera, and Siva Ganesh, "Accounting Practice Harmony, Accounting Regulation and Firm Characteristics," *Abacus* 38, 1 (2002): 90–92.

19. Gunther Gebhardt, *The Evolution of Global Standards of Accounting*, publication no. 2000/05 (Frankfurt: Centre for Financial Studies, April 2004.

20. Qingliang Tang, "Economic Consequences of the International Harmonization of Accounting Standards: Theory and Its Chinese Application," *International Journal of Accounting* (1994): 44–48.

21. Robert Bruce, "Global Harmony Hangs in the Balance," *Financial Times*, February 23, 2004.

22. "Common Ground," *Economist*, December 20, 2003, U.S. ed.

23. "Common Ground."

24. United States General Accounting Office, "Public Accounting Firms, Mandated Study on Consolidation and Competition," *Report to the Senate Committee on Banking, Housing, and Urban Affairs and the House Committee on Financial Services*, GAO-03–864 Washington, D.C.: General Accounting Office, July 2003.

25. United States General Accounting Office, "Public Accounting Firms," Washington, D.C.: General Accounting Office, July 2003, pp. 12–15.

26. United States General Accounting Office, "Public Accounting Firms," p. 31.

27. United States General Accounting Office, "Public Accounting Firms," Washington, D.C.: General Accounting Office, July 2003, pp. 13–14.

28. United States General Accounting Office, "Public Accounting Firms," Washington, D.C.: General Accounting Office, July 2003.

29. Richard M. Frankel, Marilyn F. Johnson, and Karen K. Nelson, "The Relation between Auditors' Fees for Non-Audit Services and Earnings Management," *Accounting Review*, special issue on Quality of Earnings (July 2002): 12–13.

30. Frankel, Johnson, and Nelson, "Relation between Auditors' Fees for Non-Audit Services and Earnings Management," p. 13.

31. "Accounting for Disaster: Congress, Arthur Andersen and the $60 Million Meltdown," Agency Watchdog Program, January 16, 2002, available at the website of Common Cause: www.commoncause.org/news/default.cfm?Art ID=76, accessed November 16, 2004.

32. Stephen Taub, "Splitter: Another Consulting Service to Be Spun Off," CFO.com, available online at: www.cfo.com/article/1,5309,6647,00.html?f= related, accessed February 1, 2002.

33. Arthur W. Bowman, ed., Public Accounting Report, as cited in Zeff, "How the U.S. Accounting Profession Got to Where It Is Today."

34. Zeff, "How the U.S. Accounting Profession Got to Where It Is Today."

35. AICPA Professional Ethics Committee, "A Conceptual Framework for AICPA Standards," January 22, 2004, SEC 2000 Section, available online at the website of the AICPA: www.aicpa.org/download/ethics/AICPA_Draft _Conceptual_Framework_FINAL.pdf, accessed October 16, 2004.

36. Sarah E. Bonner, Zoe-Volla Palmrose, and Susan M. Young, "The Effects of frequent and Fictitious Frauds on Auditor Litigation: An Analysis of SEC Accounting and Auditing Enforcement Releases," Working paper, Department of Accounting, Emory University, 1998.

37. R. Antle, P. A. Griffin, D. J. Teece, and O. E. Williamson, "An Economic Analysis of Auditor Independence for a Multi-Client, Multi-Service Public Accounting Firm," report prepared on behalf of the AICPA in connection with the presentation to the Independence Standards Board of "Serving the Public

Interest: A New Conceptual Framework for Auditor Independence," Law and Economics Consulting Group, Berkeley, Calif., October 20, 1997, "The Provision of Non-Audit Services by Auditors: Let the Market Evolve and Decide," *International Review of Law and Economics*, June 1999, pp. 216–240.

38. Mark L. DeFond, K. Raghunandna, and K. R. Subramanyam, "Do Non-Audit Service Fees Impair Auditor Independence? Evidence from Going-Concern Audit Opinions," January 2002.

39. De Angelo (1981).

40. Arrunada, "Provision of Non-Audit Services by Auditors."

41. Arrunada, "Provision of Non-Audit Services by Auditors."

42. Statement of Barry Melancon, president and CEO, AICPA, to Committee on Financial Services, United States House of Representatives, March 13, 2002, H.R. 3763, Hearings on the Corporate and Auditing Accountability, Responsibility and Transparency Act of 2002, available online at http://financial services.house.gov/media/pdf/031302bm.pdf, accessed September 18, 2003.

43. D. Simunic, "Auditing, Consulting and Auditor Independence," *Journal of Accounting Research* 22 (1984): 679–702; P. J. Back, T. J. Frecka, and I. Solomon, "A Model of the Market for MAS and Audit Services: Knowledge spillovers and Auditor-Auditee Bonding," *Journal of Accounting Literature* (1988): 50–64; J. D. Beeler and J. E. Hunton, *Contingent Economic Rents: Precursors to Predecisional Distortion of Client Information,* working paper, Department of Accounting, University of Southern California, 2001); all cited in Frankel, Johnson, and Nelson, "Relation between Auditors' Fees for Non-Audit Services and Earnings Management," MIT Sloan Working Paper No. 4330-02, July 2002.

44. Frankel, Johnson, and Nelson, "Relation between Auditors' Fees for Non-Audit Services and Earnings Management," p. 23.

45. Senate Subcommittee on Reports, Accounting and Management, Committee on Government Operations, "The Accounting Establishment," 95th Congress, 1st session, March 31, 1977 (commonly known as the Metcalfe Report), as cited in United States General Accounting Office, Report to the Senate Committee on Banking, Housing and Urban Affairs and the House Committee on Financial Services, *Public Accounting Firms: Mandated Study on Consolidation and Competition* (Washington, D.C., July 2003).

46. AICPA.

47. Special Committee on Financial Reporting, American Institute of Certified Public Accountants, "Improving Business Reporting—A Customer Focus: Meeting the Information Needs of Investors and Creditors," as cited in Mary Ellen Oliverio and Bernard H. Newman, "Use of Audit Firm for Non-Audit Services: Is Independence Impaired?" November 28, 2003, p. 3.

48. "Bad for CFOs, Good for Investors," *Business Week*, November 17, 2003.

49. Richard Waters and Simon London, "Cost of Employee Stock Options May Be Higher by 50 Percent," *Financial Times*, December 14, 2003.

50. Jonathan Weil, "Pro Forma Earnings Reports?" *Wall Street Journal*, April 24, 2003.

51. Robert Bruce, "Are the Big Four Responsible for Every Corporate Error?" *Financial Times*, February 23, 2004.

52. Nancy Chaffee, "The Role and Responsibility of Accountants in Today's Society," *Journal of Corporation Law* 14, 3 (spring 1988): 863.

53. Chaffee, "Role and Responsibility of Accountants in Today's Society."

54. D. R. Gwilliam, "The Auditor, Third Parties and Contributory Negli-

gence," *Accounting and Business Research* (winter 1987): 64–68, as referenced in Carl Pacini, William Hillison, Ratnam Alagaiah, and Sally Gunz, "Commonwealth Convergence toward a Narrower Scope of Auditor Liability to Third Parties for Negligent Misstatements," *Abacus* 38, 3 (2002): 142–144.

55. Zoe-Vonna Palmorose, "Who Got Sued?" *Journal of Accountancy*, Online Issues, March 1997, Auditing/Litigation, available online at www.aicpa.org/pubs/jofa/march97/whosued.htm, accessed September 20, 2003.

56. J. Siciliano, "Negligent Auditing and the Limits of Instrumental Tort Reform," *Michigan Law Review* 86, 8 (1988): 241–247.

57. Jim Cousins, Austin Mitchell, and Prem Sikka, "Auditor Liability: The Other Side of the Debate," *Critical Perspectives in Accounting* 10, 3 (1999): 112–114, as cited in Pacini, Hillison, Alagaiah, and Gunz, "Commonwealth Convergence."

58. Cousins, Mitchell, and Sikka, "Auditor Liability."

59. Palmrose, "Litigation and Independent Auditors: The Role of Business Failures and Management Fraud," *Auditing* 6 (spring 1987): 88–97, as cited in Chaffee, "Role and Responsibility of Accountants in Today's Society," p. 863.

60. *Independent*, September 28, 1983, p. 22, as cited in Cousins, Mitchell, and Sikka, "Auditor Liability."

61. *Accountancy Age*, April 21, 1994, p. 1, as cited in Cousins, Mitchell, and Sikka, "Auditor Liability."

62. *Accountant*, September 1994, as cited in Cousins, Mitchell, and Sikka, "Auditor Liability."

63. *Accountant*, July 1996, as cited in Cousins, Mitchell, and Sikka, "Auditor Liability."

64. *Accountancy Age*, June 12, 1997, p. 1, as cited in Cousins, Mitchell, and Sikka, "Auditor Liability."

65. Cousins, Mitchell, and Sikka, "Auditor Liability."

66. Peter Wyman (head of professional affairs at PricewaterhouseCoopers), "The Debate: Outrageous Calls for a Limit," *Accountancy Age*, April 15, 2004.

67. Chris Meritt, "Civil Protection for Auditors, but No Cap," *Australian Financial Review*, September 19, 2002.

68. 654 U.S. 805 (1984), as cited in Chaffee, "Role and Responsibility of Accountants in Today's Society," p. 863.

69. United States General Accounting Office, "Financial Statement Restatements—Trends, Market Impacts, Regulatory Responses and Remaining Challenges," *Report to the Chairman, Committee on Banking, Housing, and Urban Affairs, U.S. Senate*, GAO-03-138 (Washington, D.C.: October 2002).

70. GAO Report—FEI and M. Wu, "Quantitative Measures of the Quality of Financial Reporting" (Morristown, N.J.: Financial Executives International Research Foundation, 2001).

71. United States General Accounting Office, "Financial Statement Restatements."

72. United States General Accounting Office, "Financial Statement Restatements."

73. United States General Accounting Office, "Financial Statement Restatements," p. 201.

74. United States General Accounting Office, "Financial Statement Restatements," p. 201.

75. United States General Accounting Office, "Financial Statement Restatements," p. 201.

76. "SEC Settles with Ex–Andersen Partner in Sunbeam Probe," *Accountant*, February 18, 2003.

77. Adrian Michaels, "E & Y Banned from Taking New Clients," *Financial Times*, available online at the website of *Financial Times*: www.FT.com, April 16, 2004

78. John Plender, "Schooled by Scandal," *Financial Times*, January 22, 2004.

79. Reeves, "The Self-Regulation Conundrum," October 3, 2002, available online at the website of *AccountancyAge*: www.accountancyage.com/ Analysis/1130940, April 18, 2004.

80. Reeves, "Self-Regulation Conundrum."

81. "The Year in Review: The UK—A State of Limbo," *Accountant*, December 18, 2002.

82. "Firms Show Support for UK Government Report on Auditors," *Accountant*, February 18, 2003.

83. Fiona Buffini, "Auditors Forsake Self-Regulation," *Australian Financial Review*, November 25, 2002.

84. Adrian Michaels, "Germany Plans Pan-European Audit Regulator," *Financial Times*, March 12, 2003, London ed., p. 1.

85. "More Rules: Auditing Reform," *The Economist*, March 20, 2004.

Chapter 8

1. See Paul M. Healey and Krishna G. Palepu, "The Fall of Enron," *Journal of Economic Perspectives* 17, 2 (spring 2003): 144–160.

2. See Neal Batson, *Second Interim Report*, chapter 11, case no. 01-16034 (AJG), United States Bankruptcy Court, Southern District of New York, March 5.

3. See Neal Batson, *Final Report*, chapter 11, case no. 01-16034 (AJG), United States Bankruptcy Court, Southern District of New York, July 28.

4. See Batson, *Second Interim Report* and *Final Report*.

5. Adrian Michaels, "Parmalat Takes Aim at Citigroup," *Financial Times*, July 30, 2004.

6. Randall Smith, "New Inquiries Are Targeting IPO Spinning," *Wall Street Journal*, June 30, 2003.

Chapter 9

1. "The Problem of Social Cost," *Journal of Law and Economics* 3 (1960): 144–171.

2. For a good set of applications of the theory of social costs, see Robert H. Frank, *Microeconomics and Behavior*, 2nd ed. (New York: McGraw-Hill, 1994).

3. Douglas M. Branson, *Enron:When All Systems Fail: Creative Destruction or Roadmap to Corporate Governance Reform?* Villanova Public Law and Legal Theory Working Paper Series, working paper no. 2003–12 (November 2003).

4. Gene Callahan and Greg Kaza, "In Defense of Derivatives," *Reason*, February 1, 2004.

5. "The Role of the Board of Directors in Enron's Collapse," Report Prepared

by the Permanent Subcommittee on Investigations of the Committee on Governmental Affairs, United States Senate, report 107–70, July 8, 2002.

6. "Role of the Board of Directors in Enron's Collapse."

7. D. Parker, "Economic Regulation: A Review of Issues," *Annals of Public and Comparative Economics* 73, 4 (2002): 88–97.

8. Centre for Responsive Politics, "Accounting Industry, Lobbying expenditures 1997–2001" available online at http://www.opensecrets.org/news/accountants/accountants_lobbying.asp, accessed April 18, 2005.

9. "Top Business Court under Fire," *New York Times*, May 23, 1995.

10. Parker, "Economic Regulation."

11. "Federal Regulatory Reform," at http://www.ncseonline.org/NLE/CRSreprts/Risk/rsk-3.cfm?&CFID=1344729&CFTOKEN=51371271, accessed April 18, 2005.

12. G. Leach, "The Devil or the Deep Blue Sea?" in *Regulation without the State: The Debate Continues*, edited by J. Blundell and C. Robinson, Readings 52 (London: London Institute of Economic Affairs, October 2003, as cited in Parker, "Economic Regulation," pp. 27–40.

13. Ian P. Dewing and Peter O. Russell, "Regulation in UK Corporate Governance: Lessons from Accounting, Auditing and Financial Services," *Corporate Governance* 12, 1 (January 2004): 194–204.

14. Murray Weidenbaum, *Progress in Federal Regulatory Policy 1980–2000,* Contemporary Issue Series 100 (St. Louis, Mo.: Center for the Study of American Business, May 2000).

15. Weidenbaum, *Progress in Federal Regulatory Policy 1980–2000.*

Chapter 10

1. Adrian Michaels, "Bondi Targets 45 Banks in Parmalat Fall-out," *Financial Times*, Dec. 16, 2004.

2. Edward Simpkins, "Parmalat to Sue Its Former Bankers," *Telegraph*, June 13, 2004.

3. Association for Financial Professionals, 2003, located at http://news.google.com/news?q=association+for+financial+professionals&hl=en&lr=&client=firefox-a&rls=org.mozilla:en-US:official&sa=N&tab=nn&oi=newsr, accessed April 18, 2005.

4. Banks may not use their lending power "in a coercive manner" to sell nonlending services, although they may link lending and nonlending services when clients seek such "bundling." Even so, they cannot tie a given loan to a given nonlending product without allowing the client "meaningful choice." In the WestLB case, the bank required participation in debt underwriting as a condition of lending in a series of structured finance transactions. See "Fed Fines WestLB $3m for 'Tying' Loans to Products," *Financial Times*, August 28, 2002.

5. In the United States, the first type of linkage is prohibited under the antitying provisions of the Bank Holding Company Act Amendments of 1970 and by the Federal Deposit Insurance Act, while reducing the price of credit to benefit an investment banking affiliate violates section 23B of the Federal Reserve Act. However, the courts have generally upheld allegations of tying only where abuse of market power has been demonstrated. Since antitrust

cases in wholesale banking are difficult to make in light of the industry's competitive structure, very few allegations of tying have been found to violate the law. Tying can also have some perverse competitive consequences. Chris Stefanadis, *Tying and Universal Banking,* Federal Reserve Bank of New York working paper (New York: March 2003). There are no prohibitions on tying bank lending to trust services, deposit balances, etc., and investment banks are in any case exempt from antitying constraints and have actively used senior debt to obtain fee-based business. For a review, see Robert Litan, *Relationships in Financial Services: Are Anti-Tying Restrictions Out of Date?* working paper (Washington, D.C.: AEI-Brookings Joint Center on Regulatory Studies, May 2003).

6. See Seth Schiesel and Gretchen Morgenson, "ATT Is Asked for Information on Dealings with Salomon," *New York Times,* August 24, 2002.

7. In 1979, there were 182 separate director interlocks between the five largest banks and the five largest U.S. nonfinancial corporations. Anthony Saunders, "Conflicts of Interest: An Economic View," in *Deregulating Wall Street,* edited by Ingo Walter (New York: Wiley, 1985). Of the 10 largest U.S. nonfinancial corporations (by market capitalization) in 2002, 7 had senior bankers or former bank CEOs on their boards in 2002. *Database on Corporate Director Interlocks* (Portland, Me.: Corporate Library, 2003).

8. For shareholders, these costs in the United States could come through the legal doctrines of "equitable subordination" and "lender liability" in case of financial distress, which must be offset against the relationship-related and private-information benefits that board membership may contribute. This is given as a reason why bankers tend to be present mainly on the boards of large, stable corporations with low bankruptcy risk. See Randall S. Krozner and Philip E. Strahan, *Bankers on Boards, Conflicts of Interest, and Lender Liability,* working paper no. W7319 (Cambridge, Mass.: N Bureau of Economic Research, August 1999).

9. Matthew Goldstein, "Fifteen NYSE Specialists Indicted," at http://www.thestreet.com/_mktwrm/stocks/brokerages/102170061.html, accessed April 18, 2005.

10. Anthony Saunders, Anand Srinivasan, and Ingo Walter, "Price Formation in the OTC Corporate Bond Markets: A Field Study of the Inter-Dealer Market," *Journal of Economics and Business* (fall 2001): 88–97.

11. The 1999 Gramm-Leach-Bliley Act, eliminating functional barriers for U.S. financial services firms, contains privacy safeguards with respect to sharing personal information with outside firms, but not intrafirm—among banking, brokerage, asset management, and insurance affiliates. The Fair Credit Reporting Act of 1970 (as amended in 1996) allows sharing of certain data within multifunctional financial firms. This issue is complicated in the United States by state blue-sky laws versus federal authority, "opt-in" versus "opt-out" alternatives with respect to client actions, the need to track credit histories, and efforts to combat identity theft.

12. See Roni Michaely and Kent Womack, "Conflict of Interest and the Credibility of Underwriter Analyst Recommendations," *Review of Financial Studies* 12 (1999): 653–686, for example.

13. Alexander Ljungqvist, Felicia Marston, and William J. Wilhelm, *Competing for Securities Underwriting Mandates: Banking Relationships and Analyst*

Recommendations, working paper (New York: Stern School of Business, New York University, Finance Department, May 2003).

14. See Manju Puri, "The Long-Term Default Performance of Bank Underwritten Security Issues," *Journal of Banking and Finance* 18, 2 (1994): 121–140, and "Commercial Banks in Investment Banking: Conflict of Interest or Certification Role?" *Journal of Financial Economics* 40, 3 1996): 210–230, and Amar Gande, Manju Puri, and Anthony Saunders, "Bank Entry, Competition and the Market for Corporate Securities Underwriting," *Journal of Financial Economics* 54, 2 (1999): 416–430.

15. See Paul M. Healey and Krishna G. Palepu, "The Fall of Enron," *Journal of Economic Perspectives* 17, 2 (spring 2003).

16. See Marcia Millon Cornett, Alan J. Marcus, Anthony Saunders, and Hassan Tehranian, Impact of Institutional Ownership on Corporate Operating Performance, working paper (New York: New York University, Stern School of Business, Finance Department, August 2004).

17. See Victoria Ivashina, Vinay B. Naira, Anthony Saunders, Nadia Massoud, and Roger Stover, The Role of Banks in Takeovers, working paper (New York: New York University, Stern School of Business, Finance Department, August 2004).

18. See Gayle De Long and Ingo Walter, "J. P. Morgan and Banesto: An Event Study," working paper (New York: Salomon Center, New York University, April 1994), and Clifford W. Smith, "Economics and Ethics: The Case of Salomon Brothers," *Journal of Applied Corporate Finance* 5, 2 (summer 1992): 127–139.

19. See "$1 Billion Offered to Settle Suit on IPOs," *New York Times,* June 27, 2003.

20. As quoted in "Weil Apologizes to Staff," *New York Times,* September 6, 2002.

21. Such conflicts of interest are particularly problematic in the mutual funds industry, due to limited disclosure or nondisclosure of fees, incentives, and other compensation arrangements, revenue-sharing agreements, trading costs, and soft-dollar commissions to brokers.

Selected Bibliography

Aggrawal, R., N. R. Prabhala, and Manju Puri. 2002. "Institutional Allocation in IPOs: Empirical Evidence." *Journal of Finance* (June): 130–145.

Association for Financial Professionals. 2003. *Credit Access Survey: Linking Corporate Credit to the Awarding of Other Financial Services.* Bethesda, Md.: Association for Financial Professionals.

Attorney General of the State of New York. 2003. *Global Settlement: Findings of Fact.* Albany, N.Y.: Office of the State Attorney General.

Batson, Neal. 2003. *Second Interim Report,* chapter 11, case no. 01-16034 (AJG), United States Bankruptcy Court, Southern District of New York, March 5.

Batson, Neal. 2003. *Final Report,* chapter 11, case no. 01-16034 (AJG), United States Bankruptcy Court, Southern District of New York, July 28.

Beiner, S., W. Drobetz, M. Schmid, and H. Zimmermann. 2003. "Corporate Governance und Firmenbewertung." *Neue Zürcher Zeitung* 225 (fall): 16.

Boni, Leslie, and Kent Womack. 2002. "Wall Street's Credibility Problem: Misaligned Incentives and Dubious Fixes?" *Brookings-Wharton Papers in Financial Services* (May): 21–40.

Boot, Arnoud W. A., and Anjan V. Thakor. 1997. "Banking Scope and Financial Innovation." *Review of Financial Studies* 10 (winter): 124–135.

Burrows, Peter. 2003. *Backfire: Carly Fiorina's High-Stakes Battle for the Soul of Hewlett-Packard.* New York: Wiley.

Byrd, J., and K. Hickman. 2002. "Do Outside Directors Monitor Managers? Evidence from Tender Offer Bids." *Journal of Financial Economics* 32 (fall): 195–221.

Chemmanur, Thomas J., and Paolo Fulghieri. 1994. "Investment Bank Reputation, Information Production, and Financial Intermediation." *Journal of Finance* 49 (March): 210–230.

Chen, Hsuan-Chi, and Jay R. Ritter. 2000. "The Seven Percent Solution." *Journal of Finance* 55, 3: 122–140.

Choi, Jay Pil, and Chris Stefanadis. 2001. "Tying, Investment, and the Dynamic Leverage Theory." *RAND Journal of Economics* 32 (spring): 74–90.

———. 2003. *Financial Conglomerates, Informational Leverage, and Innovation: The*

Investment Banking Connection. Working paper. New York: Federal Reserve Bank of New York, February.

Corporate Library. 2003. *Database on Corporate Director Interlocks.* Portland, Me.: Corporate Library.

De Long, Gayle, and Ingo Walter. 1994. *J. P. Morgan and Banesto: An Event Study.* Working paper. New York: Salomon Center, New York University, April.

Demsky, Joel S. 2003. "Corporate Conflicts of Interest." *Journal of Economic Perspectives* 17, 2 (spring): 40–55.

Derrien, Francois, and Kent Womack. Forthcoming. "Auctions verus Bookbuilding and the Control of Underpricing in Hot IPO Markets." *Review of Financial Studies*: 126–140.

Edwards, Franklin R. 1979. "Banks and Securities Activities: Legal and Economics Perspectives on the Glass-Steagall Act." In *The Deregulation of the Banking and Securities Industries,* edited by L. Goldberg and L. J. White. Lexington, Mass.: Heath.

Erhardt, N., J. Werbel, and C. Shrader. 2003. "Board of Director Diversity and Firm Financial Performance." *Corporate Governance* 11, 2 (spring): 102–110.

Galbraith, John Kenneth. 1973. *Economics and the Public Purpose.* New York: Macmillan.

Gande, Amar, Manju Puri, Anthony Saunders, and Ingo Walter. 1997. "Bank Underwriting of Debt Securities: Modern Evidence." *Review of Financial Studies* 10, 4.

———. 1999. Manju Puri and Anthony Saunders. "Bank Entry, Competition and the Market for Corporate Securities Underwriting." *Journal of Financial Economics* 54, 2.

Gnehm, A., and C. Thalmann. 1989. *Conflicts of Interest in Financial Operations: Problems of Regulation in the National and International Context.* Basel: Swiss Bank Corporation.

Healey, Paul M., and Krishna G. Palepu. 2003. "The Fall of Enron." *Journal of Economic Perspectives* 17, 2 (spring): 280–302.

Herman, Edward S. 1975. *Conflicts of Interest: Commercial Banks and Trust Companies.* New York: Twentieth Century Fund.

Kanatas, George, and Kianping Qi. 1998. "Underwriting by Commercial Banks: Incentive Conflicts, Scope Economies, and Project Quality." *Journal of Money, Credit, and Banking* 30 (February): 119–133.

Kanatas, George, and Jianping Qi. 2003. "Integration of Lending and Underwriting: Implications of Scope Economies." *Journal of Finance* 58, 3: 410–440.

Kane, Edward J. 1987. "Competitive Financial Reregulation: An International Perspective." In *Threats to International Financial Stability,* edited by R. Portes and A. Swoboda. Cambridge: Cambridge University Press.

Kelly, Kate, and Susanne Craig. 2003. "NYSE Probe Reaches Five of Seven Specialist Firms." *Wall Street Journal,* April 18.

Krozner, Randall S., and Philip E. Strahan. 1999. *Bankers on Boards, Conflicts of Interest, and Lender Liability.* Working paper no. W7319. Cambridge, Mass.: National Bureau of Economic Research, August.

Litan, Robert. 2003. *Relationships in Financial Services: Are Anti-Tying Restrictions Out of Date?* Working paper. Washington, D.C.: AEI-Brookings Joint Center on Regulatory Studies, May.

Ljungqvist, Alexander, Felicia Marston, and William J. Wilhelm. 2003. *Compet-*

ing for Securities Underwriting Mandates: Banking Relationships and Analyst Recommendations. Working paper. New York: Stern School of Business, New York University, Finance Department, May.

Loughran, Tim, and Jay R. Ritter. 2002. "Why Don't Issuers Get Upset about Leaving Money on the Table in IPOs?" *Review of Financial Studies* 15, 2: 310–327.

Michaely, Roni, and Kent Womack. 1999. "Conflict of Interest and the Credibility of Underwriter Analyst Recommendations." *Review of Financial Studies* 12: 653–686.

Morgenson, Gretchen. 2001. "Salomon Faces Complaints over Options at WorldCom." *New York Times,* April 24.

Patel, S. 2003. "Standard & Poor's Transparency and Disclosure Study, Europe." Available online at the website of Standard & Poor's: www.standardand poors.com, fall.

Puri, Manju. 1994. "The Long-Term Default Performance of Bank Underwritten Security Issues." *Journal of Banking and Finance* 18, 2: 221–229.

———. 1996. "Commercial Banks in Investment Banking: Conflict of Interest or Certification Role?" *Journal of Financial Economics* 40, 3: 114–123.

———. 1999. "Commercial Banks as Underwriters: Implications For the Going Public Process." *Journal of Financial Economics* 54, 2: 88–97.

Rajan, Raghuram G. 1992. "Insiders and Outsiders: The Choice between Informed and Arms-Length Debt." *Journal of Finance* 47: 1367–1400.

———. 1996. "The Entry of Commercial Banks into the Securities Business: A Selective Survey of Theories and Evidence." In *Universal Banking: Financial System Design Reconsidered,* edited by Anthony Saunders and Ingo Walter. Chicago: Irwin.

Ritter, Jay R., and Ivo Welch. 2002. "A Review of IPO Activity, Pricing and Allocations." *Journal of Finance* 57, 4: 104–110.

Saunders, Anthony. 1985. "Conflicts of Interest: An Economic View." In *Deregulating Wall Street,* edited by Ingo Walter. New York: Wiley.

Saunders, Anthony, Anand Srinivasan, and Ingo Walter. 2001. "Price Formation in the OTC Corporate Bond Markets: A Field Study of the Inter-Dealer Market." *Journal of Economics and Business* (fall): 245–261.

Saunders, Anthony, and Ingo Walter. 1997. *Universal Banking in the United States: What Could We Gain? What Could We Lose?* New York: Oxford University Press.

Schiesel, Seth, and Gretchen Morgenson. 2002. "ATT Is Asked for Information on Dealings with Salomon." *New York Times,* August 24.

Schotland, R. A. 1980. *Abuse on Wall Street: Conflicts of Interest in the Securities Markets.* Westport, Conn.: Quantum Books.

Shivdasani, A., and D. Yermack. 2003. "CEO Involvement in the Selection of New Board Members: An Empirical Analysis." *Journal of Finance* 54, 5 (fall): 345–361.

Smith, Clifford W. 1992. "Economics and Ethics: The Case of Salomon Brothers." *Journal of Applied Corporate Finance* 5, 2 (summer): 181–197.

Smith, Roy C., and Ingo Walter. 1997. *Street Smarts: Linking Professional Conduct and Shareholder Value in the Securities Industry.* Boston: Harvard Business School Press.

Stefanadis, Chris. 2003. *Tying and Universal Banking.* Working paper. New York: Federal Reserve Bank of New York, March.

Tillman, H. T. 1985. "Insurance and Credit-Tied Insurance: Myth or Reality?" *Banks in Insurance* (January): 9–18.

Tschäni, R. 2003. "Ausufernder Begriff der Gruppe." *Neue Zürcher Zeitung* 256 (spring): 25.

Walter, Ingo, and Roy C. Smith. 2000. *High Finance in the Euro-Zone*. London: Prentice Hall.

Whinston, Michael D. 1990. "Tying, Foreclosure, and Exclusion." *American Economic Review* 80: 450–469.

White, Lawrence J. 1991. *The S&L Debacle: Public Policy Lessons for Bank and Thrift Regulation*. New York: Oxford University Press.

Index

The page location of figures is indicated by italics.